STERLING
Test Prep

AP Physics 1

Practice Questions

6th edition

Customer Satisfaction Guarantee

Your feedback is important because we strive to provide the highest quality prep materials. Email us comments or suggestions.

info@sterling–prep.com

We reply to emails – check your spam folder

6   5   4   3   2   1

ISBN-13: 978-1-9547257-4-4

Sterling Test Prep materials are available at quantity discounts.

Contact info@sterling–prep.com

Sterling Test Prep
6 Liberty Square #11
Boston, MA 02109

Thousands of students use our study aids to achieve high AP test scores!

Scoring well on the AP exams is essential to earn placement credits and admission into competitive colleges, which will position you for a successful future. This book prepares you to achieve a high score on the AP Physics 1 exam by developing the ability to apply your knowledge and quickly choose the correct answer. Solving targeted practice questions builds your understanding of fundamental physics concepts and is a more effective strategy than merely memorizing terms.

This book has over 730 high-yield practice questions covering AP Physics 1 topics. Physics instructors with years of teaching and applied physics experience prepared this material by analyzing the exam content and developing practice material that builds your knowledge and skills crucial for success on the exam. Our editorial team reviewed and systematized the content to match the current College Board curriculum. We are experts on preparing students for standardized tests and college admissions.

The detailed explanations describe why an answer is correct and – more important for your learning – why another attractive choice is wrong. They provide step-by-step solutions for quantitative questions and teach the scientific foundations and details of essential physics topics needed to answer conceptual exam questions. Read the explanations carefully to understand how they apply to the question and learn important physics principles and the relationships between them. With the practice material contained in this book, you will significantly improve your AP score.

We wish you great success in your academics and look forward to being an important part of your test preparation!

What some students say about this book

★★★★★ *I understand more from using this book*

I like using this book for class and to prep for the AP exam. My understanding and scores have improved. Great coverage of the AP physics topics divided into chapters of practice questions.

Feilan C. (Amazon verified purchase)

★★★★★ *I am very impressed with this book.*

I got this book to do some practice problems, and it is a great help! I learned many ways to solve physics problems because it walks you through every problem. I like that I can practice mixed-topic tests and also do practice questions for an individual AP physics 1 topic. I am very impressed with this book.

Kelly Norton (Amazon verified purchase)

★★★★★ *As a science teacher, I highly recommend this book for AP physics 1*

I'm a high school science teacher for 16 years, and I have experience with different test prep products. I am always looking for the best resources for my students. This book is the best that I have seen because it has great questions. The questions are challenging but easy to understand if a student is familiar with the concepts. Good selections of wrong answers require someone to understand the material. The diagnostic tests are a great feature to gauge your understanding before delving into the topics covered within the chapters. Several students that I suggested this book to have used it, and I see improvement in their performance. I heard from several that they did great on the ap exam.

Simon Lauder (Amazon verified purchase)

★★★★★ *Great score on the AP Physics 1 exam...great practice*

I am so happy to find this book that my physics teacher recommended. An excellent book to practice physics problems. I used it during the year and found it valuable during the school year and for the AP physics exams. I used the book to practice problems and learned from the explanations. I like that the solutions are easy to follow and very detailed for learning. Great results on the AP Physics 1 exam.

Michael Rice (Amazon verified purchase)

★★★★★ *Nice to learn and understand physics*

My teacher recommended this book for the selection of questions and explanations. I felt comfortable using this book. It was not frustrating like some other practice material I used because this book described the solutions in sufficient detail for me to understand. What a nice feeling to understand the material. I learned alot and recommend this to others. Great practice for class and the AP physics exam. Great results for me.

Dennis Brimmer. (Amazon verified purchase)

AP Physics 1 Review provides a comprehensive review of topics tested on the AP Physics 1 exam. The content covers foundational principles and concepts necessary to answer exam questions.

This review book will increase your score.

Visit our Amazon store

AP Chemistry, Biology and Physics online practice tests

Our advanced online testing platform allows you to take AP practice questions on your computer to generate a Diagnostic Report for each test.

By using our online AP tests and Diagnostic Reports, you will:

      Assess your knowledge of subjects and topics to identify your areas of strength and weakness

      Learn important scientific topics and concepts for comprehensive test preparation

      Improve your test-taking skills

To access these and other AP questions online
at a special pricing for book owners, see page 451

AP prep books by Sterling Test Prep

AP Biology Practice Questions

AP Biology Review

AP Physics 1 Practice Questions

AP Physics 1 Review

AP Physics 2 Practice Questions

AP Physics 2 Review

AP Environmental Science

AP Psychology

AP U.S. History

AP World History

AP European History

AP U.S. Government and Politics

AP Comparative Government and Politics

AP Human Geography

Visit our Amazon store

Table of Contents

College Level Examination Program (CLEP)

Biology Review

Biology Practice Questions

Chemistry Review

Chemistry Practice Questions

Introductory Business Law Review

College Algebra Practice Questions

College Mathematics Practice Questions

History of the United States I Review

History of the United States II Review

Western Civilization I Review

Western Civilization II Review

Social Sciences and History Review

American Government Review

Introductory Psychology Review

Visit our Amazon store

AP Physics Preparation and Test-Taking Strategies

Test preparation strategies

The best way to do well on AP Physics is to be good at physics. There is no way around this; proper preparation is the key to success. Prepare for the test to answer with confidence as many questions as possible.

Study in advance. Plan to devote 3 to 6 months studying for the exam. The information is manageable by studying at regular intervals during the weeks before the test. Cramming is not a successful tactic. However, do not study too far in advance. Studying more than six months ahead is not advised and may result in fatigue and poor knowledge retention.

Develop a realistic study and practice schedule. Cramming eight hours a day is unfeasible and leads to burnout, which is detrimental to performance. Commit to a realistic study and practice schedule.

Remove distractions. During this preparation period, temporarily eliminate distractions. However, it is crucial not to neglect physical well-being, as well as social or family life. Balance is key. Prepare with full intensity but do not jeopardize your health or emotional well-being.

Develop an understanding over memorization. When studying, devote time to each topic. After a study session, write a short outline of the concepts. The act of writing clarifies relationships and increases knowledge retention.

Make flashcards. Consider using self-made flashcards to develop knowledge retention and to quiz what you know. Avoid commercial flashcards because making cards helps build and retain knowledge.

Find a study partner. Occasionally studying with a friend who is preparing for the test can motivate and provide accountability. Explaining concepts to another improves and fine-tunes your understanding, integrates knowledge, bolsters competence, and identifies deficiencies in comprehension.

Take practice tests. Do not take practice tests too early. First, develop a broad and detailed understanding of concepts. In the last weeks, use practice tests to fine-tune your final preparation. If you are not scoring well on practice tests, you want time to improve without undue stress.

Alternate the days for studying and practicing. This steadily increases knowledge retention and identifies areas that require further study. Also, it accustoms you to the challenges of test-taking.

Test day strategies

Be well-rested. Get a full night's sleep before the test for proper mental and physical capacity. If you are up late the night before (i.e., you are not well prepared), you will not feel fresh and alert and will have difficulty concentrating and focusing on the test.

Eat the right foods. Avoid foods and drinks that lead to drowsiness (carbohydrates and protein) or drinks high in sugar, causing the glucose spike and crash.

Pack in advance. Check what you are allowed to bring to the test. Pay attention to the required check-in items (e.g., printed confirmation, identification). Pack the day before, so you are not frantically looking for things on test day. Prepare your clothes to avoid the stress of looking for matching socks.

Arrive at the testing center early. Allow time to check-in and remain calm before the test begins. Starting off the right way is an advantage. Map and test your route to the center in advance and determine parking locations, if applicable. If you are not familiar with the test location, visit before the test day to practice and avoid travel errors. Plan your route correctly to arrive at the center without delays or encountering additional challenges and unnecessary stress.

Maintain a positive attitude. Avoid falling into a mental spiral of negative emotions. Too much worry leads to underperformance. If you become anxious, chances are higher for lower performance in preparation and during the test. To do well on the test requires logical, systematic, and analytical thinking, so relax and remain calm. This inner peace helps during preparation and the high-stakes test.

Focus on your progress. Do not be concerned with other test-takers. It does not matter if someone appears to be proceeding rapidly through the exam; they may be rushing or guessing on questions.

Take breaks. Do not skip the available timed breaks. Your mind and body will appreciate them. If time allows, eat a light snack to replenish your energy. These refreshing breaks help you finish strong.

Pause to breathe deeply. The best approach to any test is *not* to keep your head down the whole session. While there is no time to waste, take a few seconds between questions to breathe deeply and momentarily clear your thoughts to relax your mind and muscles.

Time management strategies

Besides good preparation, time management is the critical strategy to know for the exam.

Average time per question. In advance, determine the average time allotted for each question. Use two different approaches depending on which phase of preparation you are working on.

During the first phase of preparation, acquire, fortify, and refine your knowledge. Timed practice is not the objective at this stage. While practicing, note how many questions you would have completed in the allotted time. During this regimented practice, use the time needed to develop your analytical and thought processes related to specific questions. Work systematically and note your comprehension compared to the correct answers to learn the material and identify conceptual weaknesses. Do not overlook the value of explanations to questions; these can be a great source of content, analysis, and interdependent relationships.

During the second phase of preparation, when taking practice tests, do not spend more than the average allotted time on each question. Pacing your response time helps develop a consistent pace, so you complete the test within the allotted time. If you are time-constrained during the final practice phase, you need to work more efficiently, or your score will suffer.

Focus on the easy questions and skip the unfamiliar. You get the same points for answering easy or difficult questions. This means more points for three quickly answered questions than for one hard-earned victory. Everyone has their strengths and weaknesses. For an unfamiliar question on the exam, skip it on the first round because these challenging questions require more than the average allotted time. Use your time first to answer all familiar (i.e., easy) questions, so if time runs out, you maximized points.

On the second review, questions that you cannot approach systematically or lack fundamental knowledge will likely not be answered through analysis. Use the strategy of elimination and educated guessing to select an answer and move on to another question.

Do not overinvest in any question. You may encounter questions that consume more time than the average and make you think that you will get it right by investing more time. Stop thinking that way. Do not get entangled with questions while losing track of time. The test is timed, so you cannot spend too much time on any question.

Look at every question on the exam. It would be unfortunate not to earn points for a question you could have quickly answered because you did not see it. If you are still in the first half of the test and are spending more than the required average on a question, select the best option, note the question number, and move on. You do not want to rush through the remaining questions, causing you to miss more answers. If time allows, return to marked questions and take a fresh look. However, unless you have a reason to change the original answer, do not change it. University studies show that students who hastily change answers often replace the correct answer with an incorrect answer.

Multiple-choice questions strategies

For multiple-choice questions, what matters is how many questions were answered correctly, not how much work went into selecting the answers. An educated guess earns the same points as an answer known with confidence.

On the test, you need to think and analyze information quickly. This skill cannot be gained from a college course, review prep course, or textbook. Working efficiently and effectively is a skill developed through focused effort and applied practice.

There are strategies, approaches, and perspectives to apply when answering multiple-choice questions on the AP Physics exam. These strategies help maximize points. Many strategies are known by you and seem like common sense. However, under the pressure of a timed test, these helpful approaches might be overlooked. While no strategy replaces the importance of comprehensive preparation, applying them increases the probability of successful guessing on unfamiliar questions.

Understand the question. Know what the question is asking before selecting an answer. This seems obvious, but it is surprising how many students do not read (and reread) a question carefully and rush to select the wrong answer. The test-makers anticipate these hasty mistakes, and many enticing answers are included among the specious choices.

A successful student reads the question and understands it precisely before looking at the answers. Separate the vital information from distracters and understand the design and thrust of the question. Answer the question posed and not merely pick a factually accurate statement or answer a misconstrued question.

Rephrasing the question helps articulate what precisely the correct response requires. When rephrasing, do not change the meaning of the question; assume it is direct and to the point as written. After selecting the answer, review the question and verify that the choice selected answers the question.

Answer the question before looking at choices. This valuable strategy is applicable if the question asks for generalized factual details. Answer the question by forming a thought response first, then look for the choice that matches your preordained answer. Select the predetermined statement as it is likely correct.

Factually correct, but wrong. Questions often have incorrect choices that are factually correct but do not answer the question. Therefore, with applied thought, predetermine the answer and not select a choice merely because it is a factually correct statement. Verify that the choice answers the question.

Do not fall for the familiar. When in doubt, it is comforting to choose what is familiar. If you recognize a term or concept, you may be tempted to pick that choice impetuously. However, do not go with familiar answers merely because they are familiar. Think through the answer and how it relates to the question before selecting it.

Know the equations. Since many exam questions require scientific equations, memorize the needed ones and understand when to use each. As you work with this book, learn to apply formulas and equations and use them in many questions.

Manipulate the formulas. Know how to rearrange the formulas. Many questions require manipulating equations to calculate the correct answer. Familiarity includes manipulating the terms, understanding relationships, and isolating variables.

Estimating. For quantitative questions, estimating helps choose the correct answer quickly if you have a sense of the order of magnitude. This is especially applicable to questions where the answer choices have different orders of magnitude; save time by estimating instead of computing. In most instances, estimation enables the correct answer to be identified quickly compared to the time needed for calculations.

Evaluate the units. For quantitative problems, analyze the units in the answers to build relationships between the question and the correct answer. Understand what value is sought and eliminate wrong choices with improper units.

Make visual notes. Write, draw, or graph to dissect the question. This helps determine what information is provided, the question's objective, and the concept tested by the question. Even if a question does not require a graphic answer, a graph, chart, or table often allows a solution to become apparent.

Experiments questions. Determine the purpose, methods, variables, and controls of the experiment. Understanding the presented information helps answer the question. With multiple experiments, understand variations of the same experiment by focusing on the differences. For example, focus on the changes between the first and second experiments, second and third, and first and third. This helps organize the information and apply it to the answer.

Words of caution. The words *"all," "none,"* and *"except"* require attention. Be alert with questions containing these words as they require an answer that may not be apparent on the first read of the question.

Process of elimination. If the correct answer is not immediately apparent, use the process of elimination. Use the strategy of educated guessing by eliminating one or two answers. Usually, at least one answer choice is easily identified as wrong. Eliminating even one choice increases the odds of selecting the correct one. Eliminate as many choices as possible.

- Use proportional estimations for quantitative questions to eliminate choices that are too high or low.

- Eliminate answers that are "almost right" or "half right." Consider "half right" as "wrong" since these distractor choices are purposely included.

- If two answers are direct opposites, the correct answer is likely one of them. Therefore, you can typically eliminate the other choices and narrow the search for the correct one. However, note if they are direct opposites too, or there is another reason to consider them correct.

- With factual questions where answers are numbers, eliminate the smallest and largest numbers (unless you have a reason to choose it as correct).

- *Roman numeral questions.* These questions present several statements and ask which is/are correct. These questions are tricky for most test-takers because they present more than one potentially correct statement, often included in combinations with more than one answer. Eliminating a wrong Roman numeral statement eliminates all choices that include it.

Correct ways to guess. Do not assume you must get every question right; this will add unnecessary stress during the exam. You will (most likely) need to guess some questions. Answer as many questions correctly as possible without wasting time that should be used to maximize your score.

For challenging questions, random guessing does not help. Use educated guessing after eliminating one or two choices. Guessing is a form of "partial credit" because while you might not be sure of the correct answer, you have the relevant knowledge to identify some wrong choices.

For example, if you randomly entered responses for the first 20 questions, there is a 25% chance of correctly guessing since questions have four choices. Therefore, the odds are guessing 5 questions correctly and 15 incorrectly.

After eliminating one answer as wrong, you have a 33% chance of being right. Therefore, your odds move to 6-7 questions right and 13-14 questions wrong. While this may not seem like a dramatic increase, it can make an appreciable difference in your score. If you confidently eliminate two wrong choices, you increase the chances of guessing the correct answer to 50%!

- Do not rely on gut feelings alone to answer questions quickly. Understand and recognize the difference between *knowing* and a *gut feeling* about the answer. Gut feelings should sparingly be used after the process of elimination.

- Do not fall for answers that sound "clever," and do not choose "bizarre" answers. Choose them only if you have a reason to believe they may be correct.

- *Roman numeral questions.* A workable strategy for Roman numeral questions is to guess the wrong statement. For example:

  A. I only

  B. III only

  C. I and II only

  D. I and III only

Notice that statement II does not have an answer dedicated to it. This indicates that statement II is likely wrong and eliminates choice C, narrowing your search to three choices. However, if you are confident that statement II is the answer, do not apply this strategy.

Double-check the question. After selecting an answer, return to the question to ensure the selected choice answers the question as asked and not as misconstrued for convenience.

Fill the answers carefully. This is simple but crucial. Many mistakes happen when filling in answers. Be attentive to the question number and enter the answer accordingly. If you skip a question, skip it on the answer sheet.

Strategies for free-response questions

Free-response questions typically require processing the presented information into existing conceptual frameworks. There are some personal choices for writing the desired response.

You might be required to present and discuss relevant examples, clarify or evaluate principles, perform a detailed analysis of relationships or respond to stimulus materials such as charts or graphs.

Understand the question. As with the multiple-choice questions, understand what the question asks. Mental rephrasing should not add or alter the meaning or essence of the question. Assume that the question, as written, is direct and to the point.

Answer the questions in order of competence. You are not bound to answer the questions according to their sequence. Therefore, survey all questions quickly and decide which ones you are comfortable answering with minimal effort or time. Avoid getting entangled and frustrated to use time efficiently and maximize your points.

Do not write more than needed. Additional work beyond the question's stated directives does not earn a higher score or result in extra credit. Therefore, for proper time management and keeping responses relevant, answer the question but avoid superfluous responses.

Organize your thoughts. Before writing, brainstorm the questions' topics. Outline your thoughts on scratch paper during the composition process. Organized thoughts produce a coherent response. Essential definitions, ideas, examples, or names are valid details when relevant. With practice, balance your time between brainstorming and writing your response.

Follow the structure. Structure your responses to match the order specified in the question for a grader-friendly answer. The reader should not need to search for topics used in the grading criteria. A well-structured essay has complete sentences and paragraphs. A formal introduction and conclusion are unnecessary; go directly into answering the question.

Answer questions in their entirety. It is essential to answer questions thoroughly, not just partially. For example, some questions ask to identify and explain. Performing only one step is inadequate and will be graded accordingly.

Below are *task verbs* common for free-response questions – underline these directives as you see them in practice questions and on the exam. Refer to these required tasks and verify when completed. Do not overlook them when writing your comprehensive response.

Compare – provide a description or explanation of similarities or differences.

Define – provide a specific meaning for a word or concept.

Identify – provide information about a specified topic without elaboration or explanation.

Describe – provide the relevant characteristics of a specified concept.

Develop an argument – articulate a claim and support it with evidence.

Draw a conclusion – use available information to formulate an accurate statement that demonstrates understanding based on evidence.

Explain – provide information about how or why a relationship, process, pattern, or outcome occurs, using evidence and reasoning.

Explaining "how" typically requires analyzing the relationship, process, pattern, or outcome.

Explaining "why" typically requires analysis of motivations or reasons for the relationship, process, pattern, or outcome.

Use plain language. All claims should be directly stated. You do not want the graders to guess how something demonstrates a point. Regardless of if they correctly guess your intentions, you will be graded critically for ambiguities. Present relevant information clearly and concisely to demonstrate the argument's primary points.

Use facts to bolster your arguments. Written responses should include specific facts and avoid unsubstantiated claims. Do not use long, meandering responses filled with loosely-related facts regarding specific concepts. Avoid contradictions, circular definitions, and question restatements.

Corrections. If you make a mistake, put a simple strikethrough through the error, so the grader disregards that portion.

Review your answers. If questions are completed and time remains, review each response. Assess if anything is needed to be added or requires correction. If you add content, insert an asterisk (*) and refer the reader to the end of the essay. These thoughtful last-minute revisions can earn crucial points.

Write legibly. The reader must decipher your writing so the response can be scored appropriately, so write legibly. Practice writing under a time limit to produce a readable response. If this issue may exist, ask a friend to read a sample response to understand the words expressed. Consider printing some words or key phrases or cleanly highlight (e.g., asterisk, arrow, underline) them in your work product.

Notes for active learning

Common Physics Equations and Conversions

Constants and Conversion Factors

1 unified atomic mass unit	1 u = 1.66×10^{-27} kg
	1 u = 931 MeV/c^2
Proton mass	m_p = 1.67×10^{-27} kg
Neutron mass	m_n = 1.67×10^{-27} kg
Electron mass	m_e = 9.11×10^{-31} kg
Electron charge magnitude	e = 1.60×10^{-19} C
Avogadro's number	N_0 = 6.02×10^{23} mol^{-1}
Universal gas constant	R = 8.31 J/(mol·K)
Boltzmann's constant	k_B = 1.38×10^{-23} J/K
Speed of light	c = 3.00×10^8 m/s
Planck's constant	h = 6.63×10^{-34} J·s
	h= 4.14×10^{-15} eV·s
	hc = 1.99×10^{-25} J·m
	hc = 1.24×10^3 eV·nm
Vacuum permittivity	ε_0 = 8.85×10^{-12} C^2/N·m^2
Coulomb's law constant	k = $1/4\pi\varepsilon_0$ = 9.0×10^9 N·m^2/C^2
Vacuum permeability	μ_0 = $4\pi \times 10^{-7}$ (T·m)/A
Magnetic constant	k' = $\mu_0/4\pi$ = 10^{-7} (T·m)/A
Universal gravitational constant	G = 6.67×10^{-11} m^3/kg·s^2
Acceleration due to gravity at Earth's surface	g = 9.8 m/s^2
1 atmosphere pressure	1 atm = 1.0×10^5 N/m^2
	1 atm = 1.0×10^5 Pa
1 electron volt	1 eV = 1.60×10^{-19} J
Balmer constant	B = 3.645×10^{-7} m
Rydberg constant	R = 1.097×10^7 m^{-1}
Stefan constant	σ = 5.67×10^{-8} W/m^{2}K^4

	Units			**Prefixes**	
Name	**Symbol**		**Factor**	**Prefix**	**Symbol**
meter	m		10^{12}	tera	T
kilogram	kg		10^{9}	giga	G
second	s		10^{6}	mega	M
ampere	A		10^{3}	kilo	k
kelvin	K		10^{-2}	centi	c
mole	mol		10^{-3}	mili	m
hertz	Hz		10^{-6}	micro	μ
newton	N		10^{-9}	nano	n
pascal	Pa		10^{-12}	pico	p
joule	J				
watt	W				
coulomb	C				
volt	V				
ohm	Ω				
henry	H				
farad	F				
tesla	T				
degree Celsius	°C				
electronvolt	eV				

Newtonian Mechanics

		a = acceleration
	$v = v_0 + a\Delta t$	A = amplitude
	$x = x_0 + v_0\Delta t + \frac{1}{2}a\Delta t^2$	E = energy
Translational Motion	$v^2 = v_0^2 + 2a\Delta x$	F = force
	$\vec{a} = \dfrac{\sum \vec{F}}{m} = \dfrac{\vec{F}_{net}}{m}$	f = frequency
		h = height
	$\omega = \omega_0 + \alpha t$	I = rotational inertia
	$\theta = \theta_0 + \omega_0 t + \frac{1}{2}\alpha t^2$	J = impulse
Rotational Motion	$\omega^2 = \omega_0^2 + 2\alpha\Delta\theta$	K = kinetic energy
	$\vec{\alpha} = \dfrac{\sum \vec{\tau}}{I} = \dfrac{\vec{\tau}_{net}}{I}$	k = spring constant
		ℓ = length
Force of Friction	$\lvert\vec{F}_f\rvert \le \mu\lvert\vec{F}_n\rvert$	m = mass
Centripetal Acceleration	$a_c = \dfrac{v^2}{r}$	N = normal force
		P = power
Torque	$\tau = r_\perp F = rF\sin\theta$	p = momentum
Momentum	$\vec{p} = m\vec{v}$	L = angular momentum
		r = radius of distance
Impulse	$\vec{J} = \Delta\vec{p} = \vec{F}\Delta t$	T = period
Kinetic Energy	$K = \frac{1}{2}mv^2$	t = time
		U = potential energy
Potential Energy	$\Delta U_g = mg\Delta y$	v = velocity or speed
Work	$\Delta E = W = F_\parallel d = Fd\cos\theta$	W = work done on system
		x = position
Power	$P = \dfrac{\Delta E}{\Delta t} = \dfrac{\Delta W}{\Delta t}$	y = height
		α = angular acceleration
Simple Harmonic Motion	$x = A\cos(\omega t)$	
	$x = A\cos(2\pi ft)$	

Center of Mass	$x_{cm} = \dfrac{\sum m_i x_i}{\sum m_i}$	μ = coefficient of friction
		Θ = angle
Angular Momentum	$L = I\omega$	τ = torque
Angular Impulse	$\Delta L = \tau \Delta t$	ω = angular speed
Angular Kinetic Energy	$K = \dfrac{1}{2}I\omega^2$	
Work	$W = F\Delta r \cos\theta$	
Power	$P = Fv \cos\theta$	
Spring Force	$\left|\vec{F_s}\right| = k\left|\vec{x}\right|$	
Spring Potential Energy	$U_s = \dfrac{1}{2}kx^2$	
Period of Spring Oscillator	$T_s = 2\pi\sqrt{m/k}$	
Period of Simple Pendulum	$T_p = 2\pi\sqrt{\ell/g}$	
Period	$T = \dfrac{2\pi}{\omega} = \dfrac{1}{f}$	
Gravitational Body Force	$\left|\vec{F_g}\right| = G\dfrac{m_1 m_2}{r^2}$	
Gravitational Potential Energy of Two Masses	$U_G = -\dfrac{Gm_1 m_2}{r}$	

Electrostatics, Magnetism, Circuits

Electric Field	$\vec{E} = \dfrac{\vec{F}_E}{q}$	A = area
Electric Field Strength	$\lvert\vec{E}\rvert = \dfrac{1}{4\pi\varepsilon_0}\dfrac{\lvert q\rvert}{r^2}$	B = magnetic field
Electric Field Strength	$\lvert\vec{E}\rvert = \dfrac{\lvert\Delta V\rvert}{\lvert\Delta r\rvert}$	C = capacitance
Electrostatic Force Between Charged Particles	$\lvert\vec{F}_E\rvert = \dfrac{1}{4\pi\varepsilon_0}\dfrac{\lvert q_1 q_2\rvert}{r^2}$	d = distance
Electric Potential Energy	$\Delta U_E = q\Delta V$	E = electric field
		ϵ = emf
		F = force
Electrostatic Potential due to a Charge	$V = \dfrac{1}{4\pi\varepsilon_0}\dfrac{q}{r}$	I = current
		l = length
Capacitor Voltage	$V = \dfrac{Q}{C}$	P = power
		Q = charge
Capacitance of Parallel Plate Capacitor	$C = \kappa\varepsilon_0\dfrac{A}{d}$	q = point charge
		R = resistance
Electric Field Inside a Parallel Plate Capacitor	$E = \dfrac{Q}{\varepsilon_0 A}$	r = separation
		t = time
Capacitor Potential Energy	$U_C = \frac{1}{2}Q\Delta V = \frac{1}{2}C(\Delta V)^2$	U = potential energy
Current	$I = \dfrac{\Delta Q}{\Delta t}$	V = electric potential
Resistance	$R = \dfrac{\rho l}{A}$	v = speed
		κ = dielectric constant
Power	$P = I\Delta V$	ρ = resistivity
Current	$I = \dfrac{\Delta V}{R}$	θ = angle
		Φ = flux
Resistors in Series	$R_s = \displaystyle\sum_i R_i$	
Resistors in Parallel	$\dfrac{1}{R_p} = \displaystyle\sum_i \dfrac{1}{R_i}$	
Capacitors in Parallel	$C_p = \displaystyle\sum_i C_i$	

Capacitors in Series	$\dfrac{1}{C_s} = \sum_i \dfrac{1}{C_i}$
Magnetic Field Strength (from a long straight current-carrying wire)	$B = \dfrac{\mu_0 I}{2\pi r}$
Magnetic Force	$\vec{F}_M = q\vec{v} \times \vec{B}$
	$\vec{F}_M = \|q\vec{v}\| \|\sin\theta\| \|\vec{B}\|$
	$\vec{F}_M = I\vec{l} \times \vec{B}$
	$\vec{F}_M = \|I\vec{l}\| \|\sin\theta\| \|\vec{B}\|$
Magnetic Flux	$\Phi_B = \vec{B} \cdot \vec{A}$
	$\Phi_B = \|\vec{B}\| \cos\theta \, \|\vec{A}\|$
Electromagnetic Induction	$\epsilon = \dfrac{-\Delta\Phi_B}{\Delta t}$
	$\epsilon = Blv$

Sound

Standing Wave/ Open Pipe Harmonics	$\lambda = \dfrac{2L}{n}$	f = frequency
		L = length
Closed Pipe Harmonics	$\lambda = \dfrac{4L}{n}$	m = mass
		M = molecular mass
Harmonic Frequencies	$f_n = nf_1$	n = harmonic number
		R = gas constant
Speed of Sound in Ideal Gas	$v_{sound} = \sqrt{\dfrac{yRT}{M}}$	T = tension
		v = velocity
Speed of Wave Through Wire	$v = \sqrt{\dfrac{T}{m/L}}$	y = adiabatic constant
		λ = wavelength

Doppler Effect
(approaching stationary observer)

$$f_{observed} = \left(\frac{v}{v - v_{source}}\right)f_{source}$$

Doppler Effect
(receding stationary observer)

$$f_{observed} = \left(\frac{v}{v + v_{source}}\right)f_{source}$$

Doppler Effect
(observer moving towards source)

$$f_{observed} = \left(1 + \frac{v_{observer}}{v}\right)f_{source}$$

Doppler Effect
(observer moving away from source)

$$f_{observed} = \left(1 - \frac{v_{observer}}{v}\right)f_{source}$$

Geometry and Trigonometry

Rectangle	$A = bh$	A = area
		C = circumference
Triangle	$A = \dfrac{1}{2}bh$	V = volume
		S = surface area
Circle	$A = \pi r^2$	b = base
	$C = 2\pi r$	h = height
Rectangular Solid	$V = lwh$	l = length
		w = width
Cylinder	$V = \pi r^2 l$	r = radius
	$S = 2\pi rl + 2\pi r^2$	θ = angle
Sphere	$V = \dfrac{4}{3}\pi r^3$	
	$S = 4\pi r^2$	
Right Triangle	$a^2 + b^2 = c^2$	
	$\sin \theta = \dfrac{a}{c}$	
	$\cos \theta = \dfrac{b}{c}$	
	$\tan \theta = \dfrac{a}{b}$	

Trigonometric Functions for Common Angles

θ	$\sin \theta$	$\cos \theta$	$\tan \theta$
0°	0	1	0
30°	1/2	$\sqrt{3}/2$	$\sqrt{3}/3$
37°	3/5	4/5	3/4
45°	$\sqrt{2}/2$	$\sqrt{2}/2$	1
53°	4/5	3/5	4/3
60°	$\sqrt{3}/2$	1/2	$\sqrt{3}$
90°	1	0	∞

Diagnostic Tests

Diagnostic Test 1

This Diagnostic Test is designed to assess your proficiency on each topic and NOT to mimic the test. Use your test results and identify areas of strength and weakness to adjust your study plan and enhance your fundamental knowledge. The length of the Diagnostic Tests is optimal for a single study session.

#	Answer:				Review	#	Answer:				Review
1:	A	B	C	D	___	26:	A	B	C	D	___
2:	A	B	C	D	___	27:	A	B	C	D	___
3:	A	B	C	D	___	28:	A	B	C	D	___
4:	A	B	C	D	___	29:	A	B	C	D	___
5:	A	B	C	D	___	30:	A	B	C	D	___
6:	A	B	C	D	___	31:	A	B	C	D	___
7:	A	B	C	D	___	32:	A	B	C	D	___
8:	A	B	C	D	___	33:	A	B	C	D	___
9:	A	B	C	D	___	34:	A	B	C	D	___
10:	A	B	C	D	___	35:	A	B	C	D	___
11:	A	B	C	D	___	36:	A	B	C	D	___
12:	A	B	C	D	___	37:	A	B	C	D	___
13:	A	B	C	D	___	38:	A	B	C	D	___
14:	A	B	C	D	___	39:	A	B	C	D	___
15:	A	B	C	D	___	40:	A	B	C	D	___
16:	A	B	C	D	___	41:	A	B	C	D	___
17:	A	B	C	D	___	42:	A	B	C	D	___
18:	A	B	C	D	___	43:	A	B	C	D	___
19:	A	B	C	D	___	44:	A	B	C	D	___
20:	A	B	C	D	___	45:	A	B	C	D	___
21:	A	B	C	D	___	46:	A	B	C	D	___
22:	A	B	C	D	___	47:	A	B	C	D	___
23:	A	B	C	D	___	48:	A	B	C	D	___
24:	A	B	C	D	___	49:	A	B	C	D	___
25:	A	B	C	D	___	50:	A	B	C	D	___

This page is intentionally left blank

1. What property of matter determines an object's resistance to change in its state of motion?

   I. mass   II. density   III. volume

   A. I only

   B. II only

   C. III only

   D. I and II only

2. Two forces of equal magnitude act on an object. If each force is 4.6 N and the angle between them is 40°, what is the magnitude and direction of a third force for the object to be in equilibrium?

   A. 2.3 N, to the right

   B. 4.3 N, to the right

   C. 6.5 N, to the right

   D. 8.6 N, to the right

   $\vec{F}_1$

   $\vec{F}_2$

3. How far from the heavier end must the fulcrum of a massless 10 m seesaw be if an 800 N father on one side is to balance his 200 N son at the other end?

   A. 0.5 m

   B. 2 m

   C. 1 m

   D. 8 m

4. In the absence of friction, how much work would a boy do while pulling a 10 kg sled 3.5 m with a 20 N force?

   A. 57 J

   B. 70 J

   C. 1.8 J

   D. 85 J

5. Total constructive interference is observed when two waves with the same frequency and wavelength have a:

   A. 45° phase difference

   B. 90° phase difference

   C. 180° phase difference

   D. 0° phase difference

6. The Doppler shift occurs when the source of waves and a detector move relative to each other. There is an increase in the detected frequency when the source and detector approach each other and a decrease in the detected frequency when they move away from each other. A commuter train moves at 50 m/s towards Kevin, who is standing still. The train sounds its horn at 420 Hz, and the speed of sound is 350 m/s at a temperature of 29 °C. What frequency does Kevin hear after the train passes?

   A. 335 Hz

   B. 368 Hz

   C. 424 Hz

   D. 446 Hz

7. What is the root mean square (RMS) current for a 26 μF capacitor connected across a 120 V_{rms} 60 Hz source?

   A. 1.2 A

   B. 7.3 A

   C. 2.7 A

   D. 0 A

8. Two charges, $Q_1 = 3.4 \times 10^{-10}$ C and $Q_2 = 6.8 \times 10^{-9}$ C, are separated by 1 cm. Let F_1 be the magnitude of the electrostatic force felt by Q_1 due to Q_2 and let F_2 be the magnitude of the electrostatic force felt by Q_2 due to Q_1. What is the ratio of F_1 / F_2?

A. 2
B. 1

C. 16
D. 8

9. Ignoring air resistance, how long does a coin take to reach the ground when dropped from a 42 m building? Use $g = 10$ m/s^2

A. 1.4 s
B. 2.9 s

C. 3.6 s
D. 5.4 s

10. Which of the following statements is TRUE regarding the acceleration experienced by a block moving down a frictionless plane inclined at a 20° angle?

A. It remains constant

B. It increases as the block moves down the plane

C. It increases at a rate proportional to the incline

D. It decreases at a rate proportional to the incline

11. A bullet shot from a longer barrel gun has a greater muzzle velocity because the bullet receives a greater:

    I. force   II. impulse   III. acceleration

A. I only
B. II only

C. III only
D. I and II only

12. A ball bounces on the floor three times, whereby it loses 20% of its energy with each bounce due to heating. How high is the third bounce, provided the ball was released 250 cm from the floor?

A. 115 cm
B. 150 cm

C. 75 cm
D. 128 cm

13. What is the period of a wave if its frequency is 10 Hz?

A. 0.1 s
B. 1 s

C. 100 s
D. 10 s

14. What is the frequency of a pressure wave with a wavelength of 2.5 m traveling at 1,600 m/s?

A. 640 Hz
B. 5.6 kHz

C. 0.64 Hz
D. 4 kHz

15. At terminal velocity, an object falling toward the surface of the Earth has a velocity that:

    A. is independent of the mass of the object   **C.** remains constant

    B. depends on the weight of the object   **D.** increases

16. A box that weighs 40 N is on a rough horizontal surface. An external force F is applied horizontally to the box. A normal force and a friction force are also present. When force F equals 8.8 N, the box is in motion at a constant velocity. The box decelerates when force F is removed. What is the magnitude of the acceleration of the box? (Use the acceleration due to gravity $g = 10$ m/s^2)

    A. 0.55 m/s^2 **C.** 4.4 m/s^2

    B. 1.1 m/s^2 **D.** 2.2 m/s^2

17. Two friends are standing on opposite ends of a canoe which is initially at rest with respect to the lake. Steve is on the right when he throws a very massive ball to the left, and Mike, on the left, catches it. Ignoring friction between the canoe and the water, after the ball is caught, the canoe:

    A. moves to the right before reversing direction

    B. moves to the left before reversing direction

    C. remains stationary

    D. moves to the right

18. A 1,000 kg car travels at 30 m/s on a level road when the driver slams the brakes, bringing the car to a stop. What is the change in kinetic energy during the braking if the skid marks are 35 m long?

    A. -4.5×10^5 J   **C.** -9×10^{10} J

    B. 0 J   **D.** 4.2×10^5 J

19. In a given medium with fixed boundaries, the longest wavelength that produces a standing wave is 4 m. What is the lowest possible frequency associated with a standing wave within this medium if waves propagate through the medium at 8 m/s?

    A. 0.5 Hz   **C.** 2 Hz

    B. 1 Hz   **D.** 6 Hz

20. Which of the following statements is FALSE?

    A. Waves from a vibrating string are transverse waves

    B. Sound travels much slower than light

    C. Sound waves are longitudinal pressure waves

    D. Sound can travel through a vacuum

21. The electric power of a lamp that carries 2 A at 120 V is:

A. 24 W   C. 60 W

B. 2 W   D. 240 W

22. A 3 Ω and a 1.5 Ω resistor are connected in parallel within a circuit. If the voltage drops across the 3 Ω resistor is 2 V, what is the sum of the currents through these two resistors?

A. 4/3 amps   C. 2 amps

B. 3/2 amps   D. 2/3 amps

23. A small boat moves at a velocity of 3.35 m/s when a river current perpendicular accelerates it to the initial direction of motion. Relative to the initial direction of motion, what is the new velocity of the boat after 33.5 s if the current acceleration is 0.75 m/s²?

A. 62 m/s at 7.6°   C. 25 m/s at 7.6°

B. 62 m/s at 82.4°   D. 25 m/s at 82.4°

24. Lisa is standing facing forward in a moving truck, and she suddenly falls backward because the truck's:

A. speed remained the same   C. acceleration remained the same

B. velocity decreased   D. velocity increased

25. A machinist turns the power on for a stationary grinding wheel at time $t = 0$ s. The wheel accelerates uniformly for 10 s and reaches the operating angular velocity of 58 radians/s. The wheel is run at that angular velocity for 30 s before the power is shut off. The wheel slows down uniformly at 1.4 radians/s² until it stops. What is the approximate total number of revolutions for the wheel?

A. 460   C. 380

B. 320   D. 510

26. How much work is done on a crate if pushed 2 m with a force of 20 N?

A. 10 J   C. 30 J

B. 20 J   D. 40 J

27. The graph shows the position (*x*) as a function of time (*t*) for a system undergoing simple harmonic motion. Which of the following graphs represents the acceleration of this system as a function of time?

A.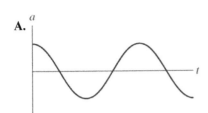

C.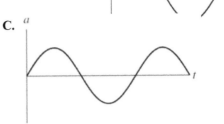

B.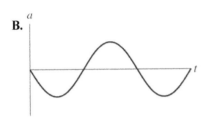

D.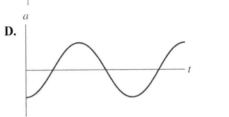

28. Sound can undergo refraction in:

    I. air   II. water   III. a vacuum

A. I only

B. II only

C. III only

D. I and II only

29. Ignoring air resistance, what is the speed of a rock as it hits the ground if it was dropped from a 50 m cliff? (Use the acceleration due to gravity $g = 10$ m/s^2)

A. 21 m/s

B. 14 m/s

C. 32 m/s

D. 42 m/s

30. A string connects a 15 kg block on a table to a 60 kg mass hanging over the edge of the table. Ignoring the frictional force, what is the acceleration of the 15 kg block when the 60 kg block is released? (Use acceleration due to gravity $g = 10$ m/s^2)

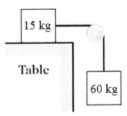

A. 9.5 m/s^2

B. 7.5 m/s^2

C. 10.5 m/s^2

D. 8 m/s^2

31. If the speed of a moving object doubles, then what else doubles?

    I. Acceleration   II. Kinetic energy   III. Momentum

A. I only

B. II only

C. III only

D. I and II only

32. Which statement is correct when a flowerpot of mass m falls from rest to the ground for a distance of h?

    A. The speed of the pot when it hits the ground is proportional to m

    B. The KE of the pot when it hits the ground does not depend on h

    C. The KE of the pot when it hits the ground is proportional to h

    D. The speed of the pot when it hits the ground is proportional to h

33. Crests of an ocean wave pass a pier every 10 s. What is the wavelength of the ocean waves if the waves are moving at 4.6 m/s?

    A. 4.4 m   **C.** 4.6 m

    B. 0.46 m   **D.** 46 m

34. Two speakers placed 3 m apart are producing in-phase sound waves with a wavelength of 1 m. A microphone is placed between the speakers to determine the intensity of the sound at various points. What kind of point exists exactly 0.5 m to the left of the speaker on the right? (Use the speed of sound $v = 340$ m/s)

    A. Node   **C.** Node and antinode

    B. Antinode   **D.** Destructive interference

35. The resistance of an object equals:

    A. length × resistivity × cross-sectional area   **C.** current / voltage

    B. length / (resistivity × cross-sectional area)   **D.** voltage / current

36. What causes an object to become electrostatically charged?

    A. Charge is created   **C.** Electrons are transferred

    B. Protons are transferred   **D.** Protons and electrons are transferred

37. Determine the distance traveled and the magnitude of the displacement when an object moves 16 m to the North and then moves 12 m to the South.

    A. 4 m, 4 m   **C.** 28 m, 4 m

    B. 28 m, 28 m   **D.** 4 m, 28 m

38. A potted plant of mass M is resting on a flat board, and one end of the board is lifted slowly until the potted plant begins to slide. What does the angle θ that the board must make for sliding depend?

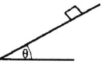

    A. M **C.** μ_k, kinetic friction

    B. μ_s, static friction   **D.** g, acceleration due to gravity

39. A 1 kg chunk of putty moving at 1 m/s collides and sticks to a stationary 6 kg box. What is the total momentum of the box and putty? (Assume the box rests on a frictionless surface)

    A. 0 kg·m/s

    B. 1 kg·m/s

    C. 2 kg·m/s

    D. 3 kg·m/s

40. A 20 kg object is dropped from a height of 100 m. Ignoring air resistance, how much gravitational PE has the object lost when its speed is 30 m/s?

    A. 2,050 J

    B. 2,850 J

    C. 9,000 J

    D. 5,550 J

41. The distance traveled by an object in one complete cycle of simple harmonic motion is how many times the amplitude?

    A. one

    B. two

    C. three

    D. four

42. With four tuning forks, what is the greatest number of different beat frequencies that can be heard by striking the forks one pair at a time?

    A. 2

    B. 4

    C. 6

    D. 8

43. Which is a unit of measuring resistance to a change of motion?

    A. N

    B. ohm

    C. sec^{-1}

    D. kg

44. At constant speed, an object following a straight-line path has:

    A. decreasing acceleration

    B. no forces acting on it

    C. zero acceleration

    D. increasing velocity

45. The masses of the blocks and the velocities before and after a collision are:

In this example, the collision is:

    A. completely inelastic

    B. completely elastic

    C. characterized by an increase in KE

    D. characterized by a decrease in momentum

46. Which statement correctly describes the situation when a 6 kg mass moves at 2 m/s and a 3 kg mass moving at 4 m/s glides over a horizontal frictionless surface? A horizontal force F, which directly opposes their motion, results in the objects coming to rest.

    A. The 6 kg mass travels twice the distance of the 3 kg mass before stopping

    B. The 3 kg mass travels farther, but less than twice the distance of the 6 kg mass before stopping

    C. The 3 kg mass travels twice the distance of the 6 kg mass before stopping

    D. The 6 kg mass loses four times more KE than the 3 kg mass before stopping

47. What is the approximate wavelength of a wave that has a speed of 360 m/s and a period of 4.2 s?

    A. 85.7 m   **C.** 1,512 m

    B. 1.86 m   **D.** 288.6 m

48. What is the effect on a system's mechanical energy if only the amplitude of a vibrating mass-and-spring system is doubled?

    A. Increases by a factor of 2   **C.** Increases by a factor of 3

    B. Increases by a factor of 4   **D.** Remains the same

49. What is the current through a 12-ohm resistor connected to a 120 V power supply?

    A. 1 A   **C.** 10 A

    B. 8 A   **D.** 20 A

50. If the distance between two electrostatic charges is doubled, how is the force between them affected?

    A. Increases by a factor of 2   **C.** Decreases by a factor of $\sqrt{2}$

    B. Increases by a factor of 4   **D.** Decreases by a factor of 4

Notes for active learning

Notes for active learning

Diagnostic Test 2

This Diagnostic Test is designed to assess your proficiency on each topic and NOT to mimic the test. Use your test results and identify areas of strength and weakness to adjust your study plan and enhance your fundamental knowledge. The length of the Diagnostic Tests is optimal for a single study session.

#	Answer:				Review	#	Answer:				Review
1:	A	B	C	D	___	26:	A	B	C	D	___
2:	A	B	C	D	___	27:	A	B	C	D	___
3:	A	B	C	D	___	28:	A	B	C	D	___
4:	A	B	C	D	___	29:	A	B	C	D	___
5:	A	B	C	D	___	30:	A	B	C	D	___
6:	A	B	C	D	___	31:	A	B	C	D	___
7:	A	B	C	D	___	32:	A	B	C	D	___
8:	A	B	C	D	___	33:	A	B	C	D	___
9:	A	B	C	D	___	34:	A	B	C	D	___
10:	A	B	C	D	___	35:	A	B	C	D	___
11:	A	B	C	D	___	36:	A	B	C	D	___
12:	A	B	C	D	___	37:	A	B	C	D	___
13:	A	B	C	D	___	38:	A	B	C	D	___
14:	A	B	C	D	___	39:	A	B	C	D	___
15:	A	B	C	D	___	40:	A	B	C	D	___
16:	A	B	C	D	___	41:	A	B	C	D	___
17:	A	B	C	D	___	42:	A	B	C	D	___
18:	A	B	C	D	___	43:	A	B	C	D	___
19:	A	B	C	D	___	44:	A	B	C	D	___
20:	A	B	C	D	___	45:	A	B	C	D	___
21:	A	B	C	D	___	46:	A	B	C	D	___
22:	A	B	C	D	___	47:	A	B	C	D	___
23:	A	B	C	D	___	48:	A	B	C	D	___
24:	A	B	C	D	___	49:	A	B	C	D	___
25:	A	B	C	D	___	50:	A	B	C	D	___

This page is intentionally left blank

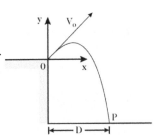

1. A projectile is fired at time $t = 0$ s from point O of a ledge. It has initial velocity components of $v_{ox} = 30$ m/s and $v_{oy} = 300$ m/s with time in flight of 75 s. The projectile lands at point P. What is the horizontal distance that the projectile travels?

    A. 3,020 m   **C.** 2,420 m

    B. 2,880 m   **D.** 2,250 m

2. A car of mass m is traveling along the roadway up a slight incline of angle θ to the horizontal when the driver sees a deer and suddenly applies the brakes. The car skids before coming to rest. Which expression gives the force of friction on the car if the coefficient of static friction between the tires and the road is μ_s and the coefficient of kinetic friction is μ_k?

    A. $\mu_k N$ **C.** mg

    B. $\mu_s N$ **D.** $mg \sin \theta$

3. A torque of 14 N·m is applied to a solid, uniform disk with a radius of 0.6 m. What is the mass of the disk if it accelerates at 5.3 rad/s²?

    A. 7.6 kg   **C.** 14.7 kg

    B. 4.2 kg   **D.** 21.4 kg

4. Energy is the:

    I. ability to do work

    II. work that can be done by an object with potential or kinetic energy

    III. work needed to generate potential or kinetic energy

    A. I only   **C.** III only

    B. II only   **D.** I, II and III

5. The displacement of a vibrating tuning fork and the resulting sound wave is related to:

    A. period   **C.** resonance

    B. amplitude   **D.** frequency

6. The decibel level of sound is related to its:

    A. velocity   **C.** wavelength

    B. frequency   **D.** intensity

7. What is the voltage across a 5.5 Ω resistor if the current through it is 10 A?

    A. 1 V   **C.** 55 V

    B. 5 V   **D.** 5.5 V

8. A positive charge Q is held fixed at the origin. A positive charge z is let go from point p on the positive x-axis. Ignoring friction, which statement describes the velocity of z after it is released?

A. Increases indefinitely

B. Decreases to zero

C. Increases, then decreases, but never reaches zero

D. Increases, but never exceeds a specific limit

9. The slope of a line at a single point on a position *vs.* time graph gives:

A. average acceleration

B. change in acceleration

C. instantaneous velocity

D. average velocity

10. What is the net force on a 1,200 kg Alfa Romeo that is moving at a constant speed of 3.5 m/s and turning to the left on a road curve that has an effective radius of 4 m?

A. 1,550 N

B. 2,160 N

C. 3,600 N

D. 8,465 N

11. An irregularly-shaped object 10 m long is placed with each end on two nearby scales. If the scale on the right reads 94 N and the left reads 69 N, how far from the left is the object's center of gravity? (Use the acceleration due to gravity $g = 9.8$ m/s^2)

A. 6.8 m

B. 6.3 m

C. 5.8 m

D. 8.1 m

12. Marshall drops a water balloon from the top of a building onto Peter on the sidewalk below. Ignoring air resistance, how tall is the building if the balloon travels at 29 m/s when it strikes Peter's head? (Use the acceleration due to gravity $g = 10$ m/s^2 and the distance of Peter's head above the ground = 1 m)

A. 50.5 m

B. 37.5 m

C. 43 m

D. 26 m

13. Assuming no change in the system's mass m, increasing the spring constant k of a spring system causes what kind of change in the resonant frequency of the system?

A. No change

B. Increase

C. Decrease only if the ratio k/m is > 1

D. Increase only if the ratio k/m is ≥ 1

14. Assuming other factors remain constant, what happens to sound velocity as the air temperature increases?

A. Does not change because it is dependent only on the state of the substance

B. Increases when atmospheric pressure is high and decreases when the pressure is low

C. Increases

D. Decreases

15. How long does it take for a rock to reach the maximum height of its trajectory if a boy throws it with an initial velocity of 3.13 m/s at 30° above the horizontal? (Use the acceleration due to gravity $g = 9.8$ m/s^2)

    A. 0.16 s   **C.** 0.333 s

    B. 0.28 s   **D.** 0.446 s

16. What is the reaction force if, as a ball falls, the action force is the pull of the Earth's mass on the ball?

    A. None present   **C.** The downward acceleration due to gravity

    B. The pull of the ball's mass on Earth   **D.** The air resistance acting against the ball

17. Shawn, with a mass of 105 kg, sits 5.5 m to the left of the center of a seesaw. Mark and John, each with a mass of 20 kg, are seated on the right side of the seesaw. If Mark sits 10 m to the right of the center, how far to the right from the center should John sit to balance the seesaw? (Use acceleration due to gravity $g = 10$ m/s^2)

    A. 5 m   **C.** 19 m

    B. 10 m   **D.** 20 m

18. Is it possible for a system to have negative potential energy?

    A. Yes, because the choice of the zero for potential energy is arbitrary

    B. No, because this has no physical meaning

    C. Yes, if the kinetic energy is positive

    D. Yes, if the total energy is positive

19. What is the speed of 2 m long water waves as they pass by a floating piece of cork that bobs up and down for one complete cycle each second?

    A. 8 m/s   **C.** 1 m/s

    B. 0.5 m/s   **D.** 2 m/s

20. A guitar has a 14 cm string and sounds a 440 Hz musical note when played without fingering. How far from the end of the string should Samantha place her fingers to play a 520 Hz note?

    A. 5.8 cm   **C.** 1.6 cm

    B. 0.8 cm   **D.** 2.2 cm

21. What is the equivalent resistance of the circuits if each has a resistance of 600 Ω?

    A. 60 Ω   **C.** 600 Ω

    B. 1,200 Ω   **D.** 175 Ω

22. A proton is traveling to the right and encounters region Y that contains an electric field where the proton speeds up. In what direction does the electric field in region Y point?

A. To the left

B. To the right

C. Down into the page

D. Up from the page

23. What is the shape of the line on a position *vs.* time graph for constant linear acceleration?

A. curve

B. sloped line

C. sinusoidal graph

D. horizontal line

24. What is true about the acceleration of an object that travels at a constant speed in a circular path?

A. It is equal to zero because the speed is constant

B. It is not equal to zero and is directed tangent to the path

C. It is not equal to zero and is directed behind the radius of the path

D. It is not equal to zero and is directed toward the center of the path

25. A steel ball A is thrown in the air with a speed of 4 m/s at an angle of 60° from the horizontal. It drops onto steel ball B, which is 1.4 times the mass of A. What is the horizontal component of ball B's velocity if ball A comes to rest after the collision and ball B bounces?

A. 0.4 m/s

B. 0.6 m/s

C. 1.4 m/s

D. 1.8 m/s

26. Susan pulls on a wagon with a force of 70 N. What is the average power generated by Susan if the wagon moves 45 m in 3 min?

A. 18 W

B. 27 W

C. 14 W

D. 21 W

27. Simple harmonic motion (SMH) is characterized by an acceleration that:

A. is proportional to displacement

B. is proportional to velocity

C. decreases linearly

D. is inversely proportional to displacement

28. An over-taut violin string was tuned with a tuning fork that produced an accurate pitch of 340 Hz. What is the period of vibration of the violin string if a beat frequency of 4 Hz is produced when the string and the fork are sounded together?

A. 1/336 sec

B. 1/321 sec

C. 1/344 sec

D. 1/327 sec

29. A ball is projected horizontally with an initial speed of 5 m/s from an initial height of 50 m. Ignoring air resistance, how far has the ball traveled horizontally from its original position when it lands? (Use the acceleration due to gravity $g = 10$ m/s^2)

A. 11 m

B. 16 m

C. 20 m

D. 7 m

30. A 200 g hockey puck slides up a metal ramp inclined at a 30° angle. The coefficients of static and kinetic friction between the hockey puck and the metal ramp are $\mu_s = 0.4$ and $\mu_k = 0.3$, respectively. The initial speed of the hockey puck is 14 m/s. What vertical height does the puck reach above its starting point? (Use the acceleration due to gravity $g = 9.8$ m/s^2)

A. 11 m

B. 4.8 m

C. 6.6 m

D. 14 m

31. A 6.5 g bullet was fired horizontally into a 2 kg wooden block suspended on a 1.5 m string. The bullet becomes embedded in the wooden block, and immediately after that, the block and the bullet move at 2 m/s. The suspended wooden block with embedded bullet swings upward by height h. How high does the block with bullet swing before it comes to rest? (Use the acceleration due to gravity $g = 9.8$ m/s^2)

A. 5.5 cm

B. 20 cm

C. 12 cm

D. 44 cm

32. A hammer of mass m is dropped from a roof and falls a distance h before striking the ground. How does the maximum velocity of the hammer, just before hitting the ground, change if h is doubled? Assume no air resistance.

A. It is multiplied by $\sqrt{2}$

B. It is multiplied by 2

C. It is increased by 200%

D. It is multiplied by 4

33. A simple pendulum has a bob of mass M and a period T. If M is doubled, what is the new period?

A. $T/\sqrt{2}$

B. T

C. $T\sqrt{2}$

D. 2T

34. Color depends on what characteristics of light?

I. frequency   II. wavelength   III. amplitude

A. I only

B. II only

C. III only

D. I and II only

35. What is the current through the 2 Ω resistor if the current through the 8 Ω resistor is 0.8 A?

A. 15.2 A

B. 18.7 A

C. 1.5 A

D. 6.6 A

36. A 0.4 kg mass is attached to a massless spring. The mass oscillates and has a total energy of 10 J. What is the oscillation frequency if the oscillation amplitude is 20 cm? (Use the conversion of 1 J = 1 N·m)

A. 3 Hz

B. 4.3 Hz

C. 2.1 Hz

D. 5.6 Hz

37. An object starting from rest accelerates uniformly along a straight line until its final velocity is v while traveling a distance d. What would be the distance traveled if the object accelerated uniformly from rest until its final velocity was $4v$?

A. $2d$

B. $4d$

C. $6d$

D. $16d$

38. Satellite #1 has mass M, which takes time T to orbit Earth. If satellite #2 has twice the mass, how long does it take for satellite #2 to orbit Earth?

A. T/2

B. T

C. 2T

D. 4T

39. Sonja is sitting on the outer edge of a carousel that is 18 m in diameter. What is the velocity of Sonja in m/s if the carousel makes 5 rev/min?

A. 3.3 m/s

B. 0.8 m/s

C. 8.8 m/s

D. 4.7 m/s

40. Two identical arrows, one with twice the kinetic energy, are fired into a hay bale. Compared to the slower arrow, the faster arrow penetrates:

A. the same distance

B. twice as far

C. four times as far

D. more than four times as far

41. The phenomena of compressions and rarefactions are characteristic of:

I. longitudinal waves

II. transverse waves

III. standing waves

A. I only

B. II only

C. III only

D. I and II only

42. What is the decibel level of a sound with an intensity of 10^{-7} W/m^2?

A. 10 dB

B. 20 dB

C. 30 dB

D. 50 dB

43. The captain of a yacht intends to travel due north. He checks his navigation gear and discovers that due to ocean currents, the yacht is traveling NE at a constant 10.7 m/s. To correct the yacht's bearing, the captain turns the vessel to point north-west and accelerates. How long does it take for the yacht to correct the bearing and achieve a due north bearing, given that the engine delivers a constant acceleration of 4.4 m/s^2?

A. 1.3 s

B. 1.8 s

C. 2.4 s

D. 3.6 s

44. A 5.5 kg box slides down an inclined plane that makes an angle of 40° with the horizontal. At what rate does the box accelerate down the slope if the coefficient of kinetic friction μ_k is 0.19? (Use the acceleration due to gravity $g = 9.8$ m/s^2)

A. 7.5 m/s^2

B. 6.4 m/s^2

C. 4.9 m/s^2

D. 5.9 m/s^2

45. An object is released from rest at a height h above the surface of the Earth, where h is much smaller than the radius of the Earth. The object's speed is v as it strikes the ground. Ignoring air resistance, at what height should the object be released from rest for it to strike the ground with a speed of $2v$? (Use g = acceleration due to gravity)

A. $4gh$

B. $4h$

C. $2gh$

D. $2h$

46. A projectile weighing 120 N is traveling horizontally with respect to the surface of the Earth at a constant velocity of 6 m/s. Ignoring air resistance, what is the power required to maintain this motion?

A. 0 W

B. 20 W

C. 120 W

D. 2 W

47. On the Moon, the acceleration of gravity is g / 6. If a pendulum has a period T on Earth, what will be the period on the Moon?

A. T$\sqrt{6}$

B. T/6

C. T/$\sqrt{6}$

D. T/3

48. Electromagnetic waves consist of:

A. particles of heat energy

B. high-frequency gravitational waves

C. compressions and rarefactions of electromagnetic pulses

D. oscillating electric and magnetic fields

49. A 9 V battery is connected to two resistors in a series. One resistance is 5 ohms, and the other is 10 ohms. Which is true about the current for the locations (A, B, C, D) marked along the circuit?

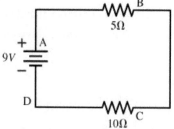

A. Current at A > current at B > current at C > current at D

B. Current at A > current at B = current at C = current at D

C. Current at A = current at B = current at C = current at D

D. Current at A = current at B = current at C > current at D

50. An object is traveling uniformly at a *v* of 5 m/s. What is its final velocity if it experiences a uniform acceleration of 2 m/s² for 6 s?

A. 12 m/s

C. 17 m/s

B. 28 m/s

D. 32 m/s

Notes for active learning

Notes for active learning

Diagnostic Test 3

This Diagnostic Test is designed to assess your proficiency on each topic and NOT to mimic the test. Use your test results and identify areas of strength and weakness to adjust your study plan and enhance your fundamental knowledge. The length of the Diagnostic Tests is optimal for a single study session.

#	Answer:				Review	#	Answer:				Review
1:	A	B	C	D	___	26:	A	B	C	D	___
2:	A	B	C	D	___	27:	A	B	C	D	___
3:	A	B	C	D	___	28:	A	B	C	D	___
4:	A	B	C	D	___	29:	A	B	C	D	___
5:	A	B	C	D	___	30:	A	B	C	D	___
6:	A	B	C	D	___	31:	A	B	C	D	___
7:	A	B	C	D	___	32:	A	B	C	D	___
8:	A	B	C	D	___	33:	A	B	C	D	___
9:	A	B	C	D	___	34:	A	B	C	D	___
10:	A	B	C	D	___	35:	A	B	C	D	___
11:	A	B	C	D	___	36:	A	B	C	D	___
12:	A	B	C	D	___	37:	A	B	C	D	___
13:	A	B	C	D	___	38:	A	B	C	D	___
14:	A	B	C	D	___	39:	A	B	C	D	___
15:	A	B	C	D	___	40:	A	B	C	D	___
16:	A	B	C	D	___	41:	A	B	C	D	___
17:	A	B	C	D	___	42:	A	B	C	D	___
18:	A	B	C	D	___	43:	A	B	C	D	___
19:	A	B	C	D	___	44:	A	B	C	D	___
20:	A	B	C	D	___	45:	A	B	C	D	___
21:	A	B	C	D	___	46:	A	B	C	D	___
22:	A	B	C	D	___	47:	A	B	C	D	___
23:	A	B	C	D	___	48:	A	B	C	D	___
24:	A	B	C	D	___	49:	A	B	C	D	___
25:	A	B	C	D	___	50:	A	B	C	D	___

This page is intentionally left blank

1. The slope of a tangent line at a given time value on a position *vs.* time graph indicates:

   A. instantaneous acceleration

   B. change in acceleration

   C. instantaneous velocity

   D. average velocity

2. Which statement must be true for an object moving with constant nonzero velocity?

   A. The net force on the object is zero

   B. The net force on the object is positive

   C. A constant force is being applied to the object in the direction opposite of motion

   D. A constant force is being applied to the object in the direction of motion

3. A 3 kg stone is dropped from a height of 5 m. Ignoring air resistance, what is its momentum on impact? (Use acceleration due to gravity $g = 10$ m/s^2)

   A. 7.5 kg·m/s

   B. 5 kg·m/s

   C. 30 kg·m/s

   D. 45 kg·m/s

4. An ideal, massless spring with a spring constant of 3 N/m has a 0.9 kg mass attached to one end, and the other end is attached to a beam. If the system is initially at equilibrium and the mass is then down 18 cm below the equilibrium length and released, what is the magnitude of the net force on the mass just after its release? (Use the acceleration due to gravity is $g = 10$ m/s^2)

   A. 0.54 N

   B. 0.75 N

   C. 6 N

   D. 0.35 N

5. A 30.0 N block is attached to the free end of an anchored spring and is allowed to slide back and forth on a frictionless table. Determine the frequency of motion if the spring constant $k = 40.0$ N/m. (Use the acceleration due to gravity $g = 9.8$ m/s^2)

   A. 0.30 Hz

   B. 0.58 Hz

   C. 2.3 Hz

   D. 3.6 Hz

6. A piano is tuned so that the third harmonic frequency of one string is 786.3 Hz. If the fundamental frequency of another string is 785.8 Hz, what is the beat frequency between the notes?

   A. 0 Hz

   B. 1 Hz

   C. 0.5 Hz

   D. 786.3 Hz

7. What quantity does the slope of this graph represent if the graph shows the power dissipated in a resistor as a function of the resistance?

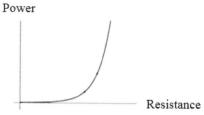

A. Maximum power transferred across the resistor

B. Square of the current across resistor

C. Current across the resistor

D. Potential difference across the resistor

8. What is the unit of the product of amps × volts?

A. Watt

B. Amp

C. Joule

D. Ohm

9. The graph shows the position of an object as a function of time. At which moment in time is the speed of the object equal to zero?

A. A

B. B

C. C

D. D

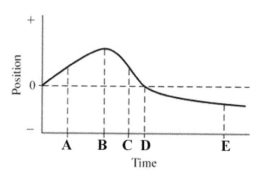

10. Why does it take more force to start moving a heavy bookcase across the carpet than to keep it moving?

A. For objects in motion, kinetic friction is a force in the same direction as the motion

B. The coefficient of static friction is greater than the forces of movement

C. The coefficient of static friction is greater than the coefficient of kinetic friction

D. The coefficient of kinetic friction is greater than the coefficient of static friction

11. A 1 kg chunk of putty moving at 1 m/s collides with and sticks to a 7 kg box initially at rest. What is the speed that the box and putty are then set in motion? (Assume the box rests on a frictionless surface)

A. 1/8 m/s

B. 1/6 m/s

C. 1/4 m/s

D. 1/7 m/s

12. A 1,500 kg car moving at 45 km/h locks its brakes and skids 30 m. How far does the same car skid if it is traveling at 150 km/h?

A. 230 m

B. 160 m

C. 445 m

D. 333 m

13. How does the frequency of vibration relate to the time it takes to complete one cycle?

A. Inversely with the time

B. Inversely with the amplitude

C. Directly with the time

D. Directly with the amplitude

14. A mosquito produces 1.5×10^{-11} W of sound energy. How many mosquitoes are needed to power a 30 W bulb if the sound energy could be used for this purpose?

A. 6×10^{11}

B. 2×10^{12}

C. 2×10^{11}

D. 6×10^{12}

15. If an object is accelerating, which values must change?

    I. Speed   II. Velocity   III. Direction

A. I only

B. II only

C. III only

D. I and II only

16. Michelle takes off down a 50 m high, 10° slope on her jet-powered skis. The skis have a thrust of 260 N. The combined mass of the skis and Michelle is 50 kg. Michelle's speed at the bottom of the slope is 40 m/s. Assuming the mass of the fuel is negligible, what is the coefficient of kinetic friction of her skis on the snow? (Use the acceleration due to gravity $g = 9.8$ m/s^2)

A. 0.23

B. 0.53

C. 0.68

D. 0.42

17. Johnny is sitting on the outer edge of a carousel that is 18 m in diameter. What is the velocity of Johnny if the carousel makes 5.3 rev/min?

A. 4.2 m/s

B. 5 m/s

C. 3.1 m/s

D. 9.8 m/s

18. A 4 kg mass is affixed to the end of a vertical spring with a spring constant of 10 N/m. When the mass comes to rest, how much has the spring stretched?

A. 1 m

B. 4 m

C. 5 m

D. 0.1 m

19. In music, the 3rd harmonic corresponds to which overtone?

A. 1st

B. 2nd

C. 3rd

D. 4th

20. What is the wavelength of the standing wave when a 12 m string, fixed at both ends, is resonating at a frequency that produces 4 nodes?

A. 6 m

B. 8 m

C. 4 m

D. 24 m

21. Which statement is correct about the equivalent resistance when four unequal resistors are connected in parallel?

    A. It is the average of the largest and smallest resistance

    B. It is less than the smallest resistance

    C. It is more than the largest resistance

    D. It is the average of the four resistances

22. A fixed distance separates two particles of like charge and equal mass. What is the effect on the repulsive force between the particles if the mass of one particle is doubled?

    A. Doubles   **C.** Increases by ½

    B. Quadruples   **D.** Remains the same

23. For constant linear acceleration, the velocity *vs.* time graph is a:

    A. sloped line   **C.** horizontal line

    B. curve   **D.** cubic graph

24. A 40 kg runner is running around a track. The curved portions of the track are arcs of a circle that has a radius of 16 m. The runner is running at a constant speed of 4 m/s. What is the net force on the runner on the curved portion of the track?

    A. 150 N   **C.** 40 N

    B. 5 N   **D.** 100 N

25. A solid cylinder with an 80 cm radius is positioned on a frictionless plane inclined at 30° above the horizontal. A string wrapped around the cylinder exerts a force (F). The center of mass of the cylinder does not move when F has a specific critical value. What is the angular acceleration of the spool when F is at this critical value? (The moment of inertia of a solid cylinder is $I = \frac{1}{2}mr^2$; use the acceleration due to gravity $g = 10$ m/s^2)

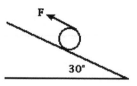

    A. 15.8 rad/s^2 **C.** 12.5 rad/s^2

    B. 23 rad/s^2 **D.** 18.6 rad/s^2

26. A stone of mass m is dropped from a height h toward the ground. Ignoring air resistance, which statement is true about the stone as it hits the ground?

    A. Its KE is proportional to h **C.** Its speed is proportional to h

    B. Its KE is proportional to h^2 **D.** Its speed is inversely proportional to h^2

27. When a light ray traveling in glass strikes an air boundary, which phase change occurs in the reflected ray?

A. 45° phase change

B. 180° phase change

C. −45° phase change

D. No phase change

28. The tension in each of two strings is adjusted so that both vibrate at precisely 822 Hz. The tension in one string is then increased slightly. Five beats per second are then heard when both strings vibrate. What is the new frequency of the string that was tightened?

A. 824 Hz

B. 816 Hz

C. 827 Hz

D. 818 Hz

29. A car and a truck are initially alongside each other at time $t = 0$. The velocity *vs.* time graph represents their motions along a straight road. At time T, which statement is true for the vehicles?

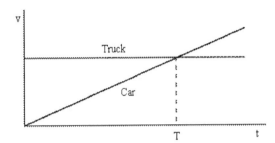

A. The car traveled farther than the truck

B. The truck traveled farther than the car

C. They traveled the same distance

D. The truck had a greater acceleration than the car

30. A hockey puck slides on a surface of frictionless ice. If the mass of the puck is 300 grams, and it moves in a straight line with a constant velocity of 5 m/s, what is the net force acting on the puck?

A. 0 N

B. 1 N

C. 30 N

D. 750 N

31. A motor can provide a maximum of 120 N·m of torque. If this torque is used to accelerate a solid, uniform flywheel of mass 12 kg and radius 4 m, what is the time necessary for the flywheel to accelerate from rest to 7.35 rad/s?

A. 4.4 s

B. 3.9 s

C. 1.1 s

D. 5.9 s

32. A 1.2 kg bowling ball is dropped from a height of 6 m. During its fall, it is constantly acted upon by air resistance, with a force of 3.4 N. Accounting for air resistance, what is the speed of the bowling ball as it hits the ground? (Use acceleration due to gravity $g = 10$ m/s^2)

A. 9.2 m/s

B. 10.6 m/s

C. 11.3 m/s

D. 13.4 m/s

33. As a water wave passes, a floating leaf oscillates up and down entirely for two cycles in 1 s. What is the wave's speed if the wave's wavelength is 12 m?

    A. 1 m/s   **C.** 24 m/s

    B. 10 m/s   **D.** 6 m/s

34. Sound intensity is defined as:

    A. power per unit time

    B. power passing through a unit of area per unit time

    C. energy passing through a unit of volume per unit time

    D. energy passing through a unit of area per unit time

35. When the current through a resistor is increased by a factor of 4, by what factor does the power dissipated by the resistor change?

    A. Increases by 16   **C.** Decreases by 4

    B. Increases by 4   **D.** Decreases by 16

36. A kilowatt-hour is a unit of:

    A. work   **C.** power

    B. current   **D.** charge

37. When an object moves with constant acceleration, can its velocity change direction?

    A. Yes, a car that starts from rest, speeds up, slows to a stop, and then backs up is an example

    B. No, because it is always slowing down

    C. No, because it is always speeding up

    D. Yes, a Frisbee thrown straight up is an example

38. A car of mass m is driving up a road with a slight incline θ above the horizontal. The driver sees a road closure and skids to a stop. The coefficient of static friction between the tires and the road is μ_s, and the coefficient of kinetic friction is μ_k. What is the magnitude of the gravity component of the force parallel to the surface of the road?

    A. $mg \sin \theta$ **C.** mg

    B. $mg \tan \theta$ **D.** $mg \cos \theta$

39. An object with a mass of 60 kg moves across a level surface at a constant speed of 13.5 m/s. If there is a frictional force, and the coefficient of kinetic friction is 0.8, which is true about the forces acting on the object?

   A. There must be an unbalanced amount of vertical force acting on the object, allowing it to move

   B. No forces are doing work on the object

   C. There must be some other horizontal force acting on the object

   D. The force exerted on the object by kinetic friction is negligible

40. What is the power output necessary for a 54 kg person to run at a constant velocity up a 10 m hillside in 4 s if the hillside is inclined at 30° above the horizontal? (Use the acceleration due to gravity $g = 9.8$ m/s^2 and 1 hp $= 745$ W)

   A. 1.92 hp   **C.** 0.89 hp

   B. 1.12 hp   **D.** 3.94 hp

41. Some of a wave's energy dissipates as heat. In time, this reduces the waves:

   A. amplitude   **C.** speed

   B. frequency   **D.** wavelength

42. A piano tuned with the third harmonic frequency of the C_3 string is 783 Hz. What is the frequency of the C_3 fundamental?

   A. 473 Hz   **C.** 387 Hz

   B. 261 Hz   **D.** 185 Hz

43. Describe the forces on a system that consists of a bicycle and a rider as the rider pedals at a constant speed in a straight line? (Ignore friction in the bearings of the bicycle)

   A. The force of air resistance is greater than the force of friction between the tires and the road

   B. The force of air resistance is less than the force of friction between the tires and the road

   C. The force of the rider's foot on the pedals is greater than the force of air resistance

   D. All external forces are balanced

44. In a binary star system, two stars revolve about their combined center of mass and are attracted to each other by the force of gravity. The force of gravity between the stars (masses M_1 and M_2) is F. If the mass of one of the stars is decreased by a factor of 2, how would this affect the force between them?

   A. Remains the same   **C.** Decreases by a factor of 4

   B. Increases by a factor of 2   **D.** Decreases by a factor of 2

45. For projectile motion with no air resistance, the vertical component of a projectile's acceleration:

A. is always positive

C. continuously increases

B. remains a nonzero constant

D. continuously decreases

46. The total mechanical energy of a system is:

A. either all kinetic energy or all potential energy, at any one instant

B. constant if there are only conservative forces acting

C. found through the product of potential energy and kinetic energy

D. equally divided between kinetic energy and potential energy in every instance

47. A 340 nm thick oil film floats on the surface of the water. The surface of the oil is illuminated from above at normal incidence with white light. What are the two wavelengths of light in the 400 nm to 800 nm wavelength band, most strongly reflected? (Use the index of refraction for oil n = 1.5 and the index of refraction for water n = 1.33)

A. 420 nm and 750 nm

C. 410 nm and 760 nm

B. 406 nm and 706 nm

D. 408 nm and 680 nm

48. A 1 m string is fixed at both ends and plucked. What is the wavelength corresponding to the fourth harmonic if the speed of the waves on this string is 4.2×10^4 m/s?

A. 1 m

C. 4/3 m

B. 0.5 m

D. 3/2 m

49. A suitcase of mass 80 kg is pushed in a straight line across a horizontal floor at a constant speed of 3 m/s. What is the net force on the suitcase? (Use the coefficient of kinetic friction $\mu_k = 0.3$)

A. 0 N

C. 800 N

B. 240 N

D. 27 N

50. A distance of 15 cm separates two point charges of +18 μC and −6 μC. What is the electric field E midway between the two charges? (Use Coulomb's constant $k = 9 \times 10^9$ N·m²·C⁻²)

A. 28.8×10^6 N/C toward the positive charge

C. 38.4×10^6 N/C toward the positive charge

B. 28.8×10^6 N/C toward the negative charge

D. 38.4×10^6 N/C toward the negative charge

Notes for active learning

Notes for active learning

Topical Practice Questions

Kinematics and Dynamics

1. Starting from rest, how long does it take for a sports car to reach 60 mi/h if it has an average acceleration of 13.1 mi/h·s?

   A. 6.6 s

   B. 3.1 s

   C. 4.5 s

   D. 4.6 s

2. A cannonball is fired with an initial speed of 20 m/s at a 30° angle with the horizontal. Ignoring air resistance, how long does it take the cannonball to reach the top of its trajectory? (Use the acceleration due to gravity $g = 10$ m/s^2)

   A. 0.5 s

   B. 1 s

   C. 1.5 s

   D. 2 s

3. Darlene starts her car from rest and accelerates at a constant 2.5 m/s^2 for 9 s to get to her cruising speed. She then drives for 15 minutes at a constant speed. She arrives at her destination, a straight-line distance of 31.5 km from where she started, the entire trip taking 1.25 hrs. What is her average velocity during 1.25 hours?

   A. 3 m/s

   B. 7 m/s

   C. 18 m/s

   D. 22.5 m/s

4. Which of the following cannot be negative?

   A. Instantaneous speed

   B. Instantaneous acceleration

   C. Acceleration of gravity

   D. Displacement

5. How far does a car travel while accelerating from 5 m/s to 21 m/s at a rate of 3 m/s^2?

   A. 15 m

   B. 21 m

   C. 69 m

   D. 105 m

6. Acceleration is sometimes expressed in multiples of g, where g is the acceleration due to gravity. How many g are experienced, on average, by the driver in a car crash if the car's velocity changes from 30 m/s to 0 m/s in 0.15 s? (Use the acceleration due to gravity $g = 9.8$ m/s^2)

   A. 22 g

   B. 28 g

   C. 20 g

   D. 14 g

7. Ignoring air resistance, how many forces act on a bullet fired horizontally after leaving the rifle?

    A. Two (one from the gunpowder explosion and one from gravity)

    B. One (from the motion of the bullet)

    C. One (from the gunpowder explosion)

    D. One (from the pull of gravity)

8. Suppose that a car traveling to the East begins to slow down as it approaches a traffic light. Which of the following statements about its acceleration is correct?

    A. The acceleration is towards the East

    B. The acceleration is towards the West

    C. Since the car is slowing, its acceleration is positive

    D. The acceleration is zero

9. On a planet where the acceleration due to gravity is 20 m/s^2, a freely falling object increases its speed each second by about:

    A. 20 m/s   **C.** 30 m/s

    B. 10 m/s   **D.** 40 m/s

10. What is a car's acceleration if it accelerates uniformly in one direction from 15 m/s to 40 m/s in 10 s?

    A. 1.75 m/s^2 **C.** 3.5 m/s^2

    B. 2.5 m/s^2 **D.** 7.6 m/s^2

11. If the fastest a person can drive is 65 mi/h, what is the longest time she can stop for lunch if she wants to travel 540 mi in 9.8 h?

    A. 1 h   **C.** 1.5 h

    B. 2.4 h   **D.** 2 h

12. What is a racecar's average velocity if it completes one lap around a 500 m track in 10 s?

    A. 10 m/s   **C.** 5 m/s

    B. 0 m/s   **D.** 20 m/s

13. What is a ball's net displacement after 5 s if it initially rolls up a slight incline at 0.2 m/s and decelerates uniformly at 0.05 m/s^2?

    A. 0.38 m   **C.** 0.9 m

    B. 0.6 m   **D.** 1.2 m

14. What does the slope of a line connecting two points on a velocity *vs.* time graph represent?

A. Change in acceleration

C. Average acceleration

B. Instantaneous acceleration

D. Instantaneous velocity

15. An airplane needs to reach a speed of 210.0 km/h to take off. On a 1,800.0 m runway, what minimum acceleration is necessary for the plane to reach this speed, assuming acceleration is constant?

A. 0.78 m/s^2

C. 1.47 m/s^2

B. 0.95 m/s^2

D. 1.1 m/s^2

16. A test rocket is fired straight up from rest with a net acceleration of 22 m/s^2. What maximum elevation does the rocket reach if the motor turns off after 4 s, but the rocket continues to coast upward? (Use the acceleration due to gravity $g = 10$ m/s^2)

A. 408 m

C. 357 m

B. 320 m

D. 563 m

17. Without any reference to direction, how fast an object moves refers to its:

A. speed

C. momentum

B. impulse

D. velocity

18. Ignoring air resistance, a 10 kg rock and a 20 kg rock are dropped simultaneously. If the 10 kg rock falls with acceleration a, what is the acceleration of the 20 kg rock?

A. $a / 2$

C. $2a$

B. a

D. $4a$

19. As an object falls freely, its magnitude of:

I. velocity increases   II. acceleration increases   III. displacement increases

A. I only

C. II and III only

B. I and II only

D. I and III only

20. A man stands in an elevator that is ascending at a constant velocity. What forces are being exerted on the man, and in which direction does the net force point?

A. Gravity pointing downward, normal force from the floor pointing upward, and tension force from the elevator cable pointing upward; net force points upward

B. Gravity pointing downward and the normal force from the floor pointing upward; net force points upward

C. Gravity pointing downward and normal force from the floor pointing upward; net force is 0

D. Gravity pointing downward; net force is 0

21. A football kicker is attempting a field goal from 44 m away, and the ball just clears the lower bar with a time of flight of 2.9 s. What was the initial speed of the ball if the angle of the kick was 45° with the horizontal?

    A. 37 m/s   **C.** 18.3 m/s

    B. 2.5 m/s   **D.** 21.4 m/s

22. Ignoring air resistance, if a rock, starting at rest, is dropped from a cliff and strikes the ground with an impact velocity of 14 m/s, from what height was it dropped? (Use the acceleration due to gravity $g = 10$ m/s^2)

    A. 10 m   **C.** 45 m

    B. 30 m   **D.** 70 m

23. An SUV is traveling at 20 m/s. Then Joseph steps on the accelerator pedal, accelerating at a constant 1.4 m/s^2 for 7 s. How far does he travel during these 7 s?

    A. 205 m   **C.** 143 m

    B. 174 m   **D.** 158 m

24. Which of the following is NOT a scalar?

    A. temperature   **C.** mass

    B. distance   **D.** force

25. Two identical balls (A and B) fall from rest from different heights to the ground. Ignoring air resistance, what is the ratio of the heights from which A and B fall if ball B takes twice as long as ball A to reach the ground?

    A. $1 : \sqrt{2}$ **C.** $1 : 2$

    B. $1 : 4$ **D.** $1 : 8$

26. How far does a car travel in 10 s when it accelerates uniformly in one direction from 5 m/s to 30 m/s?

    A. 175 m   **C.** 250 m

    B. 25 m   **D.** 650 m

27. Which graph represents an acceleration of zero?

    A. I only   **C.** I and II only

    B. II only   **D.** II and III only

28. Doubling the distance between an orbiting satellite and the Earth results in what change in the gravitational attraction between the two?

    A. Twice as much

    B. Four times as much

    C. One half as much

    D. One fourth as much

29. An object is moving in a straight line. Consider its motion during some interval of time: under what conditions is it possible for the instantaneous velocity of the object at some point during the interval to be equal to the average velocity over the interval?

    I. When velocity is constant during the interval

    II. When velocity is increasing at a constant rate during the interval

    III. When velocity is increasing at an irregular rate during the interval

    A. II only

    B. I and III only

    C. II and III only

    D. I, II and III

30. A freely falling object on Earth, 10 s after starting from rest, has a speed of about: (Use the acceleration due to gravity $g = 10$ m/s^2)

    A. 10 m/s

    B. 20 m/s

    C. 100 m/s

    D. 150 m/s

31. A truck travels a certain distance at a constant velocity v for time t. If the truck travels three times as fast, covering the same distance, then by what factor does the time of travel in relation to t change?

    A. Increases by 3

    B. Decreases by 3

    C. Decreases by $\sqrt{3}$

    D. Increases by 9

32. Assuming equal rates of acceleration, how much farther would Steve travel if he braked from 59 mi/h to rest than from 29 mi/h to rest?

    A. 2 times farther

    B. 16 times farther

    C. 4 times farther

    D. 3.2 times farther

33. What is the average speed of a racehorse if the horse makes one lap around a 400 m track in 20 s?

    A. 0 m/s

    B. 7.5 m/s

    C. 15 m/s

    D. 20 m/s

34. What was a car's initial velocity if the car is traveling up a slight slope while decelerating at 0.1 m/s^2 and comes to a stop after 5 s?

    A. 0.5 m/s

    B. 0.25 m/s

    C. 2 m/s

    D. 1.5 m/s

35. Average velocity equals the average of an object's initial and final velocity when acceleration is:

A. constantly decreasing

B. constantly increasing

C. constant

D. equal to zero

36. Ignoring air resistance, compared to a rock dropped from the same point, how much earlier does a thrown rock strike the ground if thrown downward with an initial velocity of 10 m/s from the top of a 300 m building? (Use acceleration due to gravity $g = 9.8$ m/s^2)

A. 0.75 s

B. 0.33 s

C. 0.66 s

D. 0.95 s

37. With other factors equal, what happens to the acceleration if the unbalanced force on an object of a given mass is doubled?

A. Increased by one-fourth

B. Increased by one-half

C. Increased fourfold

D. Doubled

38. How fast an object is changing speed or direction of travel is a property of motion is:

A. velocity

B. acceleration

C. speed

D. flow

39. Which statement concerning a car's acceleration must be correct if a car traveling to the North (+y direction) begins to slow down as it approaches a stop sign?

A. Acceleration is positive

B. Acceleration is zero

C. Acceleration is negative

D. Acceleration decreases in magnitude as the car slows

40. For the velocity *vs.* time graph of a basketball player traveling up and down the court in a straight-line path, what is the total distance run by the player in the 10 s?

A. 20 m

B. 22 m

C. 14 m

D. 18 m

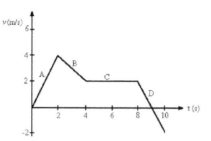

41. At the same time that a bullet is dropped into a river from a high bridge, another bullet is fired from a gun, straight down towards the water. Ignoring air resistance, the acceleration just before striking the water:

A. is greater for the dropped bullet

B. is greater for the fired bullet

C. is the same for each bullet

D. depends on how high the bullets started

42. Sarah starts her car from rest and accelerates at a constant 2.5 m/s^2 for 9 s to get to her cruising speed. What was her final velocity?

A. 22.5 m/s

B. 12.3 m/s

C. 4.6 m/s

D. 8.5 m/s

43. A bat hits a baseball, and the baseball's direction is completely reversed, and its speed is doubled. If the time of contact with the bat is 0.45 s, what is the ratio of the acceleration to the original velocity?

A. -2.5 s^{-1} : 1

B. -0.15 s^{-1} : 1

C. -9.8 s^{-1} : 1

D. -6.7 s^{-1} : 1

44. A 2 kg weight is thrown vertically upward from the surface of the Moon at a speed of 3.2 m/s, and it returns to its starting point in 4 s. What is the magnitude of acceleration due to gravity on the Moon?

A. 0.8 m/s^2

B. 1.6 m/s^2

C. 3.7 m/s^2

D. 8.4 m/s^2

45. What is the change in velocity for a bird cruising at 1.5 m/s and then accelerating at a constant 0.3 m/s^2 for 3 s?

A. 0.9 m/s

B. 0.6 m/s

C. 1.6 m/s

D. 0.3 m/s

46. All the following are vectors, except:

A. velocity

B. displacement

C. acceleration

D. mass

Questions **47-49** are based on the following:

A toy rocket is launched vertically from ground level where $y = 0$ m, at time $t = 0$ s. The rocket engine provides constant upward acceleration during the burn phase. At the instant of engine burnout, the rocket has risen to 64 m and acquired a velocity of 60 m/s. The rocket rises in unpowered flight, reaches the maximum height, and then falls back to the ground. (Use the acceleration due to gravity $g = 9.8$ m/s^2)

47. What is the maximum height reached by the rocket?

A. 274 m

B. 248 m

C. 223 m

D. 120 m

48. What is the upward acceleration of the rocket during the burn phase?

A. 9.9 m/s²   **C.** 28 m/s²

B. 4.8 m/s²   **D.** 11.8 m/s²

49. What is the time interval during which the rocket engine provides upward acceleration?

A. 1.5 s   **C.** 2.3 s

B. 1.9 s   **D.** 2.1 s

50. A car accelerates uniformly from rest along a straight track that has markers spaced at equal distances along it. As it passes Marker 2, the car reaches a speed of 140 km/h. Where on the track is the car when it is traveling at 70 km/h?

A. Close to Marker 2   **C.** Before Marker 1

B. Between Marker 1 and Marker 2   **D.** Close to the starting point

51. What are the two measurements necessary for calculating average speed?

A. Distance and time   **C.** Velocity and time

B. Distance and acceleration   **D.** Velocity and acceleration

52. A pedestrian traveling at speed v covers a distance x during a time interval t. If a bicycle travels at speed $3v$, how much time does it take to travel the same distance?

A. $t / 3$ **C.** $t + 3^2$

B. $t - 3$ **D.** $3t$

53. Ignoring air resistance, how much time passes before a ball strikes the ground if it is thrown straight upward with a velocity of 39 m/s? (Use acceleration due to gravity $g = 9.8$ m/s²)

A. 2.2 s   **C.** 12 s

B. 8 s   **D.** 4 s

54. A particle travels to the right along a horizontal axis with a constantly decreasing speed. Which one of the following describes the direction of the particle's acceleration?

A. ↑   **C.** →

B. ↓   **D.** ←

55. Larry is carrying a 25 kg package at a constant velocity of 1.8 m/s across a room for 12 s. What is the work done by Larry on the package during the 12 s? (Use the acceleration due to gravity $g = 10$ m/s²)

    A. 0 J

    B. 280 J

    C. 860 J

    D. 2,200 J

56. What does the slope of a tangent line at a time value on a velocity *vs.* time graph represent?

    A. Instantaneous acceleration

    B. Average acceleration

    C. Instantaneous velocity

    D. Position

57. A car is traveling North at 17.7 m/s. After 12 s, its velocity is 14.1 m/s in the same direction. What is the magnitude and direction of the car's average acceleration?

    A. 0.3 m/s², North

    B. 2.7 m/s², North

    C. 0.3 m/s², South

    D. 3.6 m/s², South

58. The graph below shows the position of an object as a function of time. The letters A –E represent particular moments in time. At which moment in time is the speed of the object the highest?

    A. A

    B. B

    C. C

    D. D

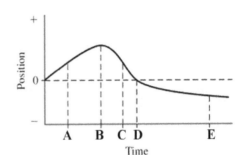

59. At a speed less than terminal velocity, what is happening to the speed of an object falling toward the surface of the Earth?

    A. Decreasing at a decreasing rate

    B. Increasing at a decreasing rate

    C. Decreasing

    D. Constant

60. How far does a car travel if it starts from rest and accelerates at a constant 2 m/s² for 10 s, then travels with the constant speed it has achieved for another 10 s, and finally slows to a stop with a constant deceleration of magnitude 2 m/s²?

    A. 150 m

    B. 200 m

    C. 350 m

    D. 400 m

61. While a car travels around a circular track at a constant speed, its:

    I. acceleration changes   II. acceleration is zero   III. velocity is zero

    A. I only

    B. II only

    C. III only

    D. I and III only

62. How long does a ball take to fall if it is dropped from a height of 10 m to the ground and experiences a constant downward acceleration of 9.8 m/s^2?

A. 1.1 s

B. 1.4 s

C. 2.4 s

D. 3.1 s

63. A car travels 95 km North at 70 km/h, then turns around and travels 21.9 km at 80 km/h. What is the difference between the average speed and the average velocity on this trip?

A. 58 km/h

B. 37 km/h

C. 19 km/h

D. 27 km/h

64. What is the acceleration of a car that accelerates uniformly from 0 to 60 mi/h in 6 s?

A. 10 mi·h^{-1}·s^{-1}

B. 10 m/h^2

C. 10 mi/h

D. 10 m/s^2

65. What is a car's average velocity when it accelerates uniformly in one dimension from 5 m/s to 30 m/s in 10 s?

A. 4.5 m/s

B. 15 m/s

C. 17.5 m/s

D. 7.5 m/s

66. Which graph represents a constant non-zero velocity?

I.

II.

III.

A. I only

B. II only

C. III only

D. II and III only

67. A train starts from rest and accelerates uniformly until it has traveled 5.6 km and has acquired a velocity of 42 m/s. The train then moves at a constant velocity of 42 m/s for 420 s. The train then slows down uniformly at 0.065 m/s^2 until it stops moving. What is the acceleration during the first 5.6 km of travel?

A. 0.29 m/s^2

B. 0.23 m/s^2

C. 0.16 m/s^2

D. 0.12 m/s^2

68. A cannonball is fired straight up at 50 m/s. Ignoring air resistance, what is the velocity at the highest point it reaches before starting to return towards Earth?

A. 0 m/s

B. 25 m/s

C. √50 m/s

D. 50 m/s

69. The tendency of a moving object to remain in unchanging motion in the absence of an unbalanced force is:

    A. impulse

    B. acceleration

    C. free fall

    D. inertia

70. Which statement is correct when an object moving in the $+x$ direction undergoes an acceleration of 2 m/s^2?

    A. It travels at 2 m/s

    B. It travels at 2 m/s^2

    C. It decreases its velocity by 2 m/s every second

    D. It increases its velocity by 2 m/s every second

71. What is the increase in speed each second for a freely falling object?

    A. 0 m/s

    B. 9.8 m/s^2

    C. 9.8 m/s

    D. 19.6 m/s

72. A marble initially rolls up a slight incline at 0.2 m/s and, starting at $t = 0$ s, decelerates uniformly at 0.05 m/s^2. At what time does the marble come to a stop?

    A. 2 s

    B. 4 s

    C. 8 s

    D. 12 s

73. An 8.7-hour trip is made at an average speed of 73 km/h. If the first third of the journey was driven at 96.5 km/h, what was the average speed for the rest of the trip?

    A. 54 km/hr

    B. 46 km/hr

    C. 28 km/hr

    D. 62 km/hr

74. The lightning flash and the thunder are not observed simultaneously because light travels much faster than sound. Therefore, it can be assumed as instantaneous when lightning occurs. What is the distance from the lightning bolt to the observer, if the delay between the sound and the lightning flash is 6 s? (Use speed of sound in air $v = 340$ m/s)

    A. 2,040 m

    B. 880 m

    C. 2,360 m

    D. 2,820 m

75. If a cat jumps at a 60° angle off the ground with an initial velocity of 2.74 m/s, what is the highest point of the cat's trajectory? (Use the acceleration due to gravity $g = 9.8$ m/s^2)

    A. 9.46 m

    B. 0.69 m

    C. 5.75 m

    D. 0.29 m

76. What is the resultant vector AB when vector A = 6 m and points 30° North of East, while vector B = 4 m and points 30° South of West?

    A. 8 m at an angle 45° East of North

    B. 8 m at an angle 30° North of East

    C. 2 m at an angle 30° North of East

    D. 2 m at an angle 45° North of East

77. How much farther would an intoxicated driver's car travel before he hits the brakes than a sober driver's car if both cars are initially traveling at 49 mi/h, and the sober driver takes 0.33 s to hit the brakes. In contrast, the intoxicated driver takes 1 s to hit the brakes?

    A. 38 ft.

    B. 52 ft.

    C. 32 ft.

    D. 48 ft.

Notes for active learning

Notes for active learning

Force, Motion, Gravitation

1. A boy attaches a weight to a string, which he swings counterclockwise in a horizontal circle. Which path does the weight follow when the string breaks at point P?

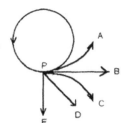

    A. path A   **C.** path C

    B. path B   **D.** path D

2. A garment bag hangs from a clothesline. The tension in the clothesline is 10 N on the right side of the garment bag and 10 N on the left side of the garment bag. The clothesline makes an angle of 60° from vertical. What is the mass of the garment bag? (Use the acceleration due to gravity g = 10.0 m/s^2)

    A. 0.5 kg   **C.** 4 kg

    B. 8 kg   **D.** 1 kg

3. A sheet of paper can be withdrawn from under a milk carton without toppling the carton if the paper is jerked away quickly. This demonstrates:

    A. the inertia of the milk carton

    B. that gravity tends to hold the milk carton secure

    C. there is an action-reaction pair of forces

    D. that the milk carton has no acceleration

4. A car of mass *m* is going up a shallow slope with an angle θ to the horizontal when the driver suddenly applies the brakes. The car skids as it comes to a stop. The coefficient of static friction between the tires and the road is μ_s, and the coefficient of kinetic friction is μ_k. Which expression represents the normal force on the car?

    A. *mg* tan θ **C.** *mg* cos θ

    B. *mg* sin θ **D.** *mg*

5. A 27 kg object is accelerated at a rate of 1.7 m/s^2. How much force does the object experience?

    A. 62 N   **C.** 7 N

    B. 74 N   **D.** 46 N

6. How are two identical masses moving if they are attached by a light string that passes over a small pulley? Assume that the table and the pulley are frictionless.

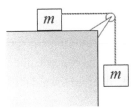

    A. With an acceleration equal to *g*

    B. With an acceleration greater than *g*

    C. At a constant speed

    D. With an acceleration less than *g*

7. An object is moving to the right in a straight line. The net force acting on the object is directed to the right, but the magnitude of the force decreases with time. What happens to the object?

    A. Continues to move to the right with its speed increasing with time

    B. Continues to move to the right with a constant speed

    C. Continues to move to the right with its speed decreasing with time

    D. Continues to move to the right, slowing quickly to a stop

8. A crate is sliding down an inclined ramp at a constant speed of 0.55 m/s. Where does the vector sum of the forces acting on this crate point?

    A. Perpendicular to the ramp   **C.** Vertically upward

    B. Vertically downward   **D.** None of the above

9. Consider an inclined plane that makes an angle θ with the horizontal. What is the relationship between the length of the ramp L and the vertical height of the ramp h?

    A. $h = L \sin \theta$ **C.** $L = h \sin \theta$

    B. $h = L \tan \theta$ **D.** $h = L \cos \theta$

10. Why is it just as difficult to accelerate a car on the Moon as it is to accelerate the same car on Earth?

    I. Moon and Earth have the same gravity

    II. weight of the car is independent of gravity

    III. mass of the car is independent of gravity

    A. I only   **C.** III only

    B. II only   **D.** I and II only

11. Sean is pulling his son in a toy wagon. His son and the wagon are 60 kg. For 3 s, Sean exerts a force that uniformly accelerates the wagon from 1.5 m/s to 3.5 m/s. What is the acceleration of the wagon with his son?

    A. 0.67 m/s^2 **C.** 1.66 m/s^2

    B. 0.84 m/s^2 **D.** 15.32 m/s^2

12. When an object moves in uniform circular motion, the direction of its acceleration is:

    A. directed away from the center of its circular path

    B. dependent on its speed

    C. in the opposite direction of its velocity vector

    D. directed toward the center of its circular path

13. What happens to a moving object in the absence of an external force?

    A. Gradually accelerates until terminal velocity, at which point it continues at a constant velocity

    B. Moves with constant velocity

    C. Stops immediately

    D. Slows and eventually stops

14. A force of 1 N causes a 1 kg mass to accelerate 1 m/s². From this information, a force of 9 N applied to a 9 kg mass would have what magnitude of acceleration?

    A. 18 m/s²

    B. 9 m/s²

    C. 1 m/s²

    D. 3 m/s²

15. Which statement is true about an object in two-dimensional projectile motion with no air resistance?

    A. The acceleration of the object is zero at its highest point

    B. The horizontal acceleration is always positive, regardless of the vertical acceleration

    C. The velocity is always in the same direction as the acceleration

    D. The horizontal acceleration is always zero, and vertical acceleration is always a nonzero constant downward

16. A can of paint with a mass of 10 kg hangs from a rope. If the can is to be pulled up to a rooftop with a constant velocity of 0.5 m/s, what must the tension on the rope be? (Use acceleration due to gravity $g = 10$ m/s²)

    A. 100 N

    B. 40 N

    C. 0 N

    D. 120 N

17. What is the magnitude of the force exerted on a 1,000 kg object that accelerates at 2 m/s²?

    A. 500 N

    B. 1,000 N

    C. 1,200 N

    D. 2,000 N

18. A 1,300 kg car is driven at a constant speed of 4 m/s and turns to the right on a curve on the road with an effective radius of 4 m. What is the acceleration of the car?

    A. 0 m/s²

    B. 3 m/s²

    C. 4 m/s²

    D. 9.8 m/s²

19. A block of mass m is resting on a 20° slope. The block has a coefficient of friction $\mu_s =$ 0.55 and $\mu_k = 0.45$ with the surface.

Block m is connected via a massless string over a massless, frictionless pulley to a hanging 2 kg block. What is the minimum mass of block m so that it does not slip? (Use the acceleration due to gravity $g = 9.8$ m/s²)

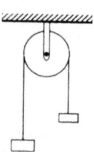

A. 0.8 kg

B. 1.3 kg

C. 3.7 kg

D. 2.3 kg

20. As shown in the figure to the right, two identical masses, attached by a light cord passing over a massless, frictionless pulley on an Atwood's machine, are hanging at different heights. If the two masses are suddenly released, then the:

A. lower mass moves down

B. masses remain stationary

C. higher mass moves down

D. motion is unpredictable

21. When Victoria jumps up in the air, which of the following statements is the most accurate?

A. The ground cannot exert the upward force necessary to lift her into the air because the ground is stationary. Instead, Victoria is propelled into the air by the internal force of her muscles acting on her body

B. When Victoria pushes down on the Earth with force greater than her weight, the Earth pushes back with the same magnitude force and propels her into the air

C. Victoria is propelled up by the upward force exerted by the ground, but this force cannot be greater than her weight

D. The Earth exerts an upward force on Victoria that is stronger than the downward force she exerts on the Earth; therefore, Victoria is able to spring up

22. If a feather is pounded with a hammer, which experiences a greater force?

A. The magnitude of the force is always the same on both

B. If the feather moves, then it feels the greater force

C. Depends on the force with which the hammer strikes the feather

D. Always the hammer

23. A block is moving down a slope of a frictionless inclined plane. Compared to the weight of the block, what is the force parallel to the surface of the plane experienced by the block?

A. Greater

B. Unrelated

C. Less than

D. Equal

24. A package falls off a truck that is moving at 30 m/s. Ignoring air resistance, the horizontal speed of the package just before it hits the ground is:

A. 0 m/s

B. 15 m/s

C. $\sqrt{60}$ m/s

D. 30 m/s

25. A carousel with the radius *r* is turning counterclockwise at a frequency *f*. How does the velocity of a seat on the carousel change when *f* is doubled?

A. Increases by a factor of 2*r*

B. Increases by a factor of *r*

C. Remains unchanged

D. Doubles

26. What is the mass of a car if it takes 4,500 N to accelerate it at a rate of 5 m/s²?

A. 900 kg

B. 1,320 kg

C. 620 kg

D. 460 kg

27. Steve is standing facing forward in a moving bus. What force causes Steve to suddenly move forward when the bus comes to an abrupt stop?

A. Force due to the air pressure inside the previously moving bus

B. Force due to kinetic friction between Steve and the floor of the bus

C. Force due to stored kinetic energy

D. No forces were responsible for Steve's movement

28. A plastic ball in a liquid is acted upon by its weight and a buoyant force. The weight of the ball is 4.4 N. The buoyant force of 8.4 N acts vertically upward. An external force acting on the ball maintains it in a state of rest. What is the magnitude and direction of the external force?

A. 4 N, upward

B. 8.4 N, downward

C. 4.4 N, upward

D. 4 N, downward

29. A passenger on a train traveling in the forward direction notices that a piece of luggage starts to slide directly toward the front of the train. From this, it can be concluded that the train is:

A. slowing down

B. speeding up

C. moving at a constant velocity forward

D. changing direction

30. An object has a mass of 36 kg and weighs 360 N at the surface of the Earth. If this object is transported to an altitude that is twice the Earth's radius, what is the object's mass and weight, respectively?

A. 9 kg and 90 N

B. 36 kg and 90 N

C. 4 kg and 90 N

D. 36 kg and 40 N

31. A truck is moving at constant velocity. Inside the storage compartment, a rock is dropped from the midpoint of the ceiling and strikes the floor below. The rock hits the floor:

A. just behind the midpoint of the ceiling

B. exactly halfway between the midpoint and the front of the truck

C. exactly below the midpoint of the ceiling

D. just ahead of the midpoint of the ceiling

32. Jason takes off across level water on his jet-powered skis. The combined mass of Jason and his skis is 75 kg (the mass of the fuel is negligible). The skis have a thrust of 200 N and a coefficient of kinetic friction on the water of 0.1. If the skis run out of fuel after only 67 s, how far has Jason traveled before he stops?

A. 5,428 m   **C.** 8,224 m

B. 3,793 m   **D.** 10,331 m

33. A 200 g hockey puck is launched up a metal ramp inclined at a 30° angle. The puck's initial speed is 63 m/s. What vertical height does the puck reach above its starting point? (Use acceleration due to gravity $g = 9.8$ m/s^2, coefficient of static friction $\mu_s = 0.40$ and kinetic friction $\mu_k = 0.30$ between the puck and the metal ramp)

A. 66 m   **C.** 170 m

B. 200 m   **D.** 130 m

34. When a 4 kg mass and a 10 kg mass are pushed from rest with equal force:

A. 4 kg mass accelerates 2.5 times faster than the 10 kg mass

B. 10 kg mass accelerates 10 times faster than the 4 kg mass

C. 4 kg mass accelerates at the same rate as the 10 kg mass

D. 10 kg mass accelerates 2.5 times faster than the 4 kg mass

35. On a different planet, a person's:

A. weight and mass decrease   **C.** weight remains the same, but mass changes

B. weight and mass remain the same   **D.** weight changes, but mass remains the same

36. Which of the following statements must be valid when a 20-ton truck collides with a 1,500 lb car?

A. During the collision, the force on the truck is equal to the force on the car

B. The truck did not slow down during the collision, but the car did

C. During the collision, the force on the truck is greater than the force on the car

D. During the collision, the force on the truck is smaller than the force on the car

37. A block is on a frictionless table on Earth. The block accelerates at 3 m/s^2 when a 20 N horizontal force is applied to it. The block and table are then transported to the Moon. What is the weight of the block on the Moon? (Use the acceleration due to gravity at the surface of the Moon = 1.62 m/s^2)

    A. 5.8 N   **C.** 8.5 N

    B. 14.2 N   **D.** 11 N

38. What is the weight of a 0.4 kg bottle of wine? (Use acceleration due to gravity $g = 9.8$ m/s^2)

    A. 0.4 N   **C.** 40 N

    B. 4 N   **D.** 20 N

39. Car A starts from rest and accelerates uniformly for time t to travel a distance of d. Car B, which has four times the mass of car A, starts from rest and accelerates uniformly. If the magnitudes of the forces accelerating car A and car B are the same, how long does it take car B to travel the same distance d?

    A. t **C.** $t/2$

    B. $2t$ **D.** $16t$

40. A 1,100 kg vehicle is traveling at 27 m/s when it starts to decelerate. What is the average braking force acting on the vehicle, if after 578 m, it comes to a complete stop?

    A. –440 N   **C.** –690 N

    B. –740 N   **D.** –540 N

41. An ornament of mass M is suspended by a string from the ceiling inside an elevator. What is the tension in the string holding the ornament when the elevator is traveling upward at a constant speed?

    A. Equal to Mg **C.** Greater than Mg

    B. Less than Mg **D.** Equal to M/g

42. An object that weighs 75 N is pulled on a horizontal surface by a force of 50 N to the right. The friction force on this object is 30 N to the left. What is the acceleration of the object? (Use the acceleration due to gravity $g = 9.8$ m/s^2)

    A. 0.46 m/s^2 **C.** 2.6 m/s^2

    B. 1.7 m/s^2 **D.** 10.3 m/s^2

43. While flying horizontally in an airplane, a string attached from the overhead luggage compartment hangs at rest 15° away from the vertical toward the front of the plane. From this observation, it can be concluded that the airplane is:

    A. accelerating forward   **C.** accelerating upward at 15° from horizontal

    B. accelerating backward   **D.** moving backward

44. An object slides down an inclined ramp at a constant speed. If the ramp's incline angle is θ, what is the coefficient of kinetic friction (μ_k) between the object and the ramp?

A. $\mu_k = 1$

C. $\mu_k = \sin\theta / \cos\theta$

B. $\mu_k = \cos\theta / \sin\theta$

D. $\mu_k = \sin\theta$

45. What is the magnitude of the net force on a 1 N apple when it is in free fall?

A. 1 N

C. 0.01 N

B. 0.1 N

D. 10 N

46. What is the acceleration of a 105 kg tiger that accelerates uniformly from rest to 20 m/s in 10 s?

A. 4.7 m/s²

C. 2 m/s²

B. 1.5 m/s²

D. 3.4 m/s²

47. Yania tries to pull an object by tugging on a rope attached to the object with a force of F. If the object does not move, what does this imply?

A. The object has reached its natural state of rest and can no longer be set into motion

B. The rope is not transmitting the force to the object

C. No other forces are acting on the object

D. There are one or more other forces that act on the object with a sum of $-F$

48. If a force F is exerted on an object, the force which the object exerts back:

A. depends on the mass of the object

C. depends on if the object is moving

B. depends on the density of the object

D. equals $-F$

49. What is the mass of an object that experiences a gravitational force of 685 N near Earth's surface? (Use the acceleration due to gravity $g = 9.8$ m/s²)

A. 76 kg

C. 70 kg

B. 62 kg

D. 81 kg

50. Sarah and her father Bob (who weighs four times as much) are standing on identical skateboards (with frictionless ball bearings), both initially at rest. For a brief time, Bob pushes Sarah on the skateboard. When Bob stops pushing:

A. Sarah and Bob move away from each other, and Sarah's speed is four times that of Bob's

B. Sarah and Bob move away from each other, and Sarah's speed is one-fourth of Bob's

C. Sarah and Bob move away from each other with equal speeds

D. Sarah moves away from Bob, and Bob is stationary

51. Considering the effects of friction, which statement best describes the motion of an object along a surface?

    A. Less force is required to start than to keep the object in motion at a constant velocity

    B. The same force is required to start to keep the object in motion at a constant velocity

    C. More force is required to start than to keep the object in motion at a constant velocity

    D. Once the object is set in motion, no force is required to keep it in motion at constant velocity

52. On the surface of Jupiter, the acceleration due to gravity is about three times that on Earth. What is the weight of a 100 kg rock when it is taken from Earth to Jupiter? (Use acceleration due to gravity $g = 10$ m/s^2)

    A. 1,800 N   **C.** 3,300 N

    B. 3,000 N   **D.** 4,000 N

53. Joe and Bill are playing tug-of-war. Joe is pulling with a force of 200 N, while Bill is simply holding onto the rope. What is the tension of the rope if neither person is moving?

    A. 75 N   **C.** 100 N

    B. 0 N   **D.** 200 N

54. A 4 kg wooden block A slides on a frictionless table pulled by a hanging 5 kg block B via a massless string and pulley system as shown. What is the acceleration of block A as it slides? (Use acceleration due to gravity $g = 9.8$ m/s^2)

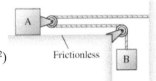

    A. 2.8 m/s^2 **C.** 3.4 m/s^2

    B. 1.6 m/s^2 **D.** 4.1 m/s^2

55. Which of the following best describes the direction in which the force of kinetic friction acts relative to the interface between the interacting bodies?

    A. Parallel to the interface and in the same direction as the relative velocity

    B. Parallel to the interface and in the opposite direction of the relative velocity

    C. Perpendicular to the interface and in the same direction as the relative velocity

    D. Perpendicular to the interface and in the opposite direction of the relative velocity

56. A person who normally weighs 600 N is standing on a scale in an elevator. The elevator is initially moving upwards at a constant speed of 8 m/s and starts to slow down at a rate of 6 m/s^2. What is the reading of the person's weight on the scale in the elevator during the slowdown? (Use acceleration due to gravity $g = 9.8$ m/s^2)

    A. 600 N   **C.** 98 N

    B. 588 N   **D.** 233 N

57. When a satellite is in orbit around the Moon, which of the two objects feels the greater force?

    A. It depends on the distance of the satellite from the Moon

    B. The Moon and the satellite feel the same force

    C. The Moon because the satellite has a smaller mass

    D. The satellite because the Moon is much more massive

58. What is the acceleration of a 40 kg crate pulled along a frictionless surface by a force of 140 N that makes an angle of 30° with the surface?

    A. 1.5 m/s^2 **C.** 2.5 m/s^2

    B. 2 m/s^2 **D.** 3 m/s^2

59. A force is a vector quantity because it has:

    I. action and reaction counterparts

    II. mass and acceleration

    III. magnitude and direction

    A. I only   **C.** III only

    B. II only   **D.** I and II only

Questions **60-61** are based on the following:

Alice pulls her daughter on a sled by a rope on level snow. Alice is 70 kg, and her daughter is 20 kg. The sled has a mass of 10 kg, which slides along the snow with a coefficient of kinetic friction of 0.09. The tension in the rope is 30 N, making an angle of 30° with the ground. They are moving at a constant 2.5 m/s for 4 s. (Use the acceleration due to gravity $g = 10$ m/s^2)

60. What is the work done by the force of gravity on the sled?

    A. −3,000 J   **C.** 1,000 J

    B. 0 J   **D.** 3,000 J

61. What is the work done by the rope on the sled?

    A. 0 J   **C.** 65 J

    B. 130 J   **D.** 260 J

62. What is the net force acting at the top of the path for an arrow shot upwards?

    A. Greater than its weight   **C.** Instantaneously equal to zero

    B. Equal to its weight   **D.** Greater than zero, but less than its weight

---

63. If an object weighs 740 N on Earth and 5,180 N on the surface of a nearby planet, what is the acceleration due to gravity on that planet? (Use acceleration due to gravity $g = 10$ m/s²)

A. 82 m/s²
C. 54 m/s²

B. 62 m/s²
D. 70 m/s²

64. Susan pushes on box G next to box H, causing both boxes to slide along the floor, as shown. The reaction force of Susan's push is the:

A. upward force of the floor on box G
C. push of box H on box G

B. push of box G against Susan
D. push of box G on box H

65. Two bodies of different masses are subjected to identical forces. Compared to the body with a smaller mass, the body with a greater mass experiences:

A. less acceleration because the ratio of force to mass is smaller
B. greater acceleration because the ratio of force to mass is greater
C. less acceleration because the product of mass and acceleration is smaller
D. greater acceleration because the product of mass and acceleration is greater

66. An object is propelled along a straight-line path by force. If the net force were doubled, the object's acceleration would:

A. halve
C. double

B. stay the same
D. quadruple

67. A 500 kg rocket ship is firing two jets at once. The two jets are at right angles, with one firing with a force of 500 N and the other with a force of 1,200 N. What is the magnitude of the acceleration of the rocket ship?

A. 1.4 m/s²
C. 3.4 m/s²

B. 2.6 m/s²
D. 5.6 m/s²

68. Assume the strings and pulleys in the diagram have negligible masses and the coefficient of kinetic friction between the 2 kg block and the table is 0.25. What is the acceleration of the 2 kg block? (Use acceleration due to gravity $g = 9.8$ m/s²)

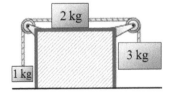

A. 3.2 m/s²
C. 0.3 m/s²

B. 4 m/s²
D. 2.5 m/s²

69. Which of the following must be true for an object moving with constant velocity in a straight line?

    A. The net force on the object is zero

    B. No forces are acting on the object

    C. A constant force is being applied in the direction opposite of motion

    D. A constant force is being applied in the direction of motion

70. A person gives a shopping cart an initial push along a horizontal floor to get it moving and then releases the cart. The cart travels forward along the floor, gradually slowing as it moves. Consider the horizontal force on the cart while it is moving forward and slowing. Which of the following statements is correct?

    A. Only a forward force is acting, which diminishes with time

    B. Only a backward force is acting; no forward force is acting

    C. Both a forward and a backward force are acting on the cart, but the forward force is larger

    D. Both a forward and a backward force are acting on the cart, but the backward force is larger

71. A truck uses a hook to tow a car whose mass is one-quarter that of the truck. If the force exerted by the truck on the car is 6,000 N, then the force exerted by the car on the truck is:

    A. 1,500 N   **C.** 6,000 N

    B. 24,000 N   **D.** 12,000 N

72. How large is the force of friction impeding the motion of a bureau when the 120 N bureau is being pulled across the sidewalk at a constant speed by a force of 30 N?

    A. 0 N   **C.** 120 N

    B. 30 N   **D.** 3 N

73. An object maintains its state of motion because it has:

    A. mass   **C.** speed

    B. acceleration   **D.** weight

74. The Earth and the Moon attract each other with the force of gravity. The Earth's radius is 3.7 times that of the Moon, and the Earth's mass is 80 times greater than the Moon's. The acceleration due to gravity on the surface of the Moon is 1/6 the acceleration due to gravity on the Earth's surface. If the distance between the Earth and Moon decreases by a factor of 4, how would the force of gravity between the Earth and Moon change?

    A. Remain the same   **C.** Decrease by a factor of 16

    B. Increase by a factor of 16   **D.** Decrease by a factor of 4

75. Two forces acting on an object have magnitudes $F_1 = -6.6$ N and $F_2 = 2.2$ N. Which third force causes the object to be in equilibrium?

    A. 4.4 N at 162° counterclockwise from F_1

    B. 4.4 N at 108° counterclockwise from F_1

    C. 7 N at 162° counterclockwise from F_1

    D. 7 N at 108° counterclockwise from F_1

76. What are the readings on the spring scales when a 17 kg fish is weighed with two spring scales if each scale has negligible weight?

    A. The top scale reads 17 kg, and the bottom scale reads 0 kg

    B. Each scale reads greater than 0 kg and less than 17 kg, but the sum of the scales is 17 kg

    C. The bottom scale reads 17 kg, and the top scale reads 0 kg

    D. The sum of the two scales is 34 kg

77. Two forces of equal magnitude are acting on an object, as shown. If the magnitude of each force is 2.3 N and the angle between them is 40°, which third force causes the object to be in equilibrium?

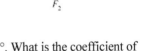

    A. 1.8 N pointing to the right   **C.** 3.5 N pointing to the right

    B. 2.2 N pointing to the right   **D.** 4.3 N pointing to the right

78. An object at rest on an inclined plane starts to slide when the incline is increased to 17°. What is the coefficient of static friction between the object and the plane? (Use the acceleration due to gravity $g = 9.8$ m/s²)

    A. 0.37   **C.** 0.24

    B. 0.43   **D.** 0.31

79. What is the force exerted by the table on a 2 kg book resting on it? (Use the acceleration due to gravity $g = 10$ m/s²)

    A. 100 N   **C.** 10 N

    B. 20 N   **D.** 0 N

Notes for active learning

Equilibrium and Momentum

1. When is the angular momentum of a system constant?

   A. When no net external torque acts on the system
   B. When the linear momentum and the energy are constant
   C. When no net external force acts on the system
   D. When the total kinetic energy is positive

2. When a rock rolls down a mountainside at 7 m/s, the horizontal component of its velocity vector is 1.8 m/s. What was the angle of the mountain surface above the horizontal?

   A. 15°   **C.** 40°
   B. 63°   **D.** 75°

3. A 200 N sled slides down a frictionless hill at an angle of 37° to the horizontal. What is the magnitude of the force that the hill exerts on the sled parallel to the surface of the hill?

   A. 170 N   **C.** 74 N
   B. 200 N   **D.** 0 N

4. Water causes a water wheel to turn as it passes by. The force of the water is 300 N, and the radius of the wheel is 10 m. What is the torque around the center of the wheel?

   A. 0 N·m   **C.** 3,000 N·m
   B. 300 N·m   **D.** 3 N·m

5. Through what angle, in degrees, does a 33 rpm record turn in 0.32 s?

   A. 44°   **C.** 113°
   B. 94°   **D.** 63°

6. A freight train rolls along a track with considerable momentum. What is its momentum if it rolls at the same speed but has twice the mass?

   A. Zero   **C.** Quadrupled
   B. Doubled   **D.** Unchanged

Questions **7-9** are based on the following:

Three carts run along a level, frictionless one-dimensional track. Furthest to the left is a 1 kg cart I, moving at 0.5 m/s to the right. In the middle is a 1.5 kg cart II, moving at 0.3 m/s to the left. Furthest to the right is a 3.5 kg cart III moving at 0.5 m/s to the left. The carts collide in sequence, sticking together. (Assume the direction to the right is the positive direction)

7. What is the total momentum of the system before the collision?

A. −2.6 kg·m/s   **C.** 0.6 kg·m/s

B. 1.4 kg·m/s   **D.** −1.7 kg·m/s

8. Assuming cart I and cart II collide first, and cart III is still independent, what is the total momentum of the system just after cart I and cart II collide?

A. −1.7 kg·m/s   **C.** 0.9 kg·m/s

B. 0.1 kg·m/s   **D.** −0.9 kg·m/s

9. What is the final velocity of the three carts?

A. −0.35 m/s   **C.** −0.87 m/s

B. −0.28 m/s   **D.** 0.35 m/s

10. A 480 kg car is moving at 14.4 m/s when it collides with another car moving at 13.3 m/s in the same direction. If the second car has a mass of 570 kg and a new velocity of 17.9 m/s after the collision, what is the velocity of the first car after the collision?

A. 19 m/s   **C.** 9 m/s

B. −9 m/s   **D.** 14 m/s

11. An 8 g bullet is shot into a 4 kg block at rest on a frictionless horizontal surface. The bullet remains lodged in the block. The block moves into a spring and compresses it by 8.9 cm. After the block comes to a stop, the spring fully decompresses and sends the block in the opposite direction. What is the magnitude of the impulse of the block (including the bullet), due to the spring, during the entire time interval in which the block and spring are in contact? (Use the spring constant = 1,400 N/m)

A. 11 N·s   **C.** 6.4 N·s

B. 8.3 N·s   **D.** 13 N·s

12. An ice skater performs a fast spin by pulling in her outstretched arms close to her body. What happens to her rotational kinetic energy about the axis of rotation?

A. Decreases   **C.** Increases

B. Remains the same   **D.** It changes, but it depends on her body mass

13. A toy car is traveling in a circular path. The force required to maintain this motion is F. If the velocity of the object is doubled, what is the force required to maintain its motion?

A. $2F$

B. F

C. $\frac{1}{2}F$

D. $4F$

14. Which of the following are units of momentum?

A. $kg \cdot m/s^2$

B. $J \cdot s/m$

C. $N \cdot m$

D. $kg \cdot s$

15. The impulse on an apple hitting the ground depends on:

    I. the speed of the apple just before it hits

    II. whether the apple bounces

    III. the time of impact with the ground

A. I only

B. II only

C. III only

D. I, II and III

16. A 55 kg girl throws a 0.8 kg ball against a wall. The ball strikes the wall horizontally with a speed of 25 m/s and bounces back at the same speed. The ball is in contact with the wall for 0.05 s. What is the average force exerted on the wall by the ball?

A. 27,500 N

B. 55,000 N

C. 400 N

D. 800 N

17. Three objects are moving along a straight line as shown. If the positive direction is to the right, what is the total momentum of this system?

A. -70 kg·m/s

B. $+70$ kg·m/s

C. $+86$ kg·m/s

D. -86 kg·m/s

6 m/s   3 m/s   2 m/s

7 kg   12 kg   4 kg

Questions **18-19** are based on the following:

Two ice skaters, Vladimir (60 kg) and Olga (40 kg), collide in midair. Before the collision, Vladimir was going North at 0.5 m/s, and Olga was going West at 1 m/s. Right after the collision and well before they land on the ground, they stick. Assume they have no vertical velocity.

18. What is the magnitude of their velocity just after the collision?

A. 0.1 m/s

B. 1.8 m/s

C. 0.9 m/s

D. 0.5 m/s

19. What is the magnitude of the total momentum just after the collision?

A. 25 kg·m/s

C. 65 kg·m/s

B. 50 kg·m/s

D. 80 kg·m/s

20. A horse is running in a straight line. If both the mass and the speed of the horse are doubled, by what factor does its momentum increase?

A. $\sqrt{2}$

C. 4

B. 2

D. 8

21. The mass of box P is greater than the mass of box Q. Both boxes are on a frictionless horizontal surface and connected by a light cord. A horizontal force F is applied to box Q, accelerating the boxes to the right. What is the magnitude of the force exerted by the connecting cord on box P?

A. equal to F

C. zero

B. equal to $2F$

D. less than F but > 0

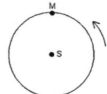

22. Which of the following is true when Melissa (M) and her friend Samantha (S) are riding on a merry-go-round, as viewed from above?

A. They have the same speed, but different angular velocity

B. They have different speeds, but the same angular velocity

C. They have the same speed and the same angular velocity

D. They have different speeds and different angular velocities

23. The relationship between impulse and impact force involves the:

A. time the force acts

B. distance the force acts

C. difference between acceleration and velocity

D. mass and its effect on resisting a change in velocity

24. Angular momentum cannot be conserved if the:

A. moment of inertia changes

C. angular velocity changes

B. system is experiencing a net force

D. system has a net torque

25. A 6.8-kg block moves on a frictionless surface with a speed of $v_i = 5.4$ m/s and makes a perfectly elastic collision with a 4.8-kg stationary block. After the collision, the 6.8-kg block recoils with a speed of $v_f = 3.2$ m/s. What is the magnitude of the average force on the 6.8-kg block while the two blocks are in contact for 2 s?

A. 4.4 N

C. 32.6 N

B. 46.1 N

D. 29.2 N

Questions **26-27** are based on the following:

A 4 kg rifle imparts a high velocity to a small 10 g bullet by exploding a charge that causes the bullet to leave the barrel at 300 m/s. Take the system as the combination of the rifle and bullet. Typically, the rifle is fired with the butt of the gun pressed against the shooter's shoulder and ignore the force of the shoulder on the rifle.

26. What is the momentum of the system just after the bullet leaves the barrel?

A. 0 kg·m/s

B. 3 kg·m/s

C. 9 kg·m/s

D. 30 kg·m/s

27. What is the recoil velocity of the rifle (i.e., the velocity of the rifle just after firing)?

A. 23 m/s

B. 1.5 m/s

C. 5.6 m/s

D. 0.75 m/s

28. A ball thrown horizontally from a point 24 m above the ground strikes the ground after traveling horizontally at a distance of 18 m. With what speed was it thrown, assuming negligible air resistance? (Use the acceleration due to gravity $g = 9.8$ m/s^2)

A. 6.8 m/s

B. 7.5 m/s

C. 8.1 m/s

D. 8.6 m/s

29. An object is moving in a circle at a constant speed. Its acceleration vector is directed:

A. toward the center of the circle

B. away from the center of the circle

C. tangent to the circle and in the direction of the motion

D. behind the normal and toward the center of the circle

30. Impulse is equal to the:

    I. force multiplied by the distance over which the force acts

    II. change in momentum

    III. momentum

A. I only

B. II only

C. III only

D. I and II only

31. A 4 kg object is at the height of 10 m above the Earth's surface. Ignoring air resistance, what is its kinetic energy immediately before impacting the ground if it is thrown straight downward with an initial speed of 20 m/s? (Use the acceleration due to gravity $g = 10$ m/s^2)

A. 150 J	**C.** 1,200 J
B. 300 J	**D.** 900 J

32. A car traveling along the highway needs a certain amount of force to stop. More stopping force may be required when the car has:

I. less stopping distance   II. more momentum   III. more mass

A. I only	**C.** III only
B. II only	**D.** I, II and III

33. A table tennis ball moving East at a speed of 4 m/s collides with a stationary bowling ball. The table tennis ball bounces back to the West, and the bowling ball moves very slowly to the East. Which ball experiences the greater magnitude of impulse during the collision?

A. Bowling ball
B. Table tennis ball
C. Neither because both experience the same magnitude of the impulse
D. It is not possible to determine since the velocities after the collision are unknown

34. Assume that a massless bar of 5 m is suspended from a rope attached to the bar at a distance of x from the bar's left end. If a 30 kg mass hangs from the right side of the bar and a 6 kg mass hangs from the left side, what value of x results in equilibrium? (Use acceleration due to gravity $g = 9.8$ m/s^2)

A. 2.8 m	**C.** 3.2 m
B. 4.2 m	**D.** 1.6 m

35. A block of mass m sits at rest on a rough inclined ramp that makes an angle θ with the horizontal. What must be true about the force of static friction (f) on the block?

A. $f > mg \sin \theta$	**C.** $f = mg$
B. $f = mg \cos \theta$	**D.** $f = mg \sin \theta$

36. A 30 kg block is pushed in a straight line across a horizontal surface. What is the coefficient of kinetic friction μ_k between the block and the surface if a constant force of 45 N must be applied to the block to maintain a constant velocity of 3 m/s? (Use the acceleration due to gravity $g = 10$ m/s^2)

A. 0.1	**C.** 0.15
B. 0.33	**D.** 0.5

37. The impulse-momentum relationship is a direct result of:

I. Newton's First Law   II. Newton's Second Law   III. Newton's Third Law

A. I only

B. II only

C. III only

D. I and II only

Questions **38-40** are based on the following:

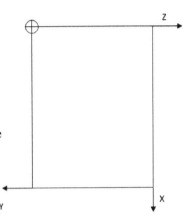

A 0.5 m by 0.6 m rectangular piece of metal is hinged (⊗) (as shown) in the upper left corner, hanging so that the long edge is vertical. A 25 N force (Y) acts to the left at the lower-left corner. A 15 N force (X) acts down at the lower right corner, and a 30 N force (Z) acts to the right at the upper right corner. Each force vector is in the plane of the metal. Use counterclockwise as the positive direction.

38. What is the torque of force X about the pivot?

A. 5 N·m

B. 3 N·m

C. −7.5 N·m

D. 0 N·m

39. What is the torque of force Z about the pivot?

A. −10 N·m

B. −4.5 N·m

C. 4.5 N·m

D. 0 N·m

40. What is the torque of force Y about the pivot?

A. −15 N·m

B. −3 N·m

C. 0 N·m

D. 3 N·m

41. A 50 g weight is tied to the end of a string and whirled at 20 m/s in a horizontal circle with a radius of 2 m. Ignoring the force of gravity, what is the tension in the string?

A. 5 N

B. 10 N

C. 50 N

D. 150 N

42. A small car collides with a large truck in a head-on collision. Which of the following statements concerning the magnitude of the average force during the collision is correct?

    A. The small car and the truck experience the same average force

    B. The force experienced by each one is inversely proportional to its velocity

    C. The truck experiences the greater average force

    D. The small car experiences the greater average force

43. A 10 kg bar that is 2 m long extends perpendicularly from a vertical wall. The free end of the bar is attached to a point on the wall by a light cable, which makes an angle of 30° with the bar. What is the tension in the cable? (Use the acceleration due to gravity $g = 10$ m/s^2)

    A. 75 N   **C.** 100 N

    B. 150 N   **D.** 125 N

44. Object A has the same size and shape as object B but is twice as heavy. When objects A and B are dropped simultaneously from a tower, they reach the ground simultaneously. Object A has greater:

    I. speed   II. momentum   III. acceleration

    A. I only   **C.** III only

    B. II only   **D.** I and II only

45. Two vehicles approach a right-angle intersection and then collide. After the collision, they become entangled. If their mass ratio was 1 : 4 and their respective speeds as they approached at 12 m/s, what is the magnitude of the velocity immediately following the collision?

    A. 16.4 m/s   **C.** 13.4 m/s

    B. 11.9 m/s   **D.** 9.9 m/s

46. A skater stands stationary on frictionless ice, and she throws a heavy ball to the right at an angle of 5° above the horizontal. With respect to the ice, if the ball weighs one-third as much as the skater and she is measured to be moving with a speed of 2.9 m/s to the left after the throw, how fast did she throw the ball?

    A. 10.2 m/s   **C.** 8.73 m/s

    B. 7.2 m/s   **D.** 9.8 m/s

47. Ignoring the forces of friction, what horizontal force must be applied to an object with a weight of 98 N to give it a horizontal acceleration of 10 m/s^2? (Use the acceleration due to gravity $g = 9.8$ m/s^2)

    A. 9.8 N   **C.** 79 N

    B. 100 N   **D.** 125 N

48. Consider a winch that pulls a cart at constant speed up an incline. Point A is at the bottom of the incline, and point B is at the top. Which of the following statements is/are true from point A to B?

      I. The KE of the cart is constant

      II. The PE of the cart is constant

      III. The sum of the KE and PE of the cart is constant

  A. I only   **C.** III only

  B. II only   **D.** I and II only

49. A high-speed dart is shot from ground level with a speed of 140 m/s at an angle of 35° above the horizontal. What is the vertical component of its velocity after 4 s if air resistance is ignored? (Use the acceleration due to gravity $g = 9.8$ m/s^2)

  A. 59 m/s   **C.** 34 m/s

  B. 75 m/s   **D.** 41 m/s

50. What does the area under the curve of a force *vs.* time graph represent for a diver as she leaves the platform during her approach to the water below?

  A. Work   **C.** Impulse

  B. Momentum   **D.** Displacement

51. A rifle of mass 2 kg is suspended by strings. The rifle fires a bullet of mass 0.01 kg at a speed of 220 m/s. What is the recoil velocity of the rifle?

  A. 0.001 m/s   **C.** 0.1 m/s

  B. 0.01 m/s   **D.** 1.1 m/s

52. How do automobile airbags reduce injury during a collision?

  A. They reduce the kinetic energy transferred to the passenger

  B. They reduce the momentum transferred to the passenger

  C. They reduce the acceleration of the automobile

  D. They reduce the forces exerted upon the passenger

Questions **53-55** are based on the following:

Tim nails a meter stick to a board at the meter stick's 0 m mark. Force I acts at the 0.5 m mark perpendicular to the meter stick with a force of 10 N, as shown in the figure. Force II acts at the end of the meter stick with a force of 5 N, making a 35° angle. Force III acts at the same point with a force of 20 N, providing tension but no shear stress. Use counterclockwise as the positive direction.

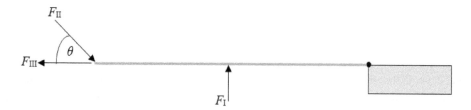

53. What is the torque of Force I about the fixed point?

A. −5 N·m   **C.** 5 N·m

B. 0 N·m   **D.** 10 N·m

54. What is the torque of Force II about the fixed point?

A. −4.8 N·m   **C.** 4.8 N·m

B. −2.9 N·m   **D.** 2.9 N·m

55. What is the torque of Force III about the fixed point?

A. −20 N·m   **C.** 10 N·m

B. 0 N·m   **D.** 20 N·m

56. Two equal mass balls (one yellow and the other red) are dropped from the same height and rebound off the floor. The yellow ball rebounds to a higher position. Which ball is subjected to the greater magnitude of impulse during its collision with the floor?

A. Both balls were subjected to the same magnitude of impulse

B. Red ball

C. Yellow ball

D. Requires the time intervals and forces

57. Calculate the impulse associated with a force of 4.5 N that lasts for 1.4 s:

A. 5.4 kg·m/s   **C.** 4.6 kg·m/s

B. 6.8 kg·m/s   **D.** 6.3 kg·m/s

58. A heavy truck and a small truck roll down a hill. Ignoring friction, at the bottom of the hill, the heavy truck has greater:

I. momentum   II. acceleration   III. speed

A. I only   **C.** III only

B. II only   **D.** I and II only

59. A 78 g steel ball is released from rest and falls vertically onto a rigid surface. The ball strikes the surface and is in contact with it for 0.5 ms. The ball rebounds elastically and returns to its original height during a round trip of 4 s. Assume that the surface does not deform during contact. What is the maximum elastic energy stored by the ball? (Use the acceleration due to gravity $g = 9.8$ m/s^2)

A. 23 J   **C.** 11 J

B. 43 J   **D.** 15 J

60. Cart A is 5 kg, and cart B is 10 kg, and they are initially stationary on a frictionless horizontal surface. A force of 3 N to the right acts on cart A for 2 s. Subsequently, it hits cart B, and the two carts stick. What is the final velocity of the two carts?

A. 1 m/s   **C.** 1.2 m/s

B. 0.4 m/s   **D.** 1.8 m/s

61. A 0.12 kg baseball is thrown with a velocity of 23 m/s. It is struck with a bat with an average force of 5,000 N, which results in a velocity of 34 m/s in the opposite direction. How long were the bat and ball in contact?

A. 3.4×10^{-2} s   **C.** 1.4×10^{-3} s

B. 4.3×10^{-3} s   **D.** 2.3×10^{-2} s

62. Which of the following represents the kinetic energy for a sailboat of mass m moving with a momentum of p?

A. p^2 / m **C.** mp

B. $\frac{1}{2}mp^2$ **D.** $p^2 / 2m$

63. A 2.2 kg block of mass m is moving on a frictionless surface with a speed of $v_i = 9.2$ m/s, and it makes a perfectly elastic collision with a stationary block of mass M. After the collision, the 2.2 kg block recoils with a speed of $v_f = 2.5$ m/s. What is the mass of M?

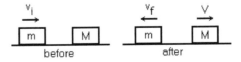

A. 5.4 kg   **C.** 2.9 kg

B. 8.4 kg   **D.** 3.8 kg

64. Carts I and II are on a level, frictionless one-dimensional track. Cart I is 1 kg and is initially going right at 7 m/s, and cart II is 3 kg and is initially going left at 2 m/s when they collide. Cart I recoils with a speed of 3 m/s. What is the velocity of cart II after the collision?

A. 2.5 m/s to the right

C. 1.3 m/s to the right

B. 3.5 m/s to the right

D. 2.5 m/s to the left

65. Two boxes, A and B, are connected by a horizontal string S on a horizontal floor. A light wire pulls horizontally on box B, as shown, with a force of 100 N. The reaction force of this pull is the:

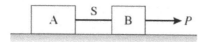

A. pull that string S exerts on box A

C. pull that box B exerts on string S

B. pull of box B on the wire

D. pull that string S exerts on box B

66. A uniform rod of mass *M* sticks out from a vertical wall and points toward the floor. The smaller angle it makes with the wall is *θ*, and the rod's end is attached to the ceiling by a string parallel to the wall. What is the tension in the supporting string?

A. *Mg* sin *θ*

C. *Mg* sin *θ* / 2

B. *Mg*

D. *Mg* / 2

67. A moving object with no forces acting on it continues to move with constant non-zero:

I. momentum   II. impulse   III. acceleration

A. I only

C. III only

B. II only

D. I and II only

68. Ignoring air resistance, the horizontal component of a projectile's velocity:

A. remains zero

B. first decreases and then increases

C. is always the same sign as the vertical component of velocity

D. remains a nonzero constant

69. A 3.3 kg object moving at 6.9 m/s makes a perfectly inelastic collision with a 3.6 kg object initially at rest. What percentage of the initial kinetic energy of the system is lost during the collision?

A. 66%

C. 71%

B. 59%

D. 52%

70. Two children are riding on a carousel. Lisa is at a greater distance from the axis of rotation than Katie is. Which girl has the larger angular displacement?

A. Lisa

B. Katie

C. Depends on the mass of each child

D. They have the same nonzero angular displacement

71. A 1,200 kg ore cart is rolling at 10 m/s across a flat surface, and a crane dumps 800 kg of ore (vertically) into the cart. Ignoring the frictional force, how fast does the cart move after being loaded with ore?

A. 8.6 m/s

B. 7.8 m/s

C. 6 m/s

D. 4 m/s

72. A small car crashes with a large truck in a head-on collision. Which of the following statements is correct regarding the magnitude of the momentum change during the collision?

A. The car and the truck experience the same change in momentum

B. The change in momentum experienced by each is inversely proportional to its mass

C. The truck experiences the greater change in momentum

D. The car experiences the greater change in momentum

73. A massless pulley is suspended from a cable attached to the beam of a building 10 m above the ground. A massless rope is slung over the pulley, and one end is attached to a bucket of bricks weighing 750 N. The free end of the rope is pulled, and the bucket is raised above the ground. The free end is then tied to a fixed point. What is the approximate downward force exerted by the cable attaching the pulley to the beam?

A. 750 N

B. 375 N

C. 1,000 N

D. 1,500 N

74. A cannon recoils after firing a cannonball. Why is the speed of the cannon's recoil smaller than that of the cannonball?

I. momentum of the cannon is smaller

II. cannon has more mass than the ball

III. momentum is mainly concentrated in the ball

A. I only

B. II only

C. III only

D. I and II only

75. A 1.2 kg asteroid is traveling toward the Orion Nebula at a speed of 2.8 m/s. Another 4.1 kg asteroid is traveling at 2.3 m/s in a perpendicular direction. The two asteroids collide and stick. What is the change in momentum from before to after the collision?

A. 0 kg·m/s   **C.** 9.4 kg·m/s
B. 2.1 kg·m/s   **D.** 12 kg·m/s

76. A 1,120 kg car experiences an impulse of 30,000 N·s during a collision with a wall. If the collision takes 0.43 s, what was the speed of the car just before the collision?

A. 12 m/s   **C.** 42 m/s
B. 64 m/s   **D.** 27 m/s

77. Does the centripetal force acting on an object do work on the object?

A. No, because the force and the displacement of the object are perpendiculars
B. Yes, since a force acts and the object moves, and work is force times distance
C. Yes, since it takes energy to turn an object
D. No, because the object has a constant speed

78. Cars with padded dashboards are safer in an accident than cars without padded dashboards because a passenger hitting the dashboard has:

    I. increased time of impact
    II. decreased impulse
    III. decreased impact force

A. I only   **C.** III only
B. II only   **D.** I and III only

79. The acceleration due to gravity on the Moon is only one-sixth of that on Earth, and the Moon has no atmosphere. If a person hit a baseball on the Moon with the same effort (therefore, at the same speed and angle) as on the Earth, how far would the ball travel on the Moon compared to Earth? (Ignore air resistance on Earth)

A. The same distance as on Earth   **C.** 1/6 as far as on Earth
B. 6 times as far as on Earth   **D.** 36 times as far as on Earth

80. A uniform meter stick weighing 20 N has a weight of 50 N attached to its left end and a weight of 30 N attached to its right end. The meter stick is hung from a rope. What is the tension in the rope, and how far from the left end of the meter stick should the rope be attached so that the meter stick remains level?

A. 100 N placed 37.5 cm from the left end of the meter stick
B. 50 N placed 40 cm from the left end of the meter stick
C. 80 N placed 37.5 cm from the left end of the meter stick
D. 100 N placed 40 cm from the left end of the meter stick

81. To catch a ball, a baseball player extends her hand forward before impact with the ball and then lets it ride backward in the direction of the ball's motion upon impact. Doing this reduces the force of impact on the player's hand principally because the:

A. time of impact is decreased

B. time of impact is increased

C. relative velocity is less

D. force of impact is reduced by $\sqrt{2}$

82. A 1,200 kg car, moving at 15.6 m/s, collides with a stationary 1,500 kg car. If the two vehicles lock, what is their combined velocity immediately after the collision?

A. 12.4 m/s

B. 5.4 m/s

C. 6.9 m/s

D. 7.6 m/s

83. A 0.05 kg golf ball, initially at rest, has a velocity of 100 m/s immediately after being struck by a golf club. If the club and ball were in contact for 0.8 ms, what is the average force exerted on the ball?

A. 5.5 kN

B. 4.9 kN

C. 11.8 kN

D. 6.3 kN

84. Which of the following is an accurate statement for a rigid body that is rotating?

A. All points on the body are moving with the same angular velocity

B. Its center of rotation is its center of gravity

C. Its center of rotation is at rest and therefore not moving

D. Its center of rotation must be moving with a constant velocity

85. Cart 1 (2 kg) and Cart 2 (2.5 kg) run along a frictionless, level, one-dimensional track. Cart 2 is initially at rest, and Cart 1 travels 0.6 m/s toward the right when it encounters Cart 2. After the collision, Cart 1 is at rest. Which of the following is true concerning the collision?

A. The collision is entirely elastic

B. Kinetic energy is conserved

C. Momentum is conserved

D. Total momentum is decreased

86. What is the reason for using a long barrel in a gun?

A. Allows the force of the expanding gases from the gunpowder to act for a longer time

B. Increases the force exerted on the bullet due to the expanding gases from the gunpowder

C. Exerts a larger force on the shells

D. Reduces frictional losses

Notes for active learning

Work and Energy

1. Consider the following ways that a girl might throw a stone from a bridge. The speed of the stone as it leaves her hand is the same in each of the three cases.

    I. Thrown straight up

    II. Thrown straight down

    III. Thrown straight out horizontally

Ignoring air resistance, in which case is the vertical speed of the stone the greatest when it hits the water below?

A. I only

B. II only

C. III only

D. I and II only

2. A package is being pulled along the ground by a 5 N force F directed 45° above the horizontal. How much work is done by the force when it pulls the package 10 m?

A. 14 J

B. 35 J

C. 70 J

D. 46 J

3. Which quantity has the greatest influence on the amount of kinetic energy that a large truck has while moving down the highway?

A. Velocity

B. Mass

C. Density

D. Direction

4. No work is done by gravity on a bowling ball that rolls along the floor of a bowling alley because:

A. no potential energy is being converted to kinetic energy

B. the force on the ball is at a right angle to the ball's motion

C. its velocity is constant

D. the total force on the ball is zero

5. A 5 kg toy car is moving along level ground. At a given time, it is traveling at a speed of 2 m/s and accelerating at 3 m/s^2. What is the cart's kinetic energy at this time?

A. 20 J

B. 8 J

C. 10 J

D. 4 J

6. A tree house is 8 m above the ground. If Peter does 360 J of work while pulling a box from the ground up to his tree house with a rope, what is the mass of a box? (Use the acceleration due to gravity $g = 10$ m/s^2)

A. 4.5 kg

B. 3.5 kg

C. 5.8 kg

D. 2.5 kg

7. For an ideal elastic spring, what does the slope of the curve represent for a displacement (x) *vs.* applied force (F) graph?

A. The acceleration of gravity   **C.** The spring constant

B. The square root of the spring constant   **D.** The reciprocal of the spring constant

8. A spring with a spring constant of 22 N/m is stretched from equilibrium to 3 m. How much work is done in the process?

A. 33 J   **C.** 99 J

B. 66 J   **D.** 198 J

9. A baseball is thrown straight up. Compare the sign of the work done by gravity while the ball goes up with the sign of the work done by gravity while it goes down:

A. negative on the way up and positive on the way down

B. negative on the way up and negative on the way down

C. positive on the way up and positive on the way down

D. positive on the way up and negative on the way down

10. Let A_1 represent the magnitude of the work done by gravity as mass A's gravitational energy increases by 400 J. Let B_1 represent the total amount of work necessary to increase mass B's kinetic energy by 400 J. How do A_1 and B_1 compare?

A. $A_1 > B_1$ **C.** $A_1 < B_1$

B. $A_1 = B_1$ **D.** $A_1 = 400 \, B_1$

11. According to the definition of work, pushing on a rock accomplishes no work unless there is:

A. an applied force equal to the rock's weight

B. movement perpendicular to the force

C. an applied force greater than the rock's weight

D. movement parallel to the force

12. A job is done slowly, while an identical job is done quickly. Both jobs require the same amount of work, but different amounts of:

     I. energy   II. power   III. torque

A. I only   **C.** I and II only

B. II only   **D.** I and III only

13. On a force (*F*) *vs.* distance (*d*) graph, what represents the work done by the force *F*?

    A. The area under the curve   **C.** The slope of the curve

    B. A line connecting two points on the curve   **D.** The length of the curve

14. A 3 kg cat leaps from a tree to the ground, which is a distance of 4 m. What is its kinetic energy just before the cat reaches the ground? (Use acceleration due to gravity $g = 10$ m/s^2)

    A. 0 J   **C.** 120 J

    B. 9 J   **D.** 60 J

15. A book is resting on a plank of wood. Jackie pushes the plank and accelerates it so that the book is stationary with respect to the plank. The work done by static friction is:

    A. zero   **C.** negative

    B. positive   **D.** parallel to the surface

16. 350 J of work is required to drive a stake into the ground fully. If the average resistive force on the stake by the ground is 900 N, how long is the stake?

    A. 2.3 m   **C.** 3 m

    B. 0.23 m   **D.** 0.39 m

17. A lightweight object and a very heavy object are sliding with equal speeds along a level, frictionless surface. They both slide up the same frictionless hill with no air resistance. Which object rises to a greater height?

    A. They both slide to the same height

    B. The heavy object because it has more kinetic energy to carry it up the hill

    C. The heavy object because it has greater potential energy

    D. The lightweight object because it has more kinetic energy to carry it up the hill

18. If Investigator II does 3 times the work of Investigator I in one-third the time, the power output of Investigator II is:

    A. 9 times greater   **C.** 1/3 times greater

    B. 3 times greater   **D.** the same

19. A diver who weighs 450 N steps off a diving board that is 9 m above the water. What is the kinetic energy when the diver strikes the water?

    A. 160 J   **C.** 45 J

    B. 540 J   **D.** 4,050 J

20. A vertical, hanging spring stretches by 23 cm when a 160 N object is attached. What is the weight of a hanging plant that stretches the spring by 34 cm?

A. 237 N   **C.** 158 N

B. 167 N   **D.** 309 N

21. A mule pulls with a horizontal force F on a covered wagon of mass M. The mule and covered wagon are traveling at a constant speed v on level ground. How much work is done by the mule on the covered wagon during time Δt? (Use acceleration due to gravity $g = 10$ m/s^2)

A. $-Fv\Delta t$ **C.** 0 J

B. $Fv\Delta t$ **D.** $-F\sqrt{v}\Delta t$

22. Jane pulls on the strap of a sled at an angle of 32° above the horizontal. If 540 J of work is done by the strap while moving the sled a horizontal distance of 18 m, what is the tension in the strap?

A. 86 N   **C.** 24 N

B. 112 N   **D.** 35 N

23. A vertical spring stretches 6 cm from equilibrium when a 120 g mass is attached to the bottom. If an additional 120 g mass is added to the spring, how does the potential energy of the spring change?

A. the same   **C.** 2 times greater

B. 4 times greater   **D.** $\sqrt{2}$ times greater

24. A Ferrari, Maserati, and Lamborghini are moving at the same speed, and each driver slams on his brakes and brings the car to a stop. The most massive is the Ferrari, and the least massive is the Lamborghini. If the tires of all three cars have identical coefficients of friction with the road surface, which car experiences the greatest amount of work done by friction?

A. Maserati   **C.** Ferrari

B. Lamborghini   **D.** The amount is the same

25. A hammer does the work of driving a nail into a wooden board. Compared to the moment before the hammer strikes the nail after it impacts the nail, the hammer's mechanical energy is:

A. the same

B. less, because work has been done on the hammer

C. greater, because the hammer has done work

D. less, because the hammer has done work

26. A 1,500 kg car travels at 25 m/s on a level road and the driver slams on the brakes. The skid marks are 10 m long. What is the work done by the road on the car?

A. -4.7×10^5 J

B. 0 J

C. 2×10^5 J

D. 3.5×10^5 J

27. A 1,000 kg car is traveling at 4.72 m/s. If a 2,000 kg truck has 20 times the kinetic energy of the car, how fast is the truck traveling?

A. 23.6 m/s

B. 47.2 m/s

C. 64.4 m/s

D. 14.9 m/s

28. A 1,500 kg car travels at 25 m/s on a level road, and the driver slams on the brakes. The skid marks are 30 m long. What forces are acting on the car while it is coming to a stop?

A. Gravity down, normal force up, and a frictional force forward

B. Gravity down, normal force up, and the engine force forward

C. Gravity down, normal force up, and a frictional force backward

D. Gravity down, normal force forward, and the engine force backward

29. A 6,000 N piano is being raised via a pulley. For every 1 m that the rope is pulled down, the piano rises 0.15 m. In this pulley system, what is the force needed to lift the piano?

A. 60 N

B. 900 N

C. 600 N

D. 300 N

30. What does the area under the curve on a force *vs.* position graph represent?

A. Kinetic energy

B. Momentum

C. Work

D. Displacement

31. What is the form in which most energy comes to and leaves the Earth?

A. Kinetic

B. Radiant

C. Chemical

D. Light

32. A driver abruptly slams on the brakes in her car, and the car skids a certain distance on a straight level road. If she had been traveling twice as fast, what distance would the car have skid under the same conditions?

A. 1.4 times farther

B. ½ as far

C. 4 times farther

D. 2 times farther

33. A crane hoists an object weighing 2,000 N to the top of a building. The crane raises the object straight upward at a constant rate. Ignoring the forces of friction, at what rate is energy consumed by the electric motor of the crane if it takes 60 s to lift the mass 320 m?

A. 2.5 kW	**C.** 3.50 kW
B. 6.9 kW	**D.** 10.7 kW

34. A barbell with a mass of 25 kg is raised 3.0 m in 3.0 s before it reaches constant velocity. What is the net power expended by all forces in raising the barbell? (Use acceleration due to gravity $g = 9.8$ m/s^2 and the acceleration of the barbell is constant)

A. 17 W	**C.** 67 W
B. 34 W	**D.** 98 W

35. Susan carried a 6.5 kg bag of groceries 1.4 m above the ground at a constant velocity for 2.4 m across the kitchen. How much work did Susan do on the bag in the process? (Use acceleration due to gravity $g = 10$ m/s^2)

A. 52 J	**C.** 164 J
B. 0 J	**D.** 138 J

36. A 1,000 kg car experiences a net force of 9,600 N while decelerating from 30 m/s to 22 m/s. How far does it travel while slowing down?

A. 17 m	**C.** 12 m
B. 22 m	**D.** 34 m

37. What is the power output in relation to the work W if a person exerts 100 J in 50 s?

A. ¼ W	**C.** 2 W
B. ½ W	**D.** 4 W

38. If a ball is released from a cliff ledge 58 m above the ground, how fast is the ball traveling when it reaches the ground? (Use the acceleration due to gravity $g = 10$ m/s^2)

A. 68 m/s	**C.** 44 m/s
B. 16 m/s	**D.** 34 m/s

39. A stone is held at a height h above the ground, and a second stone with four times the mass is held at the same height. What is the gravitational potential energy of the second stone compared to that of the first stone?

A. Four times as much	**C.** One-fourth as much
B. The same	**D.** One-half as much

40. A 1.3 kg coconut falls off a coconut tree, landing on the ground 600 cm below. How much work is done on the coconut by the gravitational force? (Use the acceleration due to gravity $g = 10$ m/s^2)

    A. 6 J

    B. 78 J

    C. 168 J

    D. 340 J

41. The potential energy of a pair of interacting objects is related to their:

    A. relative position

    B. momentum

    C. acceleration

    D. kinetic energy

42. A spring has a spring constant of 65 N/m. One end of the spring is fixed at point P, while the other is connected to a 7 kg mass *m*. The fixed end and the mass sit on a horizontal, frictionless surface so that the mass and the spring can rotate about P. The mass moves in a circle of radius $r = 4$ m, and the centripetal force of the mass is 15 N. What is the potential energy stored in the spring?

    A. 1.7 J

    B. 2.8 J

    C. 3.7 J

    D. 7.5 J

43. If electricity costs 8.16 cents/kW·h, how much would it cost to run a 120 W stereo system 3.5 hours per day for 5 weeks?

    A. $1.11

    B. $1.46

    C. $1.20

    D. $0.34

44. A boy does 120 J of work to pull his sister back on a swing with a 5.1 m chain until the swing makes an angle of 32° with the vertical. What is the mass of his sister? (Use the acceleration due to gravity $g = 9.8$ m/s^2)

    A. 18 kg

    B. 15.8 kg

    C. 13.6 kg

    D. 11.8 kg

45. What is the value of the spring constant if 111 J of work is needed to stretch a spring from 1.4 m to 2.9 m if the spring's equilibrium position is at 0.0 m?

    A. 58 N/m

    B. 53 N/m

    C. 67 N/m

    D. 34 N/m

46. The metric unit of a joule (J) is a unit of:

    I. potential energy   II. kinetic energy   III. work

    A. I only

    B. II only

    C. III only

    D. I, II and III

47. A horizontal spring-mass system oscillates on a frictionless table. Find the maximum extension of the spring if the ratio of the mass to the spring constant is 0.038 kg·m/N, and the maximum speed of the mass is 18 m/s?

A. 3.5 m

B. 0.67 m

C. 3.4 cm

D. 67 cm

48. A truck weighs twice as much as a car and is moving at twice the speed of the car. Which statement is true about the truck's kinetic energy compared to that of the car?

A. The truck has 8 times the KE

B. The truck has twice the KE

C. The truck has √2 times the KE

D. The truck has 4 times the KE

49. When a car brakes to a stop, its kinetic energy is transformed into:

A. energy of rest

B. energy of momentum

C. heat

D. stopping energy

50. A 30 kg block hangs from a spring with a spring constant of 900 N/m. How far does the spring stretch from its equilibrium position? (Use the acceleration due to gravity $g = 10$ m/s^2)

A. 12 cm

B. 33 cm

C. 50 cm

D. 0.5 cm

51. What is the kinetic energy of a 0.33 kg baseball thrown at a velocity of 40 m/s?

A. 426 J

B. 574 J

C. 318 J

D. 264 J

52. An object is acted upon by a force as represented by the force *vs.* position graph below. What is the work done as the object moves from 0 m to 4 m?

A. 10 J

B. 50 J

C. 20 J

D. 30 J

53. James and Bob throw identical balls vertically upward. James throws his ball with an initial speed twice that of Bob's. Assuming no air resistance, what is the maximum height of James's ball compared with that of Bob's ball?

A. Equal

B. Eight times

C. Four times

D. Two times

54. The graphs show the magnitude of the force (F) exerted by a spring as a function of the distance (x) the spring has been stretched. Which of the graphs shows a spring that obeys Hooke's Law?

A.

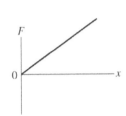

C.

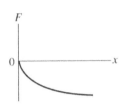

B.

D.

55. If a rocket travels through air, it loses some kinetic energy due to air resistance. Some transferred energy:

A. decreases the temperature of the air around the rocket

B. is found in increased KE of the rocket

C. is found in increased KE of the air molecules

D. decreases the temperature of the rocket

56. A car moves four times as fast as an identical car. Compared to the slower car, the faster car has how much more kinetic energy?

A. 4 times   **C.** $\sqrt{2}$ times

B. 8 times   **D.** 16 times

57. A massless, ideal spring with spring constant k is connected to a wall on one end and a massless plate on the other end. A mass m is sitting on a frictionless floor. The mass m is slid against the plate and pushed back a distance x. After release, it achieves a maximum speed v_1. In a second experiment, the same mass is pushed back a distance of $4x$. After its release, it reaches a maximum speed of v_2. How does v_2 compare with v_1?

A. $v_2 = v_1$ **C.** $v_2 = 4v_1$

B. $v_2 = 2v_1$ **D.** $v_2 = 16v_1$

58. A N·m/s is a unit of:

     I. work   II. force   III. power

A. I only   **C.** III only

B. II only   **D.** I and II only

59. For the work-energy theorem, which statement is accurate regarding the net work done?

    A. The net work done plus the initial KE is the final KE

    B. Final KE plus the net work done is the initial KE

    C. The net work done minus the final KE is the initial KE

    D. The net work done is equal to the initial KE plus the final KE

60. A 1,320 kg car climbs a 5° slope at a constant velocity of 70 km/h. Ignoring air resistance, at what rate must the engine deliver energy to drive the car? (Use the acceleration due to gravity $g = 9.8$ m/s^2)

    A. 45.1 kW   **C.** 6.3 kW

    B. 12.7 kW   **D.** 22.6 kW

61. When a pebble is dropped from height h, it reaches the ground with kinetic energy. Ignoring air resistance, from what height should the pebble be dropped to reach the ground with twice the KE?

    A. $\sqrt{2}h$ **C.** $4h$

    B. $2h$ **D.** $8h$

62. Which of the following situations requires the greatest power?

    A. 50 J of work in 20 minutes   **C.** 10 J of work in 5 minutes

    B. 200 J of work in 30 minutes   **D.** 100 J of work in 10 minutes

63. A kilowatt-hour is a unit of:

    I. work   II. force   III. power

    A. I only   **C.** III only

    B. II only   **D.** I and II only

64. A hydraulic press (like a simple lever), properly arranged, is capable of:

    I. multiplying energy input

    II. multiplying output force

    III. exerting force only vertically

    A. I only   **C.** III only

    B. II only   **D.** I and II only

65. 4.5×10^5 J of work is done on a 1,150 kg car while it accelerates from 10 m/s to some final velocity. What is this final velocity?

    A. 30 m/s   **C.** 12 m/s

    B. 37 m/s   **D.** 19 m/s

66. Which of the following is not a unit of work?

    A. N·m

    B. kw·h

    C. J

    D. kg·m/s

67. The law of conservation of energy states that:

    I. the energy of an isolated system is constant

    II. energy cannot be used faster than it is created

    III. energy cannot change forms

    A. I only

    B. II only

    C. III only

    D. I and II only

68. A crane lifts a 300 kg steel beam vertically upward a distance of 110 m. Ignoring frictional forces, how much work does the crane do on the beam if the beam accelerates upward at 1.4 m/s²? (Use the acceleration due to gravity $g = 9.8$ m/s²)

    A. 2.4×10^3 J

    B. 4.6×10^4 J

    C. 3.7×10^5 J

    D. 6.2×10^5 J

69. Steve pushes twice as hard against a stationary brick wall as Charles. Which statement is correct?

    A. Both do the same amount of positive work

    B. Both do positive work, but Steve does one-half the work of Charles

    C. Both do positive work, but Steve does four times the work of Charles

    D. Both do zero work

70. What is the change in the gravitational potential energy of an object if the height of the object above the Earth is doubled? (Assume that the object remains near the surface)

    A. Quadruple

    B. Doubled

    C. Unchanged

    D. Halved

71. If 1 N is exerted for 1 m in 1 s, the amount of power delivered is:

    A. 3 W

    B. 1/3 W

    C. 2 W

    D. 1 W

72. A brick is dropped from a roof and falls a distance h to the ground. If h were doubled, how does the maximal KE of the brick change just before it hits the ground?

    A. It doubles

    B. It increases by $\sqrt{2}$

    C. It remains the same

    D. It increases by 200

73. A helicopter with a single landing gear descends vertically to land with a speed of 4.5 m/s. Its shock absorbers have an initial length of 0.60 m, and they compress to 77% of their original length, and the air in the tires absorbs 23% of the initial energy as heat. What is the ratio of the spring constant to the helicopter's mass?

A. 0.11 kN/kg·m

C. 0.82 kN/kg·m

B. 1.1 N/kg·m

D. 11 N/kg·m

74. A 21 metric ton airplane is observed to be a vertical distance of 2.6 km from its takeoff point. What is the gravitational potential energy of the plane with respect to the ground? (Use the acceleration due to gravity $g = 9.8$ m/s^2, and a metric ton = 1,000 kg)

A. 582 J

C. 535 MJ

B. 384 J

D. 414 MJ

75. A tennis ball bounces on the floor. During each bounce, it loses 31% of its energy due to heating. How high does the ball reach after the third bounce if it is initially released 4 m from the floor?

A. 55 cm

C. 106 cm

B. 171 mm

D. 131 cm

Notes for active learning

Notes for active learning

Rotational Motion

1. Suppose a uniform solid sphere of mass M and radius R rolls without slipping down an inclined plane starting from rest. The linear velocity of the sphere at the bottom of the incline depends on:

A. the radius of the sphere

B. the mass of the sphere

C. both the mass and the radius of the sphere

D. neither the mass nor the radius of the sphere

2. A solid, uniform sphere of mass 2.0 kg and radius 1.7 m rolls from rest without slipping down an inclined plane of height 5.3 m. What is the angular velocity of the sphere at the bottom of the inclined plane?

A. 3.7 rad/s

B. 5.1 rad/s

C. 6.7 rad/s

D. 8.3 rad/s

3. A solid uniform ball with a mass of 125.0 g is rolling without slipping along the horizontal surface of a table with a speed of 4.5 m/s when it rolls off the edge and falls towards the floor, 1.1 m below. What is the rotational kinetic energy of the ball just before it hits the floor?

A. 0.51 J

B. 0.87 J

C. 1.03 J

D. 2.26 J

4. David swings a 0.38 kg ball in a circle on a string that is 1.3 m long. What is the magnitude of the ball's angular momentum if the ball makes 1.2 rev/s?

A. 0.6 kg·m²/s

B. 2.2 kg·m²/s

C. 3.6 kg·m²/s

D. 4.8 kg·m²/s

5. An ice skater has a moment of inertia of 5.0 kg·m² when her arms are outstretched, and at this time, she is spinning at 3.0 rev/s. If she pulls in her arms and decreases her moment of inertia to 2.0 kg·m², how fast will she be spinning?

A. 1.8 rev/s

B. 4.5 rev/s

C. 7.5 rev/s

D. 10.5 rev/s

6. The angular momentum of a system remains constant when:

A. its total kinetic energy is constant

B. the moment of inertia is constant

C. no net external torque acts on the system

D. no net external force acts on the system

7. A bicycle has wheels 60.0 cm in diameter. What is the angular speed of these wheels moving at 4.0 m/s?

A. 0.28 rad/s

B. 1.6 rad/s

C. 3.4 rad/s

D. 13.3 rad/s

8. What is the kinetic energy of a thin uniform rod of length 120.0 cm with a mass of 450.0 g that rotates about its center along the short axis at 3.60 rad/s? (The short axis is perpendicular to the axis of the rod. Imagine spinning the rod like an airplane propeller.)

    A. 0.350 J   **C.** 2.70 J

    B. 1.30 J   **D.** 4.96 J

9. A rope is wrapped around a wheel of radius R = 2.0 meters. The wheel is mounted with frictionless bearings on an axle through its center. A block of mass 14.0 kg is suspended from the end of the rope. When the system is released from rest, it is observed that the block descends 10.0 meters in 2.0 seconds. What is the moment of inertia of the wheel?

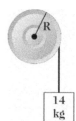

    A. 300.0 kg·m²   **C.** 53.8 kg·m²

    B. 185.0 kg·m²   **D.** 521.0 kg·m²

10. A string is wrapped tightly around a fixed frictionless pulley with a moment of inertia of 0.0352 kg·m² and a radius of 12.5 cm. The string is pulled away from the pulley with a constant force of 5.00 N, causing the pulley to rotate. If the string does not slip on the pulley, what is the speed of the string after it has unwound 1.25 m? Consider the string to be massless.

    A. 0.69 m/s   **C.** 3.62 m/s

    B. 2.36 m/s   **D.** 4.90 m/s

11. When a rigid object rotates about a fixed axis, what is true about all the points in the object?

    I. They have the same angular acceleration

    II. They have the same tangential acceleration

    III. They have the same radial acceleration

    A. I only   **C.** III only

    B. II only   **D.** I and II only

12. A small mass is placed on a record turntable that is rotating at 33.33 rpm. The linear velocity of the mass is:

    A. zero

    B. directed parallel to the line joining the mass and the center of rotation

    C. independent (in magnitude) of the position of the mass on the turntable

    D. greater the farther the mass is from the center

13. To drive a midsize car at 40.0 mph on a level road for one hour requires about 3.2×10^7 J of energy. Suppose this much energy was attempted to be stored in a spinning, solid, uniform, cylindrical flywheel. If a flywheel with a diameter of 1.2 m and mass of 400.0 kg were used, what angular speed would be required to store 3.2×10^7 J?

A. 380 rad/s

B. 620 rad/s

C. 940 rad/s

D. 1,450 rad/s

14. A wheel having a moment of inertia of 5.0 kg·m² starts from rest and accelerates for 8.0 s under a constant torque of 3.0 N·m. What is the wheel's rotational kinetic energy at the end of 8.0 s?

A. 29 J

B. 58 J

C. 83 J

D. 112 J

15. When a rigid object rotates about a fixed axis, what is true about all the points in the object?

    I. They have the same angular speed

    II. They have the same tangential speed

    III. They have the same angular acceleration

A. I only

B. II only

C. III only

D. I and III only

16. A uniform, solid cylindrical flywheel of radius 1.4 m and mass 15.0 kg rotates at 2.4 rad/s. What is the magnitude of the flywheel's angular momentum?

A. 11 kg·m²/s

B. 18 kg·m²/s

C. 25 kg·m²/s

D. 35 kg·m²/s

17. A uniform solid disk is released from rest and rolls without slipping down an inclined plane that makes an angle of 25° with the horizontal. What is the forward speed of the disk after it has rolled 3.0 m, measured along the plane?

A. 0.8 m/s

B. 1.8 m/s

C. 2.9 m/s

D. 4.1 m/s

18. A tire is rolling along a road, without slipping, with a center-of-mass velocity v. A piece of tape is attached to the tire. When the tape is opposite the road (top of the tire), what is its velocity with respect to the road?

A. $2v$

B. v

C. $1.5v$

D. $\sqrt{v}$

19. A string is wound tightly around a fixed pulley with a radius of 5.0 cm. As the string is pulled, the pulley rotates without any slipping of the string. What is the angular speed of the pulley when the string is moving at 5.0 m/s?

A. 10.0 rad/s

B. 25.0 rad/s

C. 75.0 rad/s

D. 100.0 rad/s

20. A 1.4 kg object at $x = 2.00$ m, $y = 3.10$ m moves at 4.62 m/s at an angle 45° north of east. What is the magnitude of the object's angular momentum about the origin?

A. 1.2 kg·m²/s

B. 2.6 kg·m²/s

C. 3.8 kg·m²/s

D. 5.0 kg·m²/s

21. When a fan is turned off, its angular speed decreases from 10.0 rad/s to 6.3 rad/s in 5.0 s. What is the magnitude of the average angular acceleration of the fan?

A. 0.46 rad/s²

B. 0.74 rad/s²

C. 1.86 rad/s²

D. 2.80 rad/s²

22. At time $t = 0$ s, a wheel has an angular displacement of 0 radians and an angular velocity of +26.0 rad/s. The wheel has a constant acceleration of –0.43 rad/s². In this situation, what is the time t (after $t = 0$ s), at which the kinetic energy of the wheel is twice the initial value?

A. 48 s

B. 86 s

C. 115 s

D. 146 s

23. A solid uniform disk of diameter 3.20 m and mass 42.0 kg rolls without slipping to the bottom of a hill, starting from rest. If the angular speed of the disk is 4.27 rad/s at the bottom, how high vertically did it start on the hill above the bottom?

A. 2.46 m

B. 3.57 m

C. 4.85 m

D. 6.24 m

24. When Steve rides a bicycle, in what direction is the angular velocity of the wheels?

A. to his left

B. to his right

C. forward

D. backward

25. A rolling wheel of a diameter of 68.0 cm slows down uniformly from 8.4 m/s to rest over a distance of 115.0 m. What is the magnitude of its angular acceleration if there was no slipping?

A. 0.90 rad/s²

B. 1.6 rad/s²

C. 4.2 rad/s²

D. 7.8 rad/s²

26. A uniform solid cylinder with a radius of 10.0 cm and a mass of 3.0 kg is rotating about its center axis with an angular speed of 33.4 rpm. What is the kinetic energy of the uniform solid cylinder?

A. 0.091 J

B. 0.19 J

C. 0.66 J

D. 1.14 J

27. A uniform 135.0-g meter stick rotates about an axis perpendicular to the stick, passing through its center with an angular speed of 3.50 rad/s. What is the magnitude of the angular momentum of the stick?

A. 0.0394 kg·m²/s

B. 0.0848 kg·m²/s

C. 0.286 kg·m²/s

D. 0.458 kg·m²/s

28. A 23.0 kg mass is connected to a nail on a frictionless table by a massless string of length 1.3 m. If the tension in the string is 51.0 N while the mass moves in a uniform circle on the table, how long does it take for the mass to make one complete revolution?

A. 2.8 s

B. 3.6 s

C. 4.8 s

D. 5.4 s

29. A machinist turns on the power to a grinding wheel at time $t = 0$ s. The wheel accelerates uniformly from rest for 10.0 s and reaches the operating angular speed of 38.0 rad/s. The wheel is run at that angular speed for 30.0 s, and then power is shut off. The wheel slows down uniformly at 2.1 rad/s² until the wheel stops. What is the angular acceleration of the wheel between $t = 0$ s and $t = 10.0$ s?

A. 1.21 rad/s²

B. 2.63 rad/s²

C. 3.80 rad/s²

D. 5.40 rad/s²

30. A force of 17.0 N is applied to the end of a 0.63 m long torque wrench at an angle 45° from a line joining the pivot point to the handle. What is the magnitude of the torque generated about the pivot point?

A. 4.3 N·m

B. 8.2 N·m

C. 7.6 N·m

D. 11.8 N·m

31. A solid disk of radius 1.60 m and mass 2.30 kg rolls from rest without slipping to the bottom of an inclined plane. If the angular velocity of the disk is 4.27 rad/s at the bottom, what is the height of the inclined plane?

A. 0.57 m

B. 1.08 m

C. 2.84 m

D. 3.57 m

32. A merry-go-round spins freely when Paul moves quickly to the center along a radius of the merry-go-round. As he does this, the moment of inertia of the system:

　A. increases, and the angular speed increases

　B. decreases, and the angular speed remains the same

　C. decreases, and the angular speed decreases

　D. decreases, and the angular speed increases

33. What is the angular speed of a compact disc that, at a specific instant, is rotating at 210.0 rpm?

　A. 8.5 rad/s　　　　　　　　　　　**C.** 36.4 rad/s

　B. 22.0 rad/s　　　　　　　　　　　**D.** 52.6 rad/s

34. A solid uniform sphere is rolling without slipping along a horizontal surface with a speed of 5.5 m/s when it starts up a ramp that makes an angle of 25° with the horizontal. What is the speed of the sphere after it has rolled 3.0 m up as measured along the surface of the ramp?

　A. 0.8 m/s　　　　　　　　　　　　**C.** 3.5 m/s

　B. 1.6 m/s　　　　　　　　　　　　**D.** 4.8 m/s

35. A force of 16.88 N is applied tangentially to a wheel of radius 0.340 m and gives rise to angular acceleration of 1.20 rad/s^2. What is the rotational inertia of the wheel?

　A. 1.48 kg·m^2　　　　　　　　　　**C.** 3.48 kg·m^2

　B. 2.26 kg·m^2　　　　　　　　　　**D.** 4.78 kg·m^2

36. A machine does 3.9 kJ of work on a spinning flywheel to bring it from 500.0 rpm to rest. This flywheel is in the shape of a solid uniform disk of a radius of 1.2 m. What is the mass of this flywheel?

　A. 2.6 kg　　　　　　　　　　　　**C.** 5.2 kg

　B. 4.0 kg　　　　　　　　　　　　**D.** 6.4 kg

37. A rectangular billboard with h = 20.0 cm high and w = 11.0 cm wide loses three of its four support bolts and rotates into the position as shown, with P_1 directly over P_3. It is supported by P_2, which is so tight that it holds the billboard from further rotation. What is the gravitational torque about P_2 if the mass of the billboard is 5.0 kg?

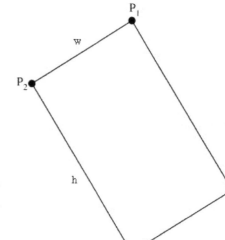

　A. 1.2 Nm　　　　　　　　　　　**C.** 4.7 Nm

　B. 2.5 Nm　　　　　　　　　　　**D.** 6.8 Nm

38. A disk, a hoop, and a solid sphere are released simultaneously at the top of an inclined plane. In which order do they reach the bottom if each is uniform and rolls without slipping?

    A. sphere, hoop, disk

    B. sphere, disk, hoop

    C. hoop, sphere, disk

    D. disk, hoop, sphere

39. A uniform disk is attached at the rim to a vertical shaft and is used as a cam. A side view and top view of the disk and shaft are shown.

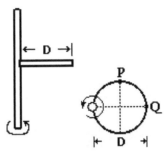

The disk has a diameter of 80.0 cm. The moment of inertia of the disk about the axis of the shaft is 6.0×10^{-3} kg·m². What is the kinetic energy of the disk as the shaft rotates uniformly about its axis at 96.0 rpm?

    A. 0.18 J

    B. 0.30 J

    C. 0.49 J

    D. 0.57 J

40. A scooter has wheels with a diameter of 240.0 mm. What is the angular speed of the wheels when the scooter is moving forward at 6.00 m/s?

    A. 128.6 rpm

    B. 248.2 rpm

    C. 472.0 rpm

    D. 478.0 rpm

41. A spinning ice skater on frictionless ice can control the rate at which she rotates by pulling in her arms. Which of the following statements are true about the skater during this process?

    I. Her kinetic energy remains constant

    II. Her moment of inertia remains constant

    III. Her angular momentum remains constant

    A. I only

    B. II only

    C. III only

    D. I and II only

42. Tanya is riding a merry-go-round with an instantaneous angular speed of 1.25 rad/s and angular acceleration of 0.745 rad/s². Tanya is standing 4.65 m from the center of the merry-go-round. What is the magnitude of the linear acceleration of Tanya?

    A. 2.45 m/s²

    B. 4.20 m/s²

    C. 6.82 m/s²

    D. 8.05 m/s²

43. Through how many degrees does a 33.0 rpm turntable rotate in 0.32 s?

A. 31°   **C.** 63°

B. 42°   **D.** 76°

44. A 50.0 kg uniform ladder, length $L = 5.00$ m long, is placed against a smooth wall at the height of $h = 3.70$ m. The ladder's base rests on a rough horizontal surface whose coefficient of static friction $\mu = 0.750$. An 80.0 kg block is suspended from the top rung of the ladder, just at the wall. What is the approximate magnitude of the force exerted on the base of the ladder due to contact with the rough horizontal surface?

A. 1,370 N   **C.** 1,580 N

B. 1,460 N   **D.** 1,640 N

45. At time $t = 0$ s, a wheel has an angular displacement of zero radians and an angular velocity of +29.0 rad/s. The wheel has a constant acceleration of –0.52 rad/s². In this situation, what is the maximum value of the angular displacement?

A. +467 rad   **C.** +1,110 rad

B. +809 rad   **D.** +1,460 rad

46. A disk lies in the *xz*-plane with its center at the origin. When viewed from the positive *y*-axis (i.e., above the disk), the direction of rotation appears clockwise. In what direction does the angular velocity of the disk point?

A. to her right   **C.** down

B. to her left   **D.** up

47. How long does it take for a rotating object to speed up from 15.0 rad/s to 33.3 rad/s if it has a uniform angular acceleration of 3.45 rad/s²?

A. 3.45 s   **C.** 8.35 s

B. 5.30 s   **D.** 14.60 s

48. A solid uniform sphere of mass 120.0 kg and radius 1.7 m starts from rest and rolls without slipping down an inclined plane of vertical height 5.3 m; the sphere starts at the top of the ramp. What is the angular speed of the sphere at the bottom of the inclined plane? The moment of inertia of a solid sphere is $(2/5)mR^2$.

A. 0.81 rad/s   **C.** 2.9 rad/s

B. 1.7 rad/s   **D.** 5.1 rad/s

49. Three solid, uniform, cylindrically shaped flywheels, each of mass 65.0 kg and radius 1.47 m, rotate independently around a common axis. Two flywheels rotate in one direction at 3.83 rad/s; the other rotates in the opposite direction at 3.42 rad/s. What is the magnitude of the net angular momentum of the system?

A. 168.0 kg·m²/s

B. 298.0 kg·m²/s

C. 456.0 kg·m²/s

D. 622.0 kg·m²/s

50. A cylinder and a sphere are released simultaneously at the top of an inclined plane. Which reaches the bottom first if they roll down the inclined plane without slipping?

A. The one of smallest diameter

B. The one of greatest mass

C. The disk

D. The sphere

51. What is the angular speed of a flywheel turning at 813.0 rpm?

A. 8.33 rad/s

C. 33.84 rad/s

B. 56.23 rad/s

D. 85.14 rad/s

52. A machinist turns the power on to a grinding wheel at time $t = 0$ s. The wheel accelerates uniformly from rest for 10.0 s and reaches the operating angular speed of 96.0 rad/s. The wheel is run at that angular velocity for 40.0 s, and then power is shut off. The wheel slows down uniformly at 1.5 rad/s² until the wheel stops. For how long after the power is shut off does it take the wheel to stop?

A. 56.0 s

B. 64.0 s

C. 72.0 s

D. 82.0 s

53. A futuristic design for a car is to have a large disk-like flywheel within the car storing kinetic energy. The flywheel has a mass 370.0 kg with a radius of 0.500 m and can rotate up to 200.0 rev/s. Assuming this stored kinetic energy could be transferred to the linear velocity of the 1500.0-kg car, what is the maximum attainable speed of the car?

A. 29.6 m/s

B. 88.4 m/s

C. 162 m/s

D. 221 m/s

54. An electrical motor spins at a constant 2,695.0 rpm. If the rotor radius is 7.165 cm, what is the linear acceleration of the edge of the rotor?

A. 707.0 m/s²

B. 1,280 m/s²

C. 3,272 m/s²

D. 5,707 m/s²

55. To drive a typical car at 40.0 mph on a level road for one hour requires about 3.2×10^7 J of energy. Suppose one tried to store this much energy in a spinning solid cylindrical flywheel which was then coupled to the wheels of the car. What angular speed would be required to store 3.2×10^7 J if the flywheel has a radius of 0.60 m and mass 400.0 kg?

A. 943.0 rad/s

C. 1,822.4 rad/s

B. 1,384.2 rad/s

D. 2,584.5 rad/s

56. A uniform, solid, cylindrical flywheel of radius 1.4 m and mass 15.0 kg rotates at 2.7 rad/s about an axis through its circular faces. What is the magnitude of the flywheel's angular momentum?

A. 22 kg·m²/s

C. 64 kg·m²/s

B. 40 kg·m²/s

D. 80 kg·m²/s

57. A particular motor can provide a maximum torque of 110.0 N·m. Assuming that this torque is used to accelerate a solid, uniform, cylindrical flywheel of mass 10.0 kg and radius 3.00 m, how long will it take for the flywheel to accelerate from rest to 8.13 rad/s?

A. 2.13 s

C. 4.65 s

B. 3.33 s

D. 5.46 s

58. A satellite is in a circular orbit around a planet. What is the satellite's orbital speed if the orbital radius is 34.0 km and the gravitational acceleration at that height is 2.3 m/s²?

A. 26 m/s

C. 280 m/s

B. 150 m/s

D. 310 m/s

Notes for active learning

Notes for active learning

Waves and Periodic Motion

1. A simple harmonic oscillator oscillates with frequency f when its amplitude is A. What is the new frequency if the amplitude is doubled to 2A?

A. $f/2$

B. f

C. $4f$

D. $2f$

2. Springs A and B are attached in series, with the free end of spring B attached to a wall. The free end of spring A is pulled, and both springs expand from their equilibrium lengths. The length of spring A increases by L_A, and the length of spring B increases by L_B. What is the expression for the spring constant k_B of spring B?

A. L_B/k_A

B. k_A^2

C. $k_A L_B$

D. $(k_A L_A)/L_B$

3. Particles of a material that move back and forth in the same direction the wave moves are:

A. Standing waves

B. Torsional waves

C. Transverse waves

D. Longitudinal waves

4. If a wave has a wavelength of 25 cm and a frequency of 1.68 kHz, what is its speed?

A. 44 m/s

B. 160 m/s

C. 420 m/s

D. 314 m/s

5. The total stored energy in a system undergoing simple harmonic motion (SHM) is proportional to the:

A. (amplitude)^2

B. wavelength

C. (spring constant)^2

D. amplitude

6. An 11 kg mass m is attached to a spring and allowed to hang in the Earth's gravitational field. The spring stretches 3 cm before reaching its equilibrium position. If the spring were allowed to oscillate, what would be its frequency? (Use acceleration due to gravity $g = 9.8$ m/s^2)

A. 0.7 Hz

B. 1.8 Hz

C. 4.1 Hz

D. 2.9 Hz

7. The time required for one cycle of any repeating event is the:

A. amplitude

B. frequency

C. period

D. rotation

8. A pendulum of length L is suspended from the ceiling of an elevator. When the elevator is at rest, the pendulum's period is T. How does the period of the pendulum change when the elevator moves upward with constant acceleration?

    A. Remains the same

    B. Decreases

    C. Increases

    D. Decreases only if the upward acceleration is less than $g / 2$

9. What is the period of a transverse wave with a frequency of 100 Hz?

    A. 0.01 s   **C.** 0.2 s

    B. 0.05 s   **D.** 20 s

10. Two radio antennae are located on a seacoast 10 km apart on a North-South axis. The antennas broadcast identical in-phase AM radio waves at a frequency of 4.7 MHz. 200 km offshore, a steamship travels North at 15 km/h, passing East of the antennae with a radio tuned to the broadcast frequency. From the moment of the maximum reception of the radio signal on the ship, what is the time interval until the next occurrence of maximum reception? (Use speed of radio waves equals speed of light $c = 3 \times 10^8$ m/s and path difference $= 1 \lambda$)

    A. 7.7 min   **C.** 3.8 min

    B. 5.1 min   **D.** 8.9 min

11. A 2.31 kg rope is stretched between supports 10.4 m apart. If one end of the rope is tweaked, how long will it take for the resulting disturbance to reach the other end? Assume that the tension in the rope is 74.4 N.

    A. 0.33 s   **C.** 0.65 s

    B. 0.74 s   **D.** 0.57 s

12. Simple pendulum A swings back and forth twice the frequency of simple pendulum B. Which statement is correct?

    A. Pendulum A is ¼ as long as B   **C.** Pendulum A is ½ as long as B

    B. Pendulum A is twice as massive as B   **D.** Pendulum B is twice as massive as A

13. A weight attached to the free end of an anchored spring is allowed to slide back and forth in simple harmonic motion on a frictionless table. How many times greater is the spring's restoring force at $x = 5$ cm compared to $x = 1$ cm (measured from equilibrium)?

    A. 2.5   **C.** 7.5

    B. 5   **D.** 15

14. A massless, ideal spring projects horizontally from a wall and is connected to a 1 kg mass. The mass is oscillating in one dimension, such that it moves 0.5 m from one end of its oscillation to the other. It undergoes 10 complete oscillations in 60 s. What is the period of the oscillation?

A. 9 s

B. 3 s

C. 6 s

D. 12 s

15. The total mechanical energy of a simple harmonic oscillating system is:

A. a nonzero constant

B. maximum when it reaches the maximum displacement

C. zero when it reaches the maximum displacement

D. zero as it passes the equilibrium point

16. What is the frequency of the oscillations when a vibrating spring moves from its maximum elongation position to its maximum compression position in 1 s?

A. 0.75 Hz

B. 0.5 Hz

C. 1 Hz

D. 2.5 Hz

17. Which of the following is not a transverse wave?

I. Radio　　　　II. Light　　　　III. Sound

A. I only

B. II only

C. III only

D. I and II only

18. If a wave has a speed of 362 m/s and a period of 4 ms, its wavelength is closest to:

A. 8.6 m

B. 1.5 m

C. 0.86 m

D. 15 m

19. Simple harmonic motion is characterized by:

A. acceleration that is proportional to the negative displacement

B. acceleration that is proportional to the velocity

C. constant positive acceleration

D. acceleration that is inversely proportional to the negative displacement

20. If the frequency of a harmonic oscillator doubles, by what factor does the maximum value of acceleration change?

A. $2/\pi$

B. $\sqrt{2}$

C. 2

D. 4

21. An object that hangs from the ceiling of a stationary elevator by an ideal spring oscillates with a period T. If the elevator were to accelerate upwards with an acceleration of $2g$, what is the period of oscillation of the object?

    A. T/2   **C.** 2T

    B. T   **D.** 4T

22. Which of the following changes made to a transverse wave must increase wavelength?

    A. An increase in frequency and a decrease in speed

    B. The wavelength is only affected by a change in amplitude

    C. A decrease in frequency and an increase in speed

    D. A decrease in frequency and a decrease in speed

23. If a wave travels 30 m in 1 s, making 60 vibrations per second, what are its frequency and speed, respectively?

    A. 30 Hz and 60 m/s   **C.** 30 Hz and 30 m/s

    B. 60 Hz and 30 m/s   **D.** 60 Hz and 15 m/s

24. Transverse waves propagate at 40 m/s in a string that is subjected to a tension of 60 N. If the string is 16 m long, what is its mass?

    A. 0.6 kg   **C.** 0.2 kg

    B. 0.9 kg   **D.** 9 kg

25. Doubling the amplitude of a vibrating mass-on-spring system changes the system frequency by what factor?

    A. Increases by 3   **C.** Increases by 5

    B. Increases by 2   **D.** Remains the same

26. A leaky faucet drips 60 times in 40 s. What is the frequency of the dripping?

    A. 0.75 Hz   **C.** 1.5 Hz

    B. 0.67 Hz   **D.** 12 Hz

27. Particles of a material that move up and down perpendicular to the direction that the wave is moving are in what type of wave?

    A. torsional   **C.** longitudinal

    B. mechanical   **D.** transverse

28. The figure shows a graph of the velocity v as a function of time t for a system undergoing simple harmonic motion. Which one of the following graphs represents the acceleration of this system as a function of time?

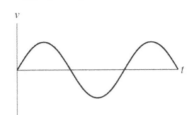

A. *a*

C. *a*

B. *a*

D. *a*

29. When compared, a transverse wave and a longitudinal wave have amplitudes of equal magnitude. Which statement is true about their speeds?

A. The waves have the same speeds
B. The transverse wave has exactly twice the speed of the longitudinal wave
C. The speeds of the two waves are unrelated to their amplitudes
D. The longitudinal wave has a slower speed

30. What is the frequency when the weight on the end of a spring bobs up and down and completes one cycle every 2 s?

A. 0.5 Hz

C. 2 Hz

B. 1 Hz

D. 2.5 Hz

31. The velocity of a given longitudinal sound wave in an ideal gas is $v = 340$ m/s at constant pressure and constant volume. Assuming an ideal gas, what is the wavelength for a 2,100 Hz sound wave?

A. 0.08 m

C. 1.6 m

B. 0.16 m

D. 7.3 m

32. When the mass of a simple pendulum is quadrupled, how does the time t required for one complete oscillation change?

A. Decreases to ¼t

B. Decreases to ¾t

C. Increases to 4t

D. Remains the same

33. An object undergoing simple harmonic motion has an amplitude of 2.5 m. If the maximum velocity of the object is 15 m/s, what is the object's angular frequency (ω)?

A. 6.0 rad/s

B. 3.6 rad/s

C. 37.5 rad/s

D. 8.8 rad/s

34. Unpolarized light is incident upon two polarization filters that do not have their transmission axes aligned. If 14% of the light passes through, what is the angle between the transmission axes of the filters?

A. 73°

B. 81°

C. 43°

D. 58°

35. A mass on a spring undergoes simple harmonic motion. Which of the statements is true when the mass is at its maximum distance from the equilibrium position?

A. KE is nonzero

B. Acceleration is at a minimum

C. Speed is zero

D. Speed is maximum

36. What is the frequency if the speed of a sound wave is 240 m/s and its wavelength is 10 cm?

A. 2.4 Hz

B. 24 Hz

C. 240 Hz

D. 2,400 Hz

37. Unlike a transverse wave, a longitudinal wave has no:

A. wavelength

B. crests or troughs

C. amplitude

D. frequency

38. The density of aluminum is 2,700 kg/m³. If transverse waves propagate at 36 m/s in a 9.2 mm diameter aluminum wire, what is the tension in the wire?

A. 43 N

B. 68 N

C. 233 N

D. 350 N

39. When a wave obliquely crosses a boundary into another medium, it is:

A. always slowed down

B. reflected

C. diffracted

D. refracted

40. A floating leaf oscillates up and down two complete cycles each second as a water wave passes. What is the wave's frequency?

A. 0.5 Hz

B. 1 Hz

C. 2 Hz

D. 3 Hz

41. A higher pitch for a sound wave means the wave has a greater:

A. frequency

B. wavelength

C. amplitude

D. period

42. An object is attached to a vertical spring and bobs up and down between points A and B. Where is the object located when its kinetic energy is at a maximum?

A. One-fourth of the way between A and B

B. One-third of the way between A and B

C. Midway between A and B

D. At either A or B

43. A pendulum consists of a 0.5 kg mass attached to the end of a 1 m rod of negligible mass. What is the magnitude of the torque τ about the pivot when the rod makes an angle θ of 60° with the vertical? (Use the acceleration due to gravity $g = 10$ m/s^2)

A. 2.7 N·m

B. 4.4 N·m

C. 5.2 N·m

D. 10.6 N·m

44. The Doppler effect is characteristic of:

I. light waves   II. sound waves   III. water waves

A. I only

B. II only

C. III only

D. I, II and III

45. A crane lifts a 2,500 kg cement block using a steel cable with a mass per unit length of 0.65 kg/m. What is the speed of the transverse waves on this cable? (Use the acceleration due to gravity $g = 10$ m/s^2)

A. 196 m/s

B. 1,162 m/s

C. 322 m/s

D. 558 m/s

46. A simple pendulum consists of a mass M attached to a weightless string of length L. Which statement about the frequency f is accurate for this system when it experiences small oscillations?

A. The f is directly proportional to the period

B. The f is independent of the mass M

C. The f is inversely proportional to the amplitude

D. The f is independent of the length L

47. A child on a swing set swings back and forth. If the length of the supporting cables for the swing is 3.3 m, what is the period of oscillation? (Use acceleration due to gravity $g = 10$ m/s^2)

A. 3.6 s

B. 5.9 s

C. 4.3 s

D. 2.7 s

48. A massless, ideal spring projects horizontally from a wall and is connected to a 0.3 kg mass. The mass is oscillating in one dimension, moving 0.4 m from one end of its oscillation to the other. It undergoes 15 complete oscillations in 60 s. How does the frequency change if the spring constant is increased by a factor of 2?

A. Increases by 200%

B. Decreases by 59%

C. Increases by 41%

D. Decreases by 41%

49. A ball swinging at the end of a massless string undergoes simple harmonic motion. At what point(s) is the instantaneous acceleration of the ball the greatest?

A. A

B. B

C. C

D. A and D

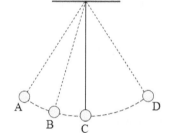

50. A simple pendulum, consisting of a 2 kg weight connected to a 10 m massless rod, is brought to an angle of 90° from the vertical and then released. What is the speed of the weight at its lowest point? (Use the acceleration due to gravity $g = 10$ m/s^2)

A. 14 m/s

B. 10 m/s

C. 20 m/s

D. 25 m/s

51. A sound source of high pitch emits a wave with a high:

      I. frequency   II. amplitude   III. speed

A. I only

B. II only

C. III only

D. I, II and III

52. Find the wavelength of a train whistle heard by a fixed observer as the train moves toward him with a velocity of 50 m/s. The wind blows at 5 m/s from the observer to the train. The whistle has a natural frequency of 500 Hz. (Use the v of sound = 340 m/s)

A. 0.75 m

B. 0.43 m

C. 0.58 m

D. 7.5 m

53. Considering a vibrating mass on a spring, what effect on the system's mechanical energy is caused by doubling the amplitude?

    A. Increases by a factor of two   **C.** Increases by a factor of three

    B. Increases by a factor of four   **D.** Produces no change

54. Which of the following is an accurate statement?

    A. Tensile stress is measured in N·m

    B. Stress is a measure of external forces on a body

    C. The ratio stress/strain is the elastic modulus

    D. Tensile strain is measured in meters

55. The efficient transfer of energy taking place at a natural frequency occurs in a phenomenon called:

    A. reverberation   **C.** beats

    B. the Doppler effect   **D.** resonance

56. A simple pendulum and a mass oscillating on an ideal spring have period T in an elevator at rest. If the elevator now accelerates downward uniformly at 2 m/s^2, what is true about the periods of these two systems?

    A. The period of the pendulum increases, but the period of the spring remains the same

    B. The period of the pendulum increases, and the period of the spring decreases

    C. The period of the pendulum decreases, but the period of the spring remains the same

    D. The periods of the pendulum and the spring both increase

57. All of the following is true of a pendulum that has swung to the top of its arc and has not yet reversed its direction, EXCEPT:

    A. The PE of the pendulum is at a maximum

    B. The acceleration of the pendulum equals zero

    C. The KE of the pendulum equals zero

    D. The velocity of the pendulum equals zero

58. The Doppler effect occurs when a source of sound moves:

        I. toward the observer

        II. away from the observer

        III. with the observer

    A. I only   **C.** III only

    B. II only   **D.** I and II only

59. Consider the wave shown in the figure. The amplitude is:

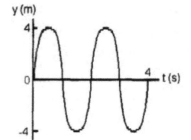

A. 1 m
B. 2 m

C. 4 m
D. 8 m

60. Increasing the mass m of a mass-and-spring system causes what kind of change on the resonant frequency f of the system?

A. The f decreases
B. There is no change in the f

C. The f decreases only if the ratio k / m is < 1
D. The f increases

61. A simple pendulum with a bob of mass M has a period T. What is the effect on the period if M is doubled while all other factors remain unchanged?

A. T/2
B. T/√2

C. 2T
D. T

62. A skipper on a boat notices wave crests passing the anchor chain every 5 s. The skipper estimates that the distance between crests is 15 m. What is the speed of the water waves?

A. 3 m/s
B. 5 m/s

C. 12 m/s
D. 9 m/s

63. For an object undergoing simple harmonic motion, the:

A. maximum potential energy is larger than the maximum kinetic energy
B. acceleration is greatest when the displacement is greatest
C. displacement is greatest when the speed is greatest
D. acceleration is greatest when the speed is greatest

64. As the frequency of a wave increases, which of the following must decrease?

A. The speed of the wave
B. The velocity of the wave

C. The amplitude of the wave
D. The period of the wave

65. What is the period for a weight on the end of a spring that bobs up and down one complete cycle every 2 s?

A. 0.5 s
B. 1 s

C. 2 s
D. 3 s

66. After a rain, one sometimes sees brightly colored oil slicks on the road. These are due to:

  A. selective absorption of different λ by oil   **C.** polarization effects

  B. diffraction effects   **D.** interference effects

67. The natural frequencies for a stretched string of length L and wave speed v are $nv / (2L)$, where n equals:

  A. 0, 1, 3, 5, ...   **C.** 2, 4, 6, 8, ...

  B. 1, 2, 3, 4, ...   **D.** 0, 1, 2, 3, ...

Notes for active learning

Sound

1. A 20 decibel (dB) noise is heard from a cricket 30 m away. How loud does it sound when the cricket is 3 m away?

A. 30 dB

B. 40 dB

C. 20 × √2 dB

D. 80 dB

2. A thunderclap occurs 6 km from a stationary person. How soon does the person hear it? (Use the speed of sound in air $v = 340$ m/s)

A. 18 s

B. 30 s

C. 48 s

D. 56 s

3. Enrico Caruso, a famous Italian opera singer, made a crystal chandelier shatter with his voice. This is a demonstration of:

A. ideal frequency

B. resonance

C. a standing wave

D. sound refraction

4. A taut 2 m string is fixed at both ends and plucked. What is the wavelength for the third harmonic?

A. 2/3 m

B. 1 m

C. 4/3 m

D. 3 m

5. High-pitched sound has a high:

      I. number of partial tones   II. frequency   III. speed

A. I only

B. II only

C. III only

D. I and II only

6. A light ray in air strikes a medium whose index of refraction is 1.5. If the angle of incidence is 60°, which of the following expressions gives the angle of refraction? (Use $n_{air} = 1$)

A. $\sin^{-1}(0.67 \sin 60°)$

B. $\sin^{-1}(1.5 \cos 60°)$

C. $\sin^{-1}(1.5 \sin 30°)$

D. $\sin^{-1}(0.67 \sin 30°)$

7. A string, 2 m in length, is fixed at both ends and tightened until the wave speed is 92 m/s. What is the frequency of the standing wave shown?

A. 46 Hz

B. 33 Hz

C. 240 Hz

D. 138 Hz

8. A 0.6 m uniform bar of metal with a diameter of 2 cm has a mass of 2.5 kg. A 1.5 MHz longitudinal wave is propagated along the length of the bar. A wave compression traverses the length of the bar in 0.14 ms. What is the wavelength of the longitudinal wave in the metal?

A. 2.9 mm   **C.** 3.2 mm

B. 1.8 mm   **D.** 4.6 mm

Questions **9-12** are based on the following:

The velocity of a wave on a wire or string is not dependent (to a close approximation) on frequency or amplitude and is given by $v^2 = T / \rho_L$. T is the tension in the wire. The linear mass density ρ_L (rho) is the mass per unit length of wire. Therefore, ρ_L is the product of the mass density and the cross-sectional area (A).

A sine wave is traveling to the right with a frequency of 250 Hz. Wire A is composed of steel and has a circular cross-section diameter of 0.6 mm, and a tension of 2,000 N. Wire B is under the same tension and is made of the same material as wire A but has a circular cross-section diameter of 0.3 mm. Wire C has the same tension as wire A and is made of a composite material. (Use the density of steel wire $\rho = 7$ g/cm^3 and the density of the composite material $\rho = 3$ g/cm^3)

9. How much does the tension need to be increased to increase the wave velocity on a wire by 30%?

A. 37%   **C.** 69%

B. 60%   **D.** 81%

10. What is the linear mass density of wire B compared to wire A?

A. $\sqrt{2}$ times   **C.** 1/8

B. 2 times   **D.** 1/4

11. What must the diameter of wire C be to have the same wave velocity as wire A?

A. 0.41 mm   **C.** 0.83 mm

B. 0.92 mm   **D.** 3.2 mm

12. How does the cross-sectional area change if the diameter increases by a factor of 4?

A. Increases by a factor of 16   **C.** Increases by a factor of 2

B. Increases by a factor of 4   **D.** Decreases by a factor of 4

13. A bird, emitting sounds with a frequency of 60 kHz, is moving at a speed of 10 m/s toward a stationary observer. What is the frequency of the sound waves detected by the observer? (Use the speed of sound in air $v = 340$ m/s)

A. 55 kHz

B. 62 kHz

C. 68 kHz

D. 76 kHz

14. What is observed for a frequency heard by a stationary person when a sound source is approaching?

A. Equal to zero

B. The same as the source

C. Higher than the source

D. Lower than the source

15. Which of the following is a false statement?

A. The transverse waves on a vibrating string are different from sound waves

B. Sound travels much slower than light

C. Sound waves are longitudinal pressure waves

D. Sound can travel through a vacuum

16. Which of the following is a real-life example of the Doppler effect?

A. Changing pitch of the siren as an ambulance passes by the observer

B. Radio signal transmission

C. Sound becomes quieter as the observer moves away from the source

D. Human hearing is most acute at 2,500 Hz

17. Two sound waves have the same frequency and amplitudes of 0.4 Pa and 0.6 Pa, respectively. When they arrive at point X, what is the range of amplitudes for sound at point X?

A. 0 – 0.4 Pa

B. 0.4 – 0.6 Pa

C. 0.2 – 1.0 Pa

D. 0.4 – 0.8 Pa

18. The intensity of the waves from a point source at a distance d from the source is I. What is the intensity at a distance $2d$ from the source?

A. I/2

B. I/4

C. 4I

D. 2I

19. Sound would be expected to travel most slowly in a medium that exhibited:

A. low resistance to compression and high density

B. high resistance to compression and low density

C. low resistance to compression and low density

D. high resistance to compression and high density

20. Which is true for a resonating pipe that is open at both ends?

   A. Displacement node at one end and a displacement antinode at the other end

   B. Displacement antinodes at each end

   C. Displacement nodes at each end

   D. Displacement node at one end and a one-fourth antinode at the other end

21. In a pipe of length L that is open at both ends, the lowest tone to resonate is 200 Hz. Which of the following frequencies does not resonate in this pipe?

   A. 400 Hz   **C.** 500 Hz

   B. 600 Hz   **D.** 800 Hz

22. In general, a sound is conducted fastest through:

   A. vacuum   **C.** liquids

   B. gases   **D.** solids

23. If an electric charge is shaken up and down:

   A. electron excitation occurs   **C.** sound is emitted

   B. a magnetic field is created   **D.** its charge changes

24. What is the wavelength of a sound wave of frequency 620 Hz in steel, given that the speed of sound in steel is 5,000 m/s?

   A. 1.8 m   **C.** 8.1 m

   B. 6.2 m   **D.** 2.6 m

25. If the sound from a constant sound source is radiating equally in all directions, as the distance doubles, by what amount is the intensity of the sound reduced?

   A. ¼   **C.** $1/\sqrt{2}$

   B. 1/16   **D.** ½

26. Why does the intensity of waves from a sound source decrease with the square of the distance from the source?

   A. The medium through which the waves travel absorbs the energy of the waves

   B. The waves speed up as they travel away from the source

   C. The waves lose energy as they travel

   D. The waves spread out as they travel

> Questions **27-30** are based on the following:

Steven is preparing a mailing tube that is 1.5 m long and 4 cm in diameter. The tube is open at one end and sealed at the other. Before he inserted his documents, the mailing tube fell to the floor and produced a note. (Use the speed of sound in air $v = 340$ m/s)

27. What is the wavelength of the fundamental?

   A. 0.04 m   **C.** 0.75 m

   B. 6 m   **D.** 1.5 m

28. If the tube was filled with helium, in which sound travels at 960 m/s, what would be the frequency of the fundamental?

   A. 160 Hz   **C.** 80 Hz

   B. 320 Hz   **D.** 640 Hz

29. What is the wavelength of the fifth harmonic?

   A. 3.2 m   **C.** 2.4 m

   B. 1.2 m   **D.** 1.5 m

30. What is the frequency of the note that Steven heard?

   A. 57 Hz   **C.** 30 Hz

   B. 85 Hz   **D.** 120 Hz

31. A 4 g string, 0.34 m long, is under tension. The string vibrates in the third harmonic. What is the wavelength of the standing wave in the string? (Use the speed of sound in air = 344 m/s)

   A. 0.56 m   **C.** 0.23 m

   B. 0.33 m   **D.** 0.61 m

32. Two pure tones are sounded together, and a particular beat frequency is heard. What happens to the beat frequency if the frequency of one of the tones is increased?

   A. Increases   **C.** Remains the same

   B. Decreases   **D.** Either increase or decrease

33. Consider a closed pipe of length L. What are the wavelengths of the three lowest tones produced?

A. $4L$, $4/3L$, $4/5L$

B. $2L$, L, $2/3L$

C. $2L$, L, $\frac{1}{2}L$

D. $4L$, $2L$, L

34. Mary hears the barely perceptible buzz of a mosquito one meter away from her ear in a quiet room. How much energy does a mosquito produce in 200 s? (Note: an almost inaudible sound has a threshold value of 9.8×10^{-12} W/m^2)

A. 6.1×10^{-8} J

B. 1.3×10^{-8} J

C. 6.4×10^{-10} J

D. 2.5×10^{-8} J

35. How long does it take for a light wave to travel 1 km through the water with a refractive index of 1.33? (Use the speed of light $c = 3 \times 10^8$ m/s)

A. 4.4×10^{-6} s

B. 4.4×10^{-9} s

C. 2.8×10^{-9} s

D. 2.8×10^{-12} s

36. In designing a music hall, an acoustical engineer deals mainly with:

A. wave interference

B. resonance

C. forced vibrations

D. modulation

37. Which curve in the figure represents the variation of wave speed (v) as a function of tension (T) for transverse waves on a stretched string?

A. A

B. B

C. C

D. D

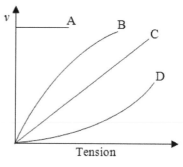

38. A string, 4 meters in length, is fixed at both ends and tightened until the wave speed is 20 m/s. What is the frequency of the standing wave shown?

A. 13 Hz

B. 8.1 Hz

C. 5.4 Hz

D. 15.4 Hz

39. Compared to the velocity of a 600 Hz sound, the velocity of a 300 Hz sound through air is:

A. one-half as great

B. the same

C. twice as great

D. four times as great

40. Consider a string with a linear mass density of 0.40 g/m stretched to a length of 0.50 m by tension of 75 N, vibrating at the 6th harmonic. It excites an open pipe into the second overtone. What is the length of the pipe?

A. 0.25 m

B. 0.1 m

C. 0.20 m

D. 0.6 m

41. A string of length L is under tension, and the speed of a wave in the string is v. What is the speed of a wave in a string of the same mass under the same tension but twice as long?

A. $v\sqrt{2}$

B. $2v$

C. $v/2$

D. $v/\sqrt{2}$

42. If a guitar string has a fundamental frequency of 500 Hz, which one of the following frequencies can set the string into resonant vibration?

A. 450 Hz

B. 760 Hz

C. 1,500 Hz

D. 2,250 Hz

43. When a light wave passes from a lower refractive index to a medium with a higher refractive index, some of the incident light is refracted, while some are reflected. What is the angle of refraction?

A. Greater than the angle of incidence and less than the angle of reflection

B. Less than the angle of incidence and greater than the angle of reflection

C. Greater than the angles of incidence and reflection

D. Less than the angles of incidence and reflection

44. The speed of a sound wave in the air depends on:

    I. the air temperature   II. wavelength   III. frequency

A. I only

B. II only

C. III only

D. I and II only

45. Which of the following statements is false?

A. The speed of a wave and the speed of the vibrating particles that constitute the wave are different entities

B. Waves transport energy and matter from one region to another

C. In a transverse wave, the particle motion is perpendicular to the velocity vector of the wave

D. Not all waves are mechanical

46. A 2.5 g string, 0.75 m long, is under tension. The string produces a 700 Hz tone when it vibrates in the third harmonic. What is the wavelength of the tone in the air? (Use the speed of sound in air $v = 344$ m/s)

A. 0.65 m

B. 0.57 m

C. 0.33 m

D. 0.5 m

47. Suppose that a source of sound is emitting waves uniformly in all directions. If an observer moves to a point twice as far away from the source, what is the frequency of the sound?

A. $\sqrt{2}$ as large

B. Twice as large

C. Unchanged

D. Half as large

48. A 2.5 kg rope is stretched between supports 8 m apart. If one end of the rope is tweaked, how long will it take for the resulting disturbance to reach the other end? Assume that the tension in the rope is 40 N.

A. 0.71 s

B. 0.62 s

C. 0.58 s

D. 0.47 s

49. An office machine is making a rattling sound with an intensity of 10^{-5} W/m² when perceived by an office worker that is sitting 3 m away. What is the sound level in decibels for the sound of the machine? (Use the threshold of hearing as $I_0 = 10^{-12}$ W/m²)

A. 10 dB

B. 35 dB

C. 70 dB

D. 95 dB

50. A taut 1 m string is plucked. Point B is midway between both ends, and a finger is placed on point B such that a waveform exists with a node at B. What is the lowest frequency that can be heard? (Use the speed of waves on the string $v = 3.8 \times 10^4$ m/s)

A. 4.8×10^5 Hz

B. 3.8×10^4 Hz

C. 9.7×10^3 Hz

D. 7.4×10^3 Hz

51. For a light wave traveling in a vacuum, which of the following properties is true?

A. Increased f results in increased amplitude

B. Increased f results in decreased speed

C. Increased f results in an increased wavelength

D. Increased f results in a decreased wavelength

52. Which wave is different from the others (i.e., does not belong to the same grouping)?

A. Pressure wave

B. Radio wave

C. Ultrasonic wave

D. Infrasonic wave

53. Two speakers are placed 2 m apart, and both produce a sound wave (in-phase) with a wavelength of 0.8 m. A microphone is placed an equal distance from both speakers to determine the intensity of the sound at various points. What point is precisely halfway between the two speakers? (Use the speed of sound $v = 340$ m/s)

A. Both an antinode and a node

B. Neither an antinode nor a node

C. A node

D. An antinode

54. The siren of an ambulance blares at 1,200 Hz when the ambulance is stationary. What frequency does a stationary observer hear after this ambulance passes her while traveling at 30 m/s? (Speed of sound $v = 342$ m/s)

A. 1,240 Hz

B. 1,128 Hz

C. 1,103 Hz

D. 1,427 Hz

55. Compared to the wavelength of a 600 Hz sound, the wavelength of a 300 Hz sound in air is:

A. one-half as long

B. the same

C. one-fourth as long

D. twice as long

56. An organ pipe that is open at both ends is tuned to a given frequency, and a second pipe with both ends open resonates with twice this frequency. What is the ratio of the length of the first pipe to the second pipe?

A. 0.5

B. 1

C. 2

D. 2.5

57. The frequency of the third harmonic of the C_4 string of a piano is 783.7 Hz. The fundamental frequency of the G_5 string is 782.4 Hz. When the key for C_4 is held down so that the string can vibrate, and the G_5 key is stricken loudly, the third harmonic of the C_4 string is excited. Then, when striking the G_5 key again more softly, the volume of the two strings is matched. What phenomenon is demonstrated when the G_5 string is used to excite the vibration of the C_4 string?

A. Resonance

B. Dispersion

C. Beats

D. Interference

58. Crests of an ocean wave pass a pier every 10 s. If the waves are moving at 4.5 m/s, what is the wavelength of the ocean waves?

A. 38 m

B. 16 m

C. 45 m

D. 25 m

59. Which statement explains why sound travels faster in water than in air?

A. Sound shifts to increased frequency

B. Sound shifts to decreased density

C. Density of water increases more quickly than its resistance to compression

D. Density of water increases more slowly than its resistance to compression

60. When visible light is incident upon clear glass, the electrons in the atoms in the glass:

I. convert the light energy into internal energy

II. resonate

III. vibrate

A. I only

B. II only

C. III only

D. I and II only

61. A sewing machine makes a rattling sound with an intensity of 10^{-6} W/m^2 where a worker sits 3 m away. If he moves to a point 9 m away, what would be the intensity?

A. 9.9×10^{-6} W/m^2

B. 3.3×10^{-6} W/m^2

C. 3.3×10^{-5} W/m^2

D. 1.1×10^{-7} W/m^2

62. A 0.5 m rope under a tension of 50 N is set into oscillation. The mass density of the rope is 140 g/cm. What is the frequency of the fundamental harmonic node (n = 1)?

A. 1.9 Hz

B. 3.8 Hz

C. 2.7 Hz

D. 1.1 Hz

63. If a person inhales a few breaths from a helium gas balloon, the person will experience an amusing change in her voice. What causes her voice to have this high-pitched effect?

A. Her voice box is resonating at the 2nd harmonic rather than at the fundamental frequency

B. Low frequencies are absorbed in helium gas, leaving the high-frequency components, which result in the high-pitched sound

C. The helium causes her vocal cords to tighten and vibrate at a higher frequency

D. Sound travels faster in helium than in air, causing the velocity to increase

64. A standing wave of the third overtone is induced in a stopped 1.4 m long pipe. A stopped pipe is open at one end and closed at the other. What is the frequency of the sound produced by the pipe? (Use the speed of sound $v = 340$ m/s)

A. 205 Hz

B. 260 Hz

C. 350 Hz

D. 425 Hz

65. Upon measuring the light waves emitted by stars, it was discovered that the measured frequency of the light was lower than the actual frequency. One explanation for this phenomenon is that the:

A. stars are accelerating

B. speed of the stars is decreasing

C. stars are moving toward the Earth

D. stars are moving away from the Earth

66. Two tuning forks have frequencies of 460 Hz and 524 Hz. What is the beat frequency if both are sounding simultaneously and resonating?

A. 52 Hz

B. 64 Hz

C. 396 Hz

D. 524 Hz

67. Which of the following is true of the properties of a light wave as it moves from a medium of lower refractive index to a medium of the higher refractive index?

A. Speed decreases

B. Speed increases

C. Frequency decreases

D. Frequency increases

68. Resonance can be looked at as forced vibration with the:

A. matching of constructive and destructive interference

B. matching of wave amplitudes

C. maximum amount of energy input

D. least amount of energy input

69. The explanation for refraction must involve a change in:

    I. frequency   II. speed   III. wavelength

A. I only

B. II only

C. III only

D. I and II only

70. Which of the following increases when a sound becomes louder?

A. Amplitude

B. Period

C. Frequency

D. Wavelength

71. Sound intensity is defined as the:

A. sound power per unit volume

B. sound power per unit time

C. sound energy passing through a unit of area

D. sound energy passing an area per unit time

72. A violin with string length 36 cm and string density 3.8 g/cm resonates with the first overtone of an organ pipe with one end closed. The pipe length is 3 m. What is the tension in the string so that the sound wave resonates at its fundamental frequency? (Use the speed of sound $v = 340$ m/s)

A. 1,390 N   **C.** 1,414 N

B. 1,946 N   **D.** 987 N

73. A speaker produces a total of 10 W of sound, and Rahul hears the music at 20 dB. His roommate turns up the power to 100 W. What level of sound does Rahul now hear?

A. 15 dB   **C.** 40 dB

B. 30 dB   **D.** 100 dB

74. Seven seconds after a flash of lightning, thunder shakes a house. Approximately how far was the lightning strike from the house? (Use the speed of sound $v = 340$ m/s)

A. Requires more information   **C.** About one kilometer away

B. About five kilometers away   **D.** About two kilometers away

75. If two traveling waves with amplitudes of 3 cm and 8 cm interfere, which of the following best describes the possible amplitudes of the resultant wave?

A. Between 5 and 11 cm   **C.** Between 3 and 5 cm

B. Between 3 and 8 cm   **D.** Between 8 and 11 cm

76. What is the source of all electromagnetic waves?

A. electric fields   **C.** heat

B. vibrating charges   **D.** magnetic fields

77. When a radio is tuned to a particular station, the frequency of the internal electrical circuit is matched to the frequency of that radio station. In tuning the radio, what is being affected?

A. Beats   **C.** Forced vibrations

B. Reverberation   **D.** Resonance

Notes for active learning

Notes for active learning

DC Circuits

1. What is the new resistance of a wire if the length of a specific wire is doubled and its radius is also doubled?

   A. It is $\sqrt{2}$ times as large

   B. It is ½ as large

   C. It stays the same

   D. It is 2 times as large

2. A 6 Ω resistor is connected across the terminals of a 12 V battery. If 0.6 A of current flows, what is the internal resistance of the battery?

   A. 2 Ω

   B. 26 Ω

   C. 20 Ω

   D. 14 Ω

3. Three 8 V batteries are connected in series to power light bulbs A and B. The resistance of light bulb A is 60 Ω and the resistance of light bulb B is 30 Ω. How does the current through light bulb A compare with the current through light bulb B?

   A. The current through light bulb A is less

   B. The current through light bulb A is greater

   C. The current through light bulb A is the same

   D. The current through light bulb A is exactly doubled that through light bulb B

4. The current flowing through a circuit of constant resistance is doubled. What is the effect on the power dissipated by that circuit?

   A. Decreases to one-half its original value

   B. Decreases to one-fourth its original value

   C. Quadruples its original value

   D. Doubles its original value

5. What current flows when a 400 Ω resistor is connected across a 220 V circuit?

   A. 0.55 A

   B. 1.8 A

   C. 5.5 A

   D. 0.18 A

6. Which statement is accurate for when different resistors are connected in parallel across an ideal battery?

   A. Power dissipated in each is the same

   B. Their equivalent resistance is greater than the resistance of any one of the individual resistors

   C. Current flowing in each is the same

   D. Potential difference across each is the same

7. For an electric motor with a resistance of 35 Ω that draws 10 A of current, what is the voltage drop?

   A. 3.5 V

   B. 25 V

   C. 350 V

   D. 3,500 V

8. The resistor R has a variable resistance. Which statement is true when R is decreased? (Neglect the tiny internal resistance r of the battery)

A. I_1 decreases, I_2 increases

B. I_1 increases, I_2 remains the same

C. I_1 remains the same, I_2 increases

D. I_1 remains the same, I_2 decreases

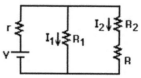

9. What physical quantity does the slope of the graph represent?

A. 1 / Current

B. Voltage

C. Current

D. Resistivity

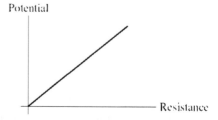

10. Kirchhoff's junction rule is a statement of:

A. Law of conservation of energy

B. Law of conservation of angular momentum

C. Law of conservation of momentum

D. Law of conservation of charge

11. When unequal resistors are connected in series across an ideal battery, the:

A. current flowing in each is the same

B. equivalent resistance of the circuit is less than that of the greatest resistor

C. power dissipated in each turn is the same

D. potential difference across each is the same

12. Electric current flows only from the point of:

A. equal potential

B. high pressure to the point of lower pressure

C. low pressure to the point of higher pressure

D. high potential to the point of lower potential

13. What is the name of a device that transforms electrical energy into mechanical energy?

A. Magnet

B. Transformer

C. Turbine

D. Motor

14. Four 6 V batteries (in a linear sequence of A → B → C → D) are connected in series to power lights A and B. The resistance of light A is 50 Ω and the resistance of light B is 25 Ω. What is the potential difference at a point between battery C and battery D? (Assume that the potential at the start of the sequence is zero)

A. 4 volts

B. 12 volts

C. 18 volts

D. 26 volts

15. What is the quantity that is calculated in units of A·s?

    A. Passivity

    B. Capacitance

    C. Potential

    D. Charge

16. Electric current can only flow:

    A. in a region of negligible resistance

    B. through a potential difference

    C. in a perfect conductor

    D. in the absence of resistance

17. A wire of resistivity ρ is replaced in a circuit by a wire of the same material but four times as long. If the total resistance remains the same, the diameter of the new wire must be:

    A. one-fourth the original diameter

    B. two times the original diameter

    C. the same as the original diameter

    D. one-half the original diameter

18. The addition of resistors in series to a resistor in an existing circuit, while voltage remains constant, would result in [   ] in the original resistor.

    A. an increase in current

    B. a decrease in resistance

    C. an increase in resistance

    D. a decrease in current

19. In an experiment, a battery is connected to a variable resistor R, where resistance can be adjusted by turning a knob. The potential difference across the resistor and the current through it are recorded for different settings of the resistor knob. The battery is an ideal potential source in series with an internal resistor. The emf of the potential source is 9 V, and the internal resistance is 0.1 Ω. What is the current if the variable resistor is set at 0.5 Ω?

    A. 15 A

    B. 0.9 A

    C. 4.5 A

    D. 45 A

20. What is the quantity calculated with units of kg·m^2/(s·C^2)?

    A. Resistance

    B. Capacitance

    C. Potential

    D. Resistivity

21. At a constant voltage, an increase in the resistance of a circuit results in:

    A. no change in I or V

    B. an increase in I

    C. an increase in power

    D. a decrease in I

22. Which change to a circuit element will always increase the current?

   A. Increased voltage and decreased resistance

   B. Decreased voltage and increased resistance

   C. Increased voltage and increased resistance

   D. Only a decrease in resistance, the voltage does not affect current

23. When three resistors are added in series to a resistor in a circuit, the original resistor's voltage [   ] and current [   ].

   A. decreases ... increases   **C.** decrease ... decreases

   B. increases ... increases   **D.** decreases ... remains the same

24. If two identical storage batteries are connected in series ("+" to "−") and placed in a circuit, the combination provides:

   A. twice the voltage, and the same current flows through each

   B. the same voltage and the same current flows through each

   C. zero volts and different currents flow through each

   D. the same voltage and different currents flow through each

25. The resistivity of gold is 2.22×10^{-8} Ω·m at a temperature of 22 °C. A gold wire, 2 mm in diameter and 18 cm long, carries a current of 500 mA. What is the power dissipated in the wire?

   A. 0.17 mW   **C.** 0.77 mW

   B. 0.54 mW   **D.** 0.32 mW

26. Consider two copper wires of equal cross-sectional area. One wire has 3 times the length of the other. How does the resistivity of these two wires compare?

   A. The longer wire has 9 times the resistivity of the shorter wire

   B. The longer wire has 27 times the resistivity of the shorter wire

   C. The longer wire has 1/3 the resistivity of the shorter wire

   D. Both wires have the same resistivity

27. A 3 Ω resistor is connected in parallel with a 6 Ω resistor and both in series with a 4 Ω resistor. All three resistors are connected to an 18 V battery, as shown. If 3 Ω resistor burnt out and exhibits infinite resistance, which of the following is true?

   A. The power dissipated in the circuit increases

   B. The current provided by the battery remains the same

   C. The current in the 6 Ω resistor decreases

   D. The current in the 6 Ω resistor increases

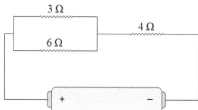

28. The resistivity of gold is 2.44×10^{-8} $\Omega \cdot$m at a temperature of 20 °C. A gold wire, 0.6 mm in diameter and 48 cm long, carries a current of 340 mA. What is the number of electrons per second passing a given cross-section of the wire? (Use the charge of an electron $= -1.6 \times 10^{-19}$ C)

    A. 2.1×10^{18} electrons   **C.** 1.2×10^{22} electrons

    B. 2.8×10^{14} electrons   **D.** 2.4×10^{17} electrons

29. For the graph shown, what physical quantity does the slope of the graph represent?

    A. 1 / Voltage   **C.** Power

    B. Resistance   **D.** Charge

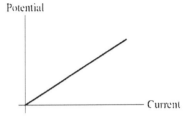

30. What is the voltage across a 15 Ω resistor with a 5 A current passing through it?

    A. 3 V   **C.** 15 V

    B. 5 V   **D.** 75 V

Notes for active learning

Electrostatics

1. How many excess electrons are present for an object that has a charge of -1 Coulomb? (Use Coulomb's constant $k = 9 \times 10^9$ N·m^2/C^2 and charge of an electron $e = -1.6 \times 10^{-19}$ C)

    A. 3.1×10^{19} electrons   **C.** 6.3×10^{18} electrons

    B. 6.3×10^{19} electrons   **D.** 1.6×10^{19} electrons

2. Two charges $Q_1 = 2.4 \times 10^{-10}$ C and $Q_2 = 9.2 \times 10^{-10}$ C are near each other, and charge Q_1 exerts a force F_1 on Q_2. How does F_1 change if the distance between Q_1 and Q_2 is increased by a factor of 4?

    A. Decreases by a factor of 4   **C.** Decreases by a factor of 16

    B. Increases by a factor of 16   **D.** Increases by a factor of 4

3. A 54,000 kg asteroid carrying a negative charge of 15 μC is 180 m from another 51,000 kg asteroid carrying a negative charge of 11 μC. What is the net force the asteroids exert upon each other? (Use the gravitational constant $G = 6.673 \times 10^{-11}$ N·m^2/kg^2 and Coulomb's constant $k = 9 \times 10^9$ N·m^2/C^2)

    A. 400,000 N   **C.** -4.0×10^{-5} N

    B. 5,700 N   **D.** 4.0×10^{-5} N

4. Two small beads are 30 cm apart with no other charges or fields present. Bead A has 20 μC of charge, and bead B has 5 μC. Which of the following statements is true about the electric forces on these beads?

    A. The force on A is 120 times the force on B

    B. The force on A is exactly equal to the force on B

    C. The force on B is 4 times the force on A

    D. The force on A is 20 times the force on B

5. A point charge $Q = -10$ μC. What is the number of excess electrons on charge Q? (Use the charge of an electron $e = -1.6 \times 10^{-19}$ C)

    A. 4.5×10^{13} electrons   **C.** 9.0×10^{13} electrons

    B. 1.6×10^{13} electrons   **D.** 6.3×10^{13} electrons

6. An electron and a proton are separated by a distance of 3 m. What happens to the magnitude of the force on the proton if the electron is moved 1.5 m closer to the proton?

    A. It increases to twice its original value   **C.** It increases to four times its original value

    B. It decreases to one-fourth its original value   **D.** It decreases to one-half its original value

7. How will the magnitude of the electrostatic force between two objects be affected if the distance between them and both of their charges are doubled?

    A. It will increase by a factor of 4   **C.** It will decrease by a factor of 2

    B. It will increase by a factor of 2   **D.** It will be unchanged

8. Two oppositely charged particles are slowly separated from each other. What happens to the force as the particles are slowly moved apart?

    A. attractive and decreasing   **C.** attractive and increasing

    B. repulsive and decreasing   **D.** repulsive and increasing

9. Two charges $Q_1 = 3 \times 10^{-8}$ C and $Q_2 = 9 \times 10^{-8}$ C are near each other and charge Q_1 exerts a force F_1 on Q_2. What is F_2, the force that charge Q_2 exerts on charge Q_1?

    A. $F_1 / 3$ **C.** $3F_1$

    B. F_1 **D.** $2F_1$

10. Two electrons are passing 30 mm apart. What is the repulsive electric force that they exert on each other? (Use Coulomb's constant $k = 9 \times 10^9$ N·m^2/C^2 and the charge of an electron $= -1.6 \times 10^{-19}$ C)

    A. 1.3×10^{-25} N   **C.** 1.3×10^{27} N

    B. 3.4×10^{-27} N   **D.** 2.56×10^{-25} N

11. Suppose a van de Graaff generator builds a negative static charge, and a grounded conductor is placed near enough to it so that an 8 μC of negative charge arcs to the conductor. What is the number of electrons transferred? (Use the charge of an electron $e = -1.6 \times 10^{-19}$ C)

    A. 1.8×10^{14} electrons   **C.** 5×10^{13} electrons

    B. 48 electrons   **D.** 74 electrons

12. Which statement must be true if two objects are electrically attracted to each other?

    A. One of the objects could be electrically neutral

    B. One object must be negatively charged, and the other must be positively charged

    C. At least one of the objects must be positively charged

    D. At least one of the objects must be negatively charged

13. Two charges ($Q_1 = 2.3 \times 10^{-8}$ C and $Q_2 = 2.5 \times 10^{-9}$ C) are a distance 0.1 m apart. How much energy is required to bring them to a distance 0.01 m apart? (Use Coulomb's constant $k = 9 \times 10^9$ N·m^2/C^2)

    A. 2.2×10^{-4} J   **C.** 1.7×10^{-5} J

    B. 8.9×10^{-5} J   **D.** 4.7×10^{-5} J

14. In the figure below, the charge in the middle is fixed and $Q = -7.5$ nC. For what fixed, positive charge q_1 will non-stationary, negative charge q_2 be in static equilibrium?

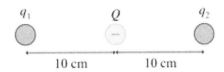

A. 53 nC

B. 7.5 nC

C. 15 nC

D. 30 nC

15. Two charges separated by 1 m exert a 1 N force on each other. If the magnitude of each charge is doubled, the force on each charge is:

A. 1 N

B. 2 N

C. 4 N

D. 6 N

16. In a water solution of NaCl, the NaCl dissociates into ions surrounded by water molecules. Consider a water molecule near a Na^+ ion. What tends to be the orientation of the water molecule?

A. The hydrogen atoms are nearer the Na^+ ion because of their positive charge

B. The hydrogen atoms are nearer the Na^+ ion because of their negative charge

C. The oxygen atom is nearer the Na^+ ion because of the oxygen's positive charge

D. The oxygen atom is nearer the Na^+ ion because of the oxygen's negative charge

17. A metal sphere is insulated electrically and is given a charge. If 30 electrons are added to the sphere in giving a charge, how many Coulombs are added to the sphere? (Use Coulomb's constant $k = 9 \times 10^9$ N·m^2/C^2 and the charge of an electron $e = -1.6 \times 10^{-19}$ C)

A. -2.4 C

B. -30 C

C. -4.8×10^{-18} C

D. -4.8×10^{-16} C

18. A positive test charge q is released near a positive fixed charge Q. As q moves away from Q, it experiences:

A. increasing acceleration

B. decreasing acceleration

C. constant velocity

D. decreasing velocity

19. A Coulomb is a unit of electrical:

A. capacity

B. resistance

C. charge

D. potential difference

20. To say that electric charge is conserved means that no case has ever been found where:

A. charge has been created or destroyed

B. the total charge on an object has increased

C. the net negative charge on an object is unbalanced by a positive charge on another object

D. the total charge on an object has changed by a significant amount

21. Two charges $Q_1 = 1.7 \times 10^{-10}$ C and $Q_2 = 6.8 \times 10^{-10}$ C are near each other. How would F change if the charges were both doubled, but the distance between them remained the same?

A. F increases by a factor of 2

C. F decreases by a factor of $\sqrt{2}$

B. F increases by a factor of 4

D. F decreases by a factor of 4

22. Two like charges of the same magnitude are 10 mm apart. If the force of repulsion they exert upon each other is 4 N, what is the magnitude of each charge? (Use Coulomb's constant $k = 9 \times 10^9$ N·m²/C²)

A. 6×10^{-5} C

C. 2×10^{-7} C

B. 6×10^5 C

D. 1.5×10^{-7} C

23. Two identical small, charged spheres are a certain distance apart, and each initially experiences an electrostatic force of magnitude F due to the other. With time, the charge gradually diminishes on each sphere. What is the magnitude of the electrostatic force when each sphere has lost half its initial charge?

A. 1/16 F

C. 1/4 F

B. 1/8 F

D. 2 F

24. A charge $Q = 3.1 \times 10^{-5}$ C is fixed in space while another charge $q = -10^{-6}$ C is 6 m away. Charge q is slowly moved 4 m in a straight line directly toward the charge Q. How much work is required to move charge q? (Use Coulomb's constant $k = 9 \times 10^9$ N·m²/C²)

A. −0.09 J

C. 0.16 J

B. −0.03 J

D. 0.08 J

25. A point charge $Q = -600$ nC. What is the number of excess electrons in charge Q? (Use the charge of an electron $e = -1.6 \times 10^{-19}$ C)

A. 5.6×10^{12} electrons

C. 2.8×10^{11} electrons

B. 2.1×10^{10} electrons

D. 3.8×10^{12} electrons

26. If an object is characterized as electrically polarized:

A. its internal electric field is zero

C. it is electrically charged

B. it is a strong insulator

D. its charges have been rearranged

27. Two equally charged spheres of mass 1 g are placed 2 cm apart. When released, they begin to accelerate at 440 m/s². What is the magnitude of the charge on each sphere? (Use Coulomb's constant $k = 9 \times 10^9$ N·m²/C²)

    A. 80 nC

    B. 65 nC

    C. 115 nC

    D. 140 nC

28. Two equal and opposite charges a certain distance apart is an electric 'dipole.' A positive test charge $+q$ is placed as shown, equidistant from the two charges.

Which choice gives the direction of the net force on the test charge?

    A. ←

    B. →

    C. ↑

    D. ↓

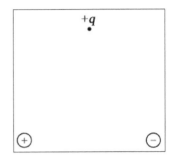

29. Find the magnitude of the electrostatic force between a +3 C point charge and a –12 C point charge if separated by 50 cm of space. (Use Coulomb's constant $k = 9 \times 10^9$ N·m²/C²)

    A. 9.2×10^{12} N

    B. 1.3×10^{12} N

    C. 7.7×10^{12} N

    D. 4.8×10^{12} N

30. Two charges separated by 1 m exert a 1 N force on each other. What is the force on each charge if the charges are pushed to a 0.25 m separation?

    A. 1 N

    B. 2 N

    C. 4 N

    D. 16 N

31. In the figure, $Q = 5.1$ nC. What is the magnitude of the electrical force on the charge Q? (Use Coulomb's constant $k = 9 \times 10^9$ N·m²/C²)

    A. 4.2×10^{-3} N

    B. 0.4×10^{-3} N

    C. 1.6×10^{-3} N

    D. 3.2×10^{-3} N

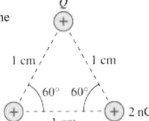

32. Two charges separated by 1 m exert a 1 N force on each other. What is the force on each charge when they are pulled to a separation distance of 3 m?

    A. 3 N

    B. 0 N

    C. 9 N

    D. 0.11 N

33. A 4 μC point charge and an 8 μC point charge are initially infinitely far apart. How much work is required to bring the 4 μC point charge to ($x = 2$ mm, $y = 0$ mm), and the 8 μC point charge to ($x = -2$ mm, $y = 0$ mm)? (Use Coulomb's constant $k = 9 \times 10^9$ N·m²/C²)

    A. 32.6 J   **C.** 47 J

    B. 9.8 J   **D.** 72 J

34. A dipole with two ±6 μC charges is positioned so that the negative charge is at the origin and the positive charge is 1 mm to the right. How much work does it take to bring a 10 μC charge from infinity to the position $x = 3$ mm, $y = 0$ mm? (Use Coulomb's constant $k = 9 \times 10^9$ N·m²/C²)

    A. 200 J   **C.** 450 J

    B. 75 J   **D.** 90 J

35. An electron is released from rest at 5 cm from a proton. How fast will the electron be moving when it is 2 cm from the proton? (Use Coulomb's constant $k = 9 \times 10^9$ N·m²/C², the mass of an electron $= 9.1 \times 10^{-31}$ kg, the charge of an electron $= -1.6 \times 10^{-19}$ C and the charge of a proton $= 1.6 \times 10^{-19}$ C)

    A. 92 m/s   **C.** 147 m/s

    B. 123 m/s   **D.** 1.3×10^3 m/s

36. What is the current in a wire if a total of 2.3×10^{13} electrons pass a given point in a wire in 15 s? (Use the charge of an electron $= -1.6 \times 10^{-19}$ C)

    A. 0.25 μA   **C.** 7.1 μA

    B. 3.2 μA   **D.** 1.3 μA

37. A kilowatt-hour is equivalent to:

    A. 3.6×10^6 J/s   **C.** 3.6×10^3 W

    B. 3.6×10^6 J   **D.** 3.6×10^3 J

Notes for active learning

Notes for active learning

Answer Keys and
Detailed Explanations:
Diagnostic Tests

Diagnostic Test 1 – Answer Key and Detailed Explanations

Answer Key

1	A	Kinematics & dynamics	26	D	Work & energy
2	D	Force, motion, gravitation	27	B	Waves & periodic motion
3	B	Equilibrium & momentum	28	D	Sound
4	B	Work & energy	29	C	Kinematics & dynamics
5	D	Waves & periodic motion	30	D	Force, motion, gravitation
6	B	Sound	31	C	Equilibrium & momentum
7	A	DC circuits	32	C	Work & energy
8	B	Electrostatics	33	D	Waves & periodic motion
9	B	Kinematics & dynamics	34	B	Sound
10	A	Force, motion, gravitation	35	D	DC circuits
11	B	Equilibrium & momentum	36	C	Electrostatics
12	D	Work & energy	37	C	Kinematics & dynamics
13	A	Waves & periodic motion	38	B	Force, motion, gravitation
14	A	Sound	39	B	Equilibrium & momentum
15	C	Kinematics & dynamics	40	C	Work & energy
16	D	Force, motion, gravitation	41	D	Waves & periodic motion
17	C	Equilibrium & momentum	42	C	Sound
18	A	Work & energy	43	D	Kinematics & dynamics
19	C	Waves & periodic motion	44	C	Force, motion, gravitation
20	D	Sound	45	B	Equilibrium & momentum
21	D	DC circuits	46	C	Work & energy
22	C	Electrostatics	47	C	Waves & periodic motion
23	D	Kinematics & dynamics	48	B	Sound
24	D	Force, motion, gravitation	49	C	DC circuits
25	D	Equilibrium & momentum	50	D	Electrostatics

1. A is correct.

An object's resistance to change in its state of motion is characterized by its inertia.

Inertia is not a physical property but is directly related to an object's mass.

Thus, mass determines resistance to change in motion.

2. D is correct.

The three forces are in equilibrium, so the net force $F_{net} = 0$

$F_{net} = F_1 + F_2 + F_3$

$0 = F_1 + F_2 + F_3$

Since the forces F_1 and F_2 are mirror images along the *x*-axis, their net force in the *y*-direction is zero.

Therefore, F_3 is also zero in the *y*-direction.

The net force along the *x*-direction must add to zero, so set the sum of the *x* components to zero.

The angles for F_1 and F_2 are equal and measured with respect to the *x*-axis, so θ_1 and θ_2 are both 20°.

Since F_3 has no *y* component, $\theta_3 = 0°$. Note that force components to the left are set as negative in this answer, and components to the right are set as positive.

$0 = F_{1x} + F_{2x} + F_{3x}$

$0 = F_1 \cos \theta_1 + F_2 \cos \theta_2 + F_3 \cos \theta_3$

$0 = (-4.6 \text{ N} \cos 20°) + (-4.6 \text{ N} \cos 20°) + (F_3 \cos 0°)$

Since $\cos 0° = 1$:

$0 = (-4.3 \text{ N}) + (-4.3 \text{ N}) + F_3$

$-F_3 = -8.6 \text{ N}$

$F_3 = 8.6 \text{ N}$, to the right

3. B is correct.

To *balance the torques* due to the weight, the fulcrum must be placed 4 times farther from the son than the man because the father weighs 4 times more.

Since the total length of the seesaw is 10 m, the fulcrum must be placed 8 m from the son and 2 m from the father, who is on the heavier end.

$x + 4x = 10 \text{ m}$

$5x = 10 \text{ m}$

$x = 2 \text{ m}$

continued…

Another method to solve the problem:

200 N _____ 800 N

$10 - x$ $\qquad\qquad$ Δ $\qquad$ x

$(200\ \text{N}){\cdot}(10 - x) = (800\ \text{N})x$

$x = 2\ \text{m}$

4. B is correct.

$W = Fd$

$W = (20\ \text{N}){\cdot}(3.5\ \text{m})$

$W = 70\ \text{J}$

5. D is correct.

Constructive interference occurs when two or more waves of equal frequency and phase produce a single amplitude wave that is the sum of amplitudes of the individual waves.

If there is a phase difference, the interference will not be the total amplitude of each wave.

If the phase difference is 180°, there will be total destructive interference.

6. B is correct.

The expression for the *Doppler shift* is:

$f = f_s[(c + v_o) / (c + v_s)]$

where f is the frequency heard by the observer, f_s is the frequency of the source, c is the speed of sound, v_o is the velocity of the observer, v_s is the velocity of the source

The velocity of the source v_s is positive when the source is moving away from the observer and negative when it is moving toward the observer

Since the train is traveling away, once it passes, the velocity of the source (i.e., train) is positive.

Kevin is standing still, so the velocity of the observer is zero.

$f = f_s[(c + v_o) / (c + v_s)]$

$f = (420\ \text{Hz}){\cdot}[(350\ \text{m/s} + 0\ \text{m/s}) / (350\ \text{m/s} + 50\ \text{m/s})]$

$f = (420\ \text{Hz}){\cdot}[(350\ \text{m/s}) / (400\ \text{m/s})]$

$f = (147{,}000\ \text{Hz}{\cdot}\text{m/s}) / (400\ \text{m/s})$

$f = 368\ \text{Hz}$

7. A is correct.

Find Capacitive Reactance:

$$X_c = 1 / 2\pi Cf$$

$$X_c = 1 / (2\pi) \cdot (26 \times 10^{-6} \text{ F}) \cdot (60 \text{ Hz})$$

$$X_c = 102 \ \Omega$$

Find rms current:

$$I = V_{rms} / X_c$$

$$I = 120 \text{ V} / 102 \ \Omega$$

$$I = 1.2 \text{ A}$$

8. B is correct.

By Newton's Third Law, F_1 and F_2 form an *action-reaction* pair.

The ratio of their magnitudes equals 1.

9. B is correct.

$$d = \tfrac{1}{2}gt^2$$

$$t^2 = 2d / g$$

$$t^2 = 2(42 \text{ m}) / 10 \text{ m/s}^2$$

$$t^2 = 8.4 \text{ s}^2$$

$$t \approx$$

$$2.9$$

10. A is correct.

$$a = g \sin \theta$$

An object's acceleration down a frictionless ramp (with an incline angle) is constant.

11. B is correct.

A longer barrel gives the propellant a longer time to impart a force upon a bullet and thus a higher velocity.

This is characterized by impulse.

$$J = F\Delta t$$

12. D is correct. The energy before release and at the top of each bounce equals gravitational PE:

$$PE = mgh$$

Gravitational potential energy is proportional to height, and mass and g stay constant.

Multiply by 0.8 (80%) to determine the height after a bounce if 20% of the energy is lost.

$h_{initial} = 250$ cm

250 cm $\times$ (0.8 $\times$ 0.8 $\times$ 0.8), equals h after 3 bounces

$h_3 = (250$ cm$)\cdot(0.8)^3$

$h_3 = 128$ cm

13. A is correct.

$T = 1 / f$

$T = 1 / (10$ Hz$)$

$T = 0.1$ s

14. A is correct.

$f = v / \lambda$

$f = (1,600$ m/s$) / (2.5$ m$)$

$f = 640$ Hz

15. C is correct.

At terminal velocity, an object has a constant velocity.

16. D is correct.

$F = ma$

$W = mg$

$m = W / g$

$F = (W / g)a$

$a = F / m$

The $F_{friction} = 8.8$ N, and the mass is known from the box's weight.

8.8 N $= (40$ N $/ 10$ m/s$^2)a$

$a = (8.8$ N$) / (4$ N/m/s$^2)$

$a = 2.2$ m/s^2

Since the box moves at constant velocity when force F is applied, F = force due to kinetic friction.

Once the force F is removed, the net force that causes its deceleration is the frictional force.

17. C is correct.

The *total momentum of the system* is always conserved. Before the ball was thrown, the momentum was zero because all mass on the canoe was stationary.

After the ball is thrown and caught on the canoe, the momentum must still be equal to zero, so the canoe must remain stationary.

$p = mv$

18. A is correct.

$KE_{final} = 0$ since $v_f = 0$

The length of the skid marks is irrelevant.

$\Delta Energy = KE_{final} - KE_{initial}$

$\Delta E = \frac{1}{2}mv_f^2 - \frac{1}{2}mv_i^2$

$\Delta E = 0 \text{ J} - \frac{1}{2}(1{,}000 \text{ kg}){\cdot}(30 \text{ m/s})^2$

$\Delta E = -4.5 \times 10^5 \text{ J}$

19. C is correct.

The *lowest* harmonic (i.e., fundamental) frequency (f_1) corresponds to the *longest* harmonic (i.e., fundamental) wavelength (λ_1).

$f_1 = v \,/\, \lambda_1$

$f_1 = (8 \text{ m/s}) \,/\, 4 \text{ m}$

$f_1 = 2 \text{ Hz}$

20. D is correct.

Sound cannot travel through a vacuum because there is no medium to propagate the wave.

In the air, sound waves travel through gas; in the ocean, they travel through liquid; and in the Earth, they travel through solids. These are all mediums in which sound waves can propagate.

Vacuums are devoid of matter; there is no medium, and the wave cannot pass.

21. D is correct.

$P = IV$

$P = (2 \text{ A}){\cdot}(120 \text{ V})$

$P = 240 \text{ W}$

An ampere (A) is a rate of electric charge flowing in a circuit in coulombs per second (C/s), where 1 A = 1 C/s.

continued...

The volt (V) measures the difference in electric potential between two points, where 1 V is defined as the electric potential difference when 1 ampere consumes 1 watt (W) of power.

Power is a measure of energy per unit time:

$$1 \text{ W} = 1 \text{ A·V}$$

$$1 \text{ W} = 1 \text{ J / s}$$

$$1 \text{ W} = 1 \text{ N·m/s}$$

$$1 \text{ W} = 1 \text{ kg·m}^2/\text{s}^3$$

22. C is correct.

If the voltage drops across the 3 Ω resistor is 2 V, the current through the 3 Ω resistor is:

$$I = V / R$$

$$I = 2 \text{ V} / 3 \text{ Ω}$$

$$I = 2/3 \text{ amps}$$

Since the 1.5 Ω resistor is connected in parallel with the 3 Ω resistor, voltage drop = 2 V (parallel resistors always share the same voltage drop).

The current through the 1.5 Ω resistor is:

$$I = 2 \text{ V} / 1.5 \text{ Ω}$$

$$I = 4/3 \text{ amps}$$

Then, sum the currents:

$$I_{total} = 2/3 \text{ amps} + 4/3 \text{ amps}$$

$$I_{total} = 2 \text{ amps}$$

23. D is correct.

Velocity is in the direction of the current:

$$v_c = at$$

$$v_c = (0.75 \text{ m/s}^2)·(33.5 \text{ s})$$

$$v_c = 25 \text{ m/s}$$

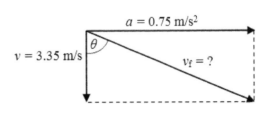

Final velocity:

$$v_f^2 = v^2 + v_c^2$$

$$v_f^2 = (3.35 \text{ m/s})^2 + (25 \text{ m/s})^2$$

$$v_f^2 = 636.2 \text{ m}^2/\text{s}^2$$

$$v_f = 25 \text{ m/s}$$

continued…

The angle of motion with respect to the initial velocity:

$\theta = \tan^{-1}(v_c / v)$

$\theta = \tan^{-1}[(25 \text{ m/s}) / (3.35 \text{ m/s})]$

$\theta = \tan^{-1} 7.5$

$\theta = 82.4°$

24. D is correct.

According to Newton's First Law: an object at rest tends to stay at rest, and an object in motion tends to stay in motion unless acted upon by an outside force.

Lisa fell backward because the truck accelerated to increase its velocity, and Lisa's body tended to stay in its original motion.

25. D is correct.

Divide the problem into three parts: initial acceleration, constant velocity & final deceleration.

1) Initial acceleration: determine α, then solve for the displacement during the acceleration. The initial velocity is zero.

Convert the displacement in radians to revolutions.

$\alpha = (\omega_f - \omega_i) / t$

$\alpha = (58 \text{ radians/s} - 0) / 10 \text{ s}$

$\alpha = 5.8 \text{ radians/s}^2$

$\theta = \tfrac{1}{2}\alpha t^2$

$\theta = \tfrac{1}{2}(5.8 \text{ radians/s}^2)\cdot(10 \text{ s})^2$

$\theta = 290 \text{ radians}$

$Rev = \theta / 2\pi$

$Rev = 290 \text{ radians} / 2\pi$

$Rev = 46 \text{ revolutions}$

2) Constant velocity: solve θ using constant angular velocity.

Convert radians to revolutions.

$\theta = \omega t$

$\theta = (58 \text{ radians/s})\cdot(30 \text{ s})$

$\theta = 1,740 \text{ radians}$

$Rev = \theta / 2\pi$

continued…

Rev = 1,740 radians / 2π

Rev = 277 revolutions

3) Final deceleration: determine *t* for the period of deceleration using the final velocity as zero.

Solve for the displacement during this constant deceleration and convert to revolutions.

$\alpha = (\omega_f - \omega_i) / t$

$t = (\omega_f - \omega_i) / \alpha$

$t = (0 - 58 \text{ radians/s}) / (-1.4 \text{ radians/s}^2)$

$t = 41$ s

$\theta = \omega_i t + \frac{1}{2}\alpha t^2$

$\theta = [(58 \text{ radians/s}) \cdot (41 \text{ s})] + [\frac{1}{2}(-1.4 \text{ radians/s}^2) \cdot (41 \text{ s})^2]$

$\theta = 1{,}201$ radians

Rev = 1,201 radians / 2π

Rev = 191 revolutions

Add the revolutions: $Rev_{total} = 46 \text{ rev} + 277 \text{ rev} + 191 \text{ rev}$

$Rev_{total} = 514 \approx 510$ revolutions

26. D is correct.

$W = Fd \cos \theta$

$W = (20 \text{ N}) \cdot (2 \text{ m})$

$W = 40$ J

27. B is correct.

The *position* of an object in simple harmonic motion (SHM) is a *function of time using sine or cosine*:

$x = A \sin (\omega t - \theta)$

where x = position, A = amplitude (i.e., max displacement of object from equilibrium position), ω = angular velocity in radians/sec (or degrees/sec), t = time elapsed, θ = phase

Here, $\theta = 0$ since the graph matches the phase of the standard sine graph, so there is no need for phase correction. $A = 1$ is used for simplicity.

$x = \sin (\omega t)$

The object's *velocity* in SHM is represented by the derivative of the position function:

$v = \omega \cos (\omega t)$

continued…

The object's *acceleration* in SHM is represented by the derivative of the velocity function:

$a = -\omega^2 \sin(\omega t)$

Therefore, the acceleration of objects in SHM is represented as the opposite value of the position, multiplied by the square of angular velocity.

ω is constant, so the graphs keep the same wavelengths.

28. D is correct.

Sound is a traveling acoustic pressure wave propagated through vibrations of particles such as air or water.

In a vacuum, no particles exist, so the wave cannot propagate, and no sound is heard.

Thus, sound can refract in air or water but not in a vacuum.

29. C is correct.

$y = v_i t + \frac{1}{2}at^2$

$50 \text{ m} = 0 + \frac{1}{2}(10 \text{ m/s}^2)t^2$

$50 \text{ m} = \frac{1}{2}(10 \text{ m/s}^2)t^2$

$t^2 = 50 \text{ m} / 5 \text{ m/s}^2$

$t^2 = 10 \text{ s}^2$

$t = 3.2 \text{ s}$

Solve for speed:

$v_f = v_i + at$

$v_f = 0 + (10 \text{ m/s}^2)\cdot(3.2 \text{ s})$

$v_f = 32 \text{ m/s}$

30. D is correct.

Newton's Second Law for each block:

$ma = F_{net}$ acting on the object.

The *tension and acceleration* on each block are equal in magnitude but act in different directions.

The only nonzero net forces will be horizontal for the 15 kg block and vertical for the 60 kg block.

For the 15 kg block:

$ma =$ tension acting to the right

$(15 \text{ kg})a = F_T$

continued…

For the 60 kg block:

ma = (weight acting downward) – (tension acting upward)

$(60 \text{ kg})a = (60 \text{ kg}) \cdot (10 \text{ m/s}^2) - F_T$

Substitute F_T from the first equation into the second:

$(60 \text{ kg})a = (60 \text{ kg}) \cdot (10 \text{ m/s}^2) - (15 \text{ kg})a$

$(60 \text{ kg})a + (15 \text{ kg})a = (60 \text{ kg}) \cdot (10 \text{ m/s}^2)$

$(75 \text{ kg})a = (60 \text{ kg}) \cdot (10 \text{ m/s}^2)$

$a = [(60 \text{ kg}) \cdot (10 \text{ m/s}^2)] / (75 \text{ kg})$

$a = 8 \text{ m/s}^2$

31. C is correct.

Momentum is the product of mass and velocity.

$p_0 = mv_0$

If velocity doubles:

$p = m(2v_0)$

$p = 2mv_0$

$p = 2p_0$

Therefore, momentum doubles.

32. C is correct.

The kinetic energy of a falling object is directly proportional to the height from which it falls.

This is because mass and gravity are constants, so only the height varies the kinetic energy of a dropped object.

$KE = PE$

$\frac{1}{2}mv^2 = mgh$

33. D is correct.

$\lambda = vt$

$\lambda = (4.6 \text{ m/s}) \cdot (10 \text{ s})$

$\lambda = 46 \text{ m}$

34. B is correct.

If the two sound sources are in phase, then there is no destructive interference.

The point can be related to the wavelength of the sound wave.

> 0.5 m = $x\lambda$
>
> 0.5 m = x(1 m)
>
> $x = \frac{1}{2}$

The microphone is located one-half wavelength from the speaker.

The speaker is a source of the sound pressure wave, so it is an antinode.

One-half wavelength from an antinode is an antinode.

35. D is correct.

> Ohm's law:
>
> $V = IR$
>
> $R = V / I$

36. C is correct.

An object becomes electrostatically charged from a charge imbalance.

A *charge* can only be transferred by electrons because protons are not mobile; thus, electron transfer creates an electrostatic charge.

37. C is correct.

Distance is direction independent

Displacement is direction dependent

> Distance = (16 m North + 12 m South) = 28 m
>
> Displacement = (16 m – 12 m) = 4 m

38. B is correct.

The angle the board makes before the pot slides depends on the static friction coefficient, as static friction influences the force of friction before the pot slides.

Kinetic friction occurs after the movement of the pot.

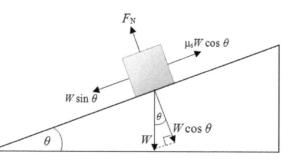

39. B is correct.

Momentum is conserved

$$m_1v_1 + m_2v_2 = m_3v_3$$

momentum *before* = momentum *after*

$$p_i = p_f$$

$$p_{total} = m_1v_1 + m_2v_2$$

$$p_{total} = (1 \text{ kg}){\cdot}(1 \text{ m/s}) + (6 \text{ kg}){\cdot}(0 \text{ m/s})$$

$$p_{total} = 1 \text{ kg}{\cdot}\text{m/s}$$

40. C is correct.

Ignoring air resistance, energy is conserved.

The loss in PE = the gain in KE.

$$KE = \tfrac{1}{2}mv^2$$

$$KE = \tfrac{1}{2}(20 \text{ kg}){\cdot}(30 \text{ m/s})^2$$

$$KE = 9{,}000 \text{ J}$$

This equals the amount of PE that is lost (i.e., converted into KE).

41. D is correct.

The wave has to travel for 4 amplitudes of distance in 1 cycle.

Simple harmonic motion can be represented by a wave of one cycle:

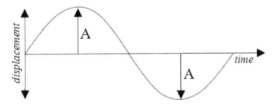

In a one-half cycle, the object travels from zero displacements to A back to zero, giving a total displacement of zero but a total distance of 2A.

Thus, in one cycle, the object travels 4A.

42. C is correct.

Label the tuning forks I, II, III, and IV.

Beats: I & II, I & III, I & IV, II & III, II & IV and III & IV

From six pairs, there is the possibility of six different beat frequencies.

This is a combination problem since order does not matter.

The formula for combinations is:

$$C(n, k) = n! / (n - k)!k!$$

where n is the given sample size and k is the number of tuning forks per pair.

When solving combination problems, the best way to choose n and k is to ask: "how do I find all the ways to pick n and k?"

$$C(4,2) = 4! / (4 - 2)!2!$$

$$C(4,2) = 4! / 2!2!$$

$$C(4,2) = 6$$

43. D is correct.

The *inertia* of an object is its resistance to change in motion and depends on its mass (units of kilograms).

44. C is correct.

velocity = acceleration × time

$$a = \Delta v / \Delta t$$

If $\Delta v = 0$, then $a = 0$

45. B is correct.

Check if KE is conserved:

$KE_{before} = KE_{after}$ if the collision is elastic

Before:

$$KE_{before} = (½)·(4 \text{ kg})·(1.8 \text{ m/s})^2 + (½)·(6 \text{ kg})·(0.2 \text{ m/s})^2$$

$$KE_{before} = 6.6 \text{ J}$$

After:

$$KE_{after} = (½)·(4 \text{ kg})·(0.6 \text{ m/s})^2 + (½)·(6 \text{ kg})·(1.4 \text{ m/s})^2$$

$$KE_{after} = 6.6 \text{ J}$$

continued…

Therefore:

$$KE_{before} = KE_{after}$$

The collision was completely elastic because kinetic energy was conserved.

46. C is correct.

The work done by the force can be related to kinetic energy.

6 kg mass:

$$KE = W$$

$$\frac{1}{2}(6 \text{ kg}) \cdot (2 \text{ m/s})^2 = Fd_1$$

$$d_1 = 12 / F$$

3 kg mass:

$$KE = W$$

$$\frac{1}{2}(3 \text{ kg}) \cdot (4 \text{ m/s})^2 = Fd_2$$

$$d_2 = 24 / F$$

$$d_2 = 2(12 / F)$$

Therefore:

$$2d_1 = d_2$$

47. C is correct.

$$\text{velocity} = \text{frequency} \times \text{wavelength}$$

$$v = f\lambda$$

$$\lambda = v / f$$

$$f = 1 / T$$

$$\lambda = v \times T$$

$$\lambda = 360 \text{ m/s} \times 4.2 \text{ s}$$

$$\lambda \approx 1,512 \text{ m}$$

48. B is correct.

$$PE = \frac{1}{2}kx^2$$

$$PE = \frac{1}{2}k(2x)^2$$

$$PE = 4(\frac{1}{2}kx^2)$$

49. C is correct.

$V = IR$

$I = V / R$

$I = (120 \text{ V}) / 12 \ \Omega$

$I = 10 \text{ A}$

50. D is correct.

From Coulomb's Law, the electrostatic force is *inversely proportional* to the square of the distance between the charges.

$F = kq_1q_2 / r^2$

If the distance increases by a factor of 2, then the force decreases by a factor of $2^2 = 4$.

Notes for active learning

Notes for active learning

Diagnostic Test 2 – Answer Key and Detailed Explanations

Answer Key

1	D	Kinematics & dynamics	26	A	Work & energy
2	A	Force, motion, gravitation	27	A	Waves & periodic motion
3	C	Equilibrium & momentum	28	C	Sound
4	D	Work & energy	29	B	Kinematics & dynamics
5	B	Waves & periodic motion	30	C	Force, motion, gravitation
6	D	Sound	31	B	Equilibrium & momentum
7	C	DC circuits	32	A	Work & energy
8	D	Electrostatics	33	B	Waves & periodic motion
9	C	Kinematics & dynamics	34	D	Sound
10	C	Force, motion, gravitation	35	A	DC circuits
11	C	Equilibrium & momentum	36	D	Waves & periodic motion
12	C	Work & energy	37	D	Kinematics & dynamics
13	B	Waves & periodic motion	38	B	Force, motion, gravitation
14	C	Sound	39	D	Equilibrium & momentum
15	A	Kinematics & dynamics	40	B	Work & energy
16	B	Force, motion, gravitation	41	A	Waves & periodic motion
17	C	Equilibrium & momentum	42	D	Sound
18	A	Work & energy	43	C	Kinematics & dynamics
19	D	Waves & periodic motion	44	C	Force, motion, gravitation
20	D	Sound	45	B	Equilibrium & momentum
21	C	DC circuits	46	A	Work & energy
22	B	Electrostatics	47	A	Waves & periodic motion
23	A	Kinematics & dynamics	48	D	Sound
24	D	Force, motion, gravitation	49	C	DC circuits
25	C	Equilibrium & momentum	50	C	Kinematics & dynamics

1. D is correct.

There is *no acceleration* in the horizontal direction, so velocity is constant.

$v_{0x} = v_x$

$d = v_x \times t$

$d = (30 \text{ m/s}) \cdot (75 \text{ s})$

$d = 2{,}250 \text{ m}$

2. A is correct.

The friction described in the scenario is between the tires and the road because the problem asks for the force of friction *on the car*.

Note that the car is skidding, meaning that the wheels are locked and are being dragged along the road; therefore, there is relative motion between the tires and the road. This is *kinetic friction*.

Static friction applies when there is no relative motion between the tires and the road at the point of contact, such as when the wheels are normally rotating.

$F_{\text{friction}} = \mu_k N$

Because the angle is described as *slight*, the incline can be ignored.

3. C is correct.

Moment of inertia I is defined as the ratio of the angular momentum L of a system to its angular velocity ω around a principal axis.

Moment of inertia:

$I = L \, / \, \omega$

Angular acceleration around a fixed axis:

$\tau = \alpha I$

Mass moment of inertia of a thin disk:

$I = \frac{1}{2}mr^2$

$\tau = \alpha(\frac{1}{2}mr^2)$

$m = (2\tau) \, / \, \alpha r^2$

$m = [(2) \cdot (14 \text{ N·m})] \, / \, [(5.3 \text{ rad/s}^2) \cdot (0.6 \text{ m})^2]$

$m = 14.7 \text{ kg}$

4. D is correct.

Energy can exist as PE, KE, heat, waves, etc.

Energy in any of its forms can be defined as the ability to do work, and the various mathematical expressions for energy specify the amount of work that can be done.

The conversion between energy and work goes both ways: work can generate any form of energy.

5. B is correct.

The *displacement* of the tines of a tuning fork from their resting positions is a measure of the amplitude of the resulting sound wave.

6. D is correct.

$$I \text{ (dB)} = 10 \log_{10}(I / I_o)$$

7. C is correct.

voltage = current × resistance

$V = IR$

$V = (10 \text{ A}) \cdot (5 \text{ } \Omega)$

$V = 55 \text{ V}$

8. D is correct.

Acceleration is always positive and away from charge Q.

Therefore, velocity increases (no opposing force of friction).

The energy of the system starts as electrical PE.

$$PE_{elec} = (kQq) / r$$

where r is the initial distance between the point charges.

Electrical PE is the energy required to bring a system together from the charges starting at infinity.

After charge Q has moved extremely far away, the energy of the system is only KE $= \frac{1}{2}mv^2$

v has a limit because KE cannot exceed kQq / r

9. C is correct.

The slope of the line is the derivative of the position *vs.* time graph.

The derivative of a position graph gives velocity.

Thus, at a single point along the line, the instantaneous velocity is given.

10. C is correct.

Centripetal acceleration

$$F_c = (m) \cdot (v^2 / r)$$

$$F_c = (1{,}200 \text{ kg}) \cdot [(3.5 \text{ m/s})^2 / 4 \text{ m}]$$

$$F_c = (1{,}200 \text{ kg}) \cdot [(12.25 \text{ m}^2/\text{s}^2) / 4 \text{ m}]$$

$$F_c = (1{,}200 \text{ kg}) \cdot (3 \text{ m/s}^2)$$

$$F_c = 3{,}600 \text{ N}$$

11. C is correct.

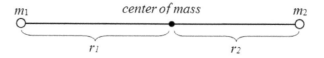

$$F = ma$$

$$m = F / a$$

$$m_1 = (69 \text{ N}) / (9.8 \text{ m/s}^2)$$

$$m_1 = 7.04 \text{ kg}$$

$$m_2 = (94 \text{ N}) / (9.8 \text{ m/s}^2)$$

$$m_2 = 9.59 \text{ kg}$$

$$m_1 r_1 = m_2 r_2$$

$$m_1 / m_2 = r_2 / r_1$$

$$m_1 / m_2 = (7.04 \text{ kg}) / (9.59 \text{ kg})$$

$$m_1 / m_2 = 0.734$$

$$r_2 / r_1 = 0.734$$

$$r_2 + r_1 = 10 \text{ m}$$

Two equations, two unknowns:

$$\text{Eq}_1: \ r_2 + r_1 = 10 \text{ m}$$

$$\text{Eq}_2: \ r_2 - (0.734) \cdot (r_1) = 0$$

Multiply Eq$_2$ by −1 and add to Eq$_1$:

$$(1.734)r_1 = 10 \text{ m}$$

$$r_1 = 5.8 \text{ m}$$

Alternatively:

For the object to be in equilibrium, the torques due to the two forces must sum to zero:

$$\tau L + \tau R = 0$$

continued…

Taking a counterclockwise torque to be positive:

$$F_L x_L - F_R x_R = 0$$

Let L be the length of the object, 10 m.

Then:

$$x_R = (L - x_L)$$

and:

$$F_L x_L - F_R (L - x_L) = 0$$

Solve for x_L:

$$x_L = L F_R / (F_L + F_R)$$

$$x_L = (10 \text{ m}) \cdot (94 \text{ N}) / (69 \text{ N} + 94 \text{ N})$$

$$x_L = 5.77 \text{ m} \approx 5.8 \text{ m}$$

12. C is correct.

$$v = v_0 + at$$

$$29 \text{ m/s} = 0 + (10 \text{ m/s}^2)t$$

$$v = at$$

$$t = v / a$$

$$t = (29 \text{ m/s}) / (10 \text{ m/s}^2)$$

$$t = 2.9 \text{ s}$$

$$y = \tfrac{1}{2}at^2$$

$$y = \tfrac{1}{2}(10 \text{ m/s}^2) \cdot (2.9 \text{ s})^2 + 1 \text{ m}$$

$$y = \tfrac{1}{2}(10 \text{ m/s}^2) \cdot (8.41 \text{ s}^2) + 1 \text{ m}$$

$$y = 42 \text{ m} + 1 \text{ m}$$

$$y = 43 \text{ m}$$

13. B is correct.

Resonant frequency of a spring-mass system:

$$\omega = \sqrt{(k / m)}$$

Increasing the spring constant k results in a higher resonant frequency.

14. C is correct.

Sound velocity in an ideal gas:

$$v_{sound} = \sqrt{(yRT / M)}$$

where y = adiabatic constant, R = gas constant, T = temperature and M = molecular mass of gas.

Increasing the temperature increases the velocity of sound in air.

15. A is correct.

$v_y = 3.13 \sin 30°$

$v_y = 1.6$ m/s

$v_f = v_o + at$

$0 = (1.6$ m/s$) + (-9.8$ m/s²$)t$

$(9.8$ m/s²$)t = (1.6$ m/s$)$

$t = (1.6$ m/s$) / (9.8$ m/s²$)$

$t = 0.16$ s

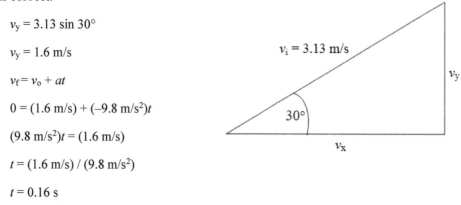

$v_i = 3.13$ m/s

v_y

30°

v_x

16. B is correct.

Newton's Third Law: when two objects interact, the force exerted on one object is equal in strength and opposite in direction to the force exerted on the other object.

17. C is correct.

To balance the seesaw, the total torque about the center must be zero.

Let the subscripts S, M, and J represent Shawn, Mark, and John, respectively. Then:

$\tau_S + \tau_M + \tau_J = 0$

Take the positive sense of torque to be counter-clockwise. Then:

$F_S x_S - F_M x_M - F_J x_J = 0$

$(m_S g)\, x_S - (m_M g)\, x_M - (m_J g)\, x_J = 0$

$m_S x_S - m_M x_M - m_J x_J = 0$

Now, solve for John's position, x_J:

$x_J = (m_S x_S - m_M x_M) / m_J$

$x_J = [(105$ kg$)·(5.5$ m$) - (20$ kg$)(10$ m$)] / (20$ kg$)$

$x_J = [(105$ kg$)·(5.5$ m$) - (20$ kg$)(10$ m$)] / (20$ kg$)$

$x_J = (377.5$ kg·m$) / (20$ kg$)$

$x_J = 18.9$ m ≈ 19 m

18. A is correct.

The potential energy of a system can be zero because PE is defined against an arbitrary reference point.

In a gravitational potential problem, if the reference point is ground level and the object is below ground level, it will have negative potential energy relative to the reference point.

19. D is correct.

$\lambda = 2$ m and T = 1 s

$f = 1 / T$

$f = 1 / 1$ s

$f = 1$ Hz

$v = f\lambda$

$v = (1$ Hz$)\cdot(2$ m$)$

$v = 2$ m/s

20. D is correct.

Frequency, length, and velocity are related by:

$f = v / 2L$

$v = f \times 2L$

$v = (440$ Hz$)\cdot(2 \times 0.14$ m$)$

$v = 123.2$ m/s ≈ 123 m/s

$L = v / 2f$

$L = (123$ m/s$) / (2)\cdot(520$ Hz$)$

$L = 0.118$ m

$\Delta L = 0.14$ m $- 0.118$ m

$\Delta L = 0.022$ m $= 2.2$ cm

21. C is correct.

First, find the total resistance of each set of resistors in parallel.

Resistors in parallel:

$1 / R_{total} = 1 / R_1 + 1 / R_2 \ldots + 1 / R_n$

$1 / R_{total} = 1 / 600$ $\Omega + 1 / 600$ Ω

$R_{total} = 300$ Ω

continued…

The two sets of parallel resistors are in series:

Resistors in series:

$$R_{total} = R_1 + R_2 \dots + R_n$$

$$R_{total} = 300 \ \Omega + 300 \ \Omega$$

$$R_{total} = 600 \ \Omega$$

22. B is correct.

Force exerted on a particle of charge q:

$$F = qE$$

The acceleration of the proton is to the right, so the force is also to the right.

Therefore, the electric field must be to the right.

23. A is correct.

For constant acceleration, the velocity increases with time.

If velocity increases with time, the position *vs.* time line of the graph is curved over each time interval.

24. D is correct.

In *a circular path*, the object's direction of motion is constantly changing.

Therefore, the velocity is not constant.

The *acceleration* (i.e., centripetal force) points toward the center of the circular path.

25. C is correct.

Use conservation of momentum for momenta in the x coordinate to solve for the x component of the second ball's final velocity.

Use m as the mass for the first ball and $1.4m$ as the mass of the second ball.

$$p_{before} = p_{after}$$

$$m(4 \text{ m/s}) \cos 60° = 1.4mv_x$$

$$v_x = (4 \text{ m/s}) \cdot (\cos 60°) / 1.4$$

$$v_x = (4 \text{ m/s}) \cdot (0.5) / 1.4$$

$$v_x = 1.4 \text{ m/s}$$

26. A is correct.

Work equation:

$$W = Fd$$

$$W = (70 \text{ N}) \cdot (45 \text{ m})$$

$$W = 3{,}150 \text{ J}$$

Power equation:

$$P = W / t$$

$$P = (3{,}150 \text{ J}) / (60 \times 30 \text{ s})$$

$$P = (3{,}150 \text{ J}) / (180 \text{ s})$$

$$P = 18 \text{ W}$$

27. A is correct.

Simple harmonic motion is described by Hooke's Law:

$$F = -kx$$

Combining it with Newton's Second Law ($F = ma$), find:

$$a = -(k/m)x$$

Acceleration is proportional to displacement.

28. C is correct.

Since a beat of frequency 4 Hz is produced, the violin string must be vibrating at either:

$$(340 \text{ Hz} - 4 \text{ Hz}) = 336 \text{ Hz}$$

or

$$(340 \text{ Hz} + 4 \text{ Hz}) = 344 \text{ Hz}$$

Since the string is too taut, the perceived *f* is too high.

Therefore, the string vibrates at 344 Hz.

The *period* is the reciprocal of the frequency.

$$T = 1 / f$$

$$T = 1 / 344 \text{ sec}$$

29. B is correct.

First determine how long it takes the ball to drop 50 m:

$$PE = KE$$

$$mgh = \tfrac{1}{2}mv_{yf}^2$$

Cancel *m* from each side of the expression:

$$gh = \tfrac{1}{2}v_{yf}^2$$

$$v_{yf}^2 = 2gh$$

$$v_{yf}^2 = (2){\cdot}(10 \text{ m/s}^2){\cdot}(50 \text{ m})$$

$$v_{yf}^2 = 1{,}000 \text{ m}^2/\text{s}^2$$

$$v_{yf} \approx 32 \text{ m/s}$$

$$t = (v_{yf} - v_{yi}) \,/\, a$$

$$t = (32 \text{ m/s} - 0) \,/\, (10 \text{ m/s}^2)$$

$$t = 3.2 \text{ s}$$

Calculate the distance traveled horizontally in 3.2 s:

$$d_x = v_x \times t$$

$$d_x = (5 \text{ m/s}){\cdot}(3.2 \text{ s}) = 16 \text{ m}$$

30. C is correct.

$$F_{tot} = F_{gravity} + F_{friction}$$

$$ma_{tot} = mg \sin \theta + \mu_k mg \cos \theta$$

Cancel *m* from each side:

$$a_{tot} = g(\sin \theta + \mu_k \cos \theta)$$

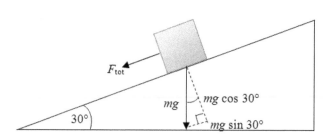

$$a_{tot} = -9.8 \text{ m/s}^2(\sin 30° + 0.3 \cos 30°)$$

$$a_{tot} = -7.44 \text{ m/s}^2$$

Find time taken to reach 0 m/s:

$$v_f = v_0 + at$$

$$0 \text{ m/s} = 14 \text{ m/s} + (-7.44 \text{ m/s}^2)t$$

$$t = 1.88 \text{ s}$$

$$x = x_0 + v_0 t + \tfrac{1}{2}at^2$$

$$x = 0 \text{ m} + (14 \text{ m/s}){\cdot}(1.88 \text{ s}) + \tfrac{1}{2}(-7.44 \text{ m/s}^2){\cdot}(1.88 \text{ s})^2$$

$$x = 13.2 \text{ m}$$

continued...

Find vertical component of x:

$$y = x \sin \theta$$

$$y = (13.2 \text{ m}) \sin 30°$$

$$y = 6.6 \text{ m}$$

31. B is correct.

The forces on the block (with the bullet) are gravity and the tension of the string.

The tension is perpendicular to the direction of travel, so the tension does no work.

This problem is solved using the conservation of energy, assuming a full transfer of KE into gravitational PE.

KE (block with a bullet at the bottom) = PE (block with a bullet at top)

$$\tfrac{1}{2}mv^2 = mgh$$

Cancel m from each side of the expression:

$$\tfrac{1}{2}v^2 = gh$$

$$\tfrac{1}{2}(2 \text{ m/s})^2 = (9.8 \text{ m/s}^2)h$$

$$\tfrac{1}{2}(4 \text{ m}^2/\text{s}^2) = (9.8 \text{ m/s}^2)h$$

$$(2 \text{ m}^2/\text{s}^2) = (9.8 \text{ m/s}^2)h$$

$$h = (2 \text{ m}^2/\text{s}^2) / (9.8 \text{ m/s}^2)$$

$$h = 0.20 \text{ m} = 20 \text{ cm}$$

32. A is correct.

Before it is released, the hammer has zero velocity and a gravitational PE of mgh.

This PE is converted entirely into KE when it reaches the ground.

PE (top) = KE (bottom)

$$mgh_0 = \tfrac{1}{2}m(v_0^2)$$

Cancel m from each side of the expression:

$$v_0 = \sqrt{(2gh_0)}$$

If h_0 increases by a factor of 2, substitute $2h_0$ for h_0

$$v = \sqrt{[2g(2h_0)]}$$

$$v = \sqrt{2} \times \sqrt{2gh_0}$$

$$v = \sqrt{2} \times (v_0)$$

The new velocity is $\sqrt{2}$ times faster.

33. B is correct.

Period of a pendulum:

$$T = 2\pi\sqrt{(L / g)}$$

The period does not depend on mass, so changes to M do not affect the period.

34. D is correct.

The perceived color of the light depends on frequency and wavelength, related through the speed of light:

$$c = f\lambda$$

35. A is correct.

The voltage through the 8 Ω resistor is:

$$V = IR$$

$$V = (8 \text{ } \Omega) \cdot (0.8 \text{ A})$$

$$V = 6.4 \text{ V}$$

Since the 8 Ω resistor is in parallel with the 16 Ω resistor, the voltage across the 16 Ω resistor is 6.4 V, and the current through it is:

$$I = V / R$$

$$I = (6.4 \text{ V}) / (16 \text{ } \Omega)$$

$$I = 0.4 \text{ A}$$

The total current in the upper branch is the sum:

$$I_{upper} = 0.4 \text{ A} + 0.8 \text{ A}$$

$$I_{upper} = 1.2 \text{ A}$$

The voltage across 20 Ω resistor:

$$V = IR$$

$$V = (1.2 \text{ A}) \cdot (20 \text{ } \Omega)$$

$$V = 24 \text{ V}$$

The total voltage across the upper branch is:

$$V_{upper} = 6.4 \text{ V} + 24 \text{ V}$$

$$V_{upper} = 30.4 \text{ V}$$

This is also the power supply voltage and the voltage across the lower branch.

continued...

The 2 Ω and 6 Ω resistors are in parallel, so it is the voltage across the 2 Ω resistor.

Therefore, the current in the 2 Ω resistor is:

$$I = V / R$$

$$I = (30.4 \text{ V}) / (2 \text{ Ω})$$

$$I = 15.2 \text{ A}$$

36. D is correct.

Solve for spring constant k:

$$PE = \tfrac{1}{2}kx^2$$

$$k = 2(PE) / x^2$$

where x is the amplitude (maximum distance traveled from rest).

$$k = 2(10 \text{ J}) / (0.2 \text{ m})^2$$

$$k = 500 \text{ N/m}$$

Solve for the period:

$$T = 2\pi[\sqrt{(m / k)}]$$

$$T = 2\pi[\sqrt{(0.4 \text{ kg} / 500 \text{ N/m})}]$$

$$T = 0.18 \text{ s}$$

Convert the period to frequency:

$$f = 1 / T$$

$$f = 1 / (0.18 \text{ s})$$

$$f = 5.6 \text{ Hz}$$

37. D is correct.

$$v_f^2 = v_0^2 + 2ad$$

where $v_0 = 0$

$$v_f^2 = 0 + 2ad$$

$$v_f^2 = 2ad$$

Since a is constant, d is proportional to v_f^2

If v_f increases by a factor of 4, then d increases by a factor of $4^2 = 16$.

38. B is correct.

The period of a satellite is found through Kepler's Third Law:

$$T = 2\pi\sqrt{(r^3 / GM)}$$

where T = period, r = distance from Earth's center, G = gravitational constant and M = mass of Earth

The period does not depend on the mass of the satellite, so the period remains the same.

39. D is correct.

Find the perimeter (i.e., circumference) of the carousel: distance traveled in one revolution.

$$\text{Perimeter} = \pi \times d$$

$$\text{Perimeter} = \pi \times 18 \text{ m}$$

$$\text{Perimeter} = 56.5 \text{ m}$$

Convert to rev/min, to rev/s:

$$v = (5 \text{ rev/min}) \cdot (1 \text{ min/60 s})$$

$$v = 0.083 \text{ rev/s}$$

Convert rev/s to m/s:

where 1 rev = 56.5 m

$$v = (0.083 \text{ rev/s}) \cdot (56.5 \text{ m/1 rev})$$

$$v = 4.7 \text{ m/s}$$

40. B is correct.

The arrows experience the same stopping force when they hit the hay bales.

The kinetic energy can be related to the work done by the force:

Arrow 1: $KE_1 = W$

             $KE_1 = Fd_1$

             $d_1 = KE_1 / F$

Arrow 2: $KE_2 = 2KE_1$

             $2KE_1 = W$

             $2KE_1 = Fd_2$

             $d_2 = 2KE_1 / F$

             $d_2 = 2d_1$

41. A is correct.

In a longitudinal wave, the particle displacement is parallel to the direction of the wave, resulting in a distribution of compressions and rarefactions.

Rarefaction is the decrease in an item's density, and it is the opposite of compression.

Like compression, which can travel in waves (e.g., sound waves), rarefaction waves exist in nature.

A common example of rarefaction is the area of low relative pressure following a shock wave.

Compression is the increase in the density of an item.

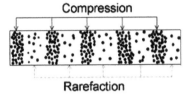

42. D is correct.

Decibels use a logarithmic scale.

$$\text{Intensity (dB)} = 10\log_{10}[I / I_0]$$

Where I_0 is the intensity at the threshold of hearing (10^{-12} W/m^2)

$$I = 10\log_{10}[10^{-7} \text{ W/m}^2 / 10^{-12} \text{ W/m}^2]$$

$$I = 10\log_{10}[10^5]$$

$$I = 50 \text{ dB}$$

43. C is correct.

To achieve a due north bearing, the east-west velocity must be made to be zero.

Find the horizontal component of the NE drift:

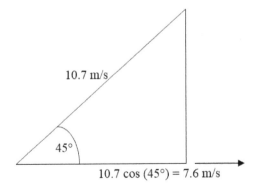

10.7 cos (45°) = 7.6 m/s

continued…

Find the horizontal component of the NW acceleration:

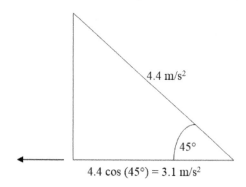

4.4 cos (45°) = 3.1 m/s²

The drift is fully corrected when there is zero east-west velocity

$v_f = v_i + a_x t$

$0 = (7.6 \text{ m/s}) + (3.1 \text{ m/s}^2)(t)$

$t = (7.6 \text{ m/s}) / (3.1 \text{ m/s}^2)$

$t = 2.4 \text{ s}$

44. C is correct.

By Newton's second law, the *acceleration* is:

$a = F_{net} / m$

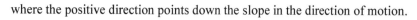

There are two forces on the object: gravity (F_g), pointing down the slope, and friction (F_f), opposing the motion, pointing up the slope.

Therefore:

$F_{net} = F_g - F_f$,

where the positive direction points down the slope in the direction of motion.

From the diagram, the *force due to gravity* is:

$F_g = mg \sin \theta$

The *force of friction* is:

$F_f = \mu_k F_{normal}$

$F_f = \mu_k mg \cos\theta$

Therefore:

$a = (mg \sin \theta - \mu_k mg \cos \theta) / m$

Cancel *m* from each side of the expression:

$a = g (\sin \theta - \mu_k \cos \theta)$

continued...

$a = (9.8 \text{ m/s}^2) \cdot (\sin 40° - 0.19 \times \cos 40°)$

$a = (9.8 \text{ m/s}^2) \cdot (0.49)$

$a = 4.9 \text{ m/s}^2$

45. B is correct.

The relationship between final speed and initial height can be found using the conservation of energy:

$PE_{initial} = KE_{final}$

$mgh = \frac{1}{2}mv^2$

Therefore:

$v^2 = 2gh$

To double v, h increases by a factor of 4.

46. A is correct.

Power = work / time

Power = (force × distance) / time

Newton's First Law: no force is required to keep the object moving with constant velocity.

The projectile maintains horizontal v since no forces are acting on the horizontal axis.

The vertical forces must be balanced since it maintains elevation (only moving horizontally).

Since there is no net force, no work is done.

Therefore, no power is required.

47. A is correct.

The period of a pendulum:

$T = 2\pi\sqrt{(L / g)}$

where L is the length of the pendulum and g is acceleration due to gravity.

Use $g / 6$ for g.

$T = 2\pi\sqrt{(L / (g / 6))}$

$T = 2\pi\sqrt{(6L / g)}$

$T = 2\pi\sqrt{(L / g)} \times \sqrt{6}$

New period = $T\sqrt{6}$

48. D is correct.

Electromagnetic waves propagate at the speed of light oscillations of electric and magnetic fields that propagate at the speed of light.

The oscillations of the two fields form a transverse wave perpendicular to each other and perpendicular to the direction of energy and wave propagation.

49. C is correct.

Resistance in series experience equal current because there is only one path for the current to travel.

50. C is correct.

$$\Delta v = at$$

$$a = \Delta v / t$$

$$a = (v_f - v_i) / t$$

$$(v_f - v_i) = at$$

$$v_f = at + v_i$$

$$v_f = (2 \text{ m/s}^2) \cdot (6 \text{ s}) + (5 \text{ m/s})$$

$$v_f = 17 \text{ m/s}$$

Notes for active learning

Notes for active learning

Diagnostic Test 3 – Answer Key and Detailed Explanations

Answer Key

1	C	Kinematics & dynamics	26	A	Work & energy
2	A	Force, motion, gravitation	27	D	Waves & periodic motion
3	C	Equilibrium & momentum	28	C	Sound
4	A	Work & energy	29	B	Kinematics & dynamics
5	B	Waves & periodic motion	30	A	Force, motion, gravitation
6	C	Sound	31	D	Equilibrium & momentum
7	B	DC circuits	32	A	Work & energy
8	A	Electrostatics	33	C	Waves & periodic motion
9	B	Kinematics & dynamics	34	D	Sound
10	C	Force, motion, gravitation	35	A	DC circuits
11	A	Equilibrium & momentum	36	A	Electrostatics
12	D	Work & energy	37	D	Kinematics & dynamics
13	A	Waves & periodic motion	38	A	Force, motion, gravitation
14	B	Sound	39	C	Equilibrium & momentum
15	B	Kinematics & dynamics	40	C	Work & energy
16	D	Force, motion, gravitation	41	A	Waves & periodic motion
17	B	Equilibrium & momentum	42	B	Sound
18	B	Work & energy	43	D	Kinematics & dynamics
19	B	Waves & periodic motion	44	D	Force, motion, gravitation
20	B	Sound	45	B	Equilibrium & momentum
21	B	DC circuits	46	B	Work & energy
22	D	Electrostatics	47	D	Waves & periodic motion
23	A	Kinematics & dynamics	48	B	Sound
24	C	Force, motion, gravitation	49	A	Force, motion, gravitation
25	C	Equilibrium & momentum	50	D	Electrostatics

1. C is correct.

The slope of a tangent line of a position *vs.* time graph at a specific time value is the instantaneous velocity, and this is equivalent to taking the derivative of the graph at this same time value.

2. A is correct.

An object in motion with constant nonzero velocity experiences no acceleration and thus no net force.

If v = constant, then:

$a = 0$

$F = ma$

$F = m(0 \text{ m/s}^2)$

$F = 0 \text{ N}$

3. C is correct.

First calculate the stone's speed at impact:

$v^2 = v_0^2 + 2ad$

where $v_0 = 0$ and $a = g$

$v^2 = 2ad$

$v^2 = 2(10 \text{ m/s}^2)\cdot(5 \text{ m})$

$v^2 = 100 \text{ m}^2/\text{s}^2$

$v = 10 \text{ m/s}$

Use the speed of impact to calculate momentum p:

$p = mv$

$p = (3 \text{ kg})\cdot(10 \text{ m/s})$

$p = 30 \text{ kg·m/s}$

Another method to solve this problem:

$PE = KE$

$mgh = \frac{1}{2}mv^2$

Cancel m from each side of the expression:

$gh = \frac{1}{2}v^2$

$2(gh) = v^2$

continued…

$$v^2 = 2(10 \text{ m/s}^2 \times 5 \text{ m})$$

$$v^2 = 100 \text{ m}^2/\text{s}^2$$

$$v = 10 \text{ m/s}$$

$$p = mv$$

$$p = (3 \text{ kg}) \cdot (10 \text{ m/s})$$

$$p = 30 \text{ kg·m/s}$$

4. A is correct.

The spring has the 0.9 kg mass attached to it, so its original equilibrium length is the length needed to counteract the force of gravity.

If the spring is stretched further, then the net force only includes the component from the spring force:

$$F_{spring} = k\Delta x$$

$$F_{spring} = (3 \text{ N/m}) \cdot (0.18 \text{ m})$$

$$F_{spring} = 0.54 \text{ N}$$

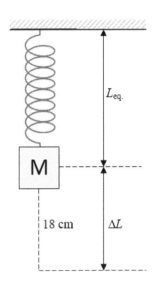

5. B is correct.

Convert weight to mass:

$$F = ma$$

$$m = F / a$$

$$m = 30 \text{ N} / (9.8 \text{ m/s}^2)$$

$$m = 3.061 \text{ kg}$$

Frequency of a spring system:

$$\omega = \sqrt{(k / m)}$$

$$\omega = \sqrt{(40.0 \text{ N/m} / 3.061 \text{ kg})}$$

$$\omega = 3.615 \text{ rad/s}$$

$$f = \omega / 2\pi$$

$$f = (3.615 \text{ rad/s}) / 2\pi$$

$$f = 0.58 \text{ Hz}$$

6. C is correct.

$$f_{beat} = |f_2 - f_1|$$

$$f_{beat} = |786.3 \text{ Hz} - 785.8 \text{ Hz}|$$

$$f_{beat} = 0.5 \text{ Hz}$$

7. B is correct.

$$P = VI$$

$$V = IR$$

Substituting into the equation:

$$P = (IR) \times I$$

$$P = I^2 \times R$$

If P is on y-axis and R is on x-axis,

$$\text{slope} = P / R$$

$$\text{slope} = I^2$$

8. A is correct.

$$\text{Power} = \text{current} \times \text{voltage}$$

$$P = IV$$

Power is measured in watts (W), current in amps (A), and voltage in volts (V).

$$W = A \times V$$

9. B is correct.

The maximum and minimum of position *vs.* time are always equal to zero velocity.

10. C is correct.

The coefficient of *static friction* (object at rest) is larger than the coefficient of *kinetic friction* (object in motion).

The coefficient of *static friction* is proportional to the force needed to take a stationary object from static equilibrium and accelerate it.

The coefficient of kinetic friction is proportional to the force needed to maintain dynamic equilibrium in an object moving at a constant speed.

Therefore, the force required to take a stationary object out of static equilibrium and accelerate it is greater than that required to keep a moving object in dynamic equilibrium. It is more challenging to set an object in motion than it is to keep it in motion.

11. A is correct.

Conservation of momentum:

$$m_1v_1 = m_2v_2$$

$$m_1 = \text{putty}$$

$$m_2 = \text{putty} + \text{bowling ball}$$

$$m_2 = (1 \text{ kg} + 7 \text{ kg})$$

$$m_2 = 8 \text{ kg}$$

$$v_2 = (m_1v_1) / m_2$$

$$v_2 = (1 \text{ kg}){\cdot}(1 \text{ m/s}) / 8 \text{ kg}$$

$$v_2 = 1/8 \text{ m/s}$$

12. D is correct.

Find *kinetic energy* and set it equal to the *work done by friction*:

$$KE = W_f$$

$$\tfrac{1}{2}mv^2 = F_f \times d$$

$$\tfrac{1}{2}m / F_f = d / v^2$$

Because the mass is constant, d / v^2 = constant regardless of velocity.

Solve for the *new skid distance*:

$$d_1 / v_1^2 = d_2 / v_2^2$$

$$d_2 = (d_1){\cdot}(v_2^2) / (v_1^2)$$

$$d_2 = (30 \text{ m}){\cdot}(150 \text{ km/h})^2 / (45 \text{ km/h})^2$$

$$d_2 = 333 \text{ m}$$

13. A is correct.

The time it takes to complete *one cycle* is period T.

$$T = 1 / f$$

The period is measured in seconds.

$$\text{Frequency} = s^{-1} \text{ or Hz}$$

14. B is correct.

$$\text{One mosquito} = 1.5 \times 10^{-11} \text{ W}$$

To power a 30 W bulb:

$$(30 \text{ W}) / (1.5 \times 10^{-11} \text{ W}) = 2 \times 10^{12} \text{ mosquitoes}$$

15. B is correct.

When an object is accelerating, its velocity must change in either speed or direction.

The speed or direction do not always change, but velocity does.

16. D is correct.

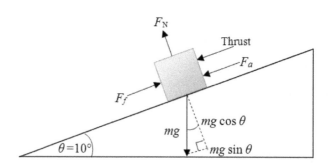

$F_f = \mu_k F_N$

$F_f = \mu_k mg \cos \theta$

Find the length of travel:

$L = 50 \text{ m} / \sin 10°$

$L = 50 \text{ m} / 0.174$

$L = 288 \text{ m}$

Find acceleration to reach 40 m/s:

$v_f^2 = v_i^2 + 2ad$

$(40 \text{ m/s})^2 = 0 + 2a(288 \text{ m})$

$1,600 \text{ m}^2/\text{s}^2 = a(576 \text{ m})$

$a = (1,600 \text{ m}^2/\text{s}^2) / (576 \text{ m})$

$a = 2.8 \text{ m/s}^2$

Find normal (F_N) and gravitational (F_G) forces:

$F_N = mg \cos \theta$

$F_N = (50 \text{ kg}) \cdot (9.8 \text{ m/s}^2) \cos 10°$

$F_N = (50 \text{ kg}) \cdot (9.8 \text{ m/s}^2) \cdot (0.985)$

$F_N = 483 \text{ N}$

$F_G = mg \sin \theta$

$F_G = (50 \text{ kg}) \cdot (9.8 \text{ m/s}^2) \sin 10°$

$F_G = (50 \text{ kg}) \cdot (9.8 \text{ m/s}^2) \cdot (0.174)$

$F_G = 85 \text{ N}$

$F_{total} = (260 \text{ N} + 85 \text{ N})$

$F_{total} = 345 \text{ N}$, total force experienced by the skier

The skier experiences acceleration down the slope that was reduced by friction.

continued…

The coefficient of kinetic friction can be calculated by:

$$F_{total} - F_{friction} = F_{experienced}$$

$$F_{total} - \mu F_N = F_{experienced}$$

$$345 \text{ N} - \mu_k 483 \text{ N} = (2.8 \text{ m/s}^2 \times 50 \text{ kg})$$

$$345 \text{ N} - \mu_k 483 \text{ N} = 140 \text{ N}$$

$$345 \text{ N} - 140 \text{ N} = \mu_K 483 \text{ N}$$

$$205 \text{ N} = \mu_k 483 \text{ N}$$

$$205 \text{ N} / 483 \text{ N} = \mu_k$$

$$\mu_k = 0.42$$

17. B is correct. Determine distance in one revolution (the perimeter or circumference):

$$P = \pi d$$

$$P = \pi (18 \text{ m})$$

$$P = 56.55 \text{ m}$$

Convert rev/min to rev/s:

$$v = (5.3 \text{ rev/min}) \cdot (1 \text{ min}/60 \text{ s})$$

$$v = 0.0883 \text{ rev/s}$$

Convert rev/s to m/s, where 1 rev = 56.55 m

$$v = (0.0883 \text{ rev/s}) \cdot (56.55 \text{ m}/1 \text{ rev})$$

$$v = 5 \text{ m/s}$$

18. B is correct.

Upward force due to the spring (Hooke's law):

$$F = k\Delta x$$

where k is the spring constant and Δx is the distance the spring is stretched

The downward force due to gravity:

$$F = mg$$

System is in equilibrium so set the expressions equal:

$$k\Delta x = mg$$

$$\Delta x = mg / k$$

$$\Delta x = (4 \text{ kg}) \cdot (10 \text{ m/s}^2) / (10 \text{ N/m})$$

$$\Delta x = 4 \text{ m}$$

19. B is correct.

The overtone or harmonic can be found by the following:

harmonic   overtone

n^{th} harmonic $(n^{th} - 1)$ overtone

Thus, the third harmonic has:

$(3 - 1) = 2^{nd}$ overtone

20. B is correct.

The two ends count as nodes.

From a standing wave with four nodes, there are three antinodes.

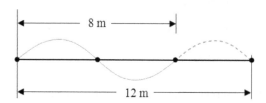

Therefore, there are three half-wavelengths.

Each dot on the curve represents one of the four nodes.

One complete wave (the solid line) includes three nodes.

> 1 wave = (2/3) entire string

> 1 wave = (2/3)·(12 m) = **8 m**

21. B is correct.

The equivalent resistance of resistors in parallel:

> $R_{eq} = 1 / (1 / R_1 + 1 / R_2 + 1 / R_3 \dots)$

The equivalent resistance is always smaller than the smallest resistance.

For example:

> $R_1 = 20\ \Omega,\ R_2 = 30\ \Omega,\ R_3 = 30\ \Omega$

> $R_{eq} = 1 / (1 / 20\ \Omega + 1 / 30\ \Omega + 1 / 30\ \Omega \dots)$

> $R_{eq} = 8.75\ \Omega$

> $R_{eq} < R_1$

22. D is correct.

Coulomb's Law, which describes the repulsive force between two particles, is given as:

> $F = kq_1q_2 / r^2$

The expression does not include mass, so the repulsive force remains the same when m changes.

Note: gravitational (attractive) forces do rely on the masses of the objects.

23. A is correct.

If acceleration is constant, velocity continuously increases or decreases and results in a sloped line (not a straight line).

24. C is correct.

$$F_{net} = ma$$

The only acceleration is centripetal:

$$a_{cent} = v^2 / r$$

$$a_{cent} = (4 \text{ m/s})^2 / 16 \text{ m}$$

$$a_{cent} = (16 \text{ m}^2/\text{s}^2) / 16 \text{ m}$$

$$a_{cent} = 1 \text{ m/s}^2$$

$$F_{net} = ma$$

$$F_{net} = (40 \text{ kg}) \cdot (1 \text{ m/s}^2)$$

$$F_{net} = 40 \text{ kg} \cdot \text{m/s}^2 = 40 \text{ N}$$

25. C is correct.

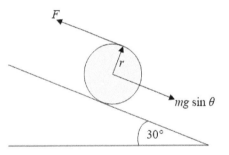

If the cylinder's center of mass does not move it must be stationary, and the forces must balance:

$$F = mg \sin \theta$$

Force produced by torque is:

$$\tau = I\alpha$$

where I is the mass moment of inertia and α is angular acceleration.

The moment of inertia for a solid cylinder is:

$$I = \tfrac{1}{2}mr^2$$

$$\tau = I\alpha$$

$$\tau = Fr$$

$$I\alpha = Fr$$

$$(\tfrac{1}{2}mr^2)\alpha = (mg \sin \theta)r$$

$$\alpha = (2g \sin \theta) / r$$

$$\alpha = (2) \cdot (10 \text{ m/s}^2) \sin 30° / (0.8 \text{ m})$$

$$\alpha = (2) \cdot (10 \text{ m/s}^2) \cdot (0.5) / (0.8 \text{ m})$$

$$\alpha = 12.5 \text{ rad/s}^2$$

26. A is correct.

Convert PE (before release) into KE (as it is about to strike the ground):

$mgh = KE$

KE is proportional to h.

27. D is correct.

A phase change occurs when waves reflect from the surface of a medium with a higher refractive index than the medium they are traveling in.

Glass has a higher refractive index than air; therefore, when a light ray moves from glass to air, no change occurs.

28. C is correct.

$f_{beat} = |f_2 - f_1|$

$\pm f_{beat} = f_2 - f_1$

$f_2 = \pm f_{beat} + f_1$

$f_2 = \pm 5\ Hz + 822\ Hz$

$f_2 = 817\ Hz,\ 827\ Hz$

Only 827 Hz is an answer choice.

29. B is correct.

Distance traveled is represented by the area under the velocity *vs.* time curve.

At the point where each of those curves intersects on this plot, there is more area under the curve of the truck velocity than there is under the curve of the car velocity.

30. A is correct.

Since the velocity is constant, the acceleration is $a = 0$.

$F_{net} = ma$

$F_{net} = 0$

31. D is correct.

$\tau = 120\ N{\cdot}m$

$\tau = I\alpha$

Mass moment of inertia: mass moment of inertia of disk about z-axis

$I = \tfrac{1}{2}mr^2$

$\tau = [\tfrac{1}{2}mr^2]\alpha$

continued…

$$120 \text{ N} = \tfrac{1}{2}(12 \text{ kg}){\cdot}(4 \text{ m})^2 \, \alpha$$

$$\alpha = (120 \text{ N}) / [\tfrac{1}{2}(12 \text{ kg}){\cdot}(4 \text{ m})^2]$$

$$\alpha = 1.25 \text{ rad/s}^2$$

$$\omega = \alpha t$$

$$7.35 \text{ rad/s} = (1.25 \text{ rad/s}^2)t$$

$$t = (7.35 \text{ rad/s}) / (1.25 \text{ rad/s}^2)$$

$$t = 5.9 \text{ s}$$

32. A is correct.

Include the term for work done by air resistance in the conservation of energy equation.

$$KE_i + PE_i + W_{\text{air resis}} = KE_f + PE_f$$

$$0 + mgh + (-F_{\text{air}} \times d) = \tfrac{1}{2}mv_f^2 + 0$$

$$mgh + (-mad) = \tfrac{1}{2}mv_f^2$$

$$(1.2 \text{ kg}){\cdot}(10 \text{ m/s}^2){\cdot}(6 \text{ m}) + (-3.4 \text{ kg·m/s}^2){\cdot}(6 \text{ m}) = \tfrac{1}{2}(1.2 \text{ kg})v_f^2$$

$$v_f^2 = 86 \text{ m}^2/\text{s}^2$$

$$v_f = 9.2 \text{ m/s}$$

33. C is correct.

Frequency = # cycles / time

$$f = 2 \text{ cycles} / 1 \text{ s}$$

$$f = 2 \text{ s}^{-1}$$

$$v = \lambda f$$

where λ is wavelength

$$v = (12 \text{ m}){\cdot}(2 \text{ s}^{-1})$$

$$v = 24 \text{ m/s}$$

34. D is correct.

Sound intensity is expressed as power / area:

Units of intensity: $\text{W/m}^2 = \text{J/s/m}^2 = \text{J/m}^2/\text{s}$

which is the unit of energy per unit area per unit time.

35. A is correct.

$$P = I^2R$$

$$P = (4I)^2R$$

$$P = (16)I^2R$$

Power increased by a factor of 16

36. A is correct.

Unit of watt = work / time

Multiply by time, time cancels, and work remains.

Alternatively, 1 kilowatt-hour:

1 watt = 1 J/s

1 watt·second = 1 J

(1 hr/60 s)·(60 min/1 hr)·(60 s/1min) = 60^2 s

1×10^3 Watt × (1 hour)·(60^2 s/1 hour) = 36×10^5 J

Work = force × distance

Joule is a unit of work.

37. D is correct.

When an object is thrown into the air, the acceleration vector is always equal to gravity (for objects in free fall).

The velocity vector changes direction when the object starts to come down.

38. A is correct.

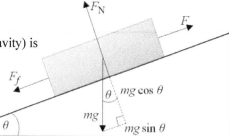

As shown in the diagram, *mg* (i.e., the force of the mass due to gravity) is broken down into two components.

The *mg* sin θ component is parallel to the slope of the road.

39. C is correct.

If the object's velocity is constant, then the net force is zero.

In the *y*-direction: $0 = F_N + F_g$

In the *x*-direction:

$$0 = F_{friction} + F$$

$$F_N + F_g = F_{friction} + F$$

$$-F = F_{friction}$$

Since kinetic friction is exerting a force opposing the object's motion, there must be an equal and opposing force propelling it forward for net force to be zero.

40. C is correct.

$$P = W / t$$

$$W = Fd$$

$$P = (Fd) / t$$

$$F = mg$$

$$P = (mgd \sin \theta) / t$$

$$P = [(54 \text{ kg}) \cdot (9.8 \text{ m/s}^2) \cdot (10 \text{ m}) \sin 30°] / (4 \text{ s})$$

$$P = [(54 \text{ kg}) \cdot (9.8 \text{ m/s}^2) \cdot (10 \text{ m}) \cdot (0.5)] / (4 \text{ s})$$

$$P = 2{,}646 \text{ J} / (4 \text{ s})$$

$$P = 661 \text{ J/s}$$

$$P = 661 \text{ W}$$

Convert watts into horsepower:

$$1 \text{ hp} = 745 \text{ W}$$

$$P = (661 \text{ W}) \cdot (1 \text{ hp} / 745 \text{ W})$$

$$P = 0.89 \text{ hp}$$

41. A is correct.

The *amplitude of a wave* is a measure of the energy of the wave.

Thus, if energy is dissipated, the amplitude is reduced.

42. B is correct.

To determine the *frequency of the fundamental*:

$$f_n = nf_1$$

where f_1 = fundamental

$$f_1 = f_3 / 3$$

$$f_1 = 783 \text{ Hz} / 3$$

$$f_1 = 261 \text{ Hz}$$

43. D is correct.

All external forces are balanced for a system consisting of a bicycle and a rider as the rider pedals at a constant speed in a straight line.

44. D is correct.

The force of gravity depends only on the *m* and the distance between their centers.

$$F_{grav} = GM_1M_2 / d^2$$

If one *m* decreases by a factor of 2, then F_{grav} decreases by a factor of 2.

45. B is correct.

In projectile motion, the acceleration due to gravity always acts in the vertical component.

Thus, the acceleration due to gravity remains a nonzero constant.

46. B is correct.

According to the *conservation of mechanical energy* principle, total mechanical energy in a system remains constant as long as the only forces acting are conservative forces.

47. D is correct.

This is a thin film interference problem. When light strikes the surface of the oil, some will be transmitted, and some light will be reflected off the surface. This process is repeated when the light reaches the oil-water interface.

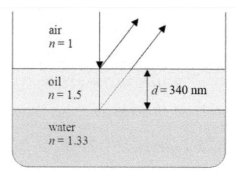

The light reflected from the oil-water interface may combine with the light initially reflected off the oil before constructive or destructive interference.

The strongly reflected light is formed through constructive interference; the rays that destructively interfere with the initially reflected light cannot be seen.

Use the thin film constructive interference equation:

$$2n_{oil}d = (m + \tfrac{1}{2})\lambda \; (m = 0, 1, 2...)$$

where m is the order of the reflected light.

$$\lambda = (2n_{oil}d) / (m + \tfrac{1}{2})$$

Solve for range: 400 nm $\leq \lambda \leq$ 800 nm

Use m = 0

$$\lambda_0 = (2) \cdot (1.5) \cdot (340 \times 10^{-9} \text{ m}) / (0 + \tfrac{1}{2}),$$

$$\lambda_0 = 1{,}020 \times 10^{-9} \text{ m} = 1{,}020 \text{ nm}$$

λ_0 is out of range

Use m = 1

$$\lambda_1 = (2) \cdot (1.5) \cdot (340 \times 10^{-9} \text{ m}) / (1 + \tfrac{1}{2})$$

$$\lambda_1 = 680 \times 10^{-9} \text{ m} = 680 \text{ nm}$$

λ_1 is in range   *continued...*

Use m = 2

$\lambda_2 = (2) \cdot (1.5) \cdot (340 \times 10^{-9} \text{ m}) / (2 + \frac{1}{2})$

$\lambda_2 = 408 \times 10^{-9} \text{ m} = 408 \text{ nm}$

λ_2 is in range

If m is a value greater than 2, it produces a wavelength outside the 400 nm to 800 nm range.

Thus, the two most strongly reflected wavelengths are:

$\lambda_1 = 680 \text{ nm}$

$\lambda_2 = 408 \text{ nm}$

48. B is correct.

The harmonic wavelength λ_n occurs when:

$\lambda_n = (2L) / n$

where L is the length of the string and n is the harmonic (n = 1, 2, 3...).

The fourth harmonic wavelength occurs at n = 4.

$\lambda_4 = (2L) / 4$

$\lambda_4 = (2 \times 1 \text{ m}) / 4$

$\lambda_4 = 0.5 \text{ m}$

49. A is correct.

$F_{net} = ma$

The suitcase is moving in a straight line, at a constant speed, so the suitcase's velocity is constant.

Therefore,

$a = 0$

$F_{net} = 0$

50. D is correct.

Electric field at a distance:

$$E = kQ / d^2$$

Solve for $Q_1 = 18$ μC, where d is half the distance:

$$E_1 = (9 \times 10^9 \text{ N·m}^2\text{·C}^{-2})\cdot(18 \times 10^{-6} \text{ C}) / (0.075 \text{ m})^2$$

$$E_1 = 28.8 \times 10^6 \text{ N/C}$$

Solve for Q_2:

$$E_2 = (9 \times 10^9 \text{ N·m}^2\text{·C}^{-2})\cdot(-6 \times 10^{-6} \text{ C}) / (0.075 \text{ m})^2$$

$$E_2 = -9.6 \times 10^6 \text{ N/C}$$

Note that the *negative sign* indicates that the electric field goes into the charge because the charge is negative.

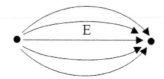

Because the electric fields generated by both charges point in the same direction, sum E_1 and E_2 to find the strength halfway between the charges:

$$E_{\text{total}} = E_1 + E_2$$

$$E_{\text{total}} = (28.8 \times 10^6 \text{ N/C}) + (9.6 \times 10^6 \text{ N/C})$$

$$E_{\text{total}} = 38.4 \times 10^6 \text{ N/C towards the negative charge}$$

Notes for active learning

Notes for active learning

Answer Keys and

Detailed Explanations:

Topical Practice Questions

Topical Practice Questions Answer Keys

Kinematics and Dynamics

1: D	11: C	21: D	31: B	41: C	51: A	61: A	71: C
2: B	12: B	22: A	32: C	42: A	52: A	62: B	72: B
3: B	13: A	23: B	33: D	43: D	53: B	63: D	73: D
4: A	14: C	24: D	34: A	44: B	54: D	64: A	74: A
5: C	15: B	25: B	35: C	45: A	55: A	65: C	75: D
6: C	16: D	26: A	36: D	46: D	56: A	66: B	76: C
7: D	17: A	27: C	37: D	47: B	57: C	67: C	77: D
8: B	18: B	28: D	38: B	48: C	58: C	68: A	
9: A	19: D	29: D	39: C	49: D	59: B	69: D	
10: B	20: C	30: C	40: A	50: C	60: D	70: D	

Force, Motion, Gravitation

1: B	11: A	21: B	31: C	41: A	51: C	61: D	71: C
2: D	12: D	22: A	32: D	42: C	52: B	62: B	72: B
3: A	13: B	23: C	33: D	43: B	53: D	63: D	73: A
4: C	14: C	24: D	34: A	44: C	54: D	64: B	74: B
5: D	15: D	25: D	35: D	45: A	55: B	65: A	75: C
6: D	16: A	26: A	36: A	46: C	56: D	66: C	76: D
7: A	17: D	27: D	37: D	47: D	57: B	67: B	77: D
8: D	18: C	28: D	38: B	48: D	58: D	68: D	78: D
9: A	19: D	29: A	39: B	49: C	59: C	69: A	79: B
10: C	20: B	30: D	40: C	50: A	60: B	70: B	

Equilibrium and Momentum

1: A	13: D	25: D	37: B	49: D	61: C	73: D	85: C
2: D	14: B	26: A	38: C	50: C	62: D	74: B	86: A
3: D	15: D	27: D	39: D	51: D	63: D	75: A	
4: C	16: D	28: C	40: A	52: D	64: C	76: D	
5: D	17: B	29: A	41: B	53: A	65: B	77: A	
6: B	18: D	30: B	42: A	54: D	66: D	78: D	
7: D	19: B	31: C	43: C	55: B	67: A	79: B	
8: A	20: C	32: D	44: B	56: C	68: D	80: D	
9: B	21: D	33: C	45: D	57: D	69: D	81: B	
10: C	22: B	34: B	46: C	58: A	70: D	82: C	
11: D	23: A	35: D	47: B	59: D	71: C	83: D	
12: C	24: D	36: C	48: A	60: B	72: A	84: A	

Work and Energy

1: D	11: D	21: B	31: B	41: A	51: D	61: B	71: D
2: B	12: B	22: D	32: C	42: A	52: C	62: D	72: A
3: A	13: A	23: B	33: D	43: C	53: C	63: A	73: C
4: B	14: C	24: C	34: A	44: B	54: B	64: B	74: C
5: C	15: B	25: D	35: B	45: D	55: C	65: A	75: D
6: A	16: D	26: A	36: B	46: D	56: D	66: D	
7: D	17: A	27: D	37: C	47: A	57: C	67: A	
8: C	18: A	28: C	38: D	48: A	58: C	68: C	
9: A	19: D	29: B	39: A	49: C	59: A	69: D	
10: B	20: A	30: C	40: B	50: B	60: D	70: B	

Rotational Motion

1: D	11: A	21: B	31: D	41: C	51: D
2: B	12: D	22: D	32: D	42: D	52: B
3: A	13: C	23: B	33: B	43: C	53: D
4: D	14: B	24: A	34: C	44: C	54: D
5: C	15: D	25: A	35: D	45: B	55: A
6: C	16: D	26: A	36: B	46: C	56: B
7: D	17: D	27: A	37: C	47: B	57: B
8: A	18: A	28: C	38: B	48: D	58: C
9: C	19: D	29: C	39: B	49: B	
10: B	20: D	30: C	40: D	50: D	

Waves and Periodic Motion

1: B	11: D	21: B	31: B	41: A	51: A	61: D
2: D	12: A	22: C	32: D	42: C	52: C	62: A
3: D	13: B	23: B	33: A	43: B	53: B	63: B
4: C	14: C	24: A	34: D	44: D	54: C	64: D
5: A	15: A	25: D	35: C	45: A	55: D	65: C
6: D	16: B	26: C	36: D	46: B	56: A	66: D
7: C	17: C	27: D	37: B	47: A	57: B	67: B
8: B	18: B	28: B	38: C	48: C	58: D	
9: A	19: A	29: C	39: D	49: D	59: C	
10: B	20: D	30: A	40: C	50: A	60: A	

Sound

1: B	11: B	21: C	31: C	41: A	51: D	61: D	71: D
2: A	12: A	22: D	32: D	42: C	52: B	62: A	72: C
3: B	13: B	23: B	33: A	43: D	53: D	63: D	73: B
4: C	14: C	24: C	34: D	44: A	54: C	64: D	74: D
5: B	15: D	25: A	35: A	45: B	55: D	65: D	75: A
6: A	16: A	26: D	36: A	46: D	56: C	66: B	76: B
7: D	17: C	27: B	37: B	47: C	57: A	67: A	77: D
8: A	18: B	28: A	38: D	48: A	58: C	68: D	
9: C	19: A	29: B	39: B	49: C	59: D	69: B	
10: D	20: B	30: A	40: C	50: B	60: C	70: A	

DC Circuits

1: B	11: A	21: D
2: D	12: D	22: A
3: C	13: D	23: C
4: C	14: C	24: A
5: A	15: D	25: D
6: D	16: B	26: D
7: C	17: B	27: D
8: C	18: D	28: A
9: C	19: A	29: B
10: D	20: A	30: D

Electrostatics

1: C	11: C	21: B	31: C
2: C	12: A	22: C	32: D
3: D	13: D	23: C	33: D
4: B	14: D	24: A	34: D
5: D	15: C	25: D	35: B
6: C	16: D	26: D	36: A
7: D	17: C	27: D	37: B
8: A	18: B	28: B	
9: B	19: C	29: B	
10: D	20: A	30: D	

Notes for active learning

Kinematics and Dynamics – Detailed Explanations

1. D is correct.

$$t = (v_f - v_i) / a$$

$$t = (60 \text{ mi/h} - 0 \text{ mi/h}) / (13.1 \text{ mi/h·s})$$

$$t = 4.6 \text{ s}$$

Acceleration is in mi/h·s, so miles and hours cancel, and the answer is in units of seconds.

2. B is correct.

At the top of the parabolic trajectory, the vertical velocity $v_{yf} = 0$

The *initial upward velocity* is the vertical component of the initial velocity:

$$v_{yi} = v \sin \theta$$

$$v_{yi} = (20 \text{ m/s}) \sin 30°$$

$$v_{yi} = (20 \text{ m/s})·(0.5)$$

$$v_{yi} = 10 \text{ m/s}$$

$$t = (v_{yf} - v_{yi}) / a$$

$$t = (0 - 10 \text{ m/s}) / (-10 \text{ m/s}^2)$$

$$t = (-10 \text{ m/s}) / (-10 \text{ m/s}^2)$$

$$t = 1 \text{ s}$$

3. B is correct.

$$\Delta d = 31.5 \text{ km} = 31,500 \text{ m}$$

$$1.25 \text{ hr} \times 60 \text{ min/hr} = 75 \text{ min}$$

$$\Delta t = 75 \text{ min} \times 60 \text{ s/min} = 4,500 \text{ s}$$

$$v_{avg} = \Delta d / \Delta t$$

$$v_{avg} = 31,500 \text{ m} / 4,500 \text{ s}$$

$$v_{avg} = 7 \text{ m/s}$$

4. A is correct.

Instantaneous speed is the scalar magnitude of the velocity.

Instantaneous speed can only be positive or zero (because magnitudes cannot be negative).

5. C is correct.

$$d = (v_f^2 - v_i^2) / 2a$$

$$d = [(21 \text{ m/s})^2 - (5 \text{ m/s})^2] / [2(3 \text{ m/s}^2)]$$

$$d = (441 \text{ m}^2/\text{s}^2 - 25 \text{ m}^2/\text{s}^2) / 6 \text{ m/s}^2$$

$$d = (416 \text{ m}^2/\text{s}^2) / 6 \text{ m/s}^2$$

$$d = 69 \text{ m}$$

6. C is correct.

$$a = (v_f - v_i) / t$$

$$a = [0 - (-30 \text{ m/s})] / 0.15 \text{ s}$$

$$a = (30 \text{ m/s}) / 0.15 \text{ s}$$

$$a = 200 \text{ m/s}^2$$

To represent the *acceleration* in terms of *g*, divide *a* by 9.8 m/s²:

$$\# \text{ of } g = (200 \text{ m/s}^2) / 9.8 \text{ m/s}^2$$

$$\# \text{ of } g = 20 \text{ } g$$

The *initial velocity* (v_i) is negative due to the acceleration of the car being a positive value.

Since the car is decelerating, its acceleration is opposite of its initial velocity.

7. D is correct.

When a bullet is fired, it is in projectile motion.

The only force in projectile motion (if air resistance is ignored) is the force of gravity.

8. B is correct.

When an object moving in a straight line is slowing its acceleration is in the direction opposite of its velocity.

If it is gaining speed, its acceleration is in the same direction as its velocity.

9. A is correct

Uniform acceleration:

$$a = \text{change in velocity} / \text{change in time}$$

$$a = \Delta v / \Delta t$$

$$\Delta v = a\Delta t$$

$$\Delta v = (20 \text{ m/s}^2) \cdot (1 \text{ s})$$

$$\Delta v = 20 \text{ m/s}$$

10. B is correct.

Uniform acceleration:

a = change in velocity / change in time

$a = \Delta v / \Delta t$

$a = (40 \text{ m/s} - 15 \text{ m/s}) / 10 \text{ s}$

$a = (25 \text{ m/s}) / 10 \text{ s}$

$a = 2.5 \text{ m/s}^2$

11. C is correct.

$t = d / v$

$t = (540 \text{ mi}) / (65 \text{ mi/h})$

$t = 8.3 \text{ h}$

The time to stop is the difference between her total allowed time and the time t that it takes to make the trip:

$t_{stop} = 9.8 \text{ h} - 8.3 \text{ h}$

$t_{stop} = 1.5 \text{ h}$

12. B is correct.

Average velocity is the change in position with respect to time:

$v = \Delta x / \Delta t$

After one lap, the racecar's final position is the same as its initial position.

Thus, $x = 0$ which implies the average velocity of 0 m/s.

13. A is correct.

$d = v_i \Delta t + \frac{1}{2} a \Delta t^2$

$d = (0.2 \text{ m/s}) \cdot (5 \text{ s}) + \frac{1}{2}(-0.05 \text{ m/s}^2) \cdot (5 \text{ s})^2$

$d = 1 \text{ m} + \frac{1}{2}(-0.05 \text{ m/s}^2) \cdot (25 \text{ s}^2)$

$d = 1 \text{ m} + (-0.625 \text{ m})$

$d = 0.375 \text{ m} \approx 0.38 \text{ m}$

Decelerating is set to negative.

The *net displacement* is the difference between the final and initial positions after 5 s.

14. C is correct.

a = change in velocity / change in time

$a = \Delta v / \Delta t$

15. B is correct.

Convert the final speed from km/h to m/s:

$v_f = (210 \text{ km/h}) \times [(1{,}000 \text{ m/1 km})] \times [(1 \text{ h/3,600 s})]$

$v_f = 58.33 \text{ m/s}$

Calculate the *acceleration necessary* to reach this speed:

$a = (v_f^2 - v_i^2) / 2d$

$a = [(58.33 \text{ m/s})^2 - (0 \text{ m/s})^2] / 2(1{,}800 \text{ m})$

$a = (3{,}402.39 \text{ m}^2/\text{s}^2) / (3{,}600 \text{ m})$

$a = 0.95 \text{ m/s}^2$

16. D is correct.

The *distance the rocket travels* during its acceleration upward is calculated by:

$d_1 = \frac{1}{2}at^2$

$d_1 = \frac{1}{2}(22 \text{ m/s}^2) \cdot (4 \text{ s})^2$

$d_1 = 176 \text{ m}$

The distance from when the motor shuts off to when the rocket reaches maximum height can be calculated using the conservation of energy:

$mgd_2 = \frac{1}{2}mv^2$

Cancel m from each side of the expression:

$gd_2 = \frac{1}{2}v^2$

where $v = at$

$gd_2 = \frac{1}{2}(at)^2$

$d_2 = \frac{1}{2}(at)^2 / g$

$d_2 = \frac{1}{2}[(22 \text{ m/s}^2) \cdot (4 \text{ s})]^2 / (10 \text{ m/s}^2)$

Magnitudes are not vectors but scalars, so no direction is needed

$d_2 = 387 \text{ m}$

For the maximum elevation, add the two distances:

$h = d_1 + d_2$

$h = 176 \text{ m} + 387 \text{ m}$

$h = 563 \text{ m}$

17. A is correct.

Speed is a *scalar* (i.e., one-dimensional physical property).

Velocity is a *vector* (i.e., has both magnitude and direction).

18. B is correct.

Acceleration due to gravity is constant and independent of mass.

19. D is correct.

As an object falls, its acceleration is constant due to gravity.

The magnitude of the *velocity* increases due to the acceleration of gravity.

Displacement increases because the object is going further away from its starting point.

20. C is correct.

The man is moving at constant velocity (no acceleration), so it is known immediately that the net force is zero.

The only objects interacting with man directly are Earth and the floor of the elevator.

The cable is not touching the man; it pulls the elevator car up, and the elevator floor pushes on the man.

21. D is correct.

Horizontal velocity (v_x):

$$v_x = d_x / t$$

$$v_x = (44 \text{ m}) / (2.9 \text{ s})$$

$$v_x = 15.2 \text{ m/s}$$

The x component of a vector is calculated by:

$$v_x = v \cos \theta$$

Rearrange the equation to determine the initial velocity of the ball:

$$v = v_x / \cos \theta$$

$$v = (15.2 \text{ m/s}) / (\cos 45°)$$

$$v = (15.2 \text{ m/s}) / 0.7$$

$$v = 21.4 \text{ m/s}$$

22. A is correct.

Conservation of energy:

$$mgh = \tfrac{1}{2}mv_{\mathrm{f}}^2$$

Cancel *m* from each side of the expression:

$$gh = \tfrac{1}{2}v_{\mathrm{f}}^2$$

$$(10 \text{ m/s}^2)h = \tfrac{1}{2}(14 \text{ m/s})^2$$

$$(10 \text{ m/s}^2)h = \tfrac{1}{2}(196 \text{ m}^2/\text{s}^2)$$

$$h = (98 \text{ m}^2/\text{s}^2) / (10 \text{ m/s}^2)$$

$$h = 9.8 \text{ m} \approx 10 \text{ m}$$

23. B is correct.

$$d = v_{\mathrm{i}}t + \tfrac{1}{2}at^2$$

$$d = (20 \text{ m/s}) \cdot (7 \text{ s}) + \tfrac{1}{2}(1.4 \text{ m/s}^2) \cdot (7 \text{ s})^2$$

$$d = (140 \text{ m}) + \tfrac{1}{2}(1.4 \text{ m/s}^2) \cdot (49 \text{ s}^2)$$

$$d = 174.3 \text{ m} \approx 174 \text{ m}$$

24. D is correct.

Force is *not* a scalar because it has a magnitude and direction.

25. B is correct.

$$d = \tfrac{1}{2}at^2$$

$$d_{\mathrm{A}} = \tfrac{1}{2}at^2$$

$$d_{\mathrm{B}} = \tfrac{1}{2}a(2t)^2$$

$$d_{\mathrm{B}} = \tfrac{1}{2}a(4t^2)$$

$$d_{\mathrm{B}} = 4 \times \tfrac{1}{2}at^2$$

$$d_{\mathrm{B}} = 4d_{\mathrm{A}}$$

26. A is correct.

$$d = v_{\text{average}} \times \Delta t$$

$$d = \tfrac{1}{2}(v_{\mathrm{i}} + v_{\mathrm{f}})\Delta t$$

$$d = \tfrac{1}{2}(5 \text{ m/s} + 30 \text{ m/s}) \cdot (10 \text{ s})$$

$$d = 175 \text{ m}$$

27. C is correct.

If there is no acceleration, then velocity is constant.

28. D is correct.

The gravitational force between two objects in space, each having masses of m_1 and m_2, is:

$F_G = Gm_1m_2 / r^2$

where G is the gravitational constant and r is the distance between the two objects.

Doubling the distance between the two objects:

$F_{G2} = Gm_1m_2 / (2r)^2$

$F_{G2} = Gm_1m_2 / (4r^2)$

$F_{G2} = \frac{1}{4}Gm_1m_2 / r^2$

$F_{G2} = \frac{1}{4}Gm_1m_2 / r^2$

$F_{G2} = \frac{1}{4}F_G$

Therefore, when the distance between the objects is doubled, the force (F_G) is one-fourth as much.

29. D is correct.

I: If the velocity is constant, the instantaneous velocity is always equal to the average velocity.

II and III: If the velocity increases, the average velocity value over an interval must lie between the initial and final velocity.

In going from its initial value to its final value, the instantaneous velocity must cross the average value at one point, regardless of whether the velocity is changing at a constant rate or changing irregularly.

30. C is correct.

velocity = acceleration × time

$v = at$

$v = (10 \text{ m/s}^2)\cdot(10 \text{ s})$

$v = 100 \text{ m/s}$

31. B is correct.

velocity = distance / time

$v = d / t$

d is constant, while t decreases by a factor of 3

32. C is correct.

The equation for distance, given a constant acceleration and each the initial and final velocity is:

$d = (v_i^2 + v_f^2) / 2a$

Since the car is coming to rest, $v_f = 0$

$d = v_i^2 / 2a$

If the initial velocity is doubled while acceleration and final velocity remain unchanged, the new distance is:

$d_2 = (2v_i)^2 / 2a$

$d_2 = 4(v_i^2 / 2a)$

$d_2 = 4d_1$

Another method to solve this problem:

$d_1 = (29 \text{ mi/h})^2 / 2a$

$d_2 = (59 \text{ mi/h})^2 / 2a$

$d_2 / d_1 = [(59 \text{ mi/h})^2 / 2a] / [(29 \text{ mi/h})^2 / 2a]$

$d_2 / d_1 = (59 \text{ mi/h})^2 / (29 \text{ mi/h})^2$

$d_2 / d_1 = (3{,}481 \text{ mi/h}) / (841 \text{ mi/h})$

$d_2 / d_1 = 4$

33. D is correct.

$\text{speed}_{average} = \text{total distance} / \text{time}$

$\text{speed} = (400 \text{ m}) / (20 \text{ s})$

$\text{speed} = 20 \text{ m/s}$

If this were velocity, it would be 0.

34. A is correct.

$\Delta v = a\Delta t$

$(v_f - v_i) = a\Delta t$

where $v_f = 0$ m/s (when the car stops)

$a = -0.1 \text{ m/s}^2$ (negative because deceleration), $\Delta t = 5$ s

$v_i = v_f - a\Delta t$

$v_i = [(0 \text{ m/s}) - (-0.1 \text{ m/s}^2)] \cdot (5 \text{ s})$

$v_i = (0.1 \text{ m/s}^2) \cdot (5 \text{ s})$

$v_i = 0.5 \text{ m/s}$

35. C is correct.

If acceleration is constant, then the velocity *vs.* time graph is linear, and the average velocity is the average of the final and initial velocity.

$$v_{\text{average}} = v_f - v_i / \Delta t$$

If acceleration is not constant, then the velocity *vs.* time graph is nonlinear.

$$v_{\text{average}} \neq v_f - v_i / \Delta t$$

36. D is correct.

Find velocity of the *thrown rock*:

$$v_{f1}^2 - v_i^2 = 2ad$$

$$v_{f1}^2 = v_i^2 + 2ad$$

$$v_{f1}^2 = (10 \text{ m/s})^2 + [2(9.8 \text{ m/s}^2)\cdot(300 \text{ m})]$$

$$v_{f1}^2 = 100 \text{ m}^2/\text{s}^2 + 5{,}880 \text{ m}^2/\text{s}^2$$

$$v_{f1}^2 = 5{,}980 \text{ m}^2/\text{s}^2$$

$$v_{f1} = 77.33 \text{ m/s}$$

$$t_1 = (v_f - v_i) / a$$

$$t_1 = (77.33 \text{ m/s} - 10 \text{ m/s}) / 9.8 \text{ m/s}^2$$

$$t_1 = (67.33 \text{ m/s}) / (9.8 \text{ m/s}^2)$$

$$t_1 = 6.87 \text{ s}$$

Find velocity of the *dropped rock*:

$$v_{f2} = \sqrt{2ad}$$

$$v_{f2} = \sqrt{[(2)\cdot(9.8 \text{ m/s}^2)\cdot(300 \text{ m})]}$$

$$v_{f2} = 76.7 \text{ m/s}$$

$$t_2 = (76.7 \text{ m/s}) / (9.8 \text{ m/s}^2)$$

$$t_2 = 7.82 \text{ s}$$

$$\Delta t = (7.82 \text{ s} - 6.87 \text{ s})$$

$$\Delta t = 0.95 \text{ s}$$

37. D is correct.

$$F = ma$$

Force and acceleration are directly proportional so doubling force doubles acceleration.

38. B is correct.

Velocity is a vector with speed and direction.

If speed or direction change, then the object is experiencing *acceleration*.

39. C is correct.

The acceleration is negative because it acts to slow the car down against the $+y$ direction.

It is unclear if the acceleration decreases in magnitude from the data provided.

40. A is correct.

Total distance is represented by the area under the velocity-time curve with respect to the x-axis.

Divide the graph into sections; calculate the area under the curve.

$$d_{total} = d_A + d_B + d_C + d_D$$

$$d_A = \frac{1}{2}(4 \text{ m/s}) \cdot (2 \text{ s}) = 4 \text{ m}$$

$$d_B = \frac{1}{2}(4 \text{ m/s} + 2 \text{ m/s}) \cdot (2 \text{ s}) = 6 \text{ m}$$

$$d_C = (2 \text{ m/s}) \cdot (4 \text{ s}) = 8 \text{ m}$$

Since the total distance traveled needs to be calculated, the area under the curve when the velocity is negative is calculated as a positive value.

Distance is a scalar quantity and therefore has no direction.

$$d_D = \frac{1}{2}(2 \text{ m/s}) \cdot (1 \text{ s}) + \frac{1}{2}(2 \text{ m/s}) \cdot (1 \text{ s}) = 2 \text{ m}$$

$$d_{total} = 4 \text{ m} + 6 \text{ m} + 8 \text{ m} + 2 \text{ m}$$

$$d_{total} = 20 \text{ m}$$

If the question asked to find the displacement, the area under the curve would be calculated as negative, and the answer would be 18 m.

41. C is correct.

The two bullets have different velocities when hitting the water, but they each only experience the force due to gravity.

Thus, the acceleration due to gravity is the same for each bullet.

42. A is correct.

$$v_f = v_i + at$$

$$v_f = 0 + (2.5 \text{ m/s}^2) \cdot (9 \text{ s})$$

$$v_f = 22.5 \text{ m/s}$$

43. D is correct.

The equation for impulse is used for contact between two objects over a specified period:

$$F\Delta t = m\Delta v$$

$$ma\Delta t = m(v_f - v_i)$$

Cancel m from each side of the expression:

$$a\Delta t = (v_f - v_i)$$

$$a = (v_f - v_i) / \Delta t$$

$$a = (-2v - v) / (0.45 \text{ s})$$

$$a = (-3v) / (0.45 \text{ s})$$

$$a = (-6.7 \text{ s}^{-1})v$$

Ratio $a : v = -6.7 \text{ s}^{-1} : 1$

44. B is correct.

The time for the round trip is 4 s.

The weight reaches the top of its path in ½ time:

$$\tfrac{1}{2}(4 \text{ s}) = 2 \text{ s}$$

where $v = 0$

$$a = \Delta v / t \text{ for the first half of the trip}$$

$$a = (v_f - v_i) / t$$

$$a = (0 - 3.2 \text{ m/s}) / 2 \text{ s}$$

$$a = -1.6 \text{ m/s}^2$$

$$|a| = 1.6 \text{ m/s}^2$$

Acceleration is a vector, and the negative direction only indicates direction.

45. A is correct.

$$\Delta v = a\Delta t$$

$$\Delta v = (0.3 \text{ m/s}^2)\cdot(3 \text{ s})$$

$$\Delta v = 0.9 \text{ m/s}$$

46. D is correct.

All of the following (velocity, displacement, and acceleration) are vectors, except mas

47. B is correct.

$$d = d_0 + (v_i^2 + v_f^2) / 2a$$

$$d = 64 \text{ m} + (0 \text{ m/s} + 60 \text{ m/s})^2 / 2(9.8 \text{ m/s}^2)$$

$$d = 64 \text{ m} + (3{,}600 \text{ m}^2/\text{s}^2) / (19.6 \text{ m/s}^2)$$

$$d = 64 \text{ m} + 184 \text{ m}$$

$$d = 248 \text{ m}$$

48. C is correct.

$$a = (v_f^2 + v_i^2) / 2d$$

$$a = [(60 \text{ m/s})^2 + (0 \text{ m/s})^2] / [2(64 \text{ m})]$$

$$a = (3{,}600 \text{ m}^2/\text{s}^2) / 128 \text{ m}$$

$$a = 28 \text{ m/s}^2$$

49. D is correct.

Expression for the time interval during constant acceleration upward:

$$d = \tfrac{1}{2}at^2$$

Solving for acceleration:

$$a = (v_f^2 + v_i^2) / 2d$$

$$a = [(60 \text{ m/s})^2 + (0 \text{ m/s})^2] / [2(64 \text{ m})]$$

$$a = (3{,}600 \text{ m}^2/\text{s}^2) / (128 \text{ m})$$

$$a = 28.1 \text{ m/s}^2$$

Solving for time:

$$t^2 = 2d / a$$

$$t^2 = 2(64 \text{ m}) / 28.1 \text{ m/s}^2$$

$$t^2 = 4.5 \text{ s}^2$$

$$t = 2.1 \text{ s}$$

50. C is correct.

$$d = (v_i^2 + v_f^2) / 2a$$

where $v_i = 0$

$$d = v_f^2 / 2a$$

For half the final velocity:

$$d_2 = (v_f / 2)^2 / 2a$$

$$d_2 = \tfrac{1}{4}v_f^2 / 2a$$

$$d_2 = \tfrac{1}{4}d$$

51. A is correct.

$$v_{average} = \Delta d / \Delta t$$

52. A is correct. Use an equation that relates v, d and t:

$$d = vt$$

$$v = d / t$$

If v increases by a factor of 3, then t decreases by a factor of 3.

Another method to solve this problem:

$d = vt$, $t = $ original time and $t_N = $ new time

$$d = 3vt_N$$

$$vt = d = 3vt_N$$

$$vt = 3vt_N$$

$$t = 3t_N$$

$$t / 3 = t_N$$

Thus, if v increases by a factor of 3, then the original time decreases by a factor of 3.

53. B is correct.

$$v_f = v_i + at$$

$$t = (v_f - v_i) / a$$

Since the ball is thrown straight up, its initial speed upward equals its final speed downward (just before hitting the ground): $v_f = -v_i$

$$t = [39 \text{ m/s} - (-39 \text{ m/s})] / 9.8 \text{ m/s}^2$$

$$t = (78 \text{ m/s}) / 9.8 \text{ m/s}^2$$

$$t = 8 \text{ s}$$

54. D is correct.

Since the speed is changing, the velocity is changing, and therefore there *is* an acceleration.

Since speed is *decreasing*, acceleration must be *in the reverse direction* (i.e., opposite to the direction of travel).

Since the particle is moving to the right, the acceleration vector points to the left.

If the speed increases, the acceleration is in the *same* direction as the direction of travel, and the acceleration vector points to the right.

55. A is correct.

The only force that Larry applies to the package is the normal force due to his hand (there is no horizontal force as the package moves with constant velocity.)

The normal force due to his hand points upward.

The displacement of the package is horizontal:

$W = Fd \cos \theta$,

where θ is the angle between the force and the displacement.

$\theta = 90°$

Since $\cos 90° = 0$,

$W = 0$ J

56. A is correct.

The *slope of a tangent line* on a velocity *vs.* time graph is the *acceleration at that time* point.

This is equivalent to taking the derivative of the velocity with respect to time to find instantaneous acceleration.

57. C is correct.

Since the car is initially traveling North, let North be the positive direction and South be the negative direction:

$a = (v_f - v_i) / t$

$a = (14.1 \text{ m/s} - 17.7 \text{ m/s}) / 12 \text{ s}$

$a = (-3.6 \text{ m/s}) / 12 \text{ s}$

$a = -0.3 \text{ m/s}^2$

$a = 0.3 \text{ m/s}^2$ South

58. C is correct.

Speed is represented by the magnitude of the slope of a position *vs.* time plot.

A steeper slope equates to a higher speed.

59. B is correct.

If the object has not reached terminal velocity, it continues to accelerate but at an ever-decreasing rate until the terminal velocity is reached.

60. D is correct.

Approach the problem by finding the distance traveled in each of the three segments.

$$d_1 = \tfrac{1}{2}a_1\Delta t_1^2$$

$$d_1 = (0.5)\cdot(2 \text{ m/s}^2)\cdot(10 \text{ s})^2 = 100 \text{ m}$$

The second segment:

$$d_2 = v_2\Delta t_2$$

where $\Delta t_2 = 10$ s, duration of interval 2 and v_2 is the speed during interval 2; the speed at the end of interval 1.

$$v_2 = v_{1f} = a_1\Delta t_1$$

$$v_2 = (2 \text{ m/s})\cdot(10 \text{ s}) = 20 \text{ m/s}$$

So:

$$d_2 = (20 \text{ m/s})\cdot(10 \text{ s}) = 200\text{m}$$

The third segment:

$$d_3 = (v^2_{3f} - v^2_{3i}) / 2a_3$$

$$d_3 = [(0 \text{ m/s})^2 - (20 \text{ m/s})^2] / 2(-2 \text{ m/s}^2)$$

$$d_3 = 100 \text{ m}$$

The total distance traveled is the sum of d_1, d_2 and d_3:

$$d = 100 \text{ m} + 200 \text{ m} + 100 \text{ m}$$

$$d = 400 \text{ m}$$

61. A is correct.

A car traveling in a circle with constant speed has an acceleration whose magnitude is constant but whose direction is changing.

Acceleration is a vector, so it is changing on account of its changing direction.

62. B is correct.

$$d = v_0 t + \tfrac{1}{2}at^2$$

where $v_0 = 0$

$$d = \tfrac{1}{2}at^2$$

$$t^2 = d / \tfrac{1}{2}a$$

$$t = \sqrt{(2d / a)}$$

$$t = \sqrt{[2\,(10 \text{ m}) / 9.8 \text{ m/s}^2]}$$

$$t = \sqrt{(2.04 \text{ s}^2)}$$

$$t = 1.4 \text{ s}$$

63. D is correct.

Before determining the average speed and velocity of the trip, first calculate the total time of the trip:

$$t_{\text{total}} = (d_{\text{North}} / v_{\text{North}}) + (d_{\text{South}} / v_{\text{South}})$$

$$t_{\text{total}} = (95 \text{ km} / 70 \text{ km/h}) + (21.9 \text{ km} / 80 \text{ km/h})$$

$$t_{\text{total}} = 1.36 \text{ h} + 0.27 \text{ h}$$

$$t_{\text{total}} = 1.63 \text{ h}$$

Calculate the average speed of the trip:

$$speed_{\text{avg}} = (d_{\text{North}} + d_{\text{South}}) / t_{\text{total}}$$

$$speed_{\text{avg}} = (95 \text{ km} + 21.9 \text{ km}) / 1.63 \text{ h}$$

$$speed_{\text{avg}} = (116.9 \text{ km}) / 1.63 \text{ h}$$

$$speed_{\text{avg}} = 72 \text{ km/h}$$

Calculate the average velocity of the trip, remembering that velocity is directional so set South as the negative direction:

$$v_{\text{avg}} = (d_{\text{North}} - d_{\text{South}}) / t_{\text{total}}$$

$$v_{\text{avg}} = (95 \text{ km} - 21.9 \text{ km}) / 1.63 \text{ h}$$

$$v_{\text{avg}} = (73.1 \text{ km}) / 1.63 \text{ h}$$

$$v_{\text{avg}} = 45 \text{ km/h}$$

The difference between the average speed and average velocity is:

$$speed_{\text{avg}} - v_{\text{avg}} = 72 \text{ km/h} - 45 \text{ km/h}$$

$$speed_{\text{avg}} - v_{\text{avg}} = 27 \text{ km/h}$$

64. A is correct.

Uniform acceleration: a = change in velocity / change in time

$a = \Delta v / \Delta t$

$a = 60$ mi/h / 6 s

$a = 10$ mi/h·s

$a = 10$ mi·h^{-1}·s^{-1}

65. C is correct.

For *uniform acceleration*:

$v_{avg} = \frac{1}{2}(v_1 + v_2)$

$v_{avg} = \frac{1}{2}(5$ m/s $+ 30$ m/s$)$

$v_{avg} = 17.5$ m/s

66. B is correct.

Graph I depicts a constant zero velocity process.

Graph II depicts a constant non-zero velocity.

Graph III depicts non-constant velocity.

67. C is correct.

$a = (v_i^2 + v_f^2) / 2d$

$a = [(0$ m/s$)^2 + (42$ m/s$)^2] / [2(5,600$ m$)]$

$a = (1,764$ m^2/s$^2) / 11,200$ m

$a = 0.16$ m/s^2

68. A is correct.

At the maximum height, the velocity $= 0$, and the cannonball stops moving up and begins to come back.

69. D is correct.

An object's inertia is its resistance to change in motion.

70. D is correct.

$v = v_0 + at$

If $a = 2$ m/s^2 then the object has a 2 m/s increase in velocity every second.

Example:

$v_0 = 0$ m/s, $a = 2$ m/s^2, $t = 1$ s

continued…

$$v = 0 \text{ m/s} + (2 \text{ m/s}^2)\cdot(1 \text{ s})$$

$$v = 2 \text{ m/s}$$

71. C is correct.

The acceleration due to gravity is 9.8 m/s^2.

If an object is in freefall, then every second it increases velocity by 9.8 m/s.

$$v = v_0 + at$$

$$v = v_0 + (9.8 \text{ m/s}^2)\cdot(1 \text{ s})$$

$$v = v_0 + 9.8 \text{ m/s}$$

72. B is correct.

To determine the time at which the marble stops:

$$v_2 - v_1 = a\Delta t$$

where $v_1 = 0.2 \text{ m/s}$ and $a = -0.05 \text{ m/s}^2$

$$\Delta t = (v_2 - v_1) / a$$

$$\Delta t = (0 \text{ m/s} - 0.2 \text{ m/s}) / (-0.05 \text{ m/s}^2)$$

$$\Delta t = (-0.2 \text{ m/s}) / (-0.05 \text{ m/s}^2)$$

$$\Delta t = 4 \text{ s}$$

73. D is correct.

$$v_{avg} = (1/3)v_1 + (2/3)v_2$$

$$73 \text{ km/h} = (1/3)\cdot(96.5 \text{ km/h}) + (2/3)v_2$$

$$73 \text{ km/h} = (32 \text{ km/h}) + (2/3)v_2$$

$$(2/3)v_2 = 41 \text{ km/h}$$

$$v_2 = (41 \text{ km/h})\cdot(3/2)$$

$$v_2 = 62 \text{ km/h}$$

74. A is correct.

The distance to the lightning bolt is calculated by determining the distance traveled by the sound.

$$\text{Distance} = \text{velocity} \times \text{time}$$

$$d = vt$$

$$d = (340 \text{ m/s})\cdot(6 \text{ s})$$

$$d = 2,040 \text{ m}$$

75. D is correct.

Calculate the vertical component of the initial velocity:

$v_{up} = v(\sin \theta)$

$v_{up} = (2.74 \text{ m/s}) \sin 60°$

$v_{up} = 2.37 \text{ m/s}$

Then solve for the upward displacement given the initial upward velocity:

$d = (v_f^2 - v_i^2) / 2a$

$d = [(0 \text{ m/s})^2 - (2.37 \text{ m/s})^2] / 2(-9.8 \text{ m/s}^2)$

$d = (-5.62 \text{ m}^2/\text{s}^2) / (-19.6 \text{ m/s}^2)$

$d = 0.29 \text{ m}$

76. C is correct.

30° North of East is the exact opposite direction of 30° South of West, so set one vector as negative, and the direction of the resultant vector will be in the direction of the larger vector between A and B.

Since the magnitude of A is greater than B and vectors were added "tip to tail," the resultant vector is:

$AB = A + B$

$AB = 6 \text{ m} + (-4 \text{ m})$

$AB = 2 \text{ m at } 30° \text{ North of East}$

77. D is correct.

The solution is measured in feet, so first convert the car velocity into feet per second:

$v = (49 \text{ mi/h}) \cdot (5280 \text{ ft./mi}) \cdot (1 \text{ h/3600 s})$

$v = 72 \text{ ft./s}$

The sober driver's distance:

$d = vt$

$d_{sober} = (72 \text{ ft./s}) \cdot (0.33 \text{ s})$

$d_{sober} = 24 \text{ ft.}$

The intoxicated driver's distance:

$d = vt$

$d_{drunk} = (72 \text{ ft./s}) \cdot (1 \text{ s})$

$d_{drunk} = 72 \text{ ft.}$

The differences between the distances:

$\Delta d = 72 \text{ ft.} - 24 \text{ ft.}$ $\Delta d = 48 \text{ ft.}$

Notes for active learning

Force, Motion, Gravitation – Detailed Explanations

1. B is correct.

The tension of the string keeps the weight traveling in a circular path; otherwise, it would move linearly on a tangent path to the circle. Without the string, there are no horizontal forces on the weight and no horizontal acceleration. The horizontal motion of the weight is in a straight line at a constant speed.

2. D is correct.

The vertical force on the garment bag from the left side of the clothesline is:

$$T_{y,left} = T \cos \theta$$

Similarly, for the right side:

$$T_{y,right} = T \cos \theta$$

where $T = 10$ N (tension) and $\theta = 60°$.

Since the garment bag is at rest, its acceleration is zero. Therefore, according to Newton's second law:

$$T_{y,left} + T_{y,right} - mg = 0 = 2T (\cos \theta) - mg$$

or: $\quad 2T (\cos \theta) = mg$

$$m = 2T (\cos \theta) / g$$

$$m = 2(10 \text{ N}) \cdot (\cos 60°) / (10.0 \text{ m/s}^2)$$

$$m = 2(10 \text{ N}) \cdot (0.5) / (10.0 \text{ m/s}^2)$$

$$m = 1 \text{ kg}$$

3. A is correct.

An object's inertia is its resistance to change in motion, and the milk carton has enough inertia to overcome the force of static friction.

4. C is correct.

$$(F_{net})_y = (F_N)_y - (F_g)_y$$

The car is not moving up or down, so $a_y = 0$:

$$(F_{net})_y = 0$$

$$0 = (F_N)_y - (F_g)_y$$

$$F_N = (F_g)_y$$

$$F_N = F_g \cos \theta$$

$$F_N = mg \cos \theta$$

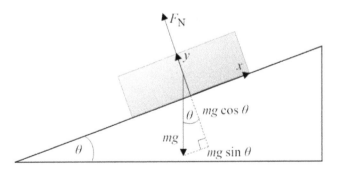

The normal force is a force that is perpendicular to the plane of contact (the slope).

5. D is correct.

$F = ma$

$F = (27 \text{ kg}) \cdot (1.7 \text{ m/s}^2)$

$F = 46 \text{ N}$

6. D is correct.

The mass on the table causes a tension force in the string that acts against the force of gravity.

7. A is correct.

Although the net force acting on the object decreases with time and the magnitude of the object's acceleration decreases, there is a positive acceleration.

Therefore, the object's speed continues to increase.

8. D is correct.

An object moving at constant velocity experiences zero net force.

9. A is correct.

The sine of an angle is equal to the opposite side over the hypotenuse:

$\sin \theta = \text{opposite} / \text{hypotenuse}$

$\sin \theta = h / L$

$h = L \sin \theta$

10. C is correct.

A car accelerating horizontally does not rely on the force of gravity to move it.

Since mass does not depend on gravity, a car on Earth and the Moon experience the same horizontal acceleration and force.

11. A is correct.

$a = (v_f - v_i) / t$

$a = (3.5 \text{ m/s} - 1.5 \text{ m/s}) / (3 \text{ s})$

$a = (2 \text{ m/s}) / (3 \text{ s})$

$a = 0.67 \text{ m/s}^2$

12. D is correct.

An object with uniform circular motion (i.e., constant angular velocity) only experiences centripetal acceleration directed toward the center of the circle.

13. B is correct.

$F = ma$, so zero force means zero acceleration in any direction.

14. C is correct.

$F = ma$

$a = F / m$

$a = 9\,\text{N} / 9\,\text{kg}$

$a = 1\,\text{m/s}^2$

15. D is correct.

The only force acting on a projectile in motion is the force due to gravity. Since that force always acts downward, there is always only a downward acceleration.

16. A is correct.

$F_{net} = ma$

If an object moves with constant v, its $a = 0$

so:

$F_{net} = 0$

Since gravity pulls down on the can with a force of mg:

$F_g = mg$

$F_g = (10\,\text{kg}){\cdot}(10\,\text{m/s}^2)$

$F_g = 100\,\text{N}$

The rope pulls *up* on the can with the same magnitude of force, so the tension is 100 N for a net force = 0.

17. D is correct.

$F = ma$

$F = (1{,}000\,\text{kg}){\cdot}(2\,\text{m/s}^2)$

$F = 2{,}000\,\text{N}$

18. C is correct.

$a_{cent} = v^2 / r$

$a_{cent} = (4\,\text{m/s})^2 / (4\,\text{m})$

$a_{cent} = (16\,\text{m}^2/\text{s}^2) / (4\,\text{m})$

$a_{cent} = 4\,\text{m/s}^2$

19. D is correct.

Solve for m_1:

$$F_{net} = 0$$

$$m_2g = F_T$$

$$m_1g \sin \theta + F_f = F_T$$

$$m_1g \sin \theta + \mu_s m_1g \cos \theta = m_2g$$

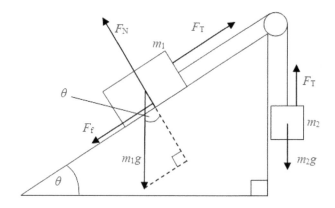

Cancel g from each side:

$$m_1(\sin \theta + \mu_s \cos \theta) = m_2$$

$$m_1 = m_2 / (\sin \theta + \mu_s \cos \theta)$$

$$m_1 = 2 \text{ kg} / [\sin 20° + (0.55) \cos 20°]$$

$$m_1 = 2 \text{ kg} / 0.86$$

$$m_1 = 2.3 \text{ kg}$$

Kinetic friction is only used when the mass is in motion.

20. B is correct.

Since the masses are identical, the force of gravity on each is the same.

The force of gravity on one of the masses produces the tension force in the string, which in turn pulls on the other mass.

Since this tension force is equal to the force of gravity, there is no net force, and the objects remain at rest.

21. B is correct.

Newton's Third Law states that for every action, there is an equal and opposite reaction.

22. A is correct.

Newton's Third Law states that for every action, there is an equal and opposite reaction.

23. C is correct.

If w denotes the magnitude of the box's weight, then the component of this force parallel to the inclined plane is $w \sin \theta$, where θ is the incline angle.

If θ is less than 90°, then $\sin \theta$ is less than 1.

The component of w parallel to the inclined plane is less than w.

24. D is correct.

The package experiences projectile motion upon leaving the truck, so it experiences no horizontal forces, and its initial velocity of 30 m/s remains unchanged.

25. D is correct.

f = revolutions / unit of time

The time (period) for one complete revolution is:

$T = 1 / f$

Each revolution represents a length of $2\pi r$.

Velocity is the distance traveled in one revolution over duration of one revolution (circumference over period):

$v = 2\pi r / t$

$v = 2\pi rf$

If f doubles, then v doubles.

26. A is correct.

$F = ma$

$m = F / a$

$m = 4{,}500 \text{ N} / 5 \text{ m/s}^2$

$m = 900 \text{ kg}$

27. D is correct.

Newton's First Law states that every object will remain at rest or in uniform motion unless acted upon by an outside force.

In this case, Steve and the bus are in uniform constant motion until the bus stops due to sudden deceleration (the ground exerts no frictional force on Steve).

There is no force acting upon Steve, and his inertia carries him forward because he is still in uniform motion while the bus comes to a stop.

28. D is correct.

The ball is in a state of rest, so $F_{net} = 0$

$F_{down} = F_{up}$

$F_{external} + F_{w} = F_{buoyant}$

$F_{external} = F_{buoyant} - F_{w}$

$F_{external} = 8.4 \text{ N} - 4.4 \text{ N}$

$F_{external} = 4 \text{ N}$, in the same direction as the weight

29. A is correct.

The luggage and the train move at the same speed, so when the luggage moves forward with respect to the train, it means the train has slowed down while the luggage continues to move at its original speed.

30. D is correct.

The mass does not change by changing the object's location.

Since the object is outside of Earth's atmosphere, the object's weight is represented by:

$F_g = GmM_{Earth} / R^2$

If the altitude is $2R_{Earth}$, then the distance from the center of the Earth is $3R_{Earth}$.

The gravitational acceleration decreases by a factor of $3^2 = 9$ ($g = GmM / R^2$).

Weight decreases by a factor of 9.

New weight = 360 N / 9 = 40 N

31. C is correct.

The velocity of the rock just after its release is the same as the truck.

Once in free fall, there are no horizontal forces on the rock, and the rock's velocity remains unchanged and is equal to that of the truck.

32. D is correct.

The acceleration of Jason due to thrust is:

$F_{net} = ma_1$

$ma_1 = F_{ski} - \mu_k mg$

$a_1 = (F_{ski} - \mu_k mg) / m$

$a_1 = [200 \text{ N} - (0.1) \cdot (75 \text{ kg}) \cdot (9.8 \text{ m/s}^2)] / 75 \text{ kg}$

$a_1 = (126.5 \text{ N}) / 75 \text{ kg}$

$a_1 = 1.69 \text{ m/s}^2$

The distance traveled during the acceleration stage is:

$d_1 = \frac{1}{2}a_1t^2$

$d_1 = \frac{1}{2}(1.69 \text{ m/s}^2) \cdot (67 \text{ s})^2$

$d_1 = 3,793 \text{ m}$

The distance traveled after the skis run out of fuel is:

$d_2 = (v_f^2 - v_i^2) / 2a_2$

continued…

a_2 is Jason's acceleration after the fuel runs out:

$F_{net} = ma_2$

$ma_2 = -\mu_k mg$

Cancel m from each side of the expression:

$a_2 = -\mu_k g$

$a_2 = -(0.1) \cdot (9.8 \text{ m/s}^2)$

$a_2 = -0.98 \text{ m/s}^2$

The acceleration is negative since the frictional force opposes the direction of motion.

v_i is the velocity at the moment when the fuel runs out:

$v_i = a_1 t$

$v_i = (1.69 \text{ m/s}^2) \cdot (67 \text{ s})$

$v_i = 113.2 \text{ m/s}$

Substitute a_2 and v_i into the equation for d_2:

$d_2 = [(0 \text{ m/s})^2 - (113.2 \text{ m/s})^2] / 2(-0.98 \text{ m/s}^2)$

$d_2 = (-12{,}814.2 \text{ m}^2/\text{s}^2) / -1.96 \text{ m/s}^2$

$d_2 = 6{,}538 \text{ m}$

The total distance Jason traveled is:

$d_{total} = d_1 + d_2$

$d_{total} = 3{,}793 \text{ m} + 6{,}538 \text{ m}$

$d_{total} = 10{,}331 \text{ m}$

33. D is correct.

Using the force analysis:

$F_{net} = F_g + F_{fk}$

$F_g = mg \sin \theta$

$F_g = (0.2 \text{ kg}) \cdot (-9.8 \text{ m/s}^2) \sin 30°$

$F_g = (0.2 \text{ kg}) \cdot (-9.8 \text{ m/s}^2) \cdot (1/2)$

$F_g = -1 \text{ N}$

$F_{fk} = \mu_k F_N$

$F_{fk} = \mu_k mg \cos \theta$

$F_{fk} = (0.3) \cdot (0.2 \text{ kg}) \cdot (-9.8 \text{ m/s}^2) \cos 30°$

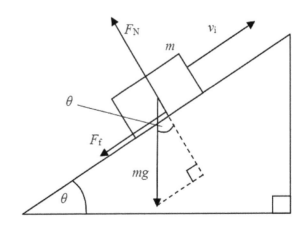

continued...

$F_{fk} = (0.3) \cdot (0.2 \text{ kg}) \cdot (-9.8 \text{ m/s}^2) \cdot (0.866)$

$F_{fk} = -0.5 \text{ N}$

$F_{net} = -1 \text{ N} + (-0.5 \text{ N})$

$F_{net} = -1.5 \text{ N}$

$a = F_{net} / m$

$a = -1.5 \text{ N} / 0.2 \text{ kg}$

$a = -7.5 \text{ m/s}^2$

The distance it travels until it reaches a velocity of 0 at its maximum height:

$d = (v_f^2 - v_i^2) / 2a$

$d = [(0 \text{ m/s})^2 - (63 \text{ m/s})^2] / 2(-7.5 \text{ m/s}^2)$

$d = (-4{,}000 \text{ m}^2/\text{s}^2) / (-15 \text{ m/s}^2)$

$d = 267 \text{ m}$

The vertical height is:

$h = d \sin \theta$

$h = (267 \text{ m}) \sin 30°$

$h = (267 \text{ m}) \cdot (0.5)$

$h = 130 \text{ m}$

Alternatively, using energy to solve the problem:

$KE = PE + W_f$

$\frac{1}{2}mv^2 = mgd \sin \theta + \mu_k mgd \cos \theta$

Cancel m from the expression:

$\frac{1}{2}v^2 = gd \sin \theta + \mu_k gd \cos \theta$

$\frac{1}{2}v^2 = d(g \sin \theta + \mu_k g \cos \theta)$

$d = v^2 / [2g(\sin \theta + \mu_k \cos \theta)]$

$d = (63 \text{ m/s})^2 / [(2) \cdot (9.8 \text{ m/s}^2) \cdot (\sin 30° + 0.3 \times \cos 30°)]$

$d = 267 \text{ m}$

$h = d \sin \theta$

$h = (267 \text{ m}) \sin 30°$

$h = 130 \text{ m}$

---

34. A is correct.

$$F = ma$$

$$a = F / m$$

$$a_1 = F / 4 \text{ kg}$$

$$a_2 = F / 10 \text{ kg}$$

$$4a_1 = 10a_2$$

$$a_1 = 2.5a_2$$

35. D is correct.

Mass is independent of gravity.

However, weight is not independent of gravity; as a person moves farther away from stars or planets, the gravitational pull decreases, and therefore, her weight decreases.

36. A is correct.

Newton's Third Law describes that when one object pushes on another, the second object pushes back with the same force. Mathematically, it can be expressed as $F_{\text{AonB}} = -F_{\text{BonA}}$

In the described scenario, the force that the truck exerts on the car is in the opposite direction to the force that the car exerts on the truck (push on each other) and, crucially, the *magnitudes* of the two forces are the same.

This may seem counterintuitive since it is known that the car will get far more damaged than the truck.

To understand this apparent contradiction, remember Newton's Second Law which states that the car will *accelerate* at a much higher rate (since it is less massive than the truck).

It is this extreme acceleration that causes the car to be destroyed.

Therefore, to understand this situation entirely, two Newton's laws must be applied:

The Third Law states that each vehicle experiences a force of the same magnitude.

The Second Law describes why the car *responds* to that force more violently due to its smaller mass.

37. D is correct.

$$m = F / a_{\text{Earth}}$$

$$m = 20 \text{ N} / 3 \text{ m/s}^2$$

$$m = 6.67 \text{ kg}$$

$$F_{\text{Moon}} = mg_{\text{Moon}}$$

$$F_{\text{Moon}} = (6.67 \text{ kg}) \cdot (1.62 \text{ m/s}^2)$$

$$F_{\text{Moon}} = 11 \text{ N}$$

38. B is correct.

weight = mass × gravity

$w = (0.4 \text{ kg}) \cdot (9.8 \text{ m/s}^2)$

$w \approx 4 \text{ N}$

39. B is correct.

Need an expression that connects time and mass.

Given information for F, v_1, and d:

$a = F / m$

$d = v_1 t + \frac{1}{2} a t^2$

Combine the expressions and set $v_i = 0$ m/s because initial velocity is zero:

$d = \frac{1}{2} a t^2$

$a = F / m$

$d = \frac{1}{2} (F / m) t^2$

$t^2 = 2dm / F$

$t = \sqrt{(2dm / F)}$

If m increases by a factor of 4, t increases by a factor of $\sqrt{4} = 2$

40. C is correct.

$a = (v_f^2 - v_i^2) / 2d$

$a = [(0 \text{ m/s})^2 - (27 \text{ m/s})^2] / 2(578 \text{ m})$

$a = (-729 \text{ m}^2/\text{s}^2) / 1{,}056 \text{ m}$

$a = -0.63 \text{ m/s}^2$

$F = ma$

$F = (1{,}100 \text{ kg}) \cdot (-0.63 \text{ m/s}^2)$

$F = -690 \text{ N}$

The car is decelerating, so the acceleration (therefore, the force) is negative.

41. A is correct.

Constant speed upward means no net force.

Tension = weight (equals Mg)

42. C is correct.

Weight $= mg$

$75 \text{ N} = mg$

$m = 75 \text{ N} / 9.8 \text{ m/s}^2$

$m = 7.65 \text{ kg}$

$F_{net} = F_{right} - F_{left}$

$F_{net} = 50 \text{ N} - 30 \text{ N}$

$F_{net} = 20 \text{ N}$

$F_{net} = ma$

$a = F_{net} / m$

$a = 20 \text{ N} / 7.65 \text{ kg}$

$a = 2.6 \text{ m/s}^2$

43. B is correct.

The string was traveling at the same velocity as the plane with respect to the ground outside.

When the plane began accelerating backward (decelerating), the string continued to move forward at its original velocity and appeared to go towards the front of the plane.

Since the string is attached to the ceiling at one end, only the bottom of the string moved.

44. C is correct.

If the object slides down the ramp with a constant speed, velocity is constant.

Acceleration and the net force $= 0$

$F_{net} = F_{grav \text{ down ramp}} - F_{friction}$

$F_{net} = mg \sin \theta - \mu_k mg \cos \theta$

$F_{net} = 0$

$mg \sin \theta - \mu_k mg \cos \theta = 0$

$mg \sin \theta = \mu_k mg \cos \theta$

$\mu_k = \sin \theta / \cos \theta$

45. A is correct.

The net force on an object in free fall is equal to its weight.

46. C is correct.

$a = \Delta v / \Delta t$

$a = (v_f - v_i) / t$

$a = (20 \text{ m/s} - 0 \text{ m/s}) / (10 \text{ s})$

$a = (20 \text{ m/s}) / (10 \text{ s})$

$a = 2 \text{ m/s}^2$

47. D is correct.

Since the object does not move, it is in a state of equilibrium, so forces act on it that equal and oppose the force *F* that Yania applies to the object.

48. D is correct.

Newton's Third Law describes that *when one object pushes on another, the second object pushes back with the same force.* Mathematically, it can be expressed as:

$F_{AonB} = -F_{BonA}$

In this situation, if one pushes on an object with force *F*, the object must push back on them equally strongly (magnitude is *F*) and in the opposite direction (hence the negative sign).

Therefore, the force vector of the object is just $-F$.

49. C is correct.

$F = mg$

$m = F / g$

$m = 685 \text{ N} / 9.8 \text{ m/s}^2$

$m = 69.9 \text{ kg} \approx 70 \text{ kg}$

50. A is correct.

$m_{Bob} = 4m_{Sarah}$

Conservation of momentum, since the system (Bob and Sarah combined) initially, had a total momentum of 0, in the final state, Sarah's momentum and Bob's momentum must add to 0 (i.e., they will be the same magnitude, but opposite directions).

$m_{Bob}v_{Bob} = m_{Sarah}v_{Sarah}$

$4m_{Sarah}\,v_{Bob} = m_{Sarah}v_{Sarah}$

$4v_{Bob} = v_{Sarah}$

51. C is correct.

For most surfaces, the coefficient of static friction is greater than the coefficient of kinetic friction.

Thus, the force needed to overcome static friction and start the object's motion is greater than the amount of force needed to overcome kinetic friction and keep the object moving at a constant velocity.

52. B is correct.

Weight on Jupiter:

$$W = mg$$

$$W = m(3g)$$

$$W = (100 \text{ kg}) \cdot (3 \times 10 \text{ m/s}^2)$$

$$W = 3{,}000 \text{ N}$$

53. D is correct.

Neither Joe nor Bill is moving, so the net force is zero:

$$F_{net} = F_{Joe} - F_T$$

$$0 = F_{Joe} - F_T$$

$$F_{Joe} = F_T$$

$$F_T = 200 \text{ N}$$

54. D is correct.

Tension in the rope is always equal to F_T.

The net force on block A to the right is:

$$F_{right} = m_A a_A = 2F_T$$

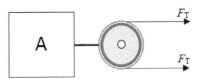

The net force of block B downward is:

$$F_{down} = m_B a_B = m_B g - F_T$$

Since block A is connected to both the pulley at the end of the table and the wall, it uses twice the rope length to travel the same distance as block B.

Therefore, the *distance* block A moves is half that of block B.

The *velocity* of block A is half the velocity of block B.

The *acceleration* of block A is half the acceleration of block B:

$$a_A = a_B / 2$$

$$F_{right} = m_A(a_B / 2)$$

$$m_A(a_B / 2) = 2F_T \qquad\qquad\qquad \textit{continued...}$$

$m_A a_B = 4F_T$

$F_T = \frac{1}{4} m_A a_B$

$m_B a_B = m_B g - \frac{1}{4} m_A a_B$

$m_B a_B + \frac{1}{4} m_A a_B = m_B g$

$a_B [m_B + \frac{1}{4} m_A] = m_B g$

$a_B = m_B g / [m_B + \frac{1}{4} m_A]$

$a_B = (5\ kg)\cdot(9.8\ m/s^2) / [5\ kg + \frac{1}{4}(4\ kg)]$

$a_B = 49\ N / 6\ kg$

$a_B = 8.2\ m/s^2$

$a_A = a_B / 2$

$a_A = (8.2\ m/s^2) / 2$

$a_A = 4.1\ m/s^2$

55. B is correct.

The force exerted by one surface on another has a perpendicular component (i.e., normal force) and a parallel component (i.e., friction force).

The force of kinetic friction on an object acts opposite to the direction of its velocity relative to the surface.

56. D is correct.

The scale measures the force of interaction between the person and the floor, the normal force.

The question asks to find the normal force.

Use Newton's Second Law:

$F = ma,$

where the net force is the result of the force of gravity and the normal force.

$F_{net} = F_{normal} - F_{gravity} = N - W$

Here, W is the normal weight of the object, $W = mg$. Therefore, Newton's Law becomes:

$N - W = ma = (W / g)\ a$

Solve for the reading of the scale, N, noting that the acceleration is negative:

$N = W (1 + a / g)$

$N = (600\ N)\cdot(1 + -6\ m/s^2 / 9.8\ m/s^2)$

$N = (600\ N)\cdot(0.388)$

$N = 233\ N$

57. B is correct.

Newton's Third Law states that when two objects interact by a mutual force, the force of the first on the second is equal in magnitude to the force of the second on the first.

58. D is correct.

Since the crate can only move in the horizontal direction, only consider the horizontal component of the applied force when computing the acceleration.

$F_x = F \cos \theta$

$F_x = (140 \text{ N}) \cos 30°$

$F_x = (140 \text{ N}) \cdot (0.866)$

$F_x = 121 \text{ N}$

$a = F_x / m$

$a = 121 \text{ N} / 40 \text{ kg}$

$a = 3 \text{ m/s}^2$

59. C is correct.

Vectors indicate magnitude and direction, while scalars only indicate magnitude.

60. B is correct.

The gravitational force and the direction of travel are perpendiculars:

$W = Fd \cos \theta$

$\cos \theta = 0$

61. D is correct.

Work = Force × distance

$W_{rope} = Fd_x$

$W_{rope} = Fd \cos \theta$

$d = vt$

$d = (2.5 \text{ m/s}) \cdot (4 \text{ s})$

$W_{rope} = (30 \text{ N}) \cdot (10 \text{ m}) \cos 30°$

$W_{rope} = 260 \text{ J}$

62. B is correct.

Arrow in flight:

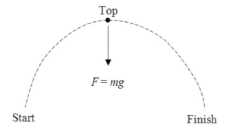

The weight of the arrow is:

W = *mg*

At the top of its flight and throughout its flight, the acceleration of gravity acts on the arrow:

F = *ma*

F = *mg*

F = W

63. D is correct.

F = *mg*

m = *F* / *g*

m = (740 N) / (10 m/s^2)

m = 74 kg

g_p = F_p / *m*

g_p = (5,180 N) / (74 kg)

g_p = 70 m/s^2

64. B is correct.

Newton's Third Law states that when two objects interact by a mutual force, the force of the first on the second is equal in magnitude to the force of the second on the first.

65. A is correct.

Newton's Second Law (*F* = *ma*) is rearranged:

a = *F* / *m*

If *F* is constant, then *a* is inversely proportional to *m*.

A larger mass implies a smaller *F* / *m* ratio; the ratio is the acceleration.

66. C is correct.

$$F = ma$$

So, doubling the force doubles the acceleration.

67. B is correct.

Pythagorean Theorem ($a^2 + b^2 = c^2$) to calculate the net force:

$$F_1^2 + F_2^2 = F_{net}^2$$

$$(500 \text{ N})^2 + (1{,}200 \text{ N})^2 = F_{net}^2$$

$$250{,}000 \text{ N}^2 + 1{,}440{,}000 \text{ N}^2 = F_{net}^2$$

$$F_{net}^2 = 1{,}690{,}000 \text{ N}^2$$

$$F_{net} = 1{,}300 \text{ N}$$

Newton's Second Law:

$$F = ma$$

$$a = F_{net} / m$$

$$a = 1{,}300 \text{ N} / 500 \text{ kg}$$

$$a = 2.6 \text{ m/s}^2$$

68. D is correct.

The acceleration of the 2 kg block is the acceleration of the system because the blocks are linked.

Balance forces and solve for acceleration:

$$F_{net} = m_3g - m_2g\mu_k - m_1g$$

$$(m_3 + m_2 + m_1)a = m_3g - m_2g\mu_k - m_1g$$

$$a = (m_3 - m_2\mu_k - m_1)g / (m_3 + m_2 + m_1)$$

$$a = [3 \text{ kg} - (2 \text{ kg}) \cdot (0.25) - 1 \text{ kg}] \cdot (9.8 \text{ m/s}^2) / (3 \text{ kg} + 2 \text{ kg} + 1 \text{ kg})$$

$$a = 2.5 \text{ m/s}^2$$

69. A is correct.

Objects moving at constant velocity experience no acceleration.

Therefore, no net force.

70. B is correct.

The cart decelerates, an acceleration in the opposite direction caused by the force of friction in the opposite direction.

71. C is correct.

Newton's Third Law states that when two objects interact by a mutual force, the force of the first on the second is equal in magnitude to the force of the second on the first.

72. B is correct.

If the bureau moves in a straight line at a constant speed, its velocity is constant.

Therefore, the bureau is experiencing zero acceleration and zero net force.

The force of kinetic friction equals the 30 N force that pulls the bureau.

73. A is correct.

Newton's First Law states that an object at rest tends to stay at rest, and an object in motion tends to maintain that motion unless acted upon by an unbalanced force.

This law depends on a property of an object called inertia, which is inherently linked to the object's mass.

More massive objects are more difficult to move and manipulate than less massive objects.

74. B is correct.

$$F_g = Gm_{Earth}m_{moon} / d^2$$

d is the distance between the Earth and the Moon.

If d decreases by a factor of 4, F_g increases by a factor of $4^2 = 16$

75. C is correct.

Find equal and opposite forces:

$$F_{Rx} = -F_1$$

$$F_{Rx} = -(-6.6 \text{ N})$$

$$F_{Rx} = 6.6 \text{ N}$$

$$F_{Ry} = -F_2$$

$$F_{Ry} = -2.2 \text{ N}$$

Pythagorean Theorem ($a^2 + b^2 = c^2$) to calculate the magnitude of the resultant force:

The magnitude of F_R:

$$F_R{}^2 = F_{Rx}{}^2 + F_{Ry}{}^2$$

$$F_R{}^2 = (6.6 \text{ N})^2 + (-2.2 \text{ N})^2$$

$$F_R{}^2 = 43.6 \text{ N}^2 + 4.8 \text{ N}^2$$

$$F_R{}^2 = 48.4 \text{ N}^2$$

$$F_R = 7 \text{ N}$$

continued…

The direction of F_R:

$\theta = \tan^{-1} (-2.2 \text{ N} / 6.6 \text{ N})$

$\theta = \tan^{-1} (-1 / 3)$

$\theta = 342°$

The direction of F_R with respect to F_1:

$\theta = 342° - 180°$

$\theta = 162°$ counterclockwise of F_1

76. D is correct.

Each scale weighs the fish at 17 kg, so the sum of the two scales is:

$17 \text{ kg} + 17 \text{ kg} = 34 \text{ kg}$

77. D is correct.

If θ is the angle with respect to a horizontal line, then:

$\theta = \frac{1}{2}(40°)$

$\theta = 20°$

Therefore, for the third force to cause equilibrium, the sum of all three forces' components must equal zero.

Since F_1 and F_2 mirror each other in the y-direction:

$F_{1y} + F_{2y} = 0$

Therefore, for F_3 to balance the forces in the y direction, its y component must equal zero:

$F_{1y} + F_{2y} + F_{3y} = 0$

$0 + F_{3y} = 0$

$F_{3y} = 0$

Since the y-component of F_3 is zero, the angle that F_3 makes with the horizontal is zero:

$\theta_3 = 0°$

The x component of F_3:

$F_{1x} + F_{2x} + F_{3x} = 0$

$F_1 \cos \theta + F_2 \cos \theta + F_3 \cos \theta = 0$

$F_3 = -(F_2 \cos \theta_2 + F_3 \cos \theta_3)$

$F_3 = -[(2.3 \text{ N}) \cos 20° + (2.3 \text{ N}) \cos 20°]$

$F_3 = -4.3 \text{ N}$

$F_3 = 4.3 \text{ N}$ to the right

78. D is correct.

At $\theta = 17°$, the force of static friction is equal to the force due to gravity:

$F_f = F_g$

$\mu_s mg \cos \theta = mg \sin \theta$

$\mu_s = \sin \theta / \cos \theta$

$\mu_s = \tan \theta$

$\mu_s = \tan 17°$

$\mu_s = 0.31$

79. B is correct.

The force of the table on the book, the normal force (F_N), is a result of Newton's Third Law of Motion, which states that there is an equal and opposite reaction for every action.

A book sitting on the table experiences a force from the table equal to the book's weight:

$W = mg$

$F_N = W$

$F_N = mg$

$F_N = (2 \text{ kg}) \cdot (10 \text{ m/s}^2)$

$F_N = 20 \text{ N}$

Notes for active learning

Notes for active learning

Equilibrium and Momentum – Detailed Explanations

1. A is correct.

The rate of change of angular momentum of a system is equal to the net external torque:

$$\tau_{net} = \Delta L / \Delta t$$

If the angular momentum is constant, then the net external torque must be zero.

2. D is correct.

If the velocity is 7 m/s down the mountain, the horizontal component v_x is:

$$v_x = v \cos \theta$$

$$1.8 \text{ m/s} = (7 \text{ m/s}) \cos \theta$$

$$\cos \theta = 0.26$$

$$\theta \approx 75°$$

3. D is correct.

The hill exerts a normal force on the sled, and this force is *perpendicular* to the surface of the hill.

There is no parallel force that the hill exerts because it is frictionless.

4. C is correct.

Assuming the water flow is tangent to the wheel, it is perpendicular to the radius vector at the point of contact.

The torque around the center of the wheel is:

$$\tau = rF$$

$$\tau = (10 \text{ m}) \cdot (300 \text{ N})$$

$$\tau = 3,000 \text{ N·m}$$

5. D is correct.

$$1 \text{ revolution} = 360°$$

$$1 \text{ min} = 60 \text{ s}$$

$$33 \text{ rpm} = 33 \text{ rev/min}$$

$$(33 \text{ rev/min}) \cdot (360°/\text{rev}) = 11,880°/\text{min}$$

$$(11,880°/\text{min}) \cdot (1 \text{ min}/60 \text{ s}) = 198°/\text{s}$$

Degrees per second is a *rate*:

$$\text{rate} \times \text{time} = \text{total degrees}$$

$$(198°/\text{s}) \cdot (0.32 \text{ s}) \approx 63°$$

6. B is correct.

momentum = mass × velocity

$p = mv$

Since *momentum is directly proportional to mass*, doubling the mass doubles the momentum.

7. D is correct.

The *total momentum before* the collision is:

$p_{total} = m_I v_I + m_{II} v_{II} + m_{III} v_{III}$

$p_{before} = (1 \text{ kg}) \cdot (0.5 \text{ m/s}) + (1.5 \text{ kg}) \cdot (-0.3 \text{ m/s}) + (3.5 \text{ kg}) \cdot (-0.5 \text{ m/s})$

$p_{before} = (0.5 \text{ kg·m/s}) + (-0.45 \text{ kg·m/s}) + (-1.75 \text{ kg·m/s})$

$p_{before} = -1.7 \text{ kg·m/s}$

8. A is correct.

The collision of I and II does not affect the momentum of the system:

$p_{before} = p_{after}$

$p_{I \& II} = (1 \text{ kg}) \cdot (0.5 \text{ m/s}) + (1.5 \text{ kg}) \cdot (-0.3 \text{ m/s})$

$p_{I \& II} = (0.5 \text{ kg·m/s}) - (0.45 \text{ kg·m/s})$

$p_{I \& II} = 0.05 \text{ kg·m/s}$

$p_{III} = (3.5 \text{ kg}) \cdot (-0.5 \text{ m/s})$

$p_{III} = -1.75 \text{ kg·m/s}$

$p_{net} = p_{I \text{ and } II} + p_{III}$

$p_{net} = (0.05 \text{ kg·m/s}) + (-1.75 \text{ kg·m/s})$

$p_{net} = -1.7 \text{ kg·m/s}$

Momentum is always conserved.

9. B is correct.

Set initial momentum equal to the final momentum after the collisions have occurred.

$p_{before} = p_{after}$

$p_{before} = (m_I + m_{II} + m_{III}) v_f$

$-1.7 \text{ kg·m/s} = (1 \text{ kg} + 1.5 \text{ kg} + 3.5 \text{ kg}) v_f$

$v_f = (-1.7 \text{ kg·m/s}) / (6 \text{ kg})$

$v_f = -0.28 \text{ m/s}$

10. C is correct.

Momentum is conserved in this system. The momentum of each car is given by mv, and the sum of the momenta before the collision must equal the sum of the momenta after the collision:

$$p_{before} = p_{after}$$

Solve for the velocity of the first car after the collision.

Each car travels in the same direction before and after the collision, so each velocity value has the same sign.

$$m_1 v_{i1} + m_2 v_{i2} = m_1 v_{f1} + m_2 v_{f2}$$

$$(480 \text{ kg})\cdot(14.4 \text{ m/s}) + (570 \text{ kg})\cdot(13.3 \text{ m/s}) = (480 \text{ kg})\cdot(v_{f2}) + (570 \text{ kg})\cdot(17.9 \text{ m/s})$$

$$(480 \text{ kg})\cdot(v_{f2}) = (480 \text{ kg})\cdot(14.4 \text{ m/s}) + (570 \text{ kg})\cdot(13.3 \text{ m/s}) - (570 \text{ kg})\cdot(17.9 \text{ m/s})$$

$$v_{f2} = [(480 \text{ kg})\cdot(14.4 \text{ m/s}) + (570 \text{ kg})\cdot(13.3 \text{ m/s}) - (570 \text{ kg})\cdot(17.9 \text{ m/s})] / (480 \text{ kg})$$

$$v_{f2} = 8.9 \text{ m/s} \approx 9 \text{ m/s}$$

11. D is correct.

Impulse is a force acting over a period of time:

$$J = F\Delta t$$

An impulse changes a system's momentum, so:

$$F\Delta t = \Delta p_{system}$$

The moving block with the lodged bullet comes to a stop when it compresses the spring, losing all momentum.

Initial velocity of the block and bullet separately can be determined by conservation of energy.

The two values of interest are the KE of the block and bullet and the PE of the spring.

$$(KE + PE)_{before} = (KE + PE)_{after}$$

$$\tfrac{1}{2}mv^2 + 0 = 0 + \tfrac{1}{2}kx^2$$

x = distance of compression of the spring

k = spring constant

$$\tfrac{1}{2}(4 \text{ kg} + 0.008 \text{ kg})v^2 = \tfrac{1}{2}(1,400 \text{ N/m})\cdot(0.089 \text{ m})^2$$

$$v^2 = (1,400 \text{ N/m})\cdot(0.089 \text{ m})^2 / (4.008 \text{ kg})$$

$$v^2 = 2.76 \text{ m}^2/\text{s}^2$$

$$v = 1.66 \text{ m/s}$$

Thus, the block with the lodged bullet hits the spring with an initial velocity of 1.66 m/s.

Since there is no friction, the block is sent in the opposite direction with the same speed of 1.66 m/s when the spring decompresses.

continued…

Calculate the momentum, with initial momentum toward the spring and final momentum away from the spring.

$\Delta p = p_{final} - p_{initial}$

$\Delta p = (4.008 \text{ kg})\cdot(-1.66 \text{ m/s}) - (4.008 \text{ kg})\cdot(1.66 \text{ m/s})$

$\Delta p = (-6.65 \text{ kg·m/s}) - (6.65 \text{ kg·m/s})$

$\Delta p \approx -13 \text{ kg·m/s}$

$\Delta p \approx -13 \text{ N·s}$

Since $F\Delta t = \Delta p$, the impulse is -13 kg·m/s $= -13$ N·s

The negative sign signifies the coordinate system chosen in this calculation: toward the spring is the positive direction, and away from the spring is the negative direction.

12. C is correct.

For a rotating body, kinetic energy is:

$K = \frac{1}{2} I \omega^2$

Angular momentum is:

$L = I \omega$

Therefore:

$I = L / \omega$

Replacing this for I in the expression for kinetic energy:

$K = L^2 / 2I$

Taking the ice to be frictionless, there is no external torque on the skater.

Thus, angular momentum is conserved and does not change as she brings in her arms.

The moment of inertia of a body of a given mass is smaller if its mass is more concentrated toward the rotation axis (e.g., when she draws her arms in close). Therefore, the moment of inertia of the skater decreases.

Consequently, the skater's kinetic energy increases.

13. D is correct.

The centripetal force is the net force required to maintain an object in uniform circular motion.

$F_{centripetal} = mv^2/r$

where r is the radius of the circular path

Since m is constant and r remains unchanged, the centripetal force is proportional to v^2.

$2^2 = 4$

Thus, if v is doubled, then $F_{centripetal}$ is quadrupled.

14. B is correct.

$$1 \text{ J} = \text{kg·m}^2/\text{s}^2$$

$$p = mv = \text{kg·m/s}$$

$$\text{J·s/m} = (\text{kg·m}^2/\text{s}^2)\cdot(\text{s/m})$$

$$\text{J·s/m} = \text{kg·m/s}$$

$$\text{kg·m/s} = p$$

$$\text{J·s/m} = p$$

15. D is correct.

Impulse is a change in momentum.

$$J = \Delta p$$

$$J = m\Delta v$$

Impulse is the product of average force and time.

$$J = F\Delta t$$

$$F\Delta t = m\Delta v$$

$$ma\Delta t = m\Delta v$$

Cancel m from each side of the expression:

$$a\Delta t = \Delta v$$

Because acceleration g is constant impulse depends only upon time and velocity.

The speed of the apple affects the impulse, as this is included in the Δv term.

Bouncing results in a change in direction; a greater change in velocity (the Δv term), so the impulse is greater.

The time of impulse changes the impulse as it is included in the Δt term.

16. D is correct.

$$F\Delta t = m\Delta v$$

$$F = m\Delta v \,/\, \Delta t$$

Choosing toward the wall as the positive direction, the initial velocity is 25 m/s, and the final is –25 m/s:

$$F = m(v_f - v_i) \,/\, \Delta t$$

$$F = (0.8 \text{ kg})\cdot(-25 \text{ m/s} - 25 \text{ m/s}) \,/\, (0.05 \text{ s})$$

$$F = -800 \text{ N}$$

Thus, the wall exerts an average force of 800 N on the ball in a negative direction.

From Newton's Third Law, the ball exerts a force of 800 N on the wall in the opposite direction.

17. B is correct.

$p = mv$

Sum momentum:

$p_{\text{total}} = m_1v_1 + m_2v_2 + m_3v_3$

All objects moving to the left have negative velocity.

$p_{\text{total}} = (7\text{ kg})\cdot(6\text{ m/s}) + (12\text{ kg})\cdot(3\text{ m/s}) + (4\text{ kg})\cdot(-2\text{ m/s})$

$p_{\text{total}} = (42\text{ kg·m/s}) + (36\text{ kg·m/s}) + (-8\text{ kg·m/s})$

$p_{\text{total}} = 70\text{ kg·m/s}$

18. D is correct.

Use conservation of momentum to determine the momentum after the collision. Since they stick, treat it as a perfectly inelastic collision.

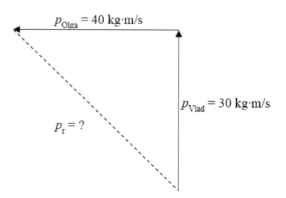

Before the collision, Vladimir's momentum is:

$(60\text{ kg})\cdot(0.5\text{ m/s}) = 30\text{ kg·m/s}$ pointing North

Before the collision, Olga's momentum is:

$(40\text{ kg})\cdot(1\text{ m/s}) = 40\text{ kg·m/s}$ pointing West

Write two expressions: one for the conservation of momentum on the *y*-axis (North-South) and one for the conservation of momentum on the *x*-axis (East-West). They do not interact since as perpendiculars.

Since Olga and Vladimir stick, the final mass is the sum of their masses.

Simply use the Pythagorean Theorem:

$a^2 + b^2 = c^2$

$(30\text{ kg·m/s})^2 + (40\text{ kg·m/s})^2 = p^2$

$900\text{ (kg·m/s)}^2 + 1{,}600\text{ (kg·m/s)}^2 = p^2$

$2{,}500\text{(kg·m/s)}^2 = p^2$

$p = 50\text{ kg·m/s}$

Use this to solve for velocity:

$p = mv$

$50\text{ kg·m/s} = (100\text{ kg})v$

$v = 50\text{ kg·m/s} / 100\text{ kg}$

$v = 0.5\text{ m/s}$

continued…

Also, this problem can be solved algebraically:

$p_{\text{before}} = p_{\text{after}}$

$p = mv$

On the y-coordinate:

$(60 \text{ kg}) \cdot (0.5 \text{ m/s}) = (60 \text{ kg} + 40 \text{ kg})v_y$

$v_y = (30 \text{ kg·m/s}) / (100 \text{ kg})$

$v_y = 0.3 \text{ m/s}$

On the x-coordinate:

$(40 \text{ kg}) \cdot (1 \text{ m/s}) = (60 \text{ kg} + 40 \text{ kg})v_x$

$v_x = (40 \text{ kg·m/s}) / (100 \text{ kg})$

$v_x = 0.4 \text{ m/s}$

Combine these final velocity components using the Pythagorean Theorem since they are perpendicular.

$v^2 = v_x^2 + v_y^2$

$v^2 = (0.4 \text{ m/s})^2 + (0.3 \text{ m/s})^2$

$v = 0.5 \text{ m/s}$

19. B is correct.

Use conservation of momentum to determine the momentum after the collision. Since they stick, treat it as a perfectly inelastic collision.

Before collision, Vladimir's momentum is:

$(60 \text{ kg}) \cdot (0.5 \text{ m/s}) = 30 \text{ kg·m/s pointing North}$

Before collision, Olga's momentum is:

$(40 \text{ kg}) \cdot (1 \text{ m/s}) = 40 \text{ kg·m/s pointing West}$

Write two expressions: one for the conservation of momentum on the y coordinate (North-South) and one for the conservation of momentum on the x coordinate (East-West).

They do not interact since they are perpendiculars. Since they stick, the final mass is the sum of their masses.

Simply use the Pythagorean Theorem:

$a^2 + b^2 = c^2$

$(30 \text{ kg·m/s})^2 + (40 \text{ kg·m/s})^2 = p^2$

$900(\text{kg·m/s})^2 + 1{,}600(\text{kg·m/s})^2 = p^2$

$2{,}500(\text{kg·m/s})^2 = p^2$

$p = 50 \text{ kg·m/s}$ *continued…*

This problem can also be solved algebraically:

$p_{before} = p_{after}$

$p = mv$

On the y-coordinate:

$(60 \text{ kg}) \cdot (0.5 \text{ m/s}) = (60 \text{ kg} + 40 \text{ kg})v_y$

$v_y = (30 \text{ kg·m/s}) / (100 \text{ kg})$

$v_y = 0.3 \text{ m/s}$

On the x-coordinate:

$(40 \text{ kg}) \cdot (1 \text{ m/s}) = (60 \text{ kg} + 40 \text{ kg})v_x$

$v_x = (40 \text{ kg·m/s}) / (100 \text{ kg})$

$v_x = 0.4 \text{ m/s}$

Combine these final velocity components using the Pythagorean Theorem since they are perpendiculars:

$v^2 = v_x{}^2 + v_y{}^2$

$v^2 = (0.4 \text{ m/s})^2 + (0.3 \text{ m/s})^2$

$v = 0.5 \text{ m/s}$

Use the final weight and final velocity to find the final momentum directly after the collision:

$p = mv$

$p = (60 \text{ kg} + 40 \text{ kg}) \cdot (0.5 \text{ m/s})$

$p = 50 \text{ kg·m/s}$

20. C is correct.

$p_0 = mv$

If m and v are doubled:

$p = (2m) \cdot (2v)$

$p = 4mv$

$p = 4p_0$

The momentum increases by a factor of 4.

21. D is correct.

Balance forces on box Q to solve for tension on box P cable:

$$m_Q a = F - T_P$$

$$T_P = F - m_Q a$$

$$0 < T_P < F$$

Thus, the tension on the cable connected to box P is less than F because it is equal to the difference between F and $m_Q a$ but is not equal because the boxes are accelerating.

22. B is correct.

At all points on a rotating body, the angular velocity is equal. The speed at different points along a rotating body is directly proportional to the radius.

$$v = \omega r$$

where v = speed, ω = angular velocity and r = radius

Thus, Melissa and her friend have different speeds due to their different radial locations.

23. A is correct.

Impulse is directly proportional to force and change in time:

$$J = F \Delta t$$

Increasing the change in time lowers the impact force while decreasing the change in time increases the force.

24. D is correct.

Angular momentum is always conserved unless a system experiences a net torque greater than zero, and this is the rotational equivalent of Newton's First Law of motion.

25. D is correct.

$$F \Delta t = m \Delta v$$

$$F = (m \Delta v) / (\Delta t)$$

$$F = (6.8 \text{ kg}) \cdot (-3.2 \text{ m/s} - 5.4 \text{ m/s}) / (2 \text{ s})$$

$$F = (-58.48 \text{ kg·m/s}) / (2 \text{ s})$$

$$F = -29.2 \text{ N}$$

$$|F| = 29.2 \text{ N}$$

26. A is correct.

Before collision, the total momentum of the system = 0 kg·m/s.

Momentum is conserved in the explosion.

The momentum of the moving rifle and bullet are in opposite directions:

Therefore, $p = 0$

The total momentum after the explosion = 0 kg·m/s

27. D is correct.

$p = mv$

Conservation of momentum:

$p_{initial} = p_{final}$

0 kg·m/s = (0.01 kg)·(300 m/s) + (4 kg)v_{recoil}

0 kg·m/s = 3 kg·m/s + (4 kg)v_{recoil}

–3 kg·m/s = (4 kg)v_{recoil}

(–3 kg·m/s) / (4 kg) = v_{recoil}

$v_{recoil} = -0.75$ m/s

Velocity is negative since the gun recoils in the opposite direction of the bullet.

28. C is correct.

Since the initial velocity only has a horizontal component, the y component of the initial velocity = 0.

Use 24 m to calculate the time the ball is in the air:

$d_y = \frac{1}{2}at^2$

$t^2 = 2d_y / a$

$t^2 = 2(24 \text{ m}) / (9.8 \text{ m/s}^2)$

$t^2 = 4.89 \text{ s}^2$

$t = 2.21$ s

Use the time in the air and the horizontal distance to calculate the horizontal speed of the ball:

$v_x = d_x / t$

$v_x = (18 \text{ m}) / (2.21 \text{ s})$

$v_x = 8.1$ m/s

29. A is correct.

An object moving in a circle at constant speed is undergoing uniform circular motion.

In uniform circular motion, the acceleration is due to centripetal acceleration and points inward towards the center of a circle.

30. B is correct.

Impulse:

$$J = F\Delta t$$

$$J = \Delta p$$

where p is momentum

31. C is correct.

Conservation of energy:

$$KE_i + PE_i = KE_f + PE_f$$

$$KE_i + PE_i = KE_f + 0$$

$$KE_f = \frac{1}{2}mv_i^2 + mgh_i$$

$$KE_f = \frac{1}{2}(4 \text{ kg}) \cdot (20 \text{ m/s})^2 + (4 \text{ kg}) \cdot (10 \text{ m/s}^2) \cdot (10 \text{ m})$$

$$KE_f = 800 \text{ J} + 400 \text{ J}$$

$$KE_f = 1,200 \text{ J}$$

32. D is correct.

The force needed to stop a car can be related to KE and work:

$$KE = W$$

$$\frac{1}{2}mv^2 = Fd$$

$$F = \frac{1}{2}mv^2 / d$$

Momentum is included in the KE term.

$$p = mv$$

$$F = \frac{1}{2}(mv)v / d$$

$$F = \frac{1}{2}(p)v / d$$

If there is less stopping distance, the force increases as they are inversely proportional.

If the momentum or mass increases, the force increases as they are directly proportional.

33. C is correct.

Impulse:

$$J = F\Delta t$$

Based on Newton's Third Law, the force experienced by these two objects is equal and opposite.

Therefore, the magnitudes of impulse are the same.

34. B is correct.

Balance the counterclockwise (CCW) torque with the clockwise (CW) torque.

Let the axis of rotation be at the point where the rope attaches to the bar.

This placement causes the torque from the rope to be zero since the lever arm is zero.

$$\Sigma \tau : \tau_1 - \tau_2 = 0$$

$$\tau_1 = \tau_2$$

The CCW torque due to the weight of the 6 kg mass:

$$\tau = r_1 F_1$$

$$r_1 F_1 = (x) \cdot (6 \text{ kg}) \cdot (9.8 \text{ m/s}^2)$$

The CW torque due to the weight of the 30 kg mass:

$$r_2 F_2 = (5 \text{ m} - x) \cdot (30 \text{ kg}) \cdot (9.8 \text{ m/s}^2)$$

Set the two expressions equal

$$(9.8 \text{ m/s}^2) \cdot (x) \cdot (6 \text{ kg}) = (5 \text{ m} - x) \cdot (30 \text{ kg}) \cdot (9.8 \text{ m/s}^2)$$

Cancel *g* and kg from each side of the equation:

$$6x = 30(5 \text{ m} - x)$$

$$6x = 150 \text{ m} - 30x$$

$$36x = 150 \text{ m}$$

$$x = 4.2 \text{ m}$$

35. D is correct.

If the block is at rest, then the force of static friction equals the force of gravity at angle *θ*.

$$F_f = mg \sin \theta$$

36. C is correct.

$F_{net} = 0$ is necessary to maintain a constant velocity.

If 45 N must be exerted on the block to maintain a constant velocity, the force of kinetic friction against the block equals 45 N.

For a horizontal surface and no other vertical forces acting, the normal force on the block equals its weight.

$$N = mg$$

$$F_{friction} = \mu_k N$$

$$F_{friction} = \mu_k mg$$

$$\mu_k = (F_{friction}) / mg$$

$$\mu_k = (45 \text{ N}) / [(30 \text{ kg}) \cdot (10 \text{ m/s}^2)]$$

$$\mu_k = 0.15$$

37. B is correct.

Newton's Second Law:

$$F = ma$$

The impulse-momentum relationship can be derived by multiplying Δt on each side:

$$F\Delta t = ma\Delta t$$

$$F\Delta t = m\Delta v$$

$$J = m\Delta v$$

Thus, the impulse is equal to the change in momentum.

38. C is correct.

Force X acts perpendicular to the short arm of the rectangle; this is the lever arm.

$$\tau = rF$$

$$\tau = (0.5 \text{ m}) \cdot (15 \text{ N})$$

$$\tau = 7.5 \text{ N·m}$$

Since the torque causes the plate to rotate clockwise its sign is negative.

$$\tau = -7.5 \text{ N·m}$$

39. D is correct.

$$\tau = rF$$

Force Z acts directly at the pivot, so the lever arm equals zero.

$$\tau = (0 \text{ m}) \cdot (30 \text{ N})$$

$$\tau = 0 \text{ N·m}$$

40. A is correct.

$$\tau = rF$$

Force Y acts perpendicular to the long arm of the rectangle; this is the lever arm.

$$\tau = (0.6 \text{ m}) \cdot (25 \text{ N})$$

$$\tau = 15 \text{ N·m}$$

The torque is clockwise, so its sign is negative.

$$\tau = -15 \text{ N·m}$$

41. B is correct.

The tension in the string provides the centripetal force.

$$T = mv^2 / r$$

$$m = 50 \text{ g} = 0.05 \text{ kg}$$

$$T = [(0.05 \text{ kg}) \cdot (20 \text{ m/s})^2] / (2 \text{ m})$$

$$T = [(0.05 \text{ kg}) \cdot (400 \text{ m}^2/\text{s}^2)] / (2 \text{ m})$$

$$T = (20 \text{ kg·m}^2/\text{s}^2) / (2 \text{ m})$$

$$T = 10 \text{ N}$$

42. A is correct.

Newton's Third Law states that each force is paired with an equal and opposite reaction force.

Therefore, the small car and the truck each receive the same force.

43. C is correct.

Choose the axis of rotation at the point where the bar attaches to the wall.

Since the lever arm of the force that the wall exerts is zero, the torque at that point is zero and can be ignored.

The two other torques present arise from the weight of the bar exerting a force downward and the cable exerting force upward.

continued…

The weight of the bar acts at the center of mass, so its lever arm is 1 m.

The lever arm for the cable is 2 m since it acts the full 2 m away from the wall at the end of the bar.

Torque is the product of the length of the lever arm and the component of force perpendicular to the arm.

The torque applied by the wire is:

$$F_T l \sin \theta$$

The sum of torques = 0 since the bar is in rotational equilibrium.

Let the torque of the cable be positive, and the torque of the weight be negative.

$$(F_T \sin 30°)·(2 \text{ m}) – (10 \text{ kg})·(10 \text{ m/s}^2)·(1 \text{ m}) = 0$$

$$F_T = [(10 \text{ kg})·(10 \text{ m/s}^2)·(1 \text{ m})] / [(2 \text{ m})·(\sin 30°)]$$

$$F_T = [(10 \text{ kg})·(10 \text{ m/s}^2)·(1 \text{ m})] / [(2 \text{ m})·(0.5)]$$

$$F_T = 100 \text{ N}$$

44. B is correct.

Momentum is defined as:

$$p = mv$$

$$m_A = 2m_B$$

$$p_A = 2m_B v$$

$$p_B = m_B v$$

$$p_A = 2p_B$$

If both objects reach the ground at the same time, they have equal velocities.

Because A is twice the mass, it has twice the momentum as object B.

45. D is correct.

Use conservation of momentum to make equations for momenta along the x-axis and the y-axis.

Since the mass ratio is 1 : 4, one car has a mass of m, and the other has a mass of $4m$.

The entangled cars after the collision have a combined mass of $5m$.

Let the car of mass m be traveling in the positive x-direction, and the car of mass $4m$ be traveling in the positive y-direction.

The choice of directions here is arbitrary, but the angle of impact is important.

$$p_{initial} = p_{final} \text{ for both the } x\text{- and } y\text{-axes}$$

$$p = mv$$

continued…

For the x-axis:

$$m_i v_i = m_f v_{fx}$$

$$m(12 \text{ m/s}) = 5mv_x$$

Cancel m from each side of the expression:

$$12 \text{ m/s} = 5v_x$$

$$v_x = 2.4 \text{ m/s}$$

For the y-axis:

$$m_i v_i = m_f v_{fy}$$

$$4m(12 \text{ m/s}) = 5mv_y$$

Cancel m from each side of the expression:

$$4(12 \text{ m/s}) = 5v_y$$

$$v_y = 9.6 \text{ m/s}$$

The question asks for the magnitude of the final velocity, so combine the x and y components of the final velocity using the Pythagorean Theorem.

$$v^2 = (2.4 \text{ m/s})^2 + (9.6 \text{ m/s})^2$$

$$v^2 = 5.76 \text{ m}^2/\text{s}^2 + 92.16 \text{ m}^2/\text{s}^2$$

$$v = 9.9 \text{ m/s}$$

46. C is correct.

Use conservation of momentum on the horizontal plane.

Before the throw, the total momentum of the skater-ball system is zero. Thus, after the throw, the total horizontal momentum must sum to zero: the horizontal component of the ball's momentum equals the momentum of the skater moving the opposite way.

Use m_s for the skater's mass and $m_s/3$ for the ball's mass.

$$p = mv$$

$$p_{\text{skater}} = p_{\text{ball}}$$

$$m_s v_s = m_b v_b$$

$$m_s(2.9 \text{ m/s}) = (1/3)m_s v \cos 5°$$

Cancel m from each side of the expression:

$$v = (2.9 \text{ m/s}) \cdot (3) / (\cos 5°)$$

$$v = (2.9 \text{ m/s}) \cdot (3) / (0.996)$$

$$v = 8.73 \text{ m/s}$$

47. B is correct.

weight = mass × gravity

W = mg

m = W / g

m = (98 N) / (9.8 m/s^2)

m = 10 kg

Newton's Second Law:

$F = ma$

F = (10 kg)·(10 m/s^2)

F = 100 N

48. A is correct.

KE is constant because speed is constant. PE increases because the cart is at a greater height at point B.

The cart as a system is not isolated since the winch does work on it, so its energy is not conserved.

Conservation of energy:

PE increase of the cart = work done by the winch

49. D is correct.

The vertical component of the initial velocity:

v_{iy} = (140 m/s) sin 35°

v_{iy} = (140 m/s)·(0.57)

v_{iy} = 79.8 m/s

The initial velocity upward, time elapsed, and acceleration due to gravity is known.

Determine the final velocity after 4 s.

$v_y = v_{iy} + at$

v_y = 79.8 m/s + (−9.8 m/s^2)·(4 s)

v_y = 41 m/s

50. C is correct.

impulse = force × time

$J = F\Delta t$

51. D is correct.

Conservation of momentum: the momentum of the fired bullet is equal and opposite to that of the rifle.

$p = mv$

$p_{before} = p_{after}$

$0 = p_{rifle} + p_{bullet}$

$-p_{rifle} = p_{bullet}$

$-(2 \text{ kg})v = (0.01 \text{ kg})\cdot(220 \text{ m/s})$

$v = (0.01 \text{ kg})\cdot(220 \text{ m/s}) / (-2 \text{ kg})$

$v = -1.1 \text{ m/s}$

Thus, the velocity of the rifle is 1.1 m/s in the opposite direction as the bullet.

52. D is correct.

Airbags reduce the force by increasing the time of contact between the passenger and the surface.

In a collision, an impulse is experienced by a passenger:

$J = F\Delta t$

$F = J / \Delta t$

The impulse is constant, but the force experienced by the passenger is inversely related to the time of contact.

Airbags increase the time of impact and thus reduce the forces experienced by the person.

53. A is correct.

Since Force I is perpendicular to the beam, the entire force produces torque without a horizontal force component.

$\tau = rF$

$\tau = (0.5 \text{ m})\cdot(10 \text{ N})$

$\tau = 5 \text{ N·m}$

Because the force causes the beam to rotate clockwise against the positive counterclockwise direction, the torque sign should be negative:

$\tau = -5 \text{ N·m}$

54. D is correct.

To calculate torque, use the 35° angle.

For torque:

$$\tau = rF \sin \theta$$

$$\tau = (1 \text{ m}) \cdot (5 \text{ N}) \sin 35°$$

$$\tau = 2.9 \text{ N·m}$$

The torque is counterclockwise, so the sign is positive.

55. B is correct.

Force III acts purely in tension with the beam and has no component acting vertically against the beam.

Torque can only be calculated using a force with some component perpendicular to the length vector.

Because Force III has no perpendicular component to the length vector, torque is zero.

$$\tau = rF$$

$$\tau = (1 \text{ m}) \cdot (0 \text{ N})$$

$$\tau = 0 \text{ N·m}$$

56. C is correct.

Impulse can be written as:

$$J = m\Delta v$$

$$J = F\Delta t$$

Impulse is the change in the momentum of an object.

Because the yellow ball bounced higher, it can be concluded that its upward velocity after the collision must be higher than that of the red ball:

$$\Delta v_{yellow} > \Delta v_{red}$$

Thus, because the mass of both balls is the same, the yellow ball must have a greater impulse according to the impulse equation:

$$m\Delta v_{yellow} > m\Delta v_{red}$$

57. D is correct.

$$J = F\Delta t$$

$$J = (4.5 \text{ N}) \cdot (1.4 \text{ s})$$

$$J = (4.5 \text{ kg·m/s}^2) \cdot (1.4 \text{ s})$$

$$J = 6.3 \text{ kg·m/s}$$

58. A is correct.

Both trucks experience the same acceleration due to gravity, so their acceleration and velocity are equal because these do not depend on mass:

$v_f = v_0 + a\Delta t$

However, their momentum is different, and the heavier truck has a larger momentum because of its larger mass.

$p = mv$

$m_H > m_L$

$p_H = m_H v$

$p_L = m_L v$

$p_H > p_L$

59. D is correct.

The time elapsed from release until a collision is:

time from release until collision = round-trip time / 2

$t = (4 \text{ s}) / 2$

$t = 2 \text{ s}$

The time of contact is negligible to the round-trip time, so this calculation ignores it.

Since this collision is elastic, the time from release until the collision is the same as the time from the collision until the ball reaches the same height again.

Given this time in the air, find the *velocity* of the ball immediately before impact:

$v = v_i + at$

$v = 0 + (9.8 \text{ m/s}^2) \cdot (2 \text{ s})$

$v = 19.6 \text{ m/s}$

Find the *KE* of the ball before impact:

$KE = \frac{1}{2}mv^2$

$KE = \frac{1}{2}(0.078 \text{ kg}) \cdot (19.6 \text{ m/s})^2$

$KE = 15 \text{ J}$

The KE of the ball is stored as elastic energy during the collision and is then converted back to KE to send the ball upward in the opposite direction.

This stored elastic energy is equivalent to the KE before the collision.

60. B is correct.

Consider the system to be the set containing both carts.

The force on the initial object provides an impulse to the system of:

$I = F\Delta t$

An impulse causes a change in the momentum of the system:

$I = \Delta p$

The initial momentum of the system is zero, and momentum is conserved during the collision.

Since the two carts stick after the collision, the final momentum is:

$p_f = v_f(m_A + m_A) = \Delta p = F\Delta t$

Therefore:

$v_f = F\Delta t / (m_A + m_A)$

$v_f = (3 \text{ N})(2 \text{ s}) / (5 \text{ kg} + 10 \text{ kg})$

$v_f = 0.4 \text{ m/s}$

61. C is correct.

$J = F\Delta t$

$J = m\Delta v$

$F\Delta t = m\Delta v$

$\Delta t = (m\Delta v) / F$

Let towards the batter be the positive direction and away from batter be the negative direction:

$t = m(v_f - v_i) / F$

$t = (0.12 \text{ kg})\cdot(-34 \text{ m/s} - 23 \text{ m/s}) / (-5,000 \text{ N})$

$t = 0.0014 \text{ s}$

$t = 1.4 \times 10^{-3} \text{ s}$

62. D is correct.

$KE = \frac{1}{2}mv^2$

$p = mv$

$m = p / v$

$v = p / m$

continued...

$$KE = \frac{1}{2}(p \,/\, v)v^2$$

$$KE = \frac{1}{2}pv$$

$$KE = \frac{1}{2}p(p \,/\, m)$$

$$KE = \frac{1}{2}(p^2 \,/\, m)$$

$$KE = p^2 \,/\, 2m$$

63. D is correct.

Conservation of momentum:

$$mv_i = mv_f + Mv$$

Conservation of energy:

$$\frac{1}{2}mv_i^2 = \frac{1}{2}mv_f^2 + \frac{1}{2}Mv^2$$

Rearranging this, the energy equation becomes:

$$m(v_i^2 - v_f^2) = Mv^2$$

Both M and v are unknown.

The question asks to find M, solving the momentum equation for v^2 eliminates v from this system of equations.

$$v^2 = (m \,/\, M)^2 \, (v_i - v_f)^2$$

Putting this into the energy equation:

$$m(v_i^2 - v_f^2) = Mv^2 = M(m \,/\, M)^2 \, (v_i - v_f)^2$$

$$(v_i^2 - v_f^2) = (m \,/\, M)\cdot(v_i - v_f)^2$$

Divide each side by $(v_i - v_f)$:

$$(v_i + v_f) = (m \,/\, M)\cdot(v_i - v_f)$$

Solve for M:

$$M = m(v_i - v_f) \,/\, (v_i + v_f)$$

$$M = (2.2 \text{ kg})\cdot[(9.2 \text{ m/s}) - (-2.5 \text{ m/s})] \,/\, [(9.2 \text{ m/s}) + (-2.5 \text{ m/s})]$$

$$M = (2.2 \text{ kg})\cdot(11.7 \text{ m/s}) \,/\, (6.7 \text{ m/s})$$

$$M = 3.8 \text{ kg}$$

64. C is correct.

Momentum is conserved:

$p = mv$

$p_{before} = p_{after}$

Set to the left as the negative direction.

$m_1 v_{1i} + m_2 v_{2i} = m_1 v_{1f} + m_2 v_{2f}$

$(1 \text{ kg}) \cdot (7 \text{ m/s}) + (3 \text{ kg}) \cdot (-2 \text{ m/s}) = (1 \text{ kg}) \cdot (-3 \text{ m/s}) + (3 \text{ kg})v$

$7 \text{ kg·m/s} + (-6 \text{ kg·m/s}) = -3 \text{ kg·m/s} + (3 \text{ kg})v_f$

$1 \text{ kg·m/s} = -3 \text{ kg·m/s} + (3 \text{ kg})v_f$

$4 \text{ kg·m/s} = (3 \text{ kg})v_f$

$(4 \text{ kg·m/s}) / (3 \text{ kg}) = v_f$

$v_f = 1.3 \text{ m/s}$, the direction of cart II is to the right because the vector is positive.

65. B is correct.

Newton's Third Law states that when two objects interact by a mutual force, the force of the first on the second is equal in magnitude to the force of the second on the first.

66. D is correct.

Equation for torque $\tau = r \times F$, where r is the length at which force is acting.

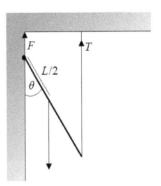

$\tau_{net} = 0$, system is in equilibrium

$0 = -\tau_{mg} + \tau_T$

The torque due to gravity is working in the clockwise direction; therefore, it is negative.

Tension is working counterclockwise, so it is positive.

Let the length of the rod be L; then the torque upward (due to the tension T in the string) $= LT \sin \theta$.

The torque downward is due to the weight of the rod, and the weight vector acts at the rod's center of mass, which is halfway ($L / 2$) down the rod.

$0 = -(L / 2)Mg \sin \theta + (L)T \sin \theta$

$0 = -(L / 2)Mg + (L)T$

$T = Mg / 2$

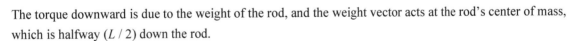

67. A is correct.

The law of conservation of momentum says that total momentum does not change in the absence of external net force.

Since the force, in this case, is zero, momentum does not change.

68. D is correct.

In projectile motion, the only force acting on the projectile (if air resistance is ignored) is the force of gravity.

The horizontal component of the velocity does not change and is constant because gravity only acts vertically.

69. D is correct.

The *percentage of energy lost* is:

$$p = [(E_{initial} - E_{final}) / E_{initial}] \times 100\%$$

The initial energy is the kinetic energy of the 3.3 kg object:

$$E_{in} = \tfrac{1}{2}\, m_1 v_1^2$$

The final kinetic energy is found from the speed and mass of the two objects stuck:

$$E_f = \tfrac{1}{2}\, (m_1 + m_2) v_2^2$$

We can express v_2 in terms of v_1 through conservation of momentum:

$$m_1 v_1 = (m_1 + m_2) v_2$$

or:

$$v_2 = v_1[m_1 / (m_1 + m_2)]$$

Therefore:

$$E_f = \tfrac{1}{2}\, (m_1 + m_2) v_2^2$$

$$E_f = \tfrac{1}{2}\, (m_1 + m_2) v_1^2 [m_1 / m_1 + m_2)]^2$$

$$E_f = \tfrac{1}{2}\, m_1 v_1^2 [m_2 / (m_1 + m_2)]$$

$$E_i - E_f = \tfrac{1}{2}\, m_1 v_1^2 [1 - m_1 / (m_1 + m_2)]$$

$$E_i - E_f = \tfrac{1}{2}\, m_1 v_1^2 [m_2 / (m_1 + m_2)]$$

Finally resulting in:

$$p = [m_2 / (m_1 + m_2)] \times 100\%$$

$$p = [3.6 \text{ kg} / (3.3 \text{ kg} + 3.6 \text{ kg})] \times 100\%$$

$$p = 52\%$$

70. D is correct.

In circular motion, all points on a rotating body experience the same angular displacement.

The angular displacement is not equal to zero if the carousel is in motion.

---

71. C is correct.

$p = mv$, or

$p = m_1v_1 = m_2v_2$

$v_2 = (m_1v_1) / m_2$

$m_2 = m_1 + m_{ore}$

$m_2 = 1,200 \text{ kg} + 800 \text{ kg}$

$m_2 = 2,000 \text{ kg}$

$v_2 = [(1,200 \text{ kg}){\cdot}(10 \text{ m/s})] / 2,000 \text{ kg}$

$v_2 = 6 \text{ m/s}$

72. A is correct.

By Newton's Third Law, the car and the truck experience equal and opposite forces during the collision, and the time of contact for the car and truck are equal.

Thus, the car and truck have the same impulse:

$J_{car} = J_{truck}$

$J = F\Delta t$

$J = \Delta p$

$\Delta p_{car} = \Delta p_{truck}$

The car and truck experience the same change in momentum.

73. D is correct.

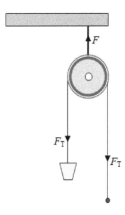

$F_{net\ pully} = 2F_T$

$F_{net\ pully} = 2(750 \text{ N})$

$F_{net\ pully} = 1,500 \text{ N}$

Since the bucket is not accelerating, the tension in the rope is 750 N.

Therefore, the pulley experiences two tension forces (one on each side of the pulley), each 750 N pulling downward.

The pulley, to remain stationary, experiences a total tension force of 1,500 N.

74. B is correct.

Momentum is conserved, so the momentum of the ball equals the momentum of the cannon.

$m_B v_B = m_C v_C$

The cannon has more mass than the ball, so its recoil velocity is much less than the velocity of the cannonball to conserve momentum.

$m_B < m_C$

$v_B > v_C$

75. A is correct.

Since the momentum is conserved during the collision, the change is $p = 0$.

$p_{initial} = p_{final}$

$m_1 v_1 + m_2 v_2 = (m_1 + m_2) v_3$

76. D is correct.

$J = \Delta p = m \Delta v$

$\Delta v = J / m$

$\Delta v = (30{,}000 \text{ N·s}) / (1{,}120 \text{ kg})$

$\Delta v = 27 \text{ m/s}$

$\Delta v = v_f - v_i$

$27 \text{ m/s} = 0 - v_i$

$v_i = 27 \text{ m/s}$

77. A is correct.

In uniform circular motion, the centripetal force does no work because the force and displacement vectors are at right angles.

$W = Fd$

The work equation is only applicable if force and displacement direction are the same.

78. D is correct.

$J = F \Delta t$

Impulse remains constant, so the time of impact increases, and the impact force decreases.

79. B is correct.

Consider a dropped baseball on Earth:

$d_E = -\frac{1}{2}gt^2$

On the Moon:

$d_M = -\frac{1}{2}(g\,/\,6)t^2$

$d_E\,/\,d_M = (-\frac{1}{2}gt^2)\,/\,(-\frac{1}{2}(g\,/\,6)t^2)$

$d_E\,/\,d_M = 1/6$, so the distance is 6 times greater on the Moon

80. D is correct.

The total downward force on the meter stick is:

20 N + 50 N + 30 N = 100 N

The total upward force on the meter stick – provided by the tension in the supporting rope – must also be 100 N to keep the meter stick in static equilibrium.

Let x be the distance from the left end of the meter stick to the suspension point.

From the pivot point, balance the torques.

The counterclockwise (CCW) torque due to the 50 N weight at the left end is 50 x.

The total clockwise (CW) torque due to the weight of the meter stick and the 30 N weight at the right end is:

(50 N)x = (20 N)·(50 cm – x) + (30 N)·(100 cm – x)

(50 N)x = [1,000 cm – (20 N)x] + [3,000 cm – (30 N)x]

(50 N)x = 4,000 cm – (50 N)x

(100 N)x = 4,000 cm

x = 40 cm

81. B is correct.

$J = F\Delta t$ is constant

increased t = decreased F

82. C is correct.

$m_1v_1 = (m_1 + m_2)v_2$

$v_2 = (m_1v_1) / (m_1 + m_2)$

$v_2 = (1,200 \text{ kg})\cdot(15.6 \text{ m/s}) / (1,200 \text{ kg} + 1,500 \text{ kg})$

$v_2 = (18,720 \text{ kg·m/s}) / (2,700 \text{ kg})$

$v_2 = 6.9 \text{ m/s}$

83. D is correct.

$F\Delta t = m\Delta v$

$F = (m\Delta v) / \Delta t$

$F = [(0.05 \text{ kg})\cdot(100 \text{ m/s} - 0 \text{ m/s})] / (0.0008 \text{ s})$

$F = (5 \text{ kg·m/s}) / (0.0008 \text{ s})$

$F = 6,250 \text{ N} = 6.3 \text{ kN}$

84. A is correct.

In circular motion, all points along the rotational body have the same angular velocity regardless of their radial distance from the center of rotation.

85. C is correct.

In both elastic and inelastic collisions, momentum is conserved.

However, in an ideal elastic collision, KE is also conserved, but not in an inelastic collision.

To determine if the collision is elastic or inelastic, compare the KE before and after the collision.

Initial KE:

$KE_i = \frac{1}{2}m_1v_1^2$

$KE_i = \frac{1}{2}(2 \text{ kg})\cdot(0.6 \text{ m/s})^2$

$KE_i = 0.36 \text{ J}$

Conservation of momentum:

$m_1v_1 + m_2v_2 = m_1u_1 + m_2u_2$

$m_1v_1 = m_2u_2$

$(m_1 / m_2)v_1 = u_2$

$u_2 = (2 \text{ kg} / 2.5 \text{ kg})\cdot(0.6 \text{ m/s})$

$u_2 = 0.48 \text{ m/s}$

continued…

Final KE:

$$KE_f = \frac{1}{2}m_2u_2^2$$

$$KE_f = \frac{1}{2}(2.5 \text{ kg}){\cdot}(0.48 \text{ m/s})^2$$

$$KE_f = 0.29 \text{ J}$$

KE_i does not equal KE_f, and thus KE is not conserved.

The collision is therefore inelastic, and only momentum is conserved.

86. A is correct.

A longer barrel gives the expanding gas more time to impart a force upon the bullet and thus increase the impulse upon the bullet.

$$J = F\Delta t$$

Notes for active learning

1. D is correct.

The final velocity in projectile motion is related to the maximum height of the projectile through conservation of energy:

$$KE = PE$$

$$\tfrac{1}{2}mv^2 = mgh$$

When the stone thrown straight up passes its starting point on its way back down, its downward speed is equal to its initial upward velocity (2D motion).

The stone thrown straight downward contains the same magnitude of initial velocity as the stone thrown upward, and thus both the stone thrown upward and the stone thrown downward have the same final speed.

A stone thrown horizontally (or, for example, a stone thrown at 45°) does not achieve the same height *h* as a stone thrown straight up, so it has a smaller final vertical velocity.

2. B is correct.

$$\text{Work} = \text{force} \times \text{displacement} \times \cos \theta$$

$$W = Fd \cos \theta$$

where θ is the angle between the vectors *F* and *d*

$$W = (5 \text{ N})\cdot(10 \text{ m}) \cos 45°$$

$$W = (50 \text{ J})\cdot(0.7)$$

$$W = 35 \text{ J}$$

3. A is correct.

$$KE = \tfrac{1}{2}mv^2$$

KE is influenced by mass and velocity.

Since velocity is squared, its influence on KE is greater than the influence of mass.

4. B is correct.

$$\text{Work} = \text{force} \times \text{displacement} \times \cos \theta$$

$$W = Fd \cos \theta$$

$$\cos 90° = 0$$

$$W = 0$$

Since the force of gravity acts perpendicular to the distance traveled by the ball, the force due to gravity does no work in moving the ball.

5. C is correct.

$$KE = \frac{1}{2}mv^2$$

$$KE = \frac{1}{2}(5 \text{ kg}) \cdot (2 \text{ m/s})^2$$

$$KE = 10 \text{ J}$$

6. A is correct.

$$W = Fd \cos \theta$$

$$\cos \theta = 1$$

$$F = W / d$$

$$F = (360 \text{ J}) / (8 \text{ m})$$

$$F = 45 \text{ N}$$

$$F = ma$$

$$m = F / a$$

$$m = (45 \text{ N}) / (10 \text{ m/s}^2)$$

$$m = 4.5 \text{ kg}$$

7. D is correct.

On a displacement (x) *vs.* force (F) graph, the displacement is the y-axis, and the force is the x-axis.

The slope is x / F (in units of m/N), which is the reciprocal of the spring constant k, measured in N/m.

8. C is correct.

Work done by a spring equation:

$$W = \frac{1}{2}kx^2$$

$$W = \frac{1}{2}(22 \text{ N/m}) \cdot (3 \text{ m})^2$$

$$W = 99 \text{ J}$$

9. A is correct.

The force of gravity always points down.

When the ball is moving upwards, the direction of its displacement is opposite of that of the force of gravity, and therefore the work done by gravity is negative.

On the way down, the direction of displacement is the same as that of the force of gravity, and therefore the work done by gravity is positive.

10. B is correct.

Work done by gravity is an object's change in gravitational PE.

$$W = -PE$$

$$A_1 = 400 \text{ J}$$

By the work-energy theorem:

$$W = KE$$

$$B_1 = 400 \text{ J}$$

11. D is correct.

Work is calculated as the product of force and displacement parallel to the direction of the applied force:

$$W = Fd \cos \theta$$

where some component of d is in the direction of the force.

12. B is correct.

Work only depends on force and distance:

$$W = Fd \cos \theta$$

Power $= W / t$ is the amount of work done in a unit of time.

13. A is correct.

The area under the curve on a graph is the product of the values of $y \times x$.

Here, the y value is the force, and the x value is distance:

$$Fd = W$$

14. C is correct.

This is the conservation of energy. The only force acting on the cat is gravity.

$$KE = PE_g$$

$$KE = mgh$$

$$KE = (3 \text{ kg}){\cdot}(10 \text{ m/s}^2){\cdot}(4 \text{ m})$$

$$KE = 120 \text{ J}$$

15. B is correct.

Although the book is stationary with respect to the plank, the plank is applying a force to the book, causing it to accelerate in the direction of the force. Since the displacement of the point of application of the force is in the same direction as the force, the work done is positive.

Choice D is not correct because work is a scalar and has no direction.

16. D is correct.

$W = Fd$

$d = W / F$

$d = (350 \text{ J}) / (900 \text{ N})$

$d = 0.39$ m

17. A is correct.

Conservation of energy between kinetic energy and potential energy:

$KE = PE$

$KE = \frac{1}{2}mv^2$ and $PE = mgh$

Set the equations equal:

$\frac{1}{2}mv^2 = mgh$

Cancel m from each side:

$\frac{1}{2}v^2 = gh$

h is only dependent on the initial v, equal between both objects, so the two objects rise to the same height.

18. A is correct.

Work = Power × time

$P_1 = W / t$

$P_2 = (3 \text{ W}) / (1/3 \ t)$

$P_2 = 3(3/1){\cdot}(W / t)$

$P_2 = 9(W / t)$

$P_2 = 9(P_1)$

19. D is correct.

Conservation of energy:

$KE = PE$

$KE = mgh$

$W = mg$

$KE = Wh$

$KE = (450 \text{ N}){\cdot}(9 \text{ m})$

$KE = 4{,}050$ J

20. A is correct.

$$F_1 = -kx_1$$

Solve for the spring constant k:

$$k = F / x_1$$

$$k = (160 \text{ N}) / (0.23 \text{ m})$$

$$k = 696 \text{ N/m}$$

$$F_2 = -kx_2$$

$$F_2 = (696 \text{ N/m}) \cdot (0.34 \text{ m})$$

$$F_2 = 237 \text{ N}$$

21. B is correct.

There is a frictional force since the net force = 0

The mule pulls in the same direction as the direction of travel so $\cos \theta = 1$

$$W = Fd \cos \theta$$

$$d = v \Delta t$$

$$W = Fv \Delta t$$

22. D is correct.

$$W = Fd \cos \theta$$

$$F_T = W / (d \times \cos \theta)$$

$$F_T = (540 \text{ J}) / (18 \text{ m} \times \cos 32°)$$

$$F_T = (540 \text{ J}) / (18 \text{ m} \times 0.848)$$

$$F_T = 35 \text{ N}$$

23. B is correct.

The spring force balances the gravitational force on the mass.

Therefore:

$$F_g = -kx$$

$$mg = -kx$$

By adding an extra 120 grams, the mass is doubled:

$$(2m)g = -kx$$

Since the weight mg and the spring constant k are constant, only x changes.

continued…

Thus, after the addition of 120 g, x doubles:

$$PE_1 = \frac{1}{2}kx^2$$

$$PE_2 = \frac{1}{2}k(2x)^2$$

$$PE_2 = \frac{1}{2}k(4x^2)$$

$$PE_2 = 4(\frac{1}{2}kx^2)$$

The potential energy increases by a factor of 4.

24. C is correct.

In each case the car's energy is reduced to zero by the work done by the frictional force:

$$KE + (-W) = 0$$

$$KE = W$$

Each car starts with kinetic energy $KE = (1/2)mv^2$.

The initial speed is the same for each car, so due to the differences in mass, the Ferrari has the most KE.

Thus, to reduce the Ferrari's energy to zero requires the most work.

25. D is correct.

The hammer does work on the nail as it drives it into the wood.

The amount of work done is equal to the amount of kinetic energy lost by the hammer:

$$\Delta KE = \Delta W$$

26. A is correct.

The only force doing work is the road's friction, so the work done by the road's friction is the total work.

This work equals the change in KE.

$$W = \Delta KE$$

$$W = KE_f - KE_i$$

$$W = \frac{1}{2}mv_2^2 - \frac{1}{2}mv_1^2$$

$$W = 0 - [\frac{1}{2}(1,500 \text{ kg}) \cdot (25 \text{ m/s})^2]$$

$$W = -4.7 \times 10^5 \text{ J}$$

27. D is correct.

$$KE = \tfrac{1}{2}mv^2$$

$$KE_{car} = \tfrac{1}{2}(1,000 \text{ kg})\cdot(4.72 \text{ m/s})^2$$

$$KE_{car} = 11,139 \text{ J}$$

Calculate the KE of the 2,000 kg truck with 20 times the KE:

$$KE_{truck} = KE_{car} \times 20$$

$$KE_{truck} = (11,139 \text{ J}) \times 20$$

$$KE_{truck} = 222.7 \text{ kJ}$$

Calculate the speed of the 2,000 kg truck:

$$KE = \tfrac{1}{2}mv^2$$

$$v^2 = 2KE \, / \, m$$

$$v^2 = 2(222.7 \text{ kJ}) \, / \, (2,000 \text{ kg})$$

$$v_{truck} = \sqrt{[2(222.7 \text{ kJ}) \, / \, (2,000 \text{ kg})]}$$

$$v_{truck} = 14.9 \text{ m/s}$$

28. C is correct.

Gravity and the normal force are balanced, vertical forces.

Since the car is slowing (i.e., accelerating backward), there is a net force backward due to friction (i.e., braking).

Newton's First Law of Motion states that the car keeps moving forward in the absence of any forces.

29. B is correct.

Energy is always conserved so the work needed to lift the piano 0.15 m is equal to the work needed to pull the rope 1 m:

$$W_1 = W_2$$

$$F_1 d_1 = F_2 d_2$$

$$F_1 d_1 \, / \, d_2 = F_2$$

$$F_2 = (6,000 \text{ N})\cdot(0.15 \text{ m}) \, / \, 1 \text{ m}$$

$$F_2 = 900 \text{ N}$$

30. C is correct.

The area under the curve on a graph is the product of the values of $y \times x$.

Here, the y value is the force, and the x value is distance:

$$Fd = W$$

31. B is correct.

Most of the Earth's energy comes from the sun, which produces radiation that penetrates the Earth's atmosphere. Likewise, radiation is emitted from the Earth's atmosphere.

32. C is correct.

$$W = Fd$$

$$W = \Delta KE$$

$$F \times d = \frac{1}{2}mv^2$$

If v is doubled:

$$F \times d_2 = \frac{1}{2}m(2v)^2$$

$$F \times d_2 = \frac{1}{2}m(4v^2)$$

$$F \times d_2 = 4(\frac{1}{2}mv^2)$$

For equations to remain equal, d_2 must be 4 times d.

33. D is correct.

$$\text{Work} = \text{Power} \times \text{time}$$

$$P = W / t$$

$$W = Fd$$

$$P = (Fd) / t$$

$$P = [(2{,}000 \text{ N}) \cdot (320 \text{ m})] / (60 \text{ s})$$

$$P = 10{,}667 \text{ W} = 10.7 \text{ kW}$$

34. A is correct.

Solution using the principle of conservation of energy.

Assuming the system consists of the barbell alone, the force of gravity and the force of the hands raising the barbell are external forces.

Since the system contains only a single object, potential energy is not defined.

The net power expended is:

$$P_{net} = W_{ext} / \Delta t$$

Conservation of energy requires:

$$W_{ext} = \Delta KE$$

$$W_{ext} = \frac{1}{2}m(v_f^2 - v_i^2)$$

continued…

For constant acceleration situations:

$$(v_f + v_i) / 2 = v_{average} = \Delta y / \Delta t$$

$$(v_f + 0.0 \text{ m/s}) / 2 = 3.0 \text{ m} / 3.0 \text{ s}$$

$$v_f = 2.0 \text{ m/s}$$

Therefore:

$$W_{ext} = \tfrac{1}{2}(25 \text{ kg}) \cdot (2.0 \text{ m/s})^2$$

$$W_{ext} = 50.0 \text{ J}$$

The net power expended is:

$$P_{net} = 50.0 \text{ J} / 3.0 \text{ s} = 17 \text{ W}$$

$$P_{net} = 17 \text{ W}$$

Solution using work

The power expended in raising the barbell is:

$$P_{net} = W_{net} / \Delta t$$

The net work is defined as:

$$W_{net} = F_{net} \Delta y$$

By Newton's Second law:

$$F_{net} = ma$$

Find the acceleration:

$$\Delta y = \tfrac{1}{2} a \Delta t^2$$

$$a = (2) \cdot (3.0 \text{ m}) / (3.0 \text{ s})^2$$

$$a = 0.67 \text{ m/s}^2$$

The net force on the barbell is:

$$F_{net} = (25 \text{ kg}) \cdot (0.67 \text{ m/s}^2)$$

$$F_{net} = (50 / 3) \text{ N}$$

The net work is:

$$W_{net} = F_{net} \Delta y$$

$$W_{net} = [(50 / 3) \text{ N}] \cdot (3.0 \text{ m})$$

$$W_{net} = 50.0 \text{ J}$$

The net power expended:

$$P_{net} = 50.0 \text{ J} / 3.0 \text{ s}$$

$$P_{net} = 17 \text{ W}$$

35. B is correct.

The bag was never lifted off the ground and moved horizontally at a constant velocity.

$F = 0$

$W = Fd$

$W = 0 \text{ J}$

Because there is no acceleration, the force is zero, and thus the work is zero.

36. B is correct.

Using energy conservation to solve the problem:

$W = |\Delta KE|$

$Fd = |\frac{1}{2}m(v_f^2 - v_0^2)|$

$d = |m(v_f^2 - v_0^2) / 2F|$

$d = |(1{,}000 \text{ kg}){\cdot}[(22 \text{ m/s})^2 - (30 \text{ m/s})^2] / (2){\cdot}(9{,}600 \text{ N})|$

$d = |(1{,}000 \text{ kg}){\cdot}(484 \text{ m}^2/\text{s}^2 - 900 \text{ m}^2/\text{s}^2) / 19{,}200 \text{ N}|$

$d = 22 \text{ m}$

Alternatively, the kinematic approach to solve the problem:

$F = ma$

$a = F / m$

$a = (9{,}600 \text{ N}) / (1{,}000 \text{ kg})$

$a = 9.6 \text{ m/s}^2$

$v_f^2 = v_0^2 + 2a\Delta d$

$(v_f^2 - v_0^2) / 2a = \Delta d$

Note that acceleration is negative due to it acting opposite the velocity.

$\Delta d = [(22 \text{ m/s})^2 - (30 \text{ m/s})^2] / 2(-9.6 \text{ m/s}^2)$

$\Delta d = (484 \text{ m}^2/\text{s}^2 - 900 \text{ m}^2/\text{s}^2) / (-19.2 \text{ m/s}^2)$

$\Delta d = (-416 \text{ m}^2/\text{s}^2) / (-19.2 \text{ m/s}^2)$

$\Delta d = 21.7 \text{ m} \approx 22 \text{ m}$

37. C is correct.

$W = 100$ J

Work = Power × time

$P = W / t$

$P = 100$ J $/ 50$ s

$P = 2$ W

38. D is correct.

All the original potential energy (with respect to the bottom of the cliff) is converted into kinetic energy.

$mgh = \frac{1}{2} mv_f^2$

Therefore:

$v_f = \sqrt{2gh}$

$v_f = \sqrt{(2) \cdot (10 \text{ m/s}^2) \cdot (58 \text{ m})}$

$v_f = 34$ m/s

Kinematic approach:

$v_f^2 = v_0^2 + 2a\Delta x$

$v_f^2 = 0 + 2a\Delta x$

$v_f = \sqrt{2a\Delta x}$

$v_f = \sqrt{[2(10 \text{ m/s}^2) \cdot (58 \text{ m})]}$

$v_f = \sqrt{(1{,}160 \text{ m}^2/\text{s}^2)}$

$v_f = 34$ m/s

39. A is correct.

PE $= mgh$

If height and gravity are constant, then potential energy is directly proportional to mass.

As such, if the second stone has four times the mass of the first, then it must have four times the potential energy of the first stone.

$m_2 = 4m_1$

$PE_2 = 4PE_1$

Therefore, the second stone has four times the potential energy.

40. B is correct.

$$W = Fd$$

Work done by gravity:

$$W = mgh$$

$$W = (1.3 \text{ kg}) \cdot (10 \text{ m/s}^2) \cdot (6 \text{ m})$$

$$W = 78 \text{ J}$$

41. A is correct.

Potential energy (PE) is the energy associated with the *relative positions* of pairs of objects, regardless of their state of motion.

Kinetic energy (KE) is the energy associated with the *motion* of single particles, regardless of their location.

42. A is correct.

$$F_{spring} = F_{centripetal}$$

$$F_{spring} = kx$$

$$kx = 15 \text{ N}$$

$$x = (15 \text{ N}) / (65 \text{ N/m})$$

$$x = 0.23 \text{ m}$$

$$PE_{spring} = \tfrac{1}{2}kx^2$$

$$PE_{spring} = \tfrac{1}{2}(65 \text{ N/m}) \cdot (0.23 \text{ m})^2$$

$$PE_{spring} = 1.7 \text{ J}$$

43. C is correct.

$$\text{total time} = (3.5 \text{ h/day}) \cdot (7 \text{ days}) \cdot (5 \text{ weeks})$$

$$\text{total time} = 122.5 \text{ h}$$

$$\text{cost} = (8.16 \text{ cents/kW·h}) \cdot (122.5 \text{ h}) \cdot (0.12 \text{ kW})$$

$$\text{cost} = 120 \text{ cents} = \$1.20$$

44. B is correct.

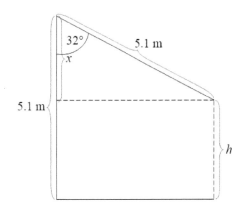

$$x = 5.1 \text{ m} \times (\cos 32°)$$

$$x = 4.33 \text{ m}$$

$$h = 5.1 \text{ m} - 4.33 \text{ m}$$

$$h = 0.775 \text{ m}$$

$$W = Fd$$

$$W = mg \times h$$

$$m = W / gh$$

$$m = (120 \text{ J}) / (9.8 \text{ m/s}^2) \cdot (0.775 \text{ m})$$

$$m = 15.8 \text{ kg}$$

45. D is correct.

Potential energy of spring:

$$PE_i + W = PE_f$$

$$\tfrac{1}{2} k x_i^2 + 111\text{J} = \tfrac{1}{2} k x_f^2$$

$$111\text{J} = \tfrac{1}{2} k (x_f^2 - x_i^2)$$

$$111\text{J} = \tfrac{1}{2} k [(2.9\text{m})^2 - (1.4\text{m})^2]$$

$$111\text{J} = \tfrac{1}{2} k [(8.41\text{m}^2) - (1.96\text{m}^2)]$$

$$111\text{J} = \tfrac{1}{2} k (6.45\text{m}^2)$$

$$k = 2(111 \text{ J}) / (6.45 \text{ m}^2)$$

$$k = 34 \text{ N/m}$$

Unit check:

$$J = \text{kg} \cdot \text{m}^2/\text{s}^2$$

$$J/\text{m}^2 = (\text{kg} \cdot \text{m}^2/\text{s}^2) \cdot (1/\text{m}^2)$$

$$J/\text{m}^2 = (\text{kg}/\text{s}^2)$$

$$N/\text{m} = (\text{kg} \cdot \text{m}/\text{s}^2) \cdot (1/\text{m})$$

$$N/\text{m} = (\text{kg}/\text{s}^2)$$

46. D is correct.

Potential energy, kinetic energy and work are all measured in joules:

$$J = kg \cdot m^2/s^2$$

$$KE = \tfrac{1}{2}mv^2 = kg(m/s)^2 = J$$

$$PE = mgh$$

$$PE = kg(m/s^2) \cdot (m) = J$$

$$W = Fd = J$$

47. A is correct.

Potential energy of spring:

$$PE = \tfrac{1}{2}kx^2$$

Kinetic energy of mass:

$$KE = \tfrac{1}{2}mv^2$$

Set equal and rearrange:

$$\tfrac{1}{2}kx^2 = \tfrac{1}{2}mv^2$$

Cancel ½ from each side of the expression:

$$kx^2 = mv^2$$

$$x^2 = (mv^2) / k$$

$$x^2 = (m / k)v^2$$

Since m / k is provided:

$$x^2 = (0.038 \text{ kg} \cdot \text{m/N}) \cdot (18 \text{ m/s})^2$$

$$x^2 = 12.3 \text{ m}^2$$

$$x = \sqrt{12.3} \text{ m} = 3.5 \text{ m}$$

48. A is correct.

$$m_t = 2m_c$$

$$v_t = 2v_c$$

KE of the truck:

$$KE_t = \tfrac{1}{2}m_t v_t^2$$

continued…

Replace mass and velocity of the truck with the equivalent mass and velocity of the car:

$$KE_t = \tfrac{1}{2}(2m_c) \cdot (2v_c)^2$$

$$KE_t = \tfrac{1}{2}(2m_c) \cdot (4v_c^2)$$

$$KE_t = \tfrac{1}{2}(8m_c v_c^2)$$

The truck has 8 times the kinetic energy of the car.

49. C is correct.

When a car stops, the KE is equal to the work done by the force of friction from the brakes.

Through friction, the KE is transformed into heat.

50. B is correct.

When the block comes to rest at the end of the spring, the upward force of the spring balances the downward force of gravity.

$$F = kx$$

$$mg = kx$$

$$x = mg / k$$

$$x = (30 \text{ kg}) \cdot (10 \text{ m/s}^2) / 900 \text{ N/m}$$

$$x = 0.33 \text{ m}$$

51. D is correct.

$$KE = \tfrac{1}{2}mv^2$$

$$KE = \tfrac{1}{2}(0.33 \text{ kg}) \cdot (40 \text{ m/s})^2$$

$$KE = 264 \text{ J}$$

52. C is correct.

Work is the area under a force *vs.* position graph.

$$\text{area} = Fd = W$$

The area of the triangle as the object moves from 0 to 4 m:

$$A = \tfrac{1}{2}bh$$

$$A = \tfrac{1}{2}(4 \text{ m} \cdot)(10 \text{ N})$$

$$A = 20 \text{ J}$$

$$W = 20 \text{ J}$$

53. C is correct.

$$KE = PE$$

$$\tfrac{1}{2}mv^2 = mgh$$

$$v^2 / 2g = h$$

If v is doubled:

$$h_B = v_B^2 / 2g$$

$$v_J = 2v_B$$

$$(2v_B)^2 / 2g = h_J$$

$$4(v_B^2 / 2g) = h_J$$

$$4h_B = h_J$$

James's ball travels 4 times higher than Bob's ball.

54. B is correct.

Hooke's Law is given as:

$$F = -kx$$

The negative is only by convention to demonstrate that the spring force is a restoring force.

Graph B is correct because the force is linearly increasing with increasing distance.

The other graphs are constant or exponential.

55. C is correct.

A decrease in the KE for the rocket causes either a gain in its gravitational PE, the transfer of heat, or a combination.

The rocket loses some KE due to air resistance (friction).

Some of the rocket's KE is converted to heat, which causes the air temperature surrounding the rocket to increase.

Therefore, the average KE of the air molecules increases.

56. D is correct.

Kinetic energy is given as:

$$KE_1 = \tfrac{1}{2}mv^2$$

$$KE_2 = \tfrac{1}{2}m(4v)^2$$

$$KE_2 = \tfrac{1}{2}m(16v^2)$$

Increasing the velocity by a factor of 4 increases the KE by a factor of 16.

57. C is correct.

The total energy of the system is conserved.

A relationship between the initial compression of the spring and the final speed of the mass can thus be found.

$E_i = E_f$

$KE_i + PE_i = KE_f + PE_f$

Initially, the spring is compressed and has PE, and the mass is at rest, so the initial KE is zero.

At the end, the spring is uncompressed, and the mass is moving, so the final PE is zero, and the mass has KE.

$PE_i = KE_f$

$\frac{1}{2}kx^2 = \frac{1}{2}mv^2$

$kx^2 = mv^2$

$x\sqrt{k} = v\sqrt{m}$

The velocity and the compression distance of the spring are directly proportional.

Thus, if the spring is compressed by four times the original distance, then the velocity is four times the original.

$x_2 = 4x_1$

$v_2 = 4v_1$

58. C is correct.

Force: $F = ma$ (N)

Work: $W = Fd$ (N·m)

Power: $P = W / t$ (N·m/s)

59. A is correct.

$W_{net} = \Delta KE$

$\Delta KE = KE_f - KE_i$

$\Delta KE + KE_i = KE_f$

60. D is correct.

$v = (70 \text{ km/h})\cdot(1{,}000 \text{ m/km})\cdot(1 \text{ h/60 min})\cdot(1 \text{ min/60 s})$

$v = 19.4 \text{ m/s}$

Force acting against the car:

$F = mg \sin \theta$

$F = (1{,}320 \text{ kg})\cdot(9.8 \text{ m/s}^2) \sin 5°$

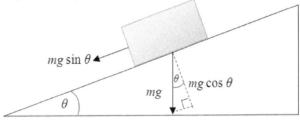

continued...

sin 5° = 0.0872, round it to 0.09

$F = (1{,}320 \text{ kg}) \cdot (9.8 \text{ m/s}^2) \cdot (0.09)$

$F = 1{,}164 \text{ N}$

$\text{N} = \text{kg} \cdot \text{m/s}^2$

Rate of energy is power:

$\text{Watts} = \text{kg} \cdot \text{m}^2/\text{s}^3$

Multiply velocity by the downward force:

$P = Fv$

$P = (1{,}164 \text{ N}) \cdot (19.4 \text{ m/s})$

$P = 22.6 \text{ kW}$

61. B is correct.

When the pebble falls, KE at impact = PE before.

$\text{PE} = \text{KE}$

$mgh = \text{KE}$

$mg(2h) = 2\text{KE}$

$2\text{PE} = 2\text{KE}$

If the mass and gravity are constant, then the height must be doubled.

62. D is correct.

Power = Work / time

A: Power = 50 J / 20 min = 2.5 J/min

B: power = 200 J / 30 min = 6.67 J/min

C: power = 10 J / 5 min = 2 J/min

D: power = 100 J / 20 min = 5 J/min

Typically, power is measured in watts or J/s.

63. A is correct.

kilowatt = unit of power

hour = unit of time

kW·h = power × time

power = work / time

kW·h = (work / time) × time

kW·h = work

64. B is correct.

Mechanical advantage:

d_1 / d_2

where d_1 and d_2 are the effort arm and load arm, respectively.

If d_1 is greater than d_2, force output is increased.

65. A is correct.

Find the final speed using conservation of energy.

Let the energy added as work be represented by W.

Then, conservation of energy requires:

$E_f = E_i + W$

$\frac{1}{2}mv^2_f = \frac{1}{2}mv^2_i + W$

Solving for v_f:

$v_f = \sqrt{v^2_i + (2W) / m}$

$v_f = \sqrt{[(10 \text{ m/s})^2 + (2) \cdot (4.5 \times 10^5 \text{ J}) / (1150 \text{ kg})]}$

$v_f = 29.7 \text{ m/s} \approx 30 \text{ m/s}$

66. D is correct.

Work = Force × distance

W = Fd

The unit kg·m/s cannot be manipulated to achieve this.

67. A is correct.

The Law of Conservation of Energy states that for an isolated system (no heat or work transferred), the energy of the system is constant.

Energy can only transform from one form to another.

68. C is correct.

The work done by this force is:

$W = Fd,$

where F = force applied by the crane and d = distance over which the force is active.

Solve for F using Newton's Second Law.

There are two forces on the beam – the applied force due to tension in the crane's cable and gravity.

$F_{net} = ma$

$F - mg = ma$

Therefore:

$W = m(a + g)d$

$W = (300 \text{ kg}) \cdot (1.4 \text{ m/s}^2 + 9.8 \text{ m/s}^2) \cdot (110 \text{ m})$

$W = 3.7 \times 10^5 \text{ J}$

69. D is correct.

Work = Force × displacement × cos θ

$W = Fd \cos \theta$

If $d = 0$, then work = 0

70. B is correct.

Relative to the ground, an object's gravitational PE = mgh, where h is the altitude.

PE is proportional to h; doubling h doubles PE.

71. D is correct.

$W = Fd$

$P = W / t$

$P = Fd / t$

$P = (1 \text{ N}) \cdot (1 \text{ m}) / 1 \text{ s}$

$P = 1 \text{ W}$

72. A is correct.

KE = PE

KE = mgh

h is directly proportional to KE.

If h doubles, then the KE doubles.

73. C is correct.

The initial KE of the helicopter is entirely converted to the potential energy of the landing gear and heat.

By conversation of energy:

$$\Delta KE = \Delta PE + Q$$

Let the equilibrium length of the landing gear's spring be L_0 and the compressed length be L.

The change in potential energy of the landing gear is:

$$\Delta PE = \tfrac{1}{2}k(\Delta x)^2$$

$$\Delta PE = \tfrac{1}{2}k(L_0 - L)^2$$

$$\Delta PE = \tfrac{1}{2}k(L_0 - (0.23)L_0)^2$$

$$\Delta PE = \tfrac{1}{2}k(0.77)^2L_0{}^2$$

The energy lost to heat is 23% of the initial kinetic energy.

The final kinetic energy is zero.

Therefore:

$$Q = (0.23)\,\Delta KE$$

$$Q = (0.23)\,\tfrac{1}{2}mv^2$$

Conservation of energy becomes:

$$\tfrac{1}{2}mv^2 = (0.23)^2L_0{}^2 + (0.23)\tfrac{1}{2}mv^2$$

Solving for k / m:

$$k / m = [(0.77)\,v^2] / [(0.23)^2L_0{}^2]$$

$$k / m = 819\ \text{s}^{-2} = 0.8\ \text{kN m}^{-1}\,\text{kg}^{-1}$$

74. C is correct.

$$PE = mgh$$

$$PE = (21 \times 10^3\,\text{kg}){\cdot}(9.8\ \text{m/s}^2){\cdot}(2.6 \times 10^3\ \text{m})$$

$$PE = 535\ \text{MJ}$$

75. D is correct.

$h_0 = 3.5$ m

$PE_0 = mgh$

$PE_1 = mgh(0.69) \rightarrow$ after first bounce

$PE_2 = mgh(0.69)^2 \rightarrow$ after second bounce

$PE_3 = mgh(0.69)^3 \rightarrow$ after third bounce

Because mass and gravity are constant, the final height is:

final height $= h(0.69)^3$

final height $= (4 \text{ m}) \cdot (0.69)^3$

final height $= 1.31$ m

final height $= 131$ cm

Notes for active learning

Notes for active learning

Rotational Motion – Detailed Explanations

1. D is correct.

An object is rolling down an incline experiences three forces, and hence three torques.

The forces are the force of gravity acting on the center of mass of the object, the normal force between the incline and the object, and the force of friction between the incline and the object.

If the origin is taken to be the center of the object, the force of gravity provides zero torque. This can be seen by noting that the distance between the origin and the point of application of the force is zero.

$$\tau_{\text{gravity}} = F_{\text{gravity}}r = mg(0) = 0$$

Similarly, the normal force contributes zero torque because the direction of the force is directed through the origin (pivot point).

$$\tau_{normal} = F_{normal}\,\text{r}\,\sin\theta = F_{normal}(R)\cdot(\sin 180°) = F_{normal}(R)\cdot(0) = 0$$

Use a coordinate system in which the x-axis is parallel to the incline and the y-axis is perpendicular.

The object is rolling in the positive x-direction.

The dynamical equation for linear motion along the x-direction is:

$$F_{\text{net}} = ma$$

$$(mg\sin\theta - f) = ma$$

Note that the normal force is only in the y-direction and thus does not directly contribute to the acceleration in the x-direction.

The dynamical equation for rotational motion is:

$$\tau_{\text{net}} = I\alpha$$

$fR = I\alpha$ (Note that the frictional force is perpendicular to the r vector, and $\sin 90° = 1$), where R is the radius of the object, f is the force of friction, and I is the moment of inertia.

A relation coupling these two dynamical equations is needed.

The equation of constraint imposed by the restriction that the object rolls without slipping:

$$\alpha = a\,/\,R$$

To find the linear acceleration, use the equation of constraint to eliminate α from the rotational equation by replacing it with $a\,/\,R$:

$$fR = I(a\,/\,R)$$

The force of friction is of no interest, so rearrange this last expression:

$$f = Ia\,/\,R^2$$

continued…

Substitute this into the linear dynamic equation from above in place of f:

$$(mg \sin \theta - Ia / R^2) = ma$$

Solving this for a:

$$a = mg \sin \theta / [m + (I / R^2)]$$

$$a = g \sin \theta / [1 + (I / mR^2)$$

The moment of inertia of any circular object can be written as NmR^2, where N is some real number different for different shapes.

For example, for a sphere,

$$I = (2/5)mR^2, \text{ so for a sphere } N = 2/5.$$

So, for any rolling object, the linear acceleration is:

$$a = g \sin \theta / (1 + N), \text{ which depends on neither the radius nor the mass of the object.}$$

Only the shape of the object is important.

2. B is correct.

Use the conservation of energy.

The initial and final states are the sphere at the top and bottom of the ramp, respectively.

Take the zero of gravitational potential energy to be the configuration in which the sphere is at the bottom.

The potential energy at the bottom is zero.

The sphere starts from rest, so the kinetic energy at the top is zero:

$$mgh = K_{\text{linear}} + K_{\text{rotation}}$$

$$mgh = \frac{1}{2}mv^2 + \frac{1}{2}I\omega^2$$

For a sphere,

$$I = (2/5)mr^2$$

Because the sphere rolls without slipping,

$$v = r\omega.$$

Substituting these into the conservation of energy equation:

$$mgh = \frac{1}{2}mr^2\omega^2 + \frac{1}{2}(2/5)mr^2\omega^2$$

$$mgh = \frac{1}{2}mr^2\omega^2 + (2/10)mr^2\omega^2$$

$$mgh = (7/10)mr^2\omega^2$$

continued…

Isolating ω:

$\omega = \sqrt{(10gh / 7r^2)}$

$\omega = \sqrt{[10 \cdot (9.8 \text{ m/s}^2) \cdot (5.3 \text{ m})] / [7 \cdot (1.7 \text{ m})^2]}$

$\omega = 5.1$ rad/s

3. A is correct.

There is no torque on the ball during the fall; its rotational speed does not change.

Therefore, the rotational KE just before the ball hits the floor is the same as rolling on the horizontal surface.

The rotational kinetic energy when it was rolling on the surface can be calculated directly.

Recall that the moment of inertia of a solid sphere is:

$I = 2/5 mR^2$

$K_{rot} = \frac{1}{2} I \omega^2$

$K_{rot} = \frac{1}{2} (2/5) mR^2 \omega^2$

Since the ball is rolling without slipping,

$\omega = v / R$

$K_{rot} = \frac{1}{2} (2/5) mR^2 (v / R)^2$

$K_{rot} = (2/10) mv^2$

$K_{rot} = (2/10) mv^2$

$K_{rot} = (2/10) \cdot (0.125 \text{ kg}) \cdot (4.5 \text{ m/s})^2$

$K_{rot} = 0.51$ J

4. D is correct.

The angular momentum of an object in circular motion is:

$L = I\omega$

where I is the moment of inertia with respect to the center of motion and ω is the angular speed.

The moment of inertia of a point mass is:

$I = mr^2$

The angular momentum is then:

$L = mr^2 \omega$

Angular speed is in rev/s.

continued…

Express in rad/s:

1.2 rev/s·$(2\pi$ rad/rev$) = 7.540$ rad/s

Finally:

$L = (0.38$ kg$)\cdot(1.3$ m$)^2\cdot(7.540$ rad/s$)$

$L = 4.8$ kg m^2/s

5. C is correct.

Conservation of angular momentum requires:

$L_f = L_i$

$I_f\omega_f = I_i\omega_i$

The final angular speed is:

$\omega_f = \omega_i\,(I_i\,/\,I_f)$

$\omega_f = (3.0$ rev/s$)\cdot(5.0$ kg·m$^2) / (2.0$ kg m$^2)$

$\omega_f = 7.5$ rev/s

6. C is correct.

An external torque changes the angular velocity of a system:

$\alpha = \sum\tau\,/\,I$, and hence its angular momentum.

To maintain a constant angular momentum, the sum of external torques must be zero.

7. D is correct.

For a rotating circular object:

$\omega = v\,/\,r$

$\omega = v\,/\,(d\,/\,2)$

$\omega = (4.0$ m/s$) / [(0.60$ m$) / 2]$

$\omega = 13.3$ rad/s

8. A is correct.

$K = \tfrac{1}{2}I\omega^2$

The moment of inertia of a rod with respect to its "short axis" is:

$I = (1/12)ml^2$

$K = (1/24)ml^2\omega^2$

$K = (1/24)\cdot(0.4500$ kg$)\cdot(1.20$ m$)^2\cdot(3.60$ rad/s$)^2$

$K = 0.350$ J

---

9. C is correct.

The moment of inertia can be found from the dynamic relation:

$$\tau = I\alpha$$

$$I = \tau / \alpha$$

where τ is the torque applied to the pulley, and α is the pulley's angular acceleration.

Torque is defined as:

$$FR \sin\theta$$

In this case, the force F is the tension force from the rope, R is the radius of the wheel, and $\theta = 90°$.

Thus, the torque is just the product of the tension of the rope and the radius of the pulley:

$$\tau = TR$$

The angular acceleration is related to the acceleration of a point on the circumference of the pulley:

$$\alpha = a / R$$

where a is the linear acceleration at the circumference, and R is the pulley's radius.

Combining these two results, the moment of inertia is:

$$I = TR^2 / a$$

If the rope does not slip on the pulley, then the rope, and hence the hanging mass, also has an acceleration a.

To continue, find the acceleration and the tension.

The tension is found by applying Newton's Second Law to the hanging mass.

There are two forces on the hanging mass; force of gravity pointing down and tension of the rope pointing up.

From Newton's Second Law (with down as the positive direction):

$$(mg - T) = ma$$

$$T = m(g - a)$$

With that, the moment of inertia becomes:

$$I = mR^2[(g - a) / a]$$

The acceleration can be found from the kinematic information given about the movement of the hanging mass.

The relation needed is:

$$\Delta y = \tfrac{1}{2}a(\Delta t)^2 + v_0(\Delta t)$$

$$a = 2\Delta y / (\Delta t)^2 = 2 \cdot (10\text{ m}) / (2\text{ s})^2$$

$$a = 5.000\text{ m/s}^2$$

continued…

Calculate the moment of inertia:

$I = (14\ \text{kg}) \cdot (2.0\ \text{m})^2 \cdot [(9.8\ \text{m/s}^2 - 5.000\ \text{m/s}^2) / (5.000\ \text{m/s}^2)]$

$I = 53.76\ \text{kg} \cdot \text{m}^2$

$I = 53.8\ \text{kg} \cdot \text{m}^2$

10. B is correct.

The *final speed* of the string can be found if the acceleration is known:

$v_f^2 = v_i^2 + 2ad = 0 + 2ad$

$v_f = \sqrt{(2ad)}$

where d is the distance over which the acceleration occurs.

The *acceleration* of the string is related to the acceleration of the pulley:

$a = r\alpha$

The *angular acceleration* follows from the dynamical equation for the rotational motion:

$\tau = I\alpha$

The *torque* is the force applied times the radius of the pulley:

$Fr = I\alpha$

Combining these equations gives:

$a = r^2 F / I$

The *final velocity* of the string is:

$v_f = \sqrt{(2r^2 Fd / I)}$

$v_f = \sqrt{[2 \cdot (0.125\ \text{m})^2 \cdot (5.00\ \text{N}) \cdot (1.25\ \text{m}) / (0.0352\ \text{kg} \cdot \text{m}^2)]}$

$v_f = 2.36\ \text{m/s}$

11. A is correct.

The angle of every point remains fixed relative to all other points.

The tangential acceleration increases as one moves away from the center ($a_t = \alpha r$).

The radial (or centripetal) acceleration also depends on the distance r from the center ($a_c = \omega^2 r$).

The only choice that does not depend on r (i.e., the same for all the points in the object) is I.

12. D is correct.

Linear velocity is related to angular velocity by $v = r\omega$.

13. C is correct.

For a rotating object:

$$K = \tfrac{1}{2}I\omega^2$$

The moment of inertia of a cylinder is:

$$I = \tfrac{1}{2}mr^2$$

Combining these:

$$K = \tfrac{1}{4}mr^2\omega^2$$

Solving for the angular speed:

$$\omega = \sqrt{(4K / mr^2)}$$

$$\omega = \sqrt{\{4\cdot(3.2 \times 10^7 \text{ J}) / [(400.0 \text{ kg}) (0.60 \text{ m})^2]\}}$$

$$\omega = 940 \text{ rad/s}$$

14. B is correct.

For a rotating object subject to a constant torque that has undergone a total angular displacement of $\Delta\theta$, the work done on the wheel is:

$$W = \tau\Delta\theta$$

Since work is the change in energy of the wheel from external forces, and since the wheel started with $E = 0$ ("from rest"), the final kinetic energy can be written as:

$$K = \tau\Delta\theta$$

By rotational kinematics:

$$\Delta\theta = \tfrac{1}{2}\alpha t^2$$

The equation of rotational dynamics is:

$$\tau = I\alpha, \text{ or } \alpha = \tau / I$$

So:

$$\Delta\theta = t^2\tau / 2I$$

and

$$K = t^2\tau^2 / 2I$$

(Note that this expression can be developed by finding the final angular velocity and using the definition of rotational kinetic energy.)

$$K = [(8.0 \text{ s})^2\cdot(3.0 \text{ N·m})^2] / [2\cdot(5.0 \text{ kg·m}^2)]$$

$$K = 58 \text{ J}$$

15. D is correct.

Tangential speed depends on the distance of the point from the fixed axis, so points at different radii have different tangential speeds.

Angular speed and acceleration of a rigid object do not depend on radius and are the same for all points (each point on the object must rotate through the same angle in the same time interval, or else it would not be rigid).

16. D is correct.

The angular momentum of a rotating object is:

$$L = I\omega$$

For a cylinder, $I = \frac{1}{2}mr^2$, giving:

$$L = \frac{1}{2}mr^2\omega$$

$$L = (0.5) \cdot (15.0 \text{ kg}) \cdot (1.4 \text{ m})^2 \cdot (2.4 \text{ rad/s})$$

$$L = 35 \text{ kg m}^2/\text{s}$$

17. D is correct.

The speed of an accelerating object is related to the distance covered by the kinematic relation:

$$v_f^2 - v_i^2 = 2ad$$

In this case, the initial speed is zero, so:

$$v_f = \sqrt{(2ad)}$$

Thus, find the linear acceleration of the disk.

An object is rolling down an incline experiences three forces, and hence three torques.

The forces are the force of gravity acting on the center of mass of the object, the normal force between the incline and the object, and the force of friction between the incline and the object.

If the origin is taken to be the center of the object, the force of gravity provides zero torque.

This can be seen by noting that the distance between the origin and the point of application of the force is zero.

$$\tau_{\text{gravity}} = F_{\text{gravity}}r = mg(0) = 0$$

Similarly, the normal force contributes zero torque because the direction of the force is directed through the origin (pivot point).

$$\tau_{normal} = F_{normal}\, r \sin \theta = F_{normal}(R) \cdot (\sin 180°) = F_{normal}(R) \cdot (0) = 0$$

Use a coordinate system in which the x-axis is parallel to the incline and the y-axis is perpendicular.

The object is rolling in the positive x-direction.

continued…

The dynamical equation for linear motion along the x-direction is:

$$F_{net} = ma$$

$$(mg \sin \theta - f) = ma$$

Note that the normal force is only in the y-direction and thus does not directly contribute to the acceleration in the x-direction.

The dynamical equation for rotational motion is:

$$\tau_{net} = I\alpha$$

$$fR = I\alpha \text{ (Note that the frictional force is perpendicular to the } r \text{ vector, and } \sin 90° = 1)$$

where R is the radius of the object, f is the force of friction, and I is the moment of inertia.

A relation coupling these two dynamical equations is needed.

Equation of constraint imposed by the restriction that the object rolls without slipping is:

$$\alpha = a / R$$

To find the linear acceleration, use the equation of constraint to eliminate α from the rotational equation by replacing it with a / R:

$$fR = I(a / R)$$

The force of friction is of no interest, so rearrange this last expression:

$$f = Ia / R^2$$

Substitute this into the linear dynamic equation from above in place of f:

$$(mg \sin \theta - Ia / R^2) = ma$$

Solving this for a:

$$a = mg \sin \theta / [m + (I / R^2)]$$

$$a = g \sin \theta / [1 + (I / mR^2)]$$

For a disk,

$$I = \tfrac{1}{2}mR^2$$

so:

$$a = g \sin \theta / (1 + \tfrac{1}{2}) = (2/3)g \sin \theta$$

Using this in the kinematic equation above:

$$v_f = \sqrt{(4gd \sin \theta / 3)}$$

$$v_f = \sqrt{[(4/3){\cdot}(9.8 \text{ m/s}^2){\cdot}(3.0 \text{ m}){\cdot}\sin (25°)]}$$

$$v_f = \sqrt{[(4/3){\cdot}(9.8 \text{ m/s}^2){\cdot}(3.0 \text{ m}){\cdot}(0.4226)]}$$

$$v_f = 4.1 \text{ m/s}$$

18. A is correct.

The center of the tire is moving at velocity v, but the bottom of the tire is in contact with the ground without slipping, so the speed at the bottom is 0 m/s.

Thus, with respect to the ground, the tire is *instantaneously* rotating about the point of contact with the ground, and all points in the tire have the same instantaneous angular speed.

The top of the tire is twice the distance from the ground as the center.

For the center of the tire:

$v = r\omega$

At the top:

$v_{top} = (2r)\omega = 2(r\omega) = 2v$

19. D is correct.

The string does not slip; the speed of the string is the same as the speed of a point on the circumference of the pulley.

The angular speed of the pulley (radius R) and the speed of a point on its circumference are related be:

$\omega = v / R$

$\omega = (5.0 \text{ m/s}) / (0.050 \text{ m})$

$\omega = 100 \text{ rad/s}$

20. D is correct.

One way of expressing the magnitude of angular momentum is:

$L = rp \sin \theta$

where r is the magnitude of the object's absolute position vector, p is the magnitude of the object's linear momentum, and θ is the angle between the position vector and the momentum vector.

The magnitude of the position vector is:

$r = \sqrt{(r_x^2 + r_y^2)}$

$r = \sqrt{[(2.00 \text{ m})^2 + (3.10 \text{ m})^2]}$

$r = 3.689 \text{ m}$

Its angle with respect to the positive x axis is:

$\theta_r = \text{atan}(r_y / r_x)$

$\theta_r = \text{atan}(3.10 / 2.00)$

$\theta_r = 0.99783 \text{ rad} = 57.17°$

continued…

The magnitude of the momentum vector is:

$$p = mv$$

$$p = (1.4 \text{ kg})(4.62 \text{ m/s})$$

$$p = 6.468 \text{ kg·m/s}$$

The angle of the momentum vector is given in the problem:

$$\theta_p = 45°$$

Thus, the angle between the two vectors is:

$$\theta = \theta_r - \theta_p$$

$$\theta = 57.17° - 45°$$

$$\theta = 12.17°$$

The angular momentum is then:

$$L = (3.689 \text{ m})·(6.468 \text{ kg m/s})·\sin(12.17°)$$

$$L = 5.0 \text{ kg·m}^2/\text{s}$$

21. B is correct.

Average angular acceleration is defined by:

$$\alpha_{avg} = \Delta\omega / \Delta t$$

$$\alpha_{avg} = |(6.3 \text{ rad/s} - 10.0 \text{ rad/s}) / (5.0 \text{ s})|$$

$$\alpha_{avg} = 0.74 \text{ rad/s}$$

22. D is correct.

The kinematic equation for angular velocity is:

$$\omega_f = \omega_i + \alpha\Delta t$$

Note that the sign of angular velocity is opposite from the sign of angular acceleration; the wheel is slowing down.

For the final kinetic energy to be larger than the initial kinetic energy, the wheel must slow and continue beyond zero speed so that it gains speed in the opposite direction.

That is, the final angular velocity must be negative.

The kinetic energy of a rotating wheel is:

$$K = \tfrac{1}{2}I\omega^2$$

continued...

The kinetic energy scales as the square of the angular speed.

To double the kinetic energy, the angular speed must increase by a factor of $\sqrt{2}$:

$\omega_f = -\omega_i \sqrt{2}$

Putting the result in the kinematic equation:

$-\omega_i \sqrt{2} = \omega_i + \alpha \Delta t$

Solving for Δt:

$\Delta t = -(1 + \sqrt{2})\omega_i / \alpha)$

$\Delta t = -(1 + \sqrt{2}) \cdot (26.0 \text{ rad/s}) / (-0.43 \text{ rad/s}^2)$

$\Delta t = 146 \text{ s}$

23. B is correct.

Apply conservation of energy.

Take the zero of gravitational potential energy to be the configuration when the disk is at the bottom of the ramp.

Conservation of energy demands:

$E_{\text{top}} = E_{\text{bottom}}$

The disk is at rest at the top of the ramp, so the kinetic energy is zero.

The total energy at the top is:

$E_{\text{top}} = K_{\text{top}} + U_{\text{top}}$

$E_{\text{top}} = 0 + mgh$

At the bottom of the ramp, the gravitational potential energy is zero, and the kinetic energy is the sum of the linear and rotational kinetic energies:

$E_{\text{bottom}} = K_{\text{bottom}} + U_{\text{bottom}}$

$E_{\text{bottom}} = K_{\text{linear}} + K_{\text{rotational}} + 0$

$E_{\text{bottom}} = \frac{1}{2} mv^2 + \frac{1}{2} I\omega^2$

Final linear velocity is not given, but the final angular velocity is given.

Eliminate the linear velocity in favor of the angular velocity by applying the constraint to a circular object rolling without slipping.

$v = \omega r$

$E_{\text{bottom}} = \frac{1}{2}m\omega^2 r^2 + \frac{1}{2}I\omega^2$

The moment of inertia of a disk is:

$I = \frac{1}{2}mr^2$

continued...

Thus:

$$E_{\text{bottom}} = \tfrac{1}{2}m\omega^2 r^2 + \tfrac{1}{2}(\tfrac{1}{2}\,mr^2)\omega^2$$

$$E_{\text{bottom}} = \tfrac{1}{2}m\omega^2 r^2 + \tfrac{1}{4}mr^2\omega^2$$

$$E_{\text{bottom}} = \tfrac{3}{4}m\omega^2 r^2$$

Combining results into the expression for conservation of energy:

$$mgh = \tfrac{3}{4}m\omega^2 r^2$$

or

$$h = 3\omega^2 r^2 / 4g$$

Note that the mass has canceled, a common occurrence in mechanics problems. The chance of error is reduced by proceeding algebraically (rather than plugging in numbers in the beginning), by which mass can be canceled.

Finally, note that diameter is given, not the radius.

$$r = d / 2 = 1.6 \text{ m}$$

$$h = [3(4.27 \text{ rad/s})^2 \cdot (1.60 \text{ m})^2] / [4(9.8 \text{ m/s}^2)]$$

$$h = 3.57 \text{ m}$$

24. A is correct.

The direction of angular velocity is taken by convention by applying the right-hand rule to the rotation.

In the case of a wheel of a forward-moving bicycle, that direction is to the left of the rider.

25. A is correct.

Angular acceleration can be found if linear acceleration is calculated from:

$$\alpha = a / R$$

The linear acceleration follows from the kinematic relationship:

$$v_f^2 - v_i^2 = 2ad$$

In this case, v_f is zero.

$$-v_i^2 = 2ad$$

Only absolute value of the acceleration is needed, so drop the minus sign and solve for a:

$$a = v_i^2 / 2d$$

The angular acceleration is:

$$\alpha = v_i^2 / 2dR$$

$$\alpha = (8.4 \text{ m/s})^2 / [2(115.0 \text{ m})(0.34 \text{ m})]$$

$$\alpha = 0.90 \text{ rad/s}^2$$

26. A is correct.

For a rotating object:

$$K = \tfrac{1}{2}I\omega^2$$

The moment of inertia of a cylinder is:

$$I = \tfrac{1}{2}mr^2$$

Combining these:

$$K = \tfrac{1}{4}mr^2\omega^2$$

The angular speed is given in rpm but needs to be in rad/s:

$$33.4 \text{ rpm} \cdot (1 \text{ min} / 60 \text{ s}) \cdot (2\pi \text{ rad/rev}) = 3.498 \text{ rad/s}$$

Thus:

$$K = (0.25) \cdot (3.0 \text{ kg}) \cdot (0.10 \text{ m})^2 \cdot (3.489 \text{ rad/s})^2$$

$$K = 0.091 \text{ J}$$

27. A is correct.

The angular momentum of a spinning object can be written as:

$$L = I\omega$$

The moment of inertia of a long thin uniform object of length *l* about an axis through the center perpendicular to the long axis is:

$$I = (1/12)ml^2$$

Giving:

$$L = (1/12)ml^2\omega$$

$$L = (1/12) \cdot (0.1350 \text{ kg}) \cdot (1.000 \text{ m})^2 \cdot (3.5 \text{ rad/s})$$

$$L = 0.0394 \text{ kg·m}^2/\text{s}$$

28. C is correct.

The period of a rotating object can be expressed as:

$$T = 2\pi / \omega$$

ω can be extracted from the definition of centripetal force:

$$F = mv^2 / r$$

Combining this with the relationship

$$v = \omega r \text{ gives:}$$

$$F = mr\omega^2$$

continued…

Thus:

$$\omega = \sqrt{(F / mr)}$$

Then:

$$T = 2\pi\sqrt{(mr / F)}$$

$$T = 2\pi\sqrt{[(23.0 \text{ kg})(1.3 \text{ m}) / (51.0 \text{ N})]}$$

$$T = 4.8 \text{ s}$$

29. C is correct.

Angular acceleration is:

$$\alpha = \Delta\omega / \Delta t$$

$$\alpha = (38.0 \text{ rad/s} - 0.00 \text{ rad/s}) / (10.0 \text{ s})$$

$$\alpha = 3.80 \text{ rad/s}$$

The other information given in the question is not needed.

30. C is correct.

The magnitude of *torque* can be expressed as:

$$\tau = rF \sin \theta$$

where r is the distance from the origin (taken here to be the pivot point) to the point of application of the force F, and θ is the angle between the position vector of the point of application and the force vector.

$$\tau = (0.63 \text{ m}) \cdot (17.0 \text{ N}) \cdot \sin (45°)$$

$$\tau = 7.6 \text{ N m}$$

31. D is correct.

Use the conservation of energy.

Take the zero of potential energy to be the configuration in which the sphere is at the bottom. The potential energy at the bottom is zero.

The disk starts from rest, so the kinetic energy at the top is zero:

$$mgh = K_{\text{linear}} + K_{\text{rotation}}$$

$$mgh = \tfrac{1}{2}mv^2 + \tfrac{1}{2}I\omega^2$$

For a disk,

$$I = \tfrac{1}{2}mr^2$$

Because the disk rolls without slipping,

$$v = r\omega$$

continued...

Substituting these into the conservation of energy equation:

$$mgh = \tfrac{1}{2}m(r^2\omega^2) + \tfrac{1}{2}(\tfrac{1}{2}mr^2)\omega^2$$

$$mgh = \tfrac{1}{2}mr^2\omega^2 + \tfrac{1}{4}mr^2\omega^2$$

$$mgh = \tfrac{3}{4}mr^2\omega^2$$

Isolating *h*:

$$h = 3r^2\omega^2 / 4g$$

$$h = [3 \cdot (1.60 \text{ m})^2 \cdot (4.27 \text{ rad/s})^2] / [4 \cdot (9.8 \text{ m/s}^2)]$$

$$h = 3.57 \text{ m}$$

32. D is correct.

The moment of inertia is proportional to the square of the distance of an object from the center of rotation.

As Paul moves toward the center, the moment of inertia decreases.

Angular momentum,

$$L = I\omega \text{ is conserved.}$$

As *I* decreases, ω, the angular speed increases to compensate.

33. B is correct.

Converting units:

$$210.0 \text{ rpm} \cdot (1 \text{ min} / 60 \text{ s}) \cdot (2\pi \text{ rad/revolution}) = 22.0 \text{ rad/s}$$

34. C is correct.

Use the conservation of energy:

$$E_f = E_i$$

$$KE_f + PE_f = KE_i + PE_i$$

Take the zero of potential energy at the initial height so that PE_i is zero.

The kinetic energy of a rolling object is the sum of the KE of translation plus the KE of rotation:

$$KE = \tfrac{1}{2}mv^2 + \tfrac{1}{2}I\omega^2$$

If the object rolls without slipping, as is the case here, then $v = r\omega$, where *R* is the radius of the sphere.

The moment of inertia of a sphere is:

$$I = (2/5)m\omega^2$$

continued...

With these, the kinetic energy of a sphere that rolls without slipping:

$$KE = \tfrac{1}{2}mv^2 + \tfrac{1}{2}(2/5)mr^2(v/r)^2$$

$$KE = \tfrac{1}{2}mv^2 + (1/5)mv^2$$

$$KE = (7/10)mv^2$$

Conservation of energy becomes:

$$(7/10)mv_f^2 + mgh = (7/10)mv_i^2$$

Canceling the mass and solving for the final speed:

$$v_f = \sqrt{[v_i^2 - (10/7)gh]}$$

The height, h, is related to the distance traveled and the angle of incline:

$$h = d \sin \theta$$

So:

$$v_f = \sqrt{[v_i^2 - (10/7)gd \sin \theta]}$$

$$v_f = \sqrt{[(5.5 \text{ m/s})^2 - (10/7) \cdot (9.8 \text{ m/s}^2) \cdot (3.0 \text{ m}) \cdot \sin (25°)]}$$

$$v_f = \sqrt{[(5.5 \text{ m/s})^2 - (10/7) \cdot (9.8 \text{ m/s}^2) \cdot (3.0 \text{ m}) \cdot (0.4226)]}$$

$$v_f = 3.5 \text{ m/s}$$

35. D is correct.

The dynamical relation for rotational motion is:

$$\tau = I\alpha$$

$$I = \tau/\alpha$$

where τ is the torque applied to the wheel, and α is the wheel's angular acceleration.

The torque is the product of the force and the radius of the pulley:

$$\tau = FR$$

Note that $\sin \theta = 1$, since $\theta = 90°$ [the problem mentions the force is applied tangentially].

So:

$$I = \tau/\alpha$$

$$I = FR/\alpha$$

$$I = (16.88 \text{ N}) \cdot (0.340 \text{ m}) / (1.20 \text{ rad/s}^2)$$

$$I = 4.78 \text{ kg·m}^2$$

36. B is correct.

The energy required to bring a rotating object to rest is:

$$E = \tfrac{1}{2}I\omega_0^2$$

The moment of inertia of a cylinder is:

$$I = \tfrac{1}{2}mr^2$$

So, the energy needed to stop the object is:

$$E = \tfrac{1}{4}mr^2\omega_0^2$$

Solving for the mass:

$$m = 4E / r^2\omega_0^2$$

The angular speed in rpm is given; convert to rad/s:

$$500.0 \text{ rpm} \cdot (1 \text{ min} / 60 \text{ sec}) \cdot (2\pi \text{ rad} / 1 \text{ rev}) = 52.36 \text{ rad/s}$$

The mass of the object is:

$$m = 4(3900 \text{ J}) / (1.2 \text{ m})^2 \cdot (52.36 \text{ rad/s})^2$$

$$m = 4.0 \text{ kg}$$

37. C is correct.

The torque at P_2 due to the weight of the billboard is:

$$\tau = r_{perp}F = r_{perp}mg$$

where r_{perp} is the perpendicular distance between P_2 and the line of application of the force.

Here, the weight of the billboard acts as if all of the mass is concentrated at the center of mass, which is the center of the billboard.

Thus, the line of application of the force of gravity is P_1P_3, the vertical line that passes through P_1 and P_3.

The length r_{perp} is the length of the horizontal line segment between P_2 and the line of application of the force (P_1P_3).

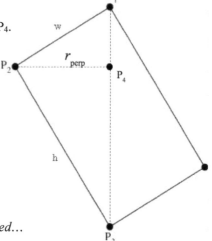

This line segment is perpendicular to P_1P_3 and intersects P_1P_3 at point P_4.

To find r_{perp}, note that the triangle $P_1P_2P_3$ is like the triangle formed by $P_1P_4P_2$.

The ratios of the lengths of corresponding sides of similar triangles are equal.

Apply this by forming the ratio of the length of the long side to the length of the hypotenuse of these two triangles:

$$h / \sqrt{(h^2 + w^2)} = r_{perp} / w$$

$$r_{perp} = hw / \sqrt{(h^2 + w^2)} \qquad \textit{continued...}$$

Giving an expression for torque:

$\tau = mg[hw / \sqrt{(h^2 + w^2)}]$

$\tau = (5.0 \text{ kg}) \cdot (9.8 \text{ m/s}^2) \cdot (0.20 \text{ m}) \cdot (0.11 \text{ m}) / \sqrt{[(0.20 \text{ m})^2 + (0.11 \text{ m})^2]}$

$\tau = 4.7 \text{ N m}$

38. B is correct.

An object is rolling down an incline experiences three forces, and hence three torques.

The forces are the force of gravity acting on the center of mass of the object, the normal force between the incline and the object, and the force of friction between the incline and the object.

If the origin is taken to be the center of the object, the force of gravity provides zero torque.

This can be seen by noting that the distance between the origin and the point of application of the force is zero.

$\tau_{\text{gravity}} = F_{\text{gravity}} r = mg(0) = 0$

Similarly, the normal force contributes zero torque because the direction of the force is directed through the origin (pivot point):

$\tau_{normal} = F_{normal} \, r \sin \theta = F_{normal}(R) \cdot (\sin 180°) = F_{normal}(R) \cdot (0) = 0$

Use a coordinate system in which the *x*-axis is parallel to the incline and the *y*-axis is perpendicular.

The object is rolling in the positive *x*-direction.

The dynamical equation for linear motion along the *x*-direction is:

$F_{\text{net}} = ma$

$(mg \sin \theta - f) = ma$

Note that the normal force is only in the *y*-direction and thus does not directly contribute to the acceleration in the *x*-direction.

The dynamical equation for rotational motion is:

$\tau_{\text{net}} = I\alpha$

$fR = I\alpha$

Note that the frictional force is perpendicular to the *r* vector, and sin 90° = 1,

where *R* is the radius of the object, *f* is the force of friction, and *I* is the moment of inertia.

A relation coupling these two dynamical equations is necessary.

The equation of constraint imposed by the restriction that the object rolls without slipping:

$\alpha = a / R$

To find the linear acceleration, use the equation of constraint to eliminate α from the rotational equation by replacing it with *a / R:*

continued…

$fR = I(a / R)$

The force of friction is of no interest, so rearrange this last expression:

$f = Ia / R^2$

Substitute this into the linear dynamic equation from above in place of f:

$(mg \sin \theta - Ia / R^2) = ma$

Solving this for a:

$a = mg \sin \theta / [m + (I / R^2)]$

$a = g \sin \theta / [1 + (I / mR^2)]$

For a sphere,

$I = (2/5)mR^2$

so:

$a_{\text{sphere}} = g \sin \theta / [1 + (2/5)]$

$a_{\text{sphere}} = (5/7)g \sin \theta$

$a_{\text{sphere}} = (0.714)g \sin \theta$

For the disk,

$I = \frac{1}{2} mR^2$

so:

$a_{\text{disk}} = g \sin \theta / (1 + \frac{1}{2})$

$a_{\text{disk}} = (2/3)g \sin \theta$

$a_{\text{disk}} = (0.667)g \sin \theta$

For the hoop,

$I = mR^2$

so:

$a_{\text{hoop}} = g \sin \theta / (1 + 1)$

$a_{\text{hoop}} = (1/2)g \sin \theta$

$a_{\text{hoop}} = (0.500)g \sin \theta$

The object with the largest acceleration will reach the bottom first.

The order is sphere, disk, hoop.

39. B is correct.

The kinetic energy of a rotation object is:

$K = \frac{1}{2}I\omega^2$

The moment of inertia is given in SI units, but the angular speed is in rpm, which is not an SI unit.

Convert:

96.0 rpm·(1 m/ 60 s)·(2π rad/rev) = 10.05 rad/s

$K = (0.5)·(6.0 \times 10^{-3}$ kg·m^2)·(10.05 rad/s)^2

$K = 0.30$ J

40. D is correct.

If a wheel of radius r rolls without slipping on the pavement, the relationship between angular speed ω and translational speed is:

$v = r\omega$

$\omega = v / r$

$\omega = (6.00$ m/s$) / (0.120$ m$)$

$\omega = 50.00$ rad/s

Converting this to rpm:

$\omega = (50.00$ rad/s$)·(1$ rev $/ 2\pi$ rad$)·(60$ s $/ 1$ min$)$

$\omega = 477.5$ rpm

$\omega = 478$ rpm

41. C is correct.

Her moment of inertia does not remain constant because the radial position of her hands is changing.

Angular momentum remains constant because there is no torque on her, assuming the ice is frictionless.

Her kinetic energy changes. To visualize this, notice that her hands initially execute uniform circular motion, and hence there is no tangential force. If this condition is maintained, her kinetic energy is constant.

However, *as she pulls her hands in,* they are no longer in uniform circular motion.

During this time, there will be a tangential component of force, and work will be done.

Another way to think about it is to recognize that because L is conserved,

$L_0 = L_f$

$I_0\omega_0 = I_f\omega_f$

I will decrease by some amount, and ω will multiply by that same amount, e.g., I halves and ω doubles.

continued…

When examining $KE = \frac{1}{2}I\omega^2$, I has gone down by half, but ω has doubled.

Since KE depends on ω squared, the change to ω has a greater impact on KE. KE increases.

42. D is correct.

There are two perpendicular components to Tanya's acceleration.

Centripetal acceleration:

$$a_c = r\omega^2$$

and tangential acceleration:

$$a_t = r\alpha$$

Since these two acceleration components are perpendiculars, find the magnitude of the total linear acceleration:

$$a = \sqrt{(a_c^2 + a_t^2)}$$

$$a = \sqrt{[(r\omega^2)^2 + (r\alpha)^2]}$$

$$a = r\sqrt{(\omega^4 + \alpha^2)}$$

$$a = (4.65 \text{ m})\cdot\sqrt{[(1.25 \text{ rad/s})^4 + (0.745 \text{ rad/s}^2)^2]}$$

$$a = 8.05 \text{ m/s}^2$$

43. C is correct.

For a rotating object:

$$\Delta\theta = \omega\Delta t$$

The angular speed is given in rpm, but needs to be in deg/s:

$$33.0 \text{ rpm}\cdot(1 \text{ min} / 60 \text{ s})\cdot(360 \text{ deg} / \text{rev}) = 198.0 \text{ deg/s}$$

$$\Delta\theta = (198.0 \text{ deg/s})\cdot(0.32 \text{ s})$$

$$\Delta\theta = 63°$$

44. C is correct.

The question asks to find the *magnitude* of the force of the floor on the bottom of the ladder.

Two forces are acting on the bottom of the ladder: the normal force of the floor, N, which acts in the vertical direction, and the force of friction, f, which acts horizontally.

These two forces are directed in mutually perpendicular directions, so the magnitude of the net force of the floor on the bottom of the ladder is:

$$F_{\text{net, bottom}} = \sqrt{(N^2 + f^2)}$$

The values of N and f can be found by applying the laws of rotational and linear static equilibrium.

Assume the ladder is static (not moving), but this is not a valid assumption until it is known whether the force of friction exceeds the limit imposed by static friction. This will be verified at the end. *continued...*

If the ladder is in equilibrium, the sum of the forces in both the x- and y-directions is zero, and the sum of the torques is zero:

$$\sum F_x = 0;\ \sum F_y = 0;\ \sum \tau = 0$$

The force equations are straightforward to fill in:

$$\sum F_x = F_w - f = 0$$

$$\sum F_y = N - Mg - mg = 0$$

where F_w is the normal force from the wall on the top of the ladder, M is the mass of the hanging block, and m is the mass of the ladder.

Since the wall is "smooth," there is no frictional force from the wall on the ladder.

The $\sum F_y$ equation has only one unknown quantity and can be solved for N:

$$N = (M + m)g = (80\text{kg} + 50\text{kg})(9.8\text{m/s}^2) = 1{,}274 \text{ N}$$

For the torque equation, choose the origin to be the point where the top of the ladder touches the wall. With that choice, the torque due to the normal force of the wall is zero, and the torque due to the hanging block is also zero (since these forces are exerted right at the origin).

There are three non-zero torques.

> One is the torque due to gravity on the ladder that acts as if all of the mass of the ladder is concentrated at the center of mass.

> The second torque is due to the normal force of the floor on the bottom of the ladder.

> The third torque is the force of friction acting on the bottom of the ladder.

Using the general formula for torque,

$$\tau = Fr \sin \phi,$$

where F is the force, r is the distance from the origin to the point where the force is being applied, and ϕ is the angle between the force vector and the r vector (which points from the origin to the point where the force is being applied):

$$\sum \tau = 0 + 0 - mg(L/2) \sin \beta - fL \sin \alpha + NL \sin \beta = 0$$

where m is the mass of the ladder and α and β are the angles in the figure shown.

Take counterclockwise torques to be positive and clockwise torques to be negative.

Use trigonometry to find α and β:

$$\alpha = \sin^{-1}(h/L) = \sin^{-1}(3.7/5) = 47.73°$$

$$\beta = 90° - \alpha = 42.27°$$

There is only one unknown quantity in the torque equation. Divide by L and rearrange.

Solve for f:

$$f \sin \alpha = N \sin \beta - \tfrac{1}{2}mg \sin \beta \qquad\qquad\qquad continued\ldots$$

$f = [(N - \frac{1}{2}mg) \cdot \sin \beta] / \sin \alpha$

$f = [1274 \text{ N} - \frac{1}{2}(50 \text{ kg}) \cdot (9.8 \text{ m/s}^2) \cdot (\sin 42.27°)] / [\sin 47.73°]$

$f = 935.3 \text{ N}$

Calculate the magnitude of the force on the bottom of the latter due to the floor:

$F_{\text{net, bottom}} = \sqrt{(N^2 + f^2)}$

$F_{\text{net, bottom}} = \sqrt{[(1,274 \text{ N})^2 + (935.3 \text{ N})^2]}$

$F_{\text{net, bottom}} = 1,580 \text{ N}$

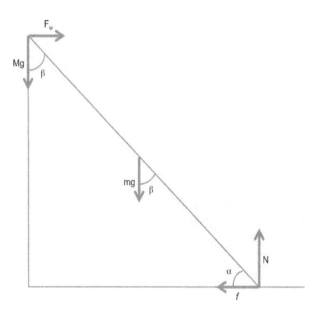

Finally, check if the force of friction is lower than the limit imposed by static friction.

$f_{max} = \mu_s N = (0.750) \cdot (1,274 \text{ N}) = 955 \text{ N}$

The calculated value for the force of static friction is 935.3 N, lower than the limit imposed by static friction,

So, the assumption that the system is in static equilibrium is valid.

If this number had been lower than the value of f, the static frictional force would *not* be able to hold the ladder stationary.

45. B is correct.

The maximum displacement occurs when the acceleration stops the forward motion and the wheel reverses direction.

Since.

$\theta_0 = 0, \Delta\theta = \theta - 0 = \theta.$

The kinematic relation is:

$\omega_f^2 - \omega_i^2 = 2\alpha\theta$

The final angular speed is zero at the instant that the wheel changes direction.

$-\omega_i^2 = 2\alpha\theta$

Thus, the angular displacement at that instant is:

$\theta = -(\omega_i^2 / 2\alpha)$

$\theta = -(29.0 \text{ rad/s})^2 / [2 \cdot (-0.52 \text{ rad/s}^2)]$

$\theta = 809 \text{ rad}$

46. C is correct.

Determine the direction of the angular momentum for a rotating object with the *right-hand rule*.

Take the fingers of your right hand and curl them in the direction that the object is rotating and stick your thumb out perpendicular to your fingers (as in a "thumbs-up" or "thumbs down" signal). The direction of your thumb points in the direction of the angular momentum – in this case, down.

For a mathematical approach, use the definition:

$L = r \times p$ applied to a point on the outer edge of the object.

Taking a point on the disk along the positive *x*-axis, the position vector *r* is in the positive *x*-direction, and the momentum vector *p* is positive *z*-direction.

The cross-product of these two vectors points down in the negative *y*-direction.

47. B is correct.

Consider this formula for rotational kinematics:

$\omega_f = \omega_i + \alpha \Delta t$

Solve for Δt:

$\Delta t = (\omega_f - \omega_i) / \alpha$

$\Delta t = (33.3 \text{ rad/s} - 15.0 \text{ rad/s}) / 3.45 \text{ rad/s}^2$

$\Delta t = 5.30 \text{ s}$

48. D is correct.

Use the conservation of energy.

Note that in the initial state, the ball is at rest, so the initial kinetic energy is zero.

Take the zero of gravitational potential energy to be the height of the ball at its final position.

The final kinetic energy has a translational part and a rotational part:

$E_f = E_i$

$KE_f = PE_i$

$KE_{\text{translation}} + KE_{\text{rotation}} = PE_i$

$\frac{1}{2}mv^2 + \frac{1}{2}I\omega^2 = mgh$

The ball is rolling without slipping, so the relationship between translational and rotational velocity is $v = r\omega$.

Then, the above becomes:

$\frac{1}{2}mr^2\omega^2 + \frac{1}{2}(2/5)mr^2\omega^2 = mgh$

$(7/10)mr^2\omega^2 = mgh$

continued...

Solving for the angular speed:

$$\omega = \sqrt{(10gh / 7r^2)}$$

$$\omega = \sqrt{\{[10 \cdot (9.8 \text{ m/s}^2) \cdot (5.3 \text{ m})] / [7 \cdot (1.7 \text{ m})^2]\}}$$

$$\omega = 5.1 \text{ rad/s}$$

49. B is correct.

There are three rotating bodies.

The total angular momentum is the sum of their angular momenta.

$$L_{total} = L_1 + L_2 + L_3$$

The angular momentum of a rotating object is:

$$L = I\omega$$

The flywheels are identical, so they each have the same rotational inertia I, so:

$$L = I(\omega_1 + \omega_2 + \omega_3)$$

The moment of inertia of the flywheels is:

$$I = \frac{1}{2}mr^2$$

$$I = 0.5(65.0 \text{ kg}) \cdot (1.47 \text{ m})^2$$

$$I = 70.23 \text{ kg m}^2$$

Thus:

$$L = (70.23 \text{ kg m}^2) \cdot (3.83 \text{ rad/s} + 3.83 \text{ rad/s} - 3.42 \text{ rad/s})$$

$$L = 298 \text{ kg m}^2/\text{s}$$

50. D is correct.

It seems that there is not enough information because neither the masses nor the radii of the sphere and cylinder are known. However, various parameters often cancel.

Try to find the acceleration of the two objects.

The object with the larger acceleration will reach the bottom first.

An object is rolling down an incline experiences three forces, and hence three torques.

The forces are the force of gravity acting on the center of mass of the object, the normal force between the incline and the object, and the force of friction between the incline and the object.

If the origin is taken to be the center of the object, the force of gravity provides zero torque.

This can be seen by noting that the distance between the origin and the point of application of the force is zero.

$$\tau_{gravity} = F_{gravity}r$$

continued…

$$F_{\text{gravity}}r = mg(0)$$

$$mg(0) = 0$$

Similarly, the normal force contributes zero torque because the direction of the force is directed through the origin (pivot point):

$$\tau_{normal} = F_{normal}\, r \sin\theta$$

$$F_{normal}\, r \sin\theta = F_{normal}(R)\cdot(\sin 180°)$$

$$F_{normal}(R)\cdot(\sin 180°) = F_{normal}(R)\cdot(0)$$

$$F_{normal}(R)\cdot(0) = 0$$

Use a coordinate system in which the x-axis is parallel to the incline and the y-axis is perpendicular. The object is rolling in the positive x-direction.

The dynamical equation for linear motion along the x-direction is:

$$F_{net} = ma$$

$$(mg \sin\theta - f) = ma$$

Note that the normal force is only in the y-direction and thus does not directly contribute to the acceleration in the x-direction.

The dynamical equation for rotational motion is:

$$\tau_{net} = I\alpha$$

$$fR = I\alpha$$

Note that the frictional force is perpendicular to the *r* vector, and sin 90° = 1,

where R is the radius of the object, f is the force of friction, and I is the moment of inertia.

A relation is needed to couple these two dynamical equations. This is the equation of constraint imposed by the restriction that the object rolls without slipping:

$$\alpha = a\,/\,R$$

To find the linear acceleration, use the equation of constraint to eliminate α from the rotational equation by replacing it with $a\,/\,R$:

$$fR = I(a\,/\,R)$$

The force of friction is of no interest, so rearrange this last expression:

$$f = Ia\,/\,R^2$$

Substitute this into the linear dynamic equation from above in place of f:

$$mg \sin\theta - (Ia\,/\,R^2) = ma$$

continued...

Solving this for *a*:

$$a = mg \sin \theta / [(m + (I / R^2)]$$

$$a = g\sin \theta / [1 + (I / mR^2)]$$

For a sphere,

$$I = (2/5)mR^2$$

So:

$$a_{\text{sphere}} = g \sin \theta / (1 + 2/5)$$

$$a_{\text{sphere}} = (5/7)g \sin \theta$$

For the cylinder,

$$I = \frac{1}{2}mR^2$$

So:

$$a_{\text{cylinder}} = g \sin \theta / (1 + \frac{1}{2})$$

$$a_{\text{cylinder}} = (2/3)g \sin \theta$$

Since 5/7 > 2/3, the acceleration of the sphere is greater than the acceleration of the cylinder so that the sphere will reach the bottom first.

Interestingly, neither the mass nor the size of the sphere or cylinder enters into the result.

Indeed, both the mass and radius cancel.

Since neither the masses nor the radii were given in the statement of the problem, it would not be possible to solve this problem by brute force numerical calculation.

51. D is correct.

$$813.0 \text{ rpm} \cdot (1 \text{ min} / 60 \text{ s}) \cdot (2\pi \text{ rad/rev}) = 85.14 \text{ rad/s}$$

52. B is correct.

The angular speed changes according to the kinematic relation:

$$\Delta\omega = \alpha\Delta t$$

$$\Delta t = \Delta\omega / \alpha$$

$$\Delta t = (0 \text{ rad/s} - 96.0 \text{ rad/s}) / (-1.5 \text{ rad/s}^2)$$

The angular acceleration is negative because the wheel is slowing down, and the initial ω is positive.

$$\Delta t = 64.0 \text{ s}$$

53. D is correct.

Apply the law of the conservation of energy.

There is no potential energy in this situation – all of the energy is kinetic (rotational kinetic energy in the initial state, translational kinetic energy in the final state).

$$E_f = E_i$$

$$K_f = K_i$$

$$\tfrac{1}{2}m_{car}v^2 = \tfrac{1}{2}I\omega^2$$

The moment of inertia of a disk is:

$$\tfrac{1}{2}mR^2,$$

where m is the mass of the disk, and R is its radius.

Then:

$$\tfrac{1}{2}m_{car}v^2 = \tfrac{1}{2}(\tfrac{1}{2}m_{wheel}R^2)\omega^2$$

Solving for velocity:

$$v = R\omega\sqrt{(m_{wheel}\,/\,2m_{car})}$$

The angular speed in rev/s must be converted to rad/s:

$$200.0 \text{ rev/s} \cdot (2\pi \text{ rad/rev}) = 1{,}256.6 \text{ rad/s}$$

Finally:

$$v = (0.50 \text{ m}) \cdot (1{,}256.6 \text{ rad/s}) \cdot \sqrt{[370.0 \text{ kg} \,/\, (2 \cdot 1{,}500.0 \text{ kg})]}$$

$$v = 221 \text{ m/s}$$

54. D is correct.

Since the motor spins at constant speed, there is no tangential component for the linear acceleration.

The linear acceleration is just the centripetal acceleration:

$$a = r\omega^2$$

Angular speed is in rpm, but needs to be in rad/s:

$$2695.0 \text{ rpm} \cdot (1 \text{ min/60 s}) \cdot (2\pi \text{ rad/rev}) = 282.22 \text{ rad/s}$$

$$a = (0.07165 \text{ m}) \cdot (282.22 \text{ rad/s})^2$$

$$a = 5{,}707 \text{ m/s}^2$$

55. A is correct.

The kinetic energy stored in a rotating object is:

$$K = \frac{1}{2} I \omega^2$$

With this, the angular speed as a function of energy is:

$$\omega^2 = 2K / I$$

The moment of inertia of a disk is:

$$I = \frac{1}{2} m r^2$$

Giving:

$$\omega^2 = 4K / mr^2$$

$$\omega = \sqrt{(4K / mr^2)}$$

$$\omega = \sqrt{[4\cdot(3.2 \times 10^7 \text{ J})] / [(400.0 \text{ kg})\cdot(0.60 \text{ m})^2]}$$

$$\omega = 943 \text{ rad/s}$$

56. B is correct.

An object having a moment of inertia I rotating with an angular speed of ω has angular momentum:

$$L = I\omega$$

The moment of inertia of a solid right circular cylinder about the axis indicated is $\frac{1}{2} m R^2$:

$$L = (\frac{1}{2} m R^2)\omega$$

$$L = 0.5(15.0 \text{ kg})\cdot(1.4 \text{ m})^2\cdot(2.7 \text{ rad/s})$$

$$L = 39.69 \text{ kg m}^2/\text{s}$$

$$L = 40 \text{ kg m}^2/\text{s}$$

57. B is correct.

The angular speed changes according to the kinematic relation:

$$\Delta\omega = \alpha\Delta t$$

$$\Delta t = \Delta\omega / \alpha$$

The torque is given, and the moment of inertia of a right circular cylinder is:

$$\frac{1}{2} m R^2$$

Find the angular acceleration from the dynamic relation:

$$\tau = I\alpha$$

$$\alpha = \tau / I$$

continued…

$\tau / I = \tau / (\frac{1}{2}mR^2)$

$\alpha = 2\tau / mR^2$

Combining the two results:

$\Delta t = mR^2 \Delta\omega / 2\tau$

$\Delta t = (10.0 \text{ kg}){\cdot}(3.00 \text{ m})^2{\cdot}(8.13 \text{ rad/s}) / [2(110.0 \text{ N m})]$

$\Delta t = 3.33 \text{ s}$

58. C is correct.

The gravitational force is the only influence making the satellite move in a circular path.

The centripetal acceleration in orbit is the gravitational acceleration at that orbital radius.

$v^2 / r = g'$

$v = \sqrt{(g'r)}$

$v = \sqrt{[(2.3 \text{ m/s}^2){\cdot}(34{,}000 \text{ m})]}$

$v = 280 \text{ m/s}$

Notes for active learning

Waves and Periodic Motion – Detailed Explanations

1. B is correct.

Frequency is the number of cycles per second a wave experiences, independent of the wave's amplitude.

2. D is correct.

Hooke's Law:

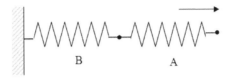

$$F = kx$$

It is known that the force on each spring must be equal if they are in static equilibrium, therefore:

$$F_A = F_B$$

Therefore, the expression can be written as:

$$k_A L_A = k_B L_B$$

Solve for the spring constant of spring B:

$$k_B = (k_A L_A) / L_B$$

3. D is correct.

In a longitudinal wave, particles of a material are displaced parallel to the direction of the wave.

4. C is correct.

$$\text{speed} = \text{wavelength} \times \text{frequency}$$

$$v = \lambda f$$

$$v = (0.25 \text{ m}) \cdot (1{,}680 \text{ Hz})$$

$$v = 420 \text{ m/s}$$

5. A is correct.

$$E_{stored} = \text{PE} = \tfrac{1}{2}kA^2$$

Stored energy is potential energy.

In simple harmonic motion (e.g., a spring), the potential energy is:

$$\text{PE} = \tfrac{1}{2}kx^2 \text{ or } \tfrac{1}{2}kA^2,$$

where k is a constant and A (or x) is the distance from equilibrium

A is the amplitude of a wave in simple harmonic motion (SHM).

6. D is correct.

The spring will oscillate around its new equilibrium position (3 cm below the equilibrium position with no mass hanging) with period $T = 2\pi\sqrt{(m / k)}$ since it is a mass-spring system undergoing simple harmonic motion.

To find k, consider how much the spring stretched when the mass was hung from it.

Since the spring found a new equilibrium point 3 cm below its natural length, the upwards force from the spring (F_s) must balance the downwards gravitational force (F_g) at that displacement:

$$|F_s| = |F_g|$$

$$kd = mg$$

$$k\,(0.03 \text{ m}) = (11 \text{ kg}){\cdot}(9.8 \text{ m/s}^2)$$

$$k = 3593 \text{ N/m}$$

Now, solve for T:

$$T = 2\pi\sqrt{(m / k)}$$

$$T = 2\pi\sqrt{(11 \text{ kg} / 3593 \text{ N/m})}$$

$$T = 0.35 \text{ s}$$

The frequency is the reciprocal of the period:

$$f = 1 / T$$

$$f = 1 / (0.35 \text{ s})$$

$$f = 2.9 \text{ Hz}$$

7. C is correct.

$$T = 1 / f$$

8. B is correct.

The period of a pendulum is:

$$T = 2\pi\sqrt{(L / g)}$$

If the elevator accelerates upwards, the constant acceleration adds to apparent acceleration due to gravity, and the period decreases.

$$g < g + a$$

The period decreases as the gravitational acceleration increases.

9. A is correct.

The period is the reciprocal of the frequency:

$$T = 1 / f$$

$$T = 1 / 100 \text{ Hz}$$

$$T = 0.01 \text{ s}$$

10. B is correct.

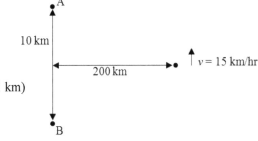

Convert v to m/s:

$$v = (15 \text{ km/1 h}) \cdot (1 \text{ h/60 min}) \cdot (1 \text{ min/60 s}) \cdot (10^3 \text{ m/1 km})$$

$$v = 4.2 \text{ m/s}$$

Convert frequency to λ:

$$\lambda = c / f$$

$$\lambda = (3 \times 10^8 \text{ m/s}) / (4.7 \times 10^6 \text{ Hz})$$

$$\lambda = 63.8 \text{ m}$$

According to Young's Equation:

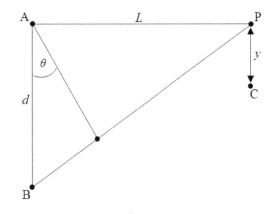

$$\lambda = yd / mL, \text{ where } m = 0, 1, 2, 3, 4...$$

Solve for y by rearranging to isolate y:

$$y = \lambda Lm / d$$

y = distance travelled by the ship:

$$y = vt$$

Since the first signal came at the point of maximum intensity, $m = 0$ at that time, at the next maximum $m = 1$.

Therefore:

$$t = L\lambda / vd$$

$$t = (200,000 \text{ m}) \cdot (63.8 \text{ m}) / (4.2 \text{ m/s}) \cdot (10,000 \text{ m})$$

$$t = 304 \text{ s}$$

Convert time from seconds to minutes:

$$t = (304 \text{ s}) \cdot (1 \text{ min/60 s})$$

$$t = 5.06 \text{ min} \approx 5.1 \text{ min}$$

For m values greater than 1, the calculated times are beyond the answer choices, so 5.1 min is the answer.

11. D is correct.

The tension in the rope is given by:

$$T = (mv^2) / L$$

where v is the velocity of the wave and L is the length of the rope.

Substituting:

$$v = L / t$$

$$T = [m(L / t)^2] / L$$

$$T = mL / t^2$$

$$t^2 = mL / T$$

$$t = \sqrt{(mL / T)}$$

$$t = \sqrt{[(2.31 \text{ kg}) \cdot (10.4 \text{ m}) / 74.4 \text{ N}]}$$

$$t = \sqrt{(0.323 \text{ s}^2)}$$

$$t = 0.57 \text{ s}$$

12. A is correct.

$$\omega_A = 2\omega_B$$

$$\omega_B = \sqrt{g / l_B}$$

Therefore:

$$l_B = g / \omega^2_B$$

Similarly, for A:

$$l_A = g / \omega^2_A$$

$$l_A = g / (2\omega_B)^2$$

$$l_A = \tfrac{1}{4}g / \omega^2_B$$

$$l_A = \tfrac{1}{4}l_B$$

13. B is correct.

$$F = -kx$$

Since the motion is simple harmonic, the restoring force is proportional to displacement.

Therefore, if the displacement is 5 times greater, then so is the restoring force.

14. C is correct.

> Period = (60 s) / (10 oscillations)
>
> T = 6 s

The period is the time for one oscillation.

If 10 oscillations take 60 s, then one oscillation takes 6 s.

15. A is correct.

Conservation of Energy:

> total ME = ΔKE + ΔPE = constant
>
> $\frac{1}{2}mv^2 + \frac{1}{2}kx^2$ = constant

16. B is correct.

A displacement from the position of maximum elongation to the position of maximum compression represents *half* a cycle.

If it takes 1 s, then the time required for a complete cycle is 2 s.

> $f = 1 / T$
>
> $f = 1 / 2$ s
>
> $f = 0.5$ Hz

17. C is correct.

Sound waves are longitudinal waves.

18. B is correct.

> speed = wavelength × frequency
>
> speed = wavelength / period
>
> $v = \lambda / T$
>
> $\lambda = vT$
>
> λ = (362 m/s)·(0.004 s)
>
> $\lambda = 1.5$ m

19. A is correct.

> $a = -A\omega^2 \cos(\omega t)$

where A is the amplitude or displacement from the resting position.

20. D is correct.

The acceleration of a simple harmonic oscillation is:

$$a = -A\omega^2 \cos(\omega t)$$

Its maximum occurs when $\cos(\omega t)$ is equal to 1

$$a_{max} = -\omega^2 x$$

If ω is doubled:

$$a = -(2\omega)^2 x$$

$$a = -4\omega^2 x$$

The maximum value of acceleration changes by a factor of 4.

21. B is correct.

Resonant frequency of a spring and mass system in any orientation:

$$\omega = \sqrt{(k/m)}$$

$$f = \omega / 2\pi$$

$$T = 1/f$$

$$T = 2\pi\sqrt{(m/k)}$$

Period of a spring does not depend on gravity.

The period remains constant because only mass and the spring constant affect the period.

22. C is correct.

$$v = \lambda f$$

$$\lambda = v/f$$

An increase in v and a decrease in f must increase λ.

23. B is correct.

Frequency is the measure of oscillations or vibrations per second.

frequency = 60 vibrations in 1 s

frequency = 60 Hz

speed = 30 m / 1 s

speed = 30 m/s

24. A is correct.

$T = (mv^2) / L$

$m = TL / v^2$

$m = (60 \text{ N})·(16 \text{ m}) / (40 \text{ m/s})^2$

$m = (960 \text{ N·m}) / (1{,}600 \text{ m}^2/\text{s}^2)$

$m = 0.6 \text{ kg}$

25. D is correct.

Amplitude is independent of frequency.

26. C is correct.

$f = \#\text{ cycles} / \text{time}$

$f = 60 \text{ drips} / 40 \text{ s}$

$f = 1.5 \text{ Hz}$

27. D is correct.

Transverse waves are characterized by their crests and valleys, caused by particles of the wave traveling "up and down" with respect to the lateral movement of the wave.

The particles in longitudinal waves travel parallel to the direction of the wave.

28. B is correct.

The velocity *vs.* time graph shows that at $t = 0$, the velocity of the particle is positive, and the speed is increasing. When speed increases, velocity and acceleration point in the same direction.

Therefore, the acceleration is non-zero and positive.

Only graph B displays a positive acceleration at $t = 0$.

29. C is correct.

The speed of a wave is determined by the characteristics of the medium (and the type of wave).

Speed is independent of amplitude.

30. A is correct.

$f = 1 / \text{period}$

$f = \#\text{ cycles} / \text{second}$

$f = 1 \text{ cycle} / 2 \text{ s}$

$f = \frac{1}{2} \text{ Hz}$

31. B is correct.

$f = v / \lambda$

$\lambda = v / f$

$\lambda = (340 \text{ m/s}) / (2{,}100 \text{ Hz})$

$\lambda = 0.16 \text{ m}$

32. D is correct.

Period $(T) = 2\pi\sqrt{(L / g)}$

The period is independent of the mass.

33. A is correct.

$v = \omega x$

$\omega = v / x$

$\omega = (15 \text{ m/s}) / (2.5 \text{ m})$

$\omega = 6.0 \text{ rad/s}$

34. D is correct.

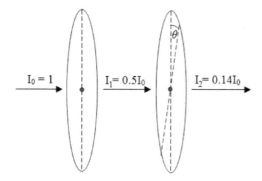

Unpolarized light on a polarizer reduces the intensity by ½.

$I = (½)I_0$

After that, the light is further reduced in intensity by the second filter.

Law of Malus:

$I = I_0 \cos^2 \theta$

$(0.14 \, I_0) = (0.5 \, I_0) \cos^2 \theta$

$0.28 = \cos^2 \theta$

$\cos^{-1} \sqrt{(0.28)} = \theta$

$\theta = 58°$

35. C is correct.

At a maximum distance from equilibrium, the energy in the system is potential energy, and the speed is zero.

Therefore, kinetic energy is zero.

Since there is no kinetic energy, the mass has no velocity.

36. D is correct.

$$v = \lambda f$$

$$f = v / \lambda$$

$$f = (240 \text{ m/s}) / (0.1 \text{ m})$$

$$f = 2{,}400 \text{ Hz}$$

37. B is correct.

In a transverse wave, the vibrations of particles are perpendicular to the direction of travel of the wave.

Transverse waves have crests and troughs that move along the wave.

In a longitudinal wave, the vibrations of particles are parallel to the direction of travel of the wave.

Longitudinal waves have compressions and rarefactions that move along the wave.

38. C is correct.

$$v = \sqrt{(T / \mu)},$$

where μ is the linear density of the wire.

$$T = v^2 \mu$$

$$\mu = \rho A$$

where A is the cross-sectional area of the wire and equals πr^2.

$$\mu = (2{,}700 \text{ kg/m}^3)\pi(4.6 \times 10^{-3} \text{ m})^2$$

$$\mu = 0.18 \text{ kg/m}$$

$$T = (36 \text{ m/s})^2 \cdot (0.18 \text{ kg/m})$$

$$T = 233 \text{ N}$$

39. D is correct.

Refraction is the change in the direction of a wave caused by the change in the wave's speed.

Examples of waves include sound waves and light waves.

Refraction is often seen when a wave passes from one medium to a different medium (e.g., from air to water and vice versa).

40. C is correct.

f = # cycles / second

f = 2 cycles / 1 s

f = 2 Hz

41. A is correct.

Pitch is how the brain perceives frequency.

Pitch becomes higher as the frequency increases.

42. C is correct.

The KE is maximum when the spring is neither stretched nor compressed.

If the object is bobbing, KE is maximum at the midpoint between fully stretched and fully compressed because all the spring's energy is KE rather than a mix of KE and PE.

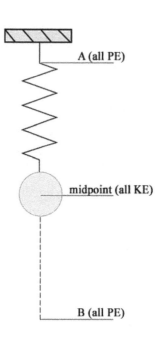

43. B is correct.

Torque = $rF \sin \theta$

$F = ma$, substitute mg for F

$\tau = rmg \sin \theta$

τ = (1 m)·(0.5 kg)·(10 m/s^2) sin 60°

τ = (5 kg·m^2/s^2) × 0.87

τ = 4.4 N·m

44. D is correct.

The Doppler effect can be observed to occur in all types of waves.

45. A is correct.

$v = \sqrt{(T / \mu)}$

where μ is the linear density of the wire.

$F_T = ma$

F_T = (2,500 kg)·(10 m/s^2)

F_T = 25,000 N

$v = \sqrt{(25,000 \text{ N} / 0.65 \text{ kg/m})}$

v = 196 m/s

The weight of the wire can be assumed to be negligible compared to the cement block.

46. B is correct.

$$f = \frac{1}{2\pi}[\sqrt{(g/L)}]$$

frequency is independent of mass.

47. A is correct.

$$T = 2\pi\sqrt{(L/g)}]$$

$$T = 2\pi\sqrt{(3.3 \text{ m} / 10 \text{ m/s}^2)}$$

$$T = 3.6 \text{ s}$$

48. C is correct.

$$f = (1/2\pi)\sqrt{(k/m)}$$

If k increases by a factor of 2, then f increases by a factor of $\sqrt{2}$ (or 1.41).

Increasing by a factor of 1.41 or 41%

49. D is correct.

In simple harmonic motion (SHM), the acceleration is greatest at the ends of motions (points A and D), where velocity is zero.

Velocity is greatest at the nadir, where acceleration is equal to zero (point C).

50. A is correct.

At the lowest point, the KE is maximum, and the PE is minimum.

The loss of gravitational PE equals the gain in KE:

$$mgh = \frac{1}{2}mv^2$$

Cancel m from each side of the expression:

$$gh = \frac{1}{2}v^2$$

$$(10 \text{ m/s}^2)\cdot(10 \text{ m}) = \frac{1}{2}v^2$$

$$(100 \text{ m}^2/\text{s}^2) = \frac{1}{2}v^2$$

$$200 \text{ m}^2/\text{s}^2 = v^2$$

$$v = 14 \text{ m/s}$$

51. A is correct.

Pitch is a psychophysical phenomenon when the sensation of a frequency is commonly referred to as the pitch of a sound.

A perception of high-pitch sound corresponds to a high-frequency sound wave, and a low-pitch sound corresponds to a low-frequency sound wave. Amplitude plays no role, and speed is constant.

52. C is correct.

Because wind is blowing in the reference frame of the train and the observer, it is not considered.

$$f_{observed} = [v_{sound} / (v_{sound} - v_{source})]f_{source}$$

$$f_{observed} = [340 \text{ m/s} / (340 \text{ m/s} - 50 \text{ m/s})] \cdot 500 \text{ Hz}$$

$$f_{observed} = 586 \text{ Hz}$$

$$\lambda = v / f$$

$$\lambda = 340 \text{ m/s} / 586 \text{ Hz}$$

$$\lambda = 0.58 \text{ m}$$

53. B is correct.

$$PE = \frac{1}{2}kx^2$$

Doubling the amplitude x increases PE by a factor of 4.

54. C is correct.

The elastic modulus is given by:

$$E = \text{tensional strength} / \text{extensional strain}$$

$$E = \sigma / \varepsilon$$

55. D is correct.

Resonance is when one system transfers its energy to another at that system's resonant frequency (natural frequency).

It is a forced vibration that produces the highest amplitude response for a given force amplitude.

56. A is correct.

Period of a pendulum:

$$T_P = 2\pi\sqrt{(L / g)}$$

Period of a spring:

$$T_S = 2\pi\sqrt{(m / k)}$$

The period of a spring does not depend on gravity and is unaffected.

57. B is correct.

At the top of its arc, the pendulum comes to rest momentarily; the KE and the velocity equal zero.

Since its height above the bottom of its arc is at a maximum at this point, its (angular) displacement from the vertical equilibrium position is at a maximum also.

The pendulum constantly experiences the forces of gravity and tension and is continuously accelerating.

58. D is correct.

The Doppler effect is the observed change in frequency when a sound source is in motion relative to an observer (away or towards).

If the sound source moves with the observer, there is no relative motion between the two, and the Doppler effect does not occur.

59. C is correct.

The amplitude of a wave is the magnitude of its oscillation from its equilibrium point.

60. A is correct.

$$f = (1/2\pi)\sqrt{(k/m)}$$

An increase in m causes a decrease in f.

61. D is correct.

$$T = 2\pi[\sqrt{(L/g)}]$$

No effect on the period because T is independent of mass.

62. A is correct.

speed = wavelength × frequency

period = 1 / frequency

$$v = \lambda f$$

$$v = \lambda / T$$

$$v = 15 \text{ m} / 5 \text{ s}$$

$$v = 3 \text{ m/s}$$

63. B is correct.

When the displacement is greatest, the force on the object is greatest.

When force is maximized, then acceleration is maximum.

64. D is correct.

$$\lambda = vf$$

$$f = v \,/\, \lambda$$

$$f = 1 \,/\, T$$

The period is the reciprocal of the frequency.

If f increases, then T decreases.

65. C is correct.

The definition of a period is the time required to complete one cycle.

Period = time / # cycles

T = 2 s / 1 cycle

T = 2 s

66. D is correct.

When it rains, the brightly colored oil slicks on the road are due to thin-film interference effects. This is when light reflects from the upper and lower boundaries of the oil layer and form a new wave due to interference effects.

These new waves are perceived as different colors.

67. B is correct.

A stretched string has all harmonics of the fundamental.

Notes for active learning

Notes for active learning

Sound – Detailed Explanations

1. B is correct.

Intensity is inversely proportional to distance (in W/m², not dB).

$$I_2 / I_1 = (d_1 / d_2)^2$$

$$I_2 / I_1 = (3 \text{ m} / 30 \text{ m})^2$$

$$100 \, I_2 = I_1$$

The intensity is 100 times greater at 3 m away than 30 m away.

Intensity to decibel relationship:

$$I \text{ (dB)} = 10 \log_{10} (I / I_0)$$

The intensity to dB relationship is logarithmic. Thus, if I_1 is 100 times the original intensity, then it is two times the dB intensity because:

$$\log_{10} (100) = 2$$

Thus, the decibel level at 3 m away is:

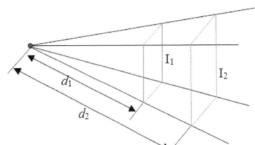

$$I \text{ (dB)} = (2) \cdot (20 \text{ dB})$$

$$I = 40 \text{ dB}$$

2. A is correct.

$$\text{distance} = \text{velocity} \times \text{time}$$

$$d = vt$$

$$t = d / v$$

$$t = (6{,}000 \text{ m}) / (340 \text{ m/s})$$

$$t = 18 \text{ s}$$

3. B is correct.

Resonance occurs when a vibrating system is driven at its resonance frequency, resulting in a relative maximum of the vibrational energy of the system.

When the force associated with the vibration exceeds the strength of the material, the glass shatters.

4. C is correct.

The third harmonic is shown in the figure below:

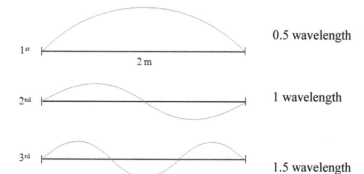

There are $(3/2)\lambda$ in the 2 m wave in the third harmonic

$L = (n / 2)\lambda$ (for n harmonic)

$L = (3 / 2)\lambda$ (for 3rd harmonic)

$L(2 / 3) = \lambda$

$\lambda = (2\text{ m})\cdot(2 / 3)$

$\lambda = 4/3$ m

5. B is correct.

High-pitched sound has a high frequency.

6. A is correct.

Snell's law:

$n_1 \sin \theta_1 = n_2 \sin \theta_2$

Solve for θ_2:

$(n_1 / n_2) \sin \theta_1 = \sin \theta_2$

$\sin \theta_1 = (n_1 / n_2) \sin \theta_2$

$\theta_2 = \sin^{-1}[(n_1 / n_2) \sin \theta_1]$

Substituting the given values:

$\theta_2 = \sin^{-1}[(1 / 1.5) \sin 60°]$

$\theta_2 = \sin^{-1}(0.67 \sin 60°)$

7. D is correct.

For a standing wave, the length and wavelength are related:

$L = (n / 2)\lambda$ (for n harmonic)

From the diagram, the wave is the 6th harmonic:

$L = (6 / 2)\lambda$

$\lambda = (2 \text{ m}) \cdot (2 / 6)$

$\lambda = 0.667 \text{ m}$

$f = v / \lambda$

$f = (92 \text{ m/s}) / (0.667 \text{ m})$

$f = 138 \text{ Hz}$

8. A is correct.

$v = d / t$

$v = (0.6 \text{ m}) / (0.00014 \text{ s})$

$v = 4,286 \text{ m/s}$

$\lambda = v / f$

$\lambda = (4,286 \text{ m/s}) / (1.5 \times 10^6 \text{ Hz})$

$\lambda = 0.0029 \text{ m} = 2.9 \text{ mm}$

9. C is correct.

The wave velocity is increased by a factor of 1.3.

$v^2 = T / \rho_L$

$T = v^2 \times \rho_L$

Increasing v by a factor of 1.3:

$T = (1.3v)^2 \rho_L$

$T = 1.69v^2 \rho_L$

T increases by 69%

10. D is correct.

$$\rho_L = \rho A$$

$$\rho_L = \rho(\pi r^2)$$

Thus, if the diameter decreases by a factor of 2, then the radius decreases by a factor of 2, and the area decreases by a factor of 4.

The linear mass density decreases by a factor of 4.

11. B is correct.

The v and period (T) of wire C are equal to wire A, so the ρ_L must be equal.

$$\rho_{LA} = \rho_{LC}$$

$$\rho_A A_A = \rho_C A_C$$

$$A_C = (\rho_A A_A) / \rho_C$$

$$(\pi / 4) \cdot (d_C)^2 = (7 \text{ g/cm}^3)(\pi / 4) \cdot (0.6 \text{ mm})^2 / (3 \text{ g/cm}^3)$$

$$(d_C)^2 = (7 \text{ g/cm}^3) \cdot (0.6 \text{ mm})^2 / (3 \text{ g/cm}^3)$$

$$d_C^2 = 0.84 \text{ mm}^2$$

$$d_C = \surd(0.84 \text{ mm}^2) = 0.92 \text{ mm}$$

12. A is correct.

$$A = \pi r^2$$

If d increases by a factor of 4, r increases by a factor of 4.

A increases by a factor of (r^2) 16.

13. B is correct.

Since the bird is moving toward the observer, the $f_{observed}$ must be higher than f_{source}.

Doppler shift for an approaching sound source:

$$f_{observed} = (v_{sound} / v_{sound} - v_{source}) f_{source}$$

$$f_{observed} = [340 \text{ m/s} / (340 \text{ m/s} - 10 \text{ m/s})] f_{source}$$

$$f_{observed} = (340 \text{ m/s} / 330 \text{ m/s}) \cdot (60 \text{ kHz})$$

$$f_{observed} = (1.03) \cdot (60 \text{ kHz})$$

$$f_{observed} = 62 \text{ kHz}$$

14. C is correct.

When an approaching sound source is heard, the observed frequency is higher than the frequency from the source due to the Doppler effect.

15. D is correct.

Sound requires a medium of solid, liquid, or gas substances to be propagated, and a vacuum is none of these.

16. A is correct.

According to the Doppler effect, frequency increases as the sound source moves towards the observer.

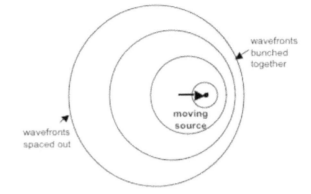

Higher frequency is perceived as a higher pitch.

Conversely, as the sound source moves away from the observer, the perceived pitch decreases.

17. C is correct.

If waves are out of phase, the combination has its minimum amplitude of (0.6 – 0.4) Pa = 0.2 Pa.

If waves are in phase, the combination has its maximum amplitude of (0.6 + 0.4) Pa = 1.0 Pa.

When the phase difference has a value between in-phase and out of phase, the amplitude will be between 0.2 Pa and 1.0 Pa.

18. B is correct.

$$I = P / A$$

$$I = P / \pi d^2$$

Intensity at $2d$:

$$I_2 = P / \pi (2d)^2$$

$$I_2 = P / 4\pi d^2$$

$$I_2 = \tfrac{1}{4} P / \pi d^2$$

The new intensity is ¼ the original.

19. A is correct.

$$\text{speed of sound} = \sqrt{[\text{resistance to compression} / \text{density}]}$$

$$v_{sound} = \sqrt{(E / \rho)}$$

Low resistance to compression and high-density results in low velocity because this minimizes the term under the radical and thus minimizes velocity.

20. B is correct.

A pipe open at each end has no constraint on displacement at the ends.

Furthermore, the pressure at the ends must equal the ambient pressure.

Thus, the pressure is maximum at the ends: an antinode.

21. C is correct.

For a pipe open at both ends, the resonance frequency:

$f_n = nf_1$

where n = 1, 2, 3, 4…

Therefore, only a multiple of 200 Hz can be a resonant frequency.

22. D is correct.

Unlike light, sound waves require a medium to travel through, and their speed depends on the medium.

Sound is fastest in solids, then liquids, and slowest in the air.

$v_{solid} > v_{liquid} > v_{air}$

23. B is correct.

Magnetic fields are induced by currents or moving charges.

24. C is correct.

$\lambda = v / f$

$\lambda = (5,000 \text{ m/s}) / (620 \text{ Hz})$

$\lambda = 8.1 \text{ m}$

25. A is correct.

Sound intensity radiating spherically:

$I = P / 4\pi r^2$

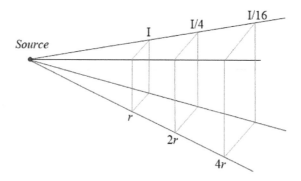

If r is doubled:

$I = P / 4\pi(2r)^2$

$I = \frac{1}{4}P / 4\pi r^2$

The intensity is reduced by a factor of ¼.

26. D is correct.

As the sound propagates through a medium, it spreads out in an spherical pattern.

The power is radiated along the surface of the sphere, and the intensity can be given by:

$I = P / (4\pi r^2)$ ← for the surface area of a sphere

Because the surface area of a sphere contains a square component with regards to radial distance, the sound intensity is inversely proportional to the square of the distance from the sound source.

27. B is correct.

The closed end is a node, and the open end is an antinode.

$\lambda = (4 / n)L$

where n = 1, 3, 5 …

For the fundamental n = 1:

$\lambda = (4 / 1)\cdot(1.5 \text{ m})$

$\lambda = 6 \text{ m}$

The 1.5 m tube (open at one end) is a quarter of a full wave, so the wavelength is 6 m.

28. A is correct.

The 1.5 m is ¼ a full wave, so the wavelength is 6 m, for the fundamental.

$f = v / \lambda$

$f = (960 \text{ m/s}) / 6 \text{ m}$

$f = 160 \text{ Hz}$

29. B is correct.

For a closed-ended pipe, the wavelength to the harmonic relationship is:

$\lambda = (4 / n)L$

where n = 1, 3, 5…

For the 5ᵗʰ harmonic n = 5

$\lambda = (4 / 5)\cdot(1.5 \text{ m})$

$\lambda_n = 1.2 \text{ m}$

Closed end tube

Harmonic # (n)	# of waves in a tube	# of nodes	# of antinodes	Wavelength to length
1	1/4	1	1	$\lambda = 4\,L$
3	3/4	2	2	$\lambda = 4/3\,L$
5	5/4	3	3	$\lambda = 4/5\,L$
7	7/4	4	4	$\lambda = 4/7\,L$

30. A is correct.

$f = v / \lambda$

$f = (340 \text{ m/s}) / (6 \text{ m})$

$f = 57 \text{ Hz}$

31. C is correct.

Wavelength to harmonic number relationship in a standing wave on a string:

$\lambda = (2L / n)$

where n = 1, 2, 3, 4, 5 …

For the 3ʳᵈ harmonic:

$\lambda = (2)\cdot(0.34 \text{ m}) / 3 = 0.23 \text{ m}$

32. D is correct.

Beat frequency equation:

$$f_{beat} = |f_2 - f_1|$$

If one of the tones increases in frequency, the beat frequency increases or decreases, but this cannot be determined unless the two tones are known.

33. A is correct.

For a closed-ended pipe, the wavelength to harmonic relationship is:

$$\lambda = (4 / n)L$$

where n = 1, 3, 5, 7...

The lowest three tones are n = 1, 3, 5

$$\lambda = (4 / 1)L; (n = 1)$$

$$\lambda = (4 / 3)L; (n = 3)$$

$$\lambda = (4 / 5)L; (n = 5)$$

34. D is correct.

The sound was barely perceptible; the intensity at Mary's ear is $I_0 = 9.8 \times 10^{-12}$ W/m^2.

Since the mosquito is 1 m away, imagine a sphere 1 m in the radius around the mosquito.

9.8×10^{-12} W emanates from each area 1 m^2.

Then, the surface area is $4\pi(1 \text{ m})^2$.

This is the power produced by one mosquito:

$$P = 4\pi r^2 I_0$$

$$P = 4\pi(1 \text{ m})^2 \times (9.8 \times 10^{-12} \text{ W/m}^2)$$

$$P = 1.2 \times 10^{-10} \text{ W}$$

energy = power × time

$$E = Pt$$

Energy produced in 200 s:

$$Pt = (1.2 \times 10^{-10} \text{ W}) \cdot (200 \text{ s})$$

$$E = 2.5 \times 10^{-8} \text{ J}$$

35. A is correct.

$$v = c / n$$

where c is the speed of light in a vacuum

$$v = \Delta x / \Delta t$$

$$\Delta x / \Delta t = c / n$$

$$\Delta t = n\Delta x / c$$

$$\Delta t = (1.33) \cdot (10^3 \text{ m}) / (3 \times 10^8 \text{ m/s})$$

$$\Delta t = 4.4 \times 10^{-6} \text{ s}$$

36. A is correct.

When waves interfere *constructively* (i.e., in-phase), the sound level is amplified.

When they interfere *destructively* (i.e., out of phase), they cancel, and no sound is heard.

Acoustic engineers work to ensure that there are no "dead spots" and the sound waves add.

An engineer should minimize destructive interference, which can distort the sound.

37. B is correct.

The *velocity of a wave on a string in tension* can be calculated by:

$$v = \sqrt{(TL / m)}$$

Graph B gives a curve of a square root relationship which is how velocity and tension are related.

$$y = x^{\frac{1}{2}}$$

38. D is correct.

From the diagram, the wave is a 6th harmonic standing wave.

Find wavelength:

$$\lambda = (2L / n)$$

$$\lambda = (2) \cdot (4 \text{ m}) / (6)$$

$$\lambda = 1.3 \text{ m}$$

Find frequency:

$$f = v / \lambda$$

$$f = (20 \text{ m/s}) / (1.3 \text{ m})$$

$$f = 15.4 \text{ Hz}$$

1st

2nd

3rd

39. B is correct.

Soundwave velocity is independent of frequency and does not change.

40. C is correct.

Find the frequency of the string, then the length of the pipe excited to the second overtone using that frequency.

The speed of sound in the string is:

$v_{string} = \sqrt{T/\mu}$

where T is the tension in the string, and μ is the linear mass density.

$v_{string} = \sqrt{[(75 \text{ N}) / (0.00040 \text{ kg})]}$

$v_{string} = 433.01 \text{ m/s}$

The wavelength of a string of length L_{string} vibrating in harmonic n_{string} is:

$\lambda_{string} = 2L_{string} / n_{string}$

Therefore, the vibration frequency of the string is:

$f = v_{string} / \lambda_{string}$

$f = [(n_{string})(v_{string})] / 2L_{string}$

$f = [(6)(433.01 \text{ m/s})] / (2 \times 0.50 \text{ m})$

$f = (2,598.06 \text{ m/s}) / 1 \text{ m}$

$f = 2,598.1 \text{ Hz}$

Now, consider the open pipe. The relationship between length, wavelength, and harmonic number for an open pipe is the same for a string.

Therefore:

$L_{pipe} = n_{pipe} (\lambda_{pipe} / 2)$

Since

$\lambda_{pipe} = v_{air} / f$

$L_{pipe} = n_{pipe} (v_{air} / 2f)$

Noting that the second overtone is the third harmonic ($n_{pipe} = 3$):

$L_{pipe} = (3 \times 345 \text{ m/s}) / (2 \times 2,598.1 \text{ Hz})$

$L_{pipe} = 0.20 \text{ m}$

Note that it is not necessary to calculate the frequency; its value cancel.

There is less chance for error if the two steps that use frequency are skipped.

$L_{pipe} = n_{pipe} (v_{air} / 2f)$

continued…

Substitute:

$$f = [(n_{string})(v_{string})] / 2L_{string}$$

which gives:

$$L_{pipe} = L_{string} (v_{air} / v_{string}) \cdot (n_{pipe} / n_{string})$$

It yields the same answer but with fewer calculations.

41. A is correct.

$$v = \sqrt{(T / \mu)}$$

$$\mu = m / L$$

$$v = \sqrt{(TL / m)}$$

$$v_2 = \sqrt{(T(2L) / m)}$$

$$v_2 = \sqrt{2} \sqrt{(TL / m)}$$

$$v_2 = v\sqrt{2}$$

42. C is correct.

For a standing wave, the resonance frequency:

$$f_n = nf_1$$

where n is the harmonic number, n = 1, 2, 3, 4 …

Therefore, only a multiple of 500 Hz can be a resonant frequency.

43. D is correct.

The angle of incidence always equals the angle of reflection.

A light beam entering a medium with a greater refractive index than the incident medium refracts *toward* the normal.

Thus, the angle of refraction is less than the angles of incidence and reflection.

Snell's law:

$$n_1 \sin \theta_1 = n_2 \sin \theta_2$$

where $n_1 < n_2$

For Snell's law to be true, then:

$$\theta_1 > \theta_2$$

44. A is correct.

Speed of sound in gas:

$$v_{sound} = \sqrt{(yRT / M)}$$

where y = adiabatic constant, R = gas constant, T = temperature and M = molecular mass

The speed of sound in a gas is only dependent upon temperature and not frequency or wavelength.

45. B is correct.

Waves only transport energy and not matter.

46. D is correct.

$$v = \lambda f$$

$$\lambda = v / f$$

$$\lambda = (344 \text{ m/s}) / (700 \text{ s}^{-1})$$

$$\lambda = 0.5 \text{ m}$$

The information about the string is unnecessary, as the only contributor to the wavelength of the sound in air is the frequency and the speed.

47. C is correct.

$$v = \lambda f$$

$$f = v / \lambda$$

Distance from a sound source is not part of the equation for frequency.

48. A is correct.

Velocity of a wave in a rope:

$$v = \sqrt{[T / (m / L)]}$$

$$t = d / v$$

$$d = L$$

$$t = d / \sqrt{[T / (m / L)]}$$

$$t = (8 \text{ m}) / [40 \text{ N} / (2.5 \text{ kg} / 8 \text{ m})]^{\frac{1}{2}}$$

$$t = 0.71 \text{ s}$$

49. C is correct.

Intensity to decibel relationship:

$$I (dB) = 10 \log_{10} (I_1 / I_0)$$

where I_0 = threshold of hearing

$$dB = 10\log_{10}[(10^{-5} \text{ W/m}^2) / (10^{-12} \text{ W/m}^2)]$$

$$I = 70 \text{ decibels}$$

50. B is correct.

The diagram represents the described scenario.

Wave is in 2nd harmonic with a wavelength of:

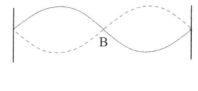

$$\lambda = (2 / n)L$$

$$\lambda = (2 / 2)\cdot(1 \text{ m})$$

$$\lambda = 1 \text{ m}$$

$$f = v / \lambda$$

$$f = (3.8 \times 10^4 \text{ m/s}) / (1 \text{ m})$$

$$f = 3.8 \times 10^4 \text{ Hz}$$

The lowest frequency corresponds to the lowest possible harmonic number.

For this problem, n = 2.

51. D is correct.

The speed of light traveling in a vacuum is *c*.

$$c = \lambda v$$

$$c = \lambda f$$

$$f = c / \lambda$$

Frequency and wavelength are inversely proportional so that an increase in frequency results in a decreased wavelength.

52. B is correct.

Radio waves are electromagnetic waves, while all other choices are mechanical waves.

53. D is correct.

Since the microphone is precisely equidistant from each speaker (i.e., equal path lengths), the sound waves take equal time to reach the microphone.

The speakers emit sound waves in phase (i.e., peaks are emitted simultaneously).

Since those peaks reach the microphone simultaneously (because of the equal path length), they combine constructively and add, forming a prominent peak or antinode.

54. C is correct.

Doppler equation for receding source of sound:

$$f_{observed} = [v_{sound} / (v_{sound} + v_{source})]f_{source}$$

$$f_{observed} = [(342 \text{ m/s}) / (342 \text{ m/s} + 30 \text{ m/s})]\cdot(1{,}200 \text{ Hz})$$

$$f_{observed} = 1{,}103 \text{ Hz}$$

The observed frequency is always lower when the source is receding.

55. D is correct.

$$f_1 = 600 \text{ Hz}$$

$$f_2 = 300 \text{ Hz}$$

$$f_2 = \tfrac{1}{2}f_1$$

$$\lambda_1 = v / f_1$$

$$\lambda_2 = v / (\tfrac{1}{2}f_1)$$

$$\lambda_2 = 2 (v / f_1)$$

The wavelength of the 300 Hz frequency is twice as long as the wavelength of the 600 Hz frequency.

56. C is correct.

$$f_2 = 2f_1$$

$$f = v / \lambda$$

$$v / \lambda_2 = (2)v / \lambda_1$$

Cancel v from each side of the expression:

$$1 / \lambda_2 = 2 / \lambda_1$$

$$\lambda = (2 / n)L, \text{ for open-ended pipes}$$

$$1 / (2 / n)L_2 = 2 / (2 / n)L_1$$

$$L_1 = 2L_2$$

$$L_1 / L_2 = 2$$

57. A is correct.

Resonance occurs when energy gets transferred from one oscillator to another of similar f by a weak coupling.

Dispersion is the spreading of waves due to the dependence of wave speed on frequency.

Interference is the addition of two waves in the same medium, which happens when waves from both strings combine, but that is not the excitation of the C_4 string.

58. C is correct.

frequency = 1 / period

$$f = 1 / T$$

$$f = 1 / 10 \text{ s}$$

$$f = 0.1 \text{ Hz}$$

Find wavelength:

$$\lambda = v / f$$

$$\lambda = (4.5 \text{ m/s}) / (0.1 \text{ Hz})$$

$$\lambda = 45 \text{ m}$$

59. D is correct.

$$v = \sqrt{K / \rho}$$

where K = bulk modulus (i.e., resistance to compression) and ρ = density.

Since ρ for water is greater than for air, the greater v for water implies that water's bulk modulus (K) must be much greater than for air.

60. C is correct.

When visible light strikes glass, it causes the electrons of atoms in the glass to vibrate at their non-resonant frequency.

The vibration is passed from one atom to the next, transferring the energy of the light.

The energy is passed to the last atom before the light is re-emitted out of the glass at its original frequency.

If the light energy were converted into internal energy, the glass would heat up and not transfer the light.

61. D is correct.

Sound intensity varies as the inverse square of the distance.

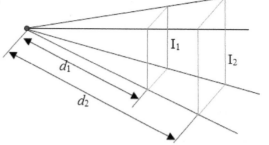

$I_2 / I_1 = (d_1 / d_2)^2$

where $d_1 = 3$ m and $d_2 = 9$ m

$I_2 = (10^{-6}$ W/m$^2) \cdot (3$ m $/ 9$ m$)^2$

$I_2 = 1.1 \times 10^{-7}$ W/m^2

62. A is correct.

Convert linear density to appropriate units:

$\mu = (140$ g/cm$) \cdot (1$ kg$/10^3$ g$) \cdot (100$ cm $/ 1$ m$)$

$\mu = 14$ kg/m

Find velocity:

$v = \sqrt{(T / \mu)}$

$v = \sqrt{(50$ N $/ 14$ kg/m$)}$

$v = 1.9$ m/s

Find frequency:

$f_n = nv / 2L$

$f_1 = (1) \cdot (1.9$ m/s$) / (2)(0.5$ m$)$

$f_1 = 1.9$ Hz

63. D is correct.

Sound travels faster in helium than in air due to its lower density.

The different speed of sound alters the timbre of her voice, but the frequency remains constant.

64. D is correct.

An overtone is any frequency higher than the fundamental.

In a stopped pipe (i.e., open at one end and closed at the other):

Harmonic #	Tone
1	fundamental tone
3	1st overtone
5	2nd overtone
7	3rd overtone

continued…

Find wavelength for the third overtone:

$$\lambda_n = (4L \,/\, n)$$

where n = 1, 3, 5, 7…

$$\lambda_n = [(4){\cdot}(1.4 \text{ m}) \,/\, (7)]$$

$$\lambda_n = 0.8 \text{ m}$$

Find frequency:

$$f = v \,/\, \lambda$$

$$f = (340 \text{ m/s}) \,/\, (0.8 \text{ m})$$

$$f = 425 \text{ Hz}$$

65. D is correct.

The Doppler effect for light is similar to that for sound.

The movement of the sound source away from the observer results in a decrease in the detected frequency.

66. B is correct.

Beat frequency equation:

$$f_{\text{beat}} = |f_2 - f_1|$$

$$f_{\text{beat}} = |\,524 \text{ Hz} - 460 \text{ Hz}\,|$$

$$f_{\text{beat}} = 64 \text{ Hz}$$

67. A is correct.

The frequency of a wave does not change when it enters a new medium.

$$v = (1 \,/\, n)c$$

where c = speed of light in a vacuum and n = refractive index.

The speed v decreases when light enters a medium with a higher refractive index.

68. D is correct.

Resonance is when one system transfers its energy to another at its resonant frequency (natural frequency).

Resonance is forced vibrations with the least energy input.

69. B is correct.

Refraction is the bending of a wave when it enters a medium where its speed is different.

Refraction occurs in sound waves and light waves.

70. A is correct.

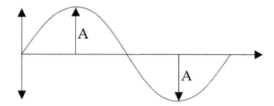

When a sound becomes louder, the energy of the sound wave becomes higher.

Amplitude is directly related to the energy of the sound wave:

more energy = higher amplitude

less energy = lower amplitude

71. D is correct.

Intensity is the power per unit area:

$I = W/m^2$

Loudness is a subjective measurement of the strength of the ear's perception to sound.

72. C is correct.

An overtone is any frequency higher than the fundamental.

In a stopped pipe (i.e., open at one end and closed at the other):

Harmonic #	Tone
1	fundamental tone
3	1st overtone
5	2nd overtone
7	3rd overtone

The first overtone is the 3rd harmonic.

Find wavelength:

$\lambda_n = (4L / n)$, for stopped pipe

where n = 1, 3, 5, 7…

$\lambda_3 = [(4) \cdot (3 \text{ m}) / 3)]$

$\lambda_3 = 4$ m

Find frequency:

$f = v / \lambda$

continued…

$f = (340 \text{ m/s}) / (4 \text{ m})$

$f = 85 \text{ Hz}$

Find velocity of a standing wave on the violin:

$f = v / 2L$

$v = (2L) \cdot (f)$

$v = (2) \cdot (0.36 \text{ m}) \cdot (85 \text{ Hz})$

$v = 61 \text{ m/s}$

Convert linear density to kg/m:

$\mu = (3.8 \text{ g/cm}) \cdot (1 \text{ kg}/10^3 \text{ g}) \cdot (100 \text{ cm} / 1 \text{ m})$

$\mu = 0.38 \text{ kg/m}$

Find tension:

$v = \sqrt{(T / \mu)}$

$T = v^2 \mu$

$T = (61 \text{ m/s})^2 \times (0.38 \text{ kg/m}) = 1{,}414 \text{ N}$

73. B is correct.

$I = \text{Power} / \text{area}$

The intensity I is proportional to the power, so an increase by a factor of 10 in power leads to an increase by a factor of 10 in intensity.

$I (\text{dB}) = 10\log_{10} (I / I_0)$

dB is related to the logarithm of intensity.

If the original intensity was 20 dB then:

$20 \text{ dB} = 10\log_{10} (I_1 / I_0)$

$2 = \log_{10} (I_1 / I_0)$

$100 = I_1 / I_0$

The new intensity is a factor of 10 higher than before:

$I_2 = 10 \, I_1$

$1{,}000 = I_2 / I_0$

$I (\text{dB}) = 10\log_{10} (1{,}000)$

$I (\text{dB}) = 30 \text{ dB}$

74. D is correct.

velocity = distance / time

$v = d / t$

$d = vt$

$d = (340 \text{ m/s}) \cdot (7 \text{ s})$

$d = 2{,}380 \text{ m} \approx 2 \text{ km}$

75. A is correct.

Constructive interference: the maximal magnitude of the amplitude of the resultant wave is the sum of the individual amplitudes:

3 cm + 8 cm = 11 cm

Destructive interference: the minimal magnitude of the amplitude of the resultant wave is the difference between the individual amplitudes:

8 cm − 3 cm = 5 cm

The magnitude of the amplitude of the resultant wave is between 5 and 11 cm.

76. B is correct.

All electromagnetic waves arise from accelerating charges.

When a charge is vibrating it is accelerating (change in the direction of motion is acceleration).

77. D is correct.

When tuning a radio, the tuner picks up specific frequencies by resonating at those frequencies. This filters out the other radio signals, so only that specific frequency is amplified.

By changing the tuner on the radio, a particular frequency is chosen that the tuner resonates at, and the signal is amplified.

Notes for active learning

Notes for active learning

DC Circuits – Detailed Explanations

1. B is correct.

$R = \rho L / A$, where ρ is the resistivity of the wire material.

If the length L is doubled, the resistance R is doubled.

If the radius r is doubled, the area $A = \pi r^2$ is quadrupled, and resistance R is decreased by ¼.

If these two changes are combined:

$$R_{new} = \rho(2L) / \pi(2r)^2$$

$$R_{new} = (2/4){\cdot}(\rho L / \pi r^2)$$

$$R_{new} = (2/4)R = \tfrac{1}{2}R$$

2. D is correct.

Internal resistance of battery is in series with resistors in circuit:

$$R_{eq} = R_1 + R_{battery}$$

where R_{eq} is equivalent resistance and R_1 is resistor connected to battery

$$V = IR_{eq}$$

$$V = I(R_1 + R_{battery})$$

$$R_{battery} = V / I - R_1$$

$$R_{battery} = (12 \text{ V} / 0.6 \text{ A}) - 6 \text{ } \Omega$$

$$R_{battery} = 14 \text{ } \Omega$$

3. C is correct.

An ohm Ω is defined as the resistance between two points of a conductor when a constant potential difference of 1 V, applied to these points, produces in the conductor a current of 1 A.

A series circuit experiences the same current through all resistors regardless of their resistance.

However, the voltage across each resistor can be different.

Since the light bulbs are in series, the current through them is the same.

4. C is correct.

$$\text{Power} = \text{current}^2 \times \text{resistance}$$

$$P = I^2R$$

Double current:

$$P_2 = (2I)^2R$$

continued…

$P_2 = 4(I^2 R)$

$P_2 = 4P$

Power is quadrupled.

5. A is correct.

$V = IR$

$I = V / R$

$I = (220 \text{ V}) / (400 \text{ } \Omega)$

$I = 0.55 \text{ A}$

6. D is correct.

A parallel circuit experiences the same potential difference across each resistor.

However, the current through each resistor can be different.

7. C is correct.

Ohm's Law:

$V = IR$

$V = (10 \text{ A}) \cdot (35 \text{ } \Omega)$

$V = 350 \text{ V}$

8. C is correct.

Resistor R_1 is connected directly across the battery.

Thus, the voltage across R_1 is V and is held constant at that value regardless of whatever happens in the circuit.

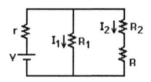

Similarly, the voltage across the series combination of R and R_2 is also held constant at V.

Since the voltage across R_1 will always be V, the current I_1 through R_1 will be unchanged as R changes (since R_1 did not change, $I_1 = V / R_1$ remains the same).

Since the voltage across the combination of R and R_2 will always be V when R is decreased, the effective resistance of the series combination $R + R_2$ decreases, and the current I_2 through R_2 increases.

9. C is correct.

$V = IR$

$I = V / R$

Ohm's law states that the current between two points is directly proportional to the potential difference between the points.

10. D is correct.

Kirchhoff's junction rule: the sum of currents coming into a junction is the sum of currents leaving a junction.

This *statement of conservation* of charge defines that no charge is created nor destroyed in the circuit.

11. A is correct.

Current is constant across resistors connected in series.

12. D is correct.

By convention, the direction of electric current is the direction that a positive charge migrates.

Therefore, current flows from the point of high potential to the point of lower potential.

13. D is correct.

Magnets provide magnetic forces.

Generators convert mechanical energy into electrical energy, turbines extract energy from fluids (e.g., air and water), and transformers transfer energy between circuits.

14. C is correct.

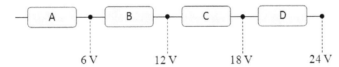

Batteries in series add voltage like resistors in series add resistance.

The resistances of the lights they power are not needed to solve the problem.

15. D is correct.

Ampere is the unit of current, which is defined as the rate of flow of charge.

The current describes how much charge (in Coulombs) passes through a point every second.

So, if the current is multiplied by the number of seconds (the time interval), one can measure just how much charge passed during that interval. Mathematically, the units are expressed as:

$$A = C / s$$

$$C = A \cdot s$$

16. B is correct.

"In a perfect conductor" and "in the absence of resistance" have the same meanings, and current can flow in conductors of varying resistances.

A semi-perfect conductor has resistance.

17. B is correct.

$R_1 = \rho L_1 / A_1$

$R_2 = \rho(4L_1) / A_2$

$R_1 = R_2$

$\rho L_1 / A_1 = \rho(4L_1) / A_2$

$A_2 = 4A_1$

$(\pi / 4)d_2^2 = (\pi / 4)\cdot(4)d_1^2$

$d_2^2 = 4d_1^2$

$d_2 = 2d_1$

18. D is correct.

The total resistance of a network of series resistors increases as more resistors are added.

$V = IR$

An increase in the total resistance results in a decrease in the total current through the network.

19. A is correct.

This is a circuit with two resistors in series.

Combine the two resistors into one resistor:

$R_T = R + R_{int}$

$R_T = 0.5 \ \Omega + 0.1 \ \Omega$

$R_T = 0.6 \ \Omega$

Ohm's law:

$V = IR$

$I = V / R$

$I = 9 \text{ V} / 0.6 \ \Omega$

$I = 15 \text{ A}$

20. A is correct.

Resistance = Ohms

$\Omega = V / A$

$\Omega = [(kg\cdot m^2/s^2)/C] / [C/s]$

$\Omega = kg\cdot m^2/(C^2/s)$

21. D is correct.

Ohm's Law:

$$V = IR$$

If V is constant, then I and R are inversely proportional.

An increase in R results in a decrease in I.

22. A is correct.

Ohm's law:

$$V = IR$$

Increasing V and decreasing R then increases I.

23. C is correct.

The total resistance of a network of series resistors increases as more resistors are added to the network.

An increase in the total resistance results in a decrease in the total current through the network.

A decrease in current results in a decrease in the voltage across the original resistor:

$$V = IR$$

24. A is correct.

Batteries in series add voltage (like resistors in series), the same current flows through each.

25. D is correct.

Calculate resistance:

$$R = \rho L / A$$

$$A = \pi r^2 = (\pi / 4)d^2$$

$$R = [(2.22 \times 10^{-8}\,\Omega \cdot m) \cdot (0.18\,m)] / (\pi / 4) \cdot (0.002\,m)^2$$

$$R = 1.3 \times 10^{-3}\,\Omega$$

$$P = I^2 R$$

$$P = (0.5\,A)^2 \times (1.3 \times 10^{-3}\,\Omega)$$

$$P = 0.32\,mW$$

26. D is correct.

Because the material of both wires is the same (copper), the resistivity of each wire is equal.

27. D is correct.

The equivalent resistance of the 3 Ω and 6 Ω resistors is:

$$1 / R_{eq} = 1 / (3\ \Omega) + 1 / (6\ \Omega)$$

$$R_{eq} = 2\ \Omega$$

The voltage across the equivalent resistor (i.e., the 6 Ω resistor) is given by the voltage divider relationship:

$$V_6 = 18\ V\ (2\ \Omega) / (2\ \Omega + 4\ \Omega) = 6\ V$$

The current through the 6 Ω resistor is:

$$I_6 = V_6 / 6\ \Omega = 1\ A$$

After the 3 Ω resistor burns out, the voltage across the 6 Ω resistor is found by the voltage divider relationship:

$$V_6{}' = 18\ V\ (6\ \Omega) / (6\ \Omega + 4\ \Omega) = 10.8\ V$$

Now the current through the 6 Ω resistor is:

$$I_6{}' = V_6{}' / 6\ \Omega = 1.8\ A$$

The current has increased.

28. A is correct.

Use the definition of one ampere:

$$1\ amp = 1\ C/s$$

Let the current expressed in electrons per second be denoted by I_e.

Solve:

$$I_e = (340 \times 10^{-3}\ C\ /\ 1\ s)\cdot(1\ electron\ /\ 1.6 \times 10^{-19}\ C)$$

$$I_e = 2.1 \times 10^{18}\ electrons/s$$

29. B is correct.

$$V = IR$$

$$R = V / I$$

30. D is correct.

Voltage = current × resistance

$$V = IR$$

$$V = (5\ A)\cdot(15\ \Omega)$$

$$V = 75\ V$$

Notes for active learning

Notes for active learning

Electrostatics – Detailed Explanations

1. C is correct.

Since charge is quantized, the charge Q must be a whole number (n) times the charge on a single electron:

Charge = # electrons × electron charge

$$Q = n(e^-)$$

$$n = Q / e^-$$

$$n = (-1 \text{ C}) / (-1.6 \times 10^{-19} \text{ C})$$

$$n = 6.25 \times 10^{18} \approx 6.3 \times 10^{18} \text{ electrons}$$

2. C is correct.

Coulomb's law:

$$F_1 = kQ_1Q_2 / r^2$$

If r is increased by a factor of 4:

$$F_e = kQ_1Q_2 / (4r)^2$$

$$F_e = kQ_1Q_2 / (16r^2)$$

$$F_e = (1/16)kQ_1Q_2 / r^2$$

$$F_e = (1/16)F_1$$

As the distance increases by a factor of 4, the force decreases by a factor of $4^2 = 16$.

3. D is correct.

Use a coordinate system in which a repulsive force is in the positive direction, and an attractive force is in the negative direction.

Gravitational Force: F_g

$$F_g = -Gm_1m_2 / r^2$$

$$F_g = -[(6.673 \times 10^{-11} \text{ N·m}^2/\text{kg}^2) \cdot (54,000 \text{ kg}) \cdot (51,000 \text{ kg})] / (180 \text{ m})^2$$

$$F_g = -0.18 \text{ N·m}^2 / (32,400 \text{ m}^2)$$

$$F_g = -5.7 \times 10^{-6} \text{ N}$$

Electrostatic Force: F_e

$$F_e = kQ_1Q_2 / r^2$$

$$F_e = [(9 \times 10^9 \text{ N·m}^2/\text{C}^2) \cdot (-15 \times 10^{-6} \text{ C}) \cdot (-11 \times 10^{-6} \text{ C})] / (180 \text{ m})^2$$

$$F_e = (1.49 \text{ N·m}^2) / (32,400 \text{ m}^2)$$

$$F_e = 4.6 \times 10^{-5} \text{ N}$$

continued...

Net Force:

$$F_{net} = F_g + F_e$$

$$F_{net} = (-5.7 \times 10^{-6} \, \text{N}) + (4.6 \times 10^{-5} \, \text{N})$$

$$F_{net} = 4 \times 10^{-5} \, \text{N}$$

F_{net} is positive, which means there is a net repulsive force on the asteroids.

Thus, the repulsive electrostatic force between them is stronger than the attractive gravitational force.

4. B is correct.

Newton's Third Law states that *for every force, there is an equal and opposite reaction force*, and this applies to electrostatic forces.

Electrostatic Force:

$$F_1 = kQ_1Q_2 \, / \, r^2$$

$$F_2 = kQ_1Q_2 \, / \, r^2$$

$$F_1 = F_2$$

5. D is correct.

charge = # electrons × electron charge

$$Q = ne^-$$

$$n = Q \, / \, e^-$$

$$n = (-10 \times 10^{-6} \, \text{C}) \, / \, (-1.6 \times 10^{-19} \, \text{C})$$

$$n = 6.3 \times 10^{13} \, \text{electrons}$$

6. C is correct.

Coulomb's law:

$$F_e = kQ_1Q_2 / r^2$$

If the separation is halved, then r decreases by ½:

$$F_2 = kq_1q_2 / (½r)^2$$

$$F_2 = 4(kq_1q_2 / r^2)$$

$$F_2 = 4F_e$$

7. D is correct.

Coulomb's law:

$$F = kQ_1Q_2 / r^2$$

Doubling both the charges and distance:

$$F = [k(2Q_1)\cdot(2Q_2)] / (2r)^2$$

$$F = [4k(Q_1)\cdot(Q_2)] / (4r^2)$$

$$F = (4/4)[kQ_1Q_2 / (r^2)]$$

$$F = kQ_1Q_2 / r^2, \text{ remains the same}$$

8. A is correct.

Coulomb's law:

$$F = kQ_1Q_2 / r^2$$

The Coulomb force between opposite charges is attractive.

Since the strength of the force is inversely proportional to the square of the separation distance (r^2), the force decreases as the charges are pulled apart.

9. B is correct. Coulomb's Law:

$$F_1 = kQ_1Q_2 / r^2$$

$$F_2 = kQ_1Q_2 / r^2$$

$$F_1 = F_2$$

Newton's Third Law: the force exerted by one charge on the other has the same magnitude as the force the other exerts on the first.

10. D is correct.

$$F_e = kQ_1Q_2 / r^2$$

$$F_e = (9 \times 10^9 \text{ N·m}^2/\text{C}^2)\cdot(-1.6 \times 10^{-19} \text{ C})\cdot(-1.6 \times 10^{-19} \text{ C}) / (0.03 \text{ m})^2$$

$$F_e = 2.56 \times 10^{-25} \text{ N}$$

11. C is correct.

Charge = # electrons × electron charge

$$Q = ne^-$$

$$n = Q / e^-$$

$$n = (8 \times 10^{-6} \text{ C}) / (1.6 \times 10^{-19} \text{ C})$$

$$n = 5 \times 10^{13} \text{ electrons}$$

12. A is correct.

An object with a charge can attract another object of opposite charge or a neutral charge.

Like charges cannot attract, but the type of charge does not matter otherwise.

13. D is correct.

$$W = Q\Delta V$$

$$V = kQ / r$$

Consider the charge Q_1 to be fixed and move charge Q_2 from initial distance r_i to final distance r_f.

$$W = Q_2(V_f - V_i)$$

$$W = Q_2[(kQ_1 / r_f) - (kQ_1 / r_i)]$$

$$W = kQ_1Q_2(1 / r_f - 1 / r_i)$$

$$W = (9 \times 10^9 \text{ N·m}^2/\text{C})·(2.3 \times 10^{-8} \text{ C})·(2.5 \times 10^{-9} \text{ C})·[(1 / 0.01 \text{ m}) - (1 / 0.1 \text{ m})]$$

$$W = 4.7 \times 10^{-5} \text{ J}$$

14. D is correct.

Equilibrium:

$$F = kq_1q_2 / r_1^2$$

$$F_{\text{attractive on } q2} = F_{\text{repulsive on } q2}$$

$$kq_1q_2 / r_1^2 = kq_2Q / r_2^2$$

$$q_1 = Qr_1^2 / r_2^2$$

$$q_1 = (7.5 \times 10^{-9} \text{ C})·(0.2 \text{ m})^2 / (0.1 \text{ m})^2$$

$$q_1 = 30 \times 10^{-9} \text{ C}$$

15. C is correct.

Coulomb's law:

$$F_e = kQ_1Q_2 / r^2$$

$$1 \text{ N} = kQ_1Q_2 / r^2$$

Doubling charges and keeping distance constant:

$$k(2Q_1)·(2Q_2) / r^2 = 4kQ_1Q_2 / r^2$$

$$4kQ_1Q_2 / r^2 = 4F_e$$

$$4F_e = 4(1 \text{ N}) = 4 \text{ N}$$

16. D is correct.

The Na^+ ion is positively charged and attracts the oxygen atom.

Oxygen is slightly negative because it is more electronegative than the hydrogen atoms to which it is bonded.

17. C is correct.

Charge = # of electrons × electron charge

$$Q = ne^-$$
$$Q = (30)\cdot(-1.6 \times 10^{-19}\ C)$$
$$Q = -4.8 \times 10^{-18}\ C$$

18. B is correct.

The repulsive force between two particles is:

$$F = kQ_1Q_2 / r^2$$

As r increases, F decreases

Using $F = ma$, a also decreases

19. C is correct.

The Coulomb is the basic unit of electrical charge in the SI unit system.

20. A is correct.

By the Law of Conservation of Charge, a charge cannot be created nor destroyed.

21. B is correct.

Coulomb's Law:

$$F = kQ_1Q_2 / r^2$$

If both charges are doubled,

$$F = k(2Q_1)\cdot(2Q_2) / r^2$$
$$F = 4kQ_1Q_2 / r^2$$

F increases by a factor of 4.

22. C is correct.

Coulomb's law:

$$F = kQ_1Q_2 / r^2$$
$$Q_1 = Q_2$$

continued…

Therefore:

$$Q_1 Q_2 = Q^2$$

$$F = kQ^2 / r^2$$

Rearranging:

$$Q^2 = Fr^2 / k$$

$$Q = \sqrt{(Fr^2 / k)}$$

$$Q = \sqrt{[(4 \text{ N}) \cdot (0.01 \text{ m})^2 / (9 \times 10^9 \text{ N·m}^2/\text{C}^2)]}$$

$$Q = 2 \times 10^{-7} \text{ C}$$

23. C is correct. Coulomb's law:

$$F = kQ_1 Q_2 / r^2$$

When each particle has lost ½ its charge:

$$F_2 = k(\tfrac{1}{2}Q_1) \cdot (\tfrac{1}{2}Q_2) / r^2$$

$$F_2 = (\tfrac{1}{4})kQ_1 Q_2 / r^2$$

$$F_2 = (\tfrac{1}{4})F$$

F decreases by a factor of ¼

24. A is correct.

$$W = Q\Delta V$$

$$V = kq / r$$

$$W = (kQq) \cdot (1 / r_2 - 1 / r_1)$$

$$W = (kQq) \cdot (1 / 2 \text{ m} - 1 / 6 \text{ m})$$

$$W = (kQq) \cdot (1 / 3 \text{ m})$$

$$W = (9 \times 10^9 \text{ N·m}^2/\text{C}^2) \cdot (3.1 \times 10^{-5} \text{ C}) \cdot (-10^{-6} \text{ C}) / (1 / 3 \text{ m})$$

$$W = -0.093 \text{ J} \approx -0.09 \text{ J}$$

The negative sign indicates that the electric field does the work on charge q.

25. D is correct.

charge = # electrons × electron charge

$$Q = ne^-$$

$$n = Q / e^-$$

$$n = (-600 \times 10^{-9} \text{ C}) / (-1.6 \times 10^{-19} \text{ C})$$

$$n = 3.8 \times 10^{12} \text{ electrons}$$

26. D is correct.

An object that is electrically polarized has had its charge separated into opposites and thus rearrange themselves within distinct regions.

27. D is correct.

Force due to motion:

$$F = ma$$

$$F = (0.001 \text{ kg}) \cdot (440 \text{ m/s}^2)$$

$$F = 0.44 \text{ N}$$

Force due to charge:

$$F = kQ_1Q_2 / r^2$$

$$Q_1 = Q_2$$

$$Q_1Q_2 = Q^2$$

$$F = kQ^2 / r^2$$

Rearranging:

$$Q^2 = Fr^2 / k$$

$$Q = \sqrt{(Fr^2 / k)}$$

$$Q = \sqrt{[(0.44 \text{ N}) \cdot (0.02 \text{ m})^2 / (9 \times 10^9 \text{ N} \cdot \text{m}^2/\text{C}^2)]}$$

$$Q = 1.4 \times 10^{-7} \text{ C} = 140 \text{ nC}$$

28. B is correct.

$$F = kQ_1Q_2 / r^2$$

	Force from +	Force from −
x direction	$\rightarrow$	$\rightarrow$
y direction	$\uparrow$	$\downarrow$

Net force $= \rightarrow$

29. B is correct.

Coulomb's law: the strength of the electrostatic force between two point charges.

$$F = kQ_1Q_2 / r^2$$

$$F = [(9 \times 10^9 \text{ N} \cdot \text{m}^2/\text{C}^2) \cdot (+3 \text{ C}) \cdot (-12 \text{ C})] / (0.5 \text{ m})^2$$

$$F = -1.3 \times 10^{12} \text{ N}$$

F is positive to indicate an attractive force; thus, the magnitude of the force is 1.3×10^{12} N.

30. D is correct.

Coulomb's law:

$$F_1 = kQ_1Q_2 / r^2$$

$$F_2 = kQ_1Q_2 / (0.25r)^2$$

$$F_2 = 16kQ_1Q_2 / r^2$$

$$F_2 = 16F_1$$

F increases by a factor of 16,

$$(1 \text{ N}) \cdot (16) = 16 \text{ N}$$

31. C is correct.

$$F_e = kQ_1Q_2 / r^2$$

$$F_e = [(9 \times 10^9 \text{ N} \cdot \text{m}^2/\text{C}^2) \cdot (5.1 \times 10^{-9} \text{ C})(2 \times 10^{-9} \text{ C})] / (0.1 \text{ m})^2$$

$$F_e = 9.18 \times 10^{-4} \text{ N}$$

$F_e \sin (60°)$ represents the force from one of the positive 2 nC charges.

Double to find the total force:

$$F_{total} = 2F_e \sin (60°)$$

$$F_{total} = 2(9.18 \times 10^{-4} \text{ N}) \sin (60°)$$

$$F_{total} = 1.6 \times 10^{-3} \text{ N}$$

The sine of the angle is used since only the vertical forces are added because the horizontal forces are equal and opposite, and therefore they cancel.

32. D is correct.

Coulomb's law:

$$F_e = kQ_1Q_2 / r^2$$

If r is increased by a factor of 3:

$$F_{new} = kQ_1Q_2 / (3r)^2$$

$$F_{new} = kQ_1Q_2 / (9r^2)$$

$$F_{new} = (1/9)kQ_1Q_2 / r^2$$

$$F_{new} = F_{original} (1/9)$$

$$F_{new} = (1 \text{ N}) \cdot (1/9)$$

$$F_{new} = 0.11 \text{ N}$$

33. D is correct.

$W = kq_1q_2 / r$

$r = \Delta x$

$r = 2\ \text{mm} - (-2\ \text{mm})$

$r = 4\ \text{mm}$

$W = [(9 \times 10^9\ \text{N·m}^2/\text{C}^2)·(4 \times 10^{-6}\ \text{C})·(8 \times 10^{-6}\ \text{C})] / (4 \times 10^{-3}\ \text{m})$

$W = (0.288\ \text{N·m}^2) / (4 \times 10^{-3}\ \text{m})$

$W = 72\ \text{J}$

34. D is correct.

$W = kQq(1 / r - 1 / \infty)$

$W_1 = (kQ_1q) / r_1$

$W_2 = (kQ_2q) / r_2$

$W_{total} = W_1 + W_2$

$W_{total} = kq(Q_1 / r_1 + Q_2 / r_2)$

$W_{total} = (9 \times 10^9\ \text{N·m}^2/\text{C}^2)·(10 \times 10^{-6}\ \text{C})·(+6\ \mu\text{C} / 0.002\ \text{m} + -6\ \mu\text{C} / 0.003\ \text{m})$

$W_{total} = 90\ \text{J}$

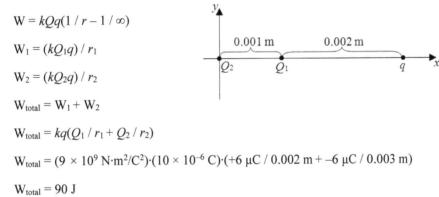

35. B is correct.

Use the energy relationship:

$PE_{before} = PE_{after} + KE$

Electrostatic Potential Energy:

$PE = kQq / r$

Solve:

$kQq / r_1 = kQq / r_2 + \tfrac{1}{2}mv^2$

$\tfrac{1}{2}mv^2 = kQq(1 / r_1 - 1 / r_2)$

$v^2 = (2kQq / m)·(1 / r_1 - 1 / r_2)$

$v = \sqrt{[(2kQq / m)·(1 / r_1 - 1 / r_2)]}$

$v = \sqrt{[(2)·(9 \times 10^9\ \text{N·m}^2/\text{C}^2)·(1.6 \times 10^{-19}\ \text{C})·(1.6 \times 10^{-19}\ \text{C}) /}$

$(9.1 \times 10^{-31}\ \text{kg})]·[(1 / 0.02\ \text{m}) - (1 / 0.05\ \text{m})]$

$v = 123\ \text{m/s}$

Note: only the magnitude of the charge is used.

36. A is correct.

1 amp = 1 C/s

$I = (2.3 \times 10^{13}$ electrons $/ 1) \cdot (1.6 \times 10^{-19}$ C $/ 1$ electron$) \cdot (1 / 15$ s$)$

$I = 0.25 \times 10^{-6}$ amps

$I = 0.25$ μA

37. B is correct.

1 kW = 1,000 W

1,000 W = 1,000 J/s

1 hr = (60 min)·(60 sec/min)

1 hr = 3,600 s

kW·hr = (1,000 J/s)·(3,600 s)

kW·hr = 3.6×10^3 J

Notes for active learning

Notes for active learning

Glossary of Physics Terms

A

Absolute humidity (or saturation value) – the maximum amount of water vapor that could be present in 1 m³ of air at a given temperature.

Absolute magnitude – a classification scheme that compensates for the differences in the distance to stars; calculates the brightness that stars would appear to have if they were at a defined, standard distance of 10 parsecs.

Absolute scale – temperature scale set so that zero is the theoretically lowest temperature possible (this would occur when random motion of molecules has ceased).

Absolute zero – the theoretically lowest temperature possible, at which temperature the molecular motion vanishes; –273.16 °C or 0 K.

Absorptance – the ratio of the total absorbed radiation to the total incident radiation.

Acceleration – the rate of change of velocity of a moving object with respect to time; the SI units are m/s²; by definition, this change in velocity can result from a change in speed, a change in direction, or a combination of changes in speed and direction.

Acceleration due to gravity – the rate of change in velocity produced in a body due to the Earth's attraction; denoted by the letter g (SI unit – m/s²); on the surface of the Earth, its average value is 9.8 m/s²; increases when going towards the poles from the equator; decreases with altitude and with depth inside the Earth; the value of g at the center of the Earth is zero.

Achromatic – capable of transmitting light without decomposing it into its constituent colors.

Acid rain – rainwater with a pH of less than 5.7 is acid rain. It is caused by the gases NO_2 (from car exhaust fumes) and SO_2 (from the burning of fossil fuels) dissolving in the rain. Acid rain kills fish, kills trees, and destroys buildings and lakes.

Acoustics – the science of the production, transmission, and effects of sound.

Acoustic shielding – a sound barrier that prevents the transmission of acoustic energy.

Adiabatic – any change in which there is no gain or loss of heat.

Adiabatic cooling – the decrease in temperature of an expanding gas that involves no additional heat flowing out of the gas; the cooling from the energy lost by expansion.

Adiabatic heating – the increase in temperature of the compressed gas that involves no additional heat flowing into the gas; the heating from the energy gained by compression.

Afocal lens – a lens of zero convergent power whose focal points are infinitely distant.

Air mass – a large, uniform body of air with nearly identical temperature and moisture conditions throughout.

Albedo – the fraction of the total light incident on a reflecting surface, especially a celestial body, which is reflected in all directions.

Allotropic forms – elements with several structures with different physical properties (e.g., graphite and diamond).

Alpha (α) particle – the nucleus of a helium atom (i.e., two protons and two neutrons) emitted as radiation from a decaying heavy nucleus (α-decay).

Alternating current – the flow of charge (i.e., current) traveling in one direction for one-hundredth of a second but the opposite direction for the next hundredth of a second. An electric current that first moves in one direction, then in the opposite direction with a regular frequency.

Amorphous – term that describes solids that have neither definite form nor structure.

Amp – unit of electric current; equivalent to coulomb/second.

Ampere – the unit amp; the SI unit of electric current; one ampere is the flow of one coulomb of charge per second.

Amplitude – the maximum absolute value attained by the disturbance of a wave or by any quantity that varies periodically. The height of the wave crest above the average position.

Amplitude (of an oscillation) – the maximum displacement of a body from its mean position during an oscillatory motion.

Amplitude (of waves) – the maximum displacement of particles of the medium from their mean positions during the propagation of a wave.

Angle of contact – the angle between tangents to the liquid surface and the solid surface inside the liquid; both tangents are drawn at the point of contact.

Angle of incidence – the angle of an incident (arriving) ray or particle to a surface; measured from a line perpendicular to the surface (the normal).

Angle of reflection – the angle of a reflected ray or particle from a surface; measured from a line perpendicular to the surface (the normal).

Angle of refraction – the angle between the refracted ray and the normal.

Angle of repose – the degree of inclination of a plane with the horizontal such that a body placed on the plane is on the verge of sliding but does not.

Angstrom – a unit of length; $1 = 10^{-10}$ m.

Angular acceleration – the rate of change of angular velocity of a body moving along a circular path; denoted by a.

Angular displacement – the angle described at the center of the circle by a moving body along a circular path. It is measured in radians.

Angular momentum (or *moment of momentum*) – the cross-product of position vector and momentum.

Angular momentum quantum number – from the quantum mechanics model of the atom, one of four descriptions of the energy state of an electron wave; describes the energy sublevels of electrons within the principal energy levels of an atom.

Angular velocity – the rate of change of angular displacement per unit of time.

Annihilation – when a particle and an antiparticle combine and release their rest energies in other particles.

Antineutrino – the antiparticle of neutrino; has zero mass and spin ½.

Archimedes principle – a body immersed in a fluid experiences an apparent loss of weight equal to the weight of the fluid displaced by the body.

Area – the amount of surface enclosed within the boundary lines.

Astronomical unit – the radius of the Earth's orbit is defined as one astronomical unit (A.U.).

Atom − the smallest unit of an element that can exist alone or in combination with other elements.

Atomic mass unit − relative mass unit (amu) of an isotope based on the standard of the ^{12}carbon isotope; one atomic mass unit (1 amu) = 1/12 the mass of a ^{12}C atom = 1.66×10^{-27} Kg.

Atomic number − the number of protons in the nucleus of an atom.

Atomic weight − weighted average of the masses of stable isotopes of an element as they occur in nature; based on the abundance of each isotope of the element and the atomic mass of the isotope compared to ^{12}carbon.

Avogadro's number − the number of ^{12}carbon atoms in exactly 12.00 g of C is 6.02×10^{23} atoms or other chemical units; the number of chemical units in one mole of a substance.

Avogadro's Law − under the same temperature and pressure conditions, equal volumes of gases contain an equal number of molecules.

Axis − the imaginary line about which a planet or other object rotates.

B

Background radiation − ionizing radiation (e.g., alpha, beta, gamma rays) from natural sources.

Balanced forces − when some forces act on a body and the resultant force is zero; see *Resultant forces*.

Balmer lines − lines in the spectrum of the hydrogen atom in the visible range; produced by the transition between a high energy level to n = 2, with n being the principal quantum number.

Balmer series − a set of four-line spectra; narrow lines of color emitted by hydrogen atom electrons as they drop from excited states to the ground state.

Bar − a unit of pressure; equal to 10^5 Pascal.

Barometer − an instrument that measures atmospheric pressure; used in weather forecasting and determining elevation above sea level.

Baryon − subatomic particle composed of three quarks.

Beat − a phenomenon of the periodic variation in sound intensity due to the superposition of waves differing slightly in frequency; rhythmic increases and decreases of volume from constructive and destructive interference between two sound waves of slightly different frequencies.

Bernoulli's theorem − states that the total energy per unit volume of a non-viscous, incompressible fluid in a streamline flow will remain constant.

Beta (β) particle − high-energy electron emitted as ionizing radiation from a decaying nucleus (β-decay); also a *beta ray*.

Big bang theory − the current model of galactic evolution in which the universe is assumed to have been created by an intense and brilliant explosion from a primeval fireball.

Binding energy − the net energy required to break a nucleus into its constituent protons and neutrons; also, the energy equivalent released when a nucleus is formed.

Biomass – the chemical energy stored in fast growing plants.

Black body – an ideal body which would absorb all incident radiation and reflect none.

Black body radiation – electromagnetic radiation emitted by an ideal material (the black body) perfectly absorbs and perfectly emits radiation.

Black hole – the remaining theoretical core of a supernova that is so dense that even light cannot escape.

Bohr model – model of the structure of the atom that attempted to correct the deficiencies of the solar system model and account for the Balmer series.

Boiling point – the temperature at which a phase change of liquid to gas occurs through boiling; the same temperature as the condensation point.

Boundary – the division between two regions of differing physical properties.

Boyle's Law – for a given mass of a gas at a constant temperature, the volume of the gas is inversely proportional to the pressure.

Brewster's Law – states that the refractive index of a material is equal to the tangent of the polarizing angle for the material.

British thermal unit (Btu) – the amount of energy or heat needed to increase the temperature of one pound of water one-degree Fahrenheit.

Brownian motion – the continuous random motion of solid microscopic particles suspended in a fluid medium due to their ongoing bombardment by atoms and molecules.

Bulk modulus of elasticity – the ratio of normal stress to the volumetric strain produced in a body.

Buoyant force – the upward force on an object immersed in a fluid.

C

Calorie – a unit of heat; 1 Calorie = 4.186 joule.

Candela – the SI unit of luminous intensity defined as the luminous intensity in each direction of a source that emits monochromatic photons of frequency 540×10^{12} Hz and has a radiant intensity in that direction of 1/683 W/sr.

Capacitance – the ratio of the charge stored per increase in potential difference.

Capacitor – an electrical device used to store charge and energy in the electrical field.

Capillarity – the rise or fall of a liquid in a tube of a fine bore.

Carnot's theorem – no engine operating between two temperatures can be more efficient than a reversible engine working between the same two temperatures.

Cathode rays – negatively charged particles (electrons) emitted from a negative terminal in an evacuated glass tube.

Celsius scale of temperature – the ice-point is taken as the lower fixed point (0 °C), and the steam-point is taken as the upper fixed point (100 °C); the interval between the ice-point and the steam-point is divided into 100 equal divisions; the unit division on this scale is 1 °C; previously called the centigrade scale; the relationship relates the temperatures on the Celsius scale and the Fahrenheit scale, C/100 = (F – 32) / 180; the temperature of a healthy person is 37 °C or 98.6 °F.

Center of gravity – the point through which all the weight of an object appears to act.

Centrifugal force – an apparent outward force on an object in circular motion; a consequence of the third law of motion.

Centripetal force – the radial force required to keep an object moving in a circular path.

Chain reaction – a self-sustaining reaction where some of the products can produce more reactions of the same kind (e.g., in a nuclear chain reaction, neutrons are the products that produce more nuclear reactions in a self-sustaining series).

Charles' Law – for a given mass of a gas at constant pressure, the volume is directly proportional to the temperature.

Chromatic aberration – an optical lens defect causing color fringes due to the lens bringing different colors of light to focus at different points.

Circular motion – the motion of a body along a circular path.

Closed system – the system which cannot exchange heat or matter with the surroundings.

Coefficient of areal expansion – the fractional change in surface area per degree of temperature change; see *Coefficient of thermal expansion.*

Coefficient of linear expansion – the fractional change in length per degree of temperature change; see *Coefficient of thermal expansion.*

Coefficient of thermal expansion – the fractional change in the size of an object per degree of change in temperature at constant pressure; the SI unit is K^{-1}.

Coefficient of volumetric expansion – the fractional change in volume per degree of temperature change; see *Coefficient of thermal expansion.*

Coherent source – when there is a constant phase difference between waves emitted from different parts of the source.

Combustion (or *burning*) – the combining of a substance with oxygen.

Compass – a magnet, which is free to rotate and indicate direction.

Complementary colors – two colors which, when mixed, give white. For examples: blue + yellow = white; red + cyan = white and green + magenta = white.

Compound – a substance made up of two or more elements chemically combined.

Compression – a part of a longitudinal wave in which the density of the particles of the medium is higher than the typical density.

Compressive stress – a force that tends to compress the surface as the Earth's plates move into each other.

Concave lens – a lens that spreads out light rays.

Condensation – the changing of a gas to a liquid state.

Condensation (sound) – a compression of gas molecules; a pulse of increased density and pressure that moves through the air at the speed of sound.

Condensation (water vapor) – where more vapor or gas molecules are returning to the liquid state than are evaporating.

Condensation nuclei – tiny particles such as dust, soot, or salt crystals suspended in the air on which water condenses.

Condensation point – the temperature at which a gas or vapor changes back to liquid; see *Boiling point*.

Conduction – the transfer of heat from a region of higher temperature to a region of lower temperature by increased kinetic energy moving from molecule to molecule, without the movement of the solid.

Constructive interference – the condition in which two waves are arriving at the same place at the same time and in phase add amplitudes to create a new wave.

Control rods – material inserted between fuel rods in a nuclear reactor to absorb neutrons and control the rate of the nuclear chain reaction.

Convection – transfer of heat from a region of higher temperature to a region of lower temperature by the displacement of high-energy molecules. For example, the displacement of warmer, less dense air (higher kinetic energy) by cooler, denser air (lower kinetic energy).

Conventional current – the opposite of electron current; considers an electric current to consist of a drift of positive charges that flow from the positive terminal to the negative terminal of a battery.

Convex lens – a lens that brings light rays together.

Corrosion – an undesired process where a metal is converted to one of its compounds (e.g., rusting).

Coulomb – a unit used to measure the quantity of electric charge; equivalent to the charge resulting from the transfer of 6.24 billion particles such as the electron.

Coulomb's Law – the relationship between charge, distance, and magnitude of the electrical force between two bodies; the force between two charges is directly proportional to the product of charges and inversely proportional to the square of the distance between the charges.

Covalent bond – a chemical bond formed by the sharing of a pair of electrons.

Covalent compound – chemical compound held by covalent bonds.

Crest – the point of maximum positive displacement on a transverse wave.

Critical angle – the limit to the angle of incidence when all light rays are reflected internally.

Critical mass – the mass of fissionable material needed to sustain a chain reaction.

Current – a flow of charge. Unit is Ampere (A).

Curvilinear motion – the motion of a body along a curved path.

Cycle – a complete vibration.

Cyclotron – a device used to accelerate the charged particles.

D

De-acceleration – negative acceleration when the velocity of a body decreases with time.

Decibel – unit of sound level; if P_1 & P_2 are two amounts of power, the first is said to be n decibels greater, where n = 10 log10 (P_1/P_2).

Decibel scale – a nonlinear scale of loudness based on the ratio of the intensity level of a sound to the intensity at the hearing threshold.

Density – the mass of a substance per unit volume.

Destructive interference – the condition in which two waves arriving at the same point at the same time out of phase add amplitudes that cancel to create zero total disturbance; see *constructive interference*.

Dewpoint temperature – the temperature at which condensation begins.

Dew – condensation of water vapor into droplets of liquid on surfaces.

Diffraction – the bending of light around the edge of an opaque object.

Diffuse reflection – light rays reflected in many random directions, as opposed to the parallel rays reflected from a perfectly smooth surface such as a mirror.

Diopter – unit of measure of the refractive power of a lens.

Direct current – an electrical current that always flows in one direction only (i.e., from the positive terminal to the negative terminal).

Direct proportion – when two variables increase or decrease in the same ratio (at the same rate).

Dispersion – the splitting of white light into its component colors of the spectrum.

Displacement – a vector quantity for the change in the position of an object as it moves in a particular direction; also the shortest distance between the initial position and the final position of a moving body.

Distance – a scalar quantity for the length of the path traveled by a body irrespective of its direction.

Distillation – the vaporization of a liquid by heating and then the condensation of the vapor by cooling.

Doppler effect – an apparent change in the frequency of sound or light due to the relative motion between the source of the sound or light and the observer.

E

Echo – a reflected sound distinguished from the original sound, usually arriving 0.1 s or more after the original sound.

Einstein mass-energy relation – $E = mc^2$; E is the energy released, m is the mass defect, and c is the speed of light.

Elastic potential energy – the potential energy of a body by its configuration (i.e., shape).

Elastic strain – an adjustment to stress in which materials recover their original shape after stress is released.

Electric circuit – consists of a voltage source that maintains an electrical potential, a continuous conducting path for a current to follow, and a device where the electrical potential does work; a switch in the circuit is used to complete or interrupt the conducting path.

Electric current – the flow of electric charge; the electric force field produced by an electrical charge.

Electric field line – an imaginary curve tangent to which at any given point gives the direction of the electric field at that point.

Electric field lines – a map of an electric field representing the direction of the force that a test charge would experience; the direction of an electric field shown by lines of force.

Electric generator – a mechanical device that uses wire loops rotating in a magnetic field to produce electromagnetic induction to generate electricity.

Electric potential energy – potential energy due to the position of a charge near other charges.

Electrical conductors – materials that have electrons free to move throughout the material (e.g., metals); allows electric current to flow through the material.

Electrical energy – a form of energy from electromagnetic interactions.

Electric force – a fundamental force that results from the interaction of electrical charges; it is the most powerful force in the universe.

Electrical insulators – electrical nonconductors, or materials that obstruct the flow of electric current.

Electrical nonconductors – materials with electrons that do not move easily within the material (e.g., rubber); also called *electrical insulators*.

Electrical resistance – the property of opposing or reducing electric current.

Electrode – a conductor, which dips into an electrolyte and allows the electrons to flow to and from the electrolyte.

Electrolysis – the production of a chemical change using electricity. Electrolysis can be used to split up water into hydrogen and oxygen.

Electrolyte – water solution of ionic substances that will conduct an electric current.

Electromagnet – a magnet formed by a solenoid that can be turned on and off by turning the current on and off.

Electromagnetic force – one of four fundamental forces; the force of attraction or repulsion between two charged particles.

Electromagnetic induction – the process in which current is induced in a coil whenever there is a change in the magnetic flux linked with the coil.

Electromagnetic waves – the waves due to oscillating electrical and magnetic fields and do not need any material medium for their propagation; can travel through a material medium (e.g., light waves and radio waves); travel in a vacuum with a speed 3.0×10^8 m/s.

Electron – a subatomic particle that has the smallest negative charge possible; usually found in an orbital of an atom but is gained or lost when atoms become ions.

Electron configuration – the arrangement of electrons in orbits and sub-orbits about the nucleus of an atom.

Electron current – the opposite of conventional current; considers electric current to consist of a drift of negative charges that flows from the negative terminal to the positive terminal of a battery.

Electron pair – a pair of electrons with different spin quantum numbers that may occupy an orbital.

Electron volt – the energy gained by an electron moving across a potential difference of 1 V equals 1.60×10^{-19} Joules.

Electronegativity – the comparative ability of atoms of an element to attract bonding electrons.

Electroplating – where metal is covered with a layer of another metal using electricity.

Electrostatic charge – an accumulated electric charge on an object from a surplus of electrons or a deficiency of electrons.

Element – a pure chemical substance that cannot be broken down into anything simpler by chemical or physical means; there are over 100 known elements, the fundamental materials of which matter is made.

Endothermic process – the process in which heat is absorbed.

Energy – the capacity of a body to do work; a scalar quantity; the SI unit is the Joule; there are five forms: mechanical, chemical, radiant, electrical, and nuclear.

Equilibrium – the condition of a system when neither its state of motion nor its internal energy state tends to change with time; a balanced object is in equilibrium.

Escape velocity – the minimum velocity with which an object must be thrown upward to overcome the gravitational pull and escape into space; the escape velocity depends on the mass and radius of the planet/star, but not on the mass of the body being thrown upward.

Evaporation – a process of more molecules leaving a liquid for the gaseous state than returning from the gas to the liquid; can occur at any given temperature from the surface of a liquid; takes place from the surface of the liquid; causes cooling; faster if the surface of the liquid is large, the temperature is higher, and the surrounding atmosphere does not contain a large amount of vapor of the liquid.

Exothermic process – the process in which heat is evolved.

F

Fahrenheit scale of temperature – the ice-point (lower fixed point) is taken as 32 °F, and the steam-point (upper fixed point) is taken as 212 °F; the interval between these two points is divided into 180 equal divisions; the unit division on the Fahrenheit scale is 1 °F; the relationship relates the temperatures on the Celsius scale and the Fahrenheit scale, C/100 = (°F − 32) / 180; the temperature of a healthy person is 37 °C or 98.6 °F.

Farad – the SI unit of capacitance; the capacitance of a capacitor that, if charged to 1 C, has a potential difference of 1 V.

Faraday – the electric charge required to liberate a gram equivalent of a substance; 1 Faraday = 9,6485 coulomb/mole.

Fermat's principle – an electromagnetic wave takes a path involving the least time when propagating between two points.

First Law of Motion – every object remains at rest or in a state of uniform straight-line motion unless acted on by an unbalanced force.

Fluid – matter that can flow or be poured; the individual molecules of fluid can move, rolling by another.

Focus – the point to which rays that are initially parallel to the axis of a lens or mirror converge or from which they appear to diverge.

Force (F) – a push or pull which tends to change the state of rest or uniform motion, the direction of motion or the shape and size of a body; a vector quantity; the SI unit is a Newton, denoted by N; one N is the force which when acting on a body of mass 1 kg produces an acceleration of 1 m/s².

Force of gravitation – the force with which two objects attract by their masses; acts even if the two objects are not connected; an action-at-a-distance force.

Fossil fuels – formed from the remains of plants and animals that lived millions of years ago.

Fracture strain – an adjustment to stress in which materials crack or break because of the stress.

Fraunhofer lines – the dark lines in the spectrum of the sun or a star.

Freefall – the motion of a body falling to Earth with no other force except the force of gravity acting on it; free-falling bodies are weightless.

Freezing – the changing of a liquid to a solid state.

Freezing point – the temperature at which a phase change of liquid to solid occurs; the same temperature as the melting point for a given substance.

Frequency – the number of oscillations completed in 1 second by an oscillating body.

Frequency (of oscillations) – the number of oscillations made by an oscillating body per second.

Frequency (of waves) – the number of waves produced per second.

Friction – the force that resists the motion of one surface relative to another with which it is in contact; caused by the humps and crests of surfaces, even those on a microscopic scale; the area of contact is small, and the consequent high pressure leads to local pressure welding of the surface; in motion, the welds are broken and remade continually.

Fuel – any substance that burns in oxygen to produce heat.

Fuel rod – long zirconium alloy tubes are containing fissionable material for use in a nuclear reactor.

Fundamental charge – the smallest common charge known; the magnitude of the charge of an electron and a proton, which is 1.60×10^{-19} coulombs.

Fundamental frequency – the lowest frequency (longest wavelength) at which a system vibrates freely and can set up standing waves in an air column or on a string.

Fundamental properties – a property that cannot be defined in more straightforward terms other than to describe how it is measured; the fundamental properties are length, mass, time, and charge.

Fuse – a safety device in an electric circuit. If the current (i.e., the flow of charge) gets too high, the wire in the fuse melts, which breaks the circuit switching off the current.

G

g – a symbol representing the acceleration of an object in free fall due to the force of gravity; its magnitude is 9.80 m/s².

Gamma (γ) ray – a high energy photon of short wavelength electromagnetic radiation emitted by decaying nuclei (γ-decay).

Gases – a phase of matter composed of molecules that are relatively far apart moving freely in constant, random motion and have weak cohesive forces acting between them, resulting in the characteristic indefinite shape and indefinite volume of a gas.

Graham's Law of Diffusion – the diffusion rate of a gas is inversely proportional to the square root of its density.

Gram-atomic weight – the mass in grams of one mole of an element that is numerically equal to its atomic weight.

Gram-formula weight – the mass in grams of one mole of a compound that is numerically equal to its formula weight.

Gram-molecular weight – the gram-formula weight of a molecular compound.

Gravitational constant (G) – term in the equation for Newton's Law of Gravitation; numerically, equal to the force of gravitation, which acts between two bodies with a mass of 1 kg each separated by 1 m; the value of G is 6.67×10^{-11} Nm²/kg².

Gravitational potential at a point – the amount of work done against the gravitational forces to move a particle of unit mass from infinity to that point.

Gravitational potential energy (PE) – the energy possessed by a body by its height from the ground; equals *mgh*.

Gravity – the gravitational attraction at the surface of a planet or other celestial body.

Greenhouse effect – the process of increasing the temperature of the lower parts of the atmosphere through redirecting energy back toward the surface; the absorption and re-emission of infrared radiation by carbon dioxide (CO_2), water vapor and a few other gases in the atmosphere.

Ground state – the energy state of an atom with its electrons at the lowest energy state possible for that atom.

H

Half-life – time required for one-half of the unstable nuclei in a radioactive substance to decay into a new element.

Halogens – the elements in group seven in the periodic table.

Hard water – water that finds it difficult to form lather with soap.

Heat – a form of energy that makes a body hot or cold; measured by the temperature-effect, it produces in any material body; the SI unit is the Joule (J).

Heisenberg uncertainty principle – states that there is a fundamental limit to the precision with which certain pairs of physical properties of a particle (i.e., **complementary** variables) can be known simultaneously (e.g., one cannot measure the exact momentum and position of a subatomic particle at the same time – the more certain is one, the less certain is the other).

Hertz (Hz) − unit of frequency; equivalent to one cycle per second.

Hooke's Law − within the elastic limit, stress is directly proportional to strain.

Horsepower − unit of power; 1 hp = 746 Watts.

Humidity − the ratio of water vapor in a sample of air to the volume of the sample.

Huygens' principle − each point on a light wavefront can be regarded as a source of secondary waves, the envelope of these secondary waves determining the position of the wavefront later.

Hypothesis − a tentative explanation of a phenomenon that is compatible with the data and provides a framework for understanding and describing that phenomenon.

I

Ice-point − the melting point of ice under 1 atm pressure; equal to 0 °C or 32 °F.

Ideal gas equation − $PV = nRT$.

Immiscible liquids – liquids that do not mix to form a solution, e.g. oil and water.

Impulse − equal to the product of the force acting on a body and the time for which it acts; if the force is variable, the impulse is the integral of Fd_t from t_0 to t_1; the impulse of a force acting for a given time interval is equal to change in momentum produced over that interval; $J = m(v − u)$, assuming that the mass m remains constant while the velocity changes from v to u; the SI units are kg m/s.

Impulsive force − acts on a body for a short time but produces a large change in the momentum of the body.

Incandescent − matter emitting visible light because of high temperature (e.g., a light bulb, a flame from any burning source, the Sun).

Incident ray − line representing the direction of motion of incoming light approaching a boundary.

Index of refraction − the ratio of the speed of light in a vacuum to the speed of light in a material.

Indicator – a substance, which shows using a color change if a substance is acidic or basic.

Inertia − the property of matter that causes it to resist any change in its state of rest or of uniform motion; there are three kinds of inertia: the inertia of rest, the inertia of motion and the inertia of direction; the mass of a body is a measure of its inertia.

Infrasonic − sound waves at a frequency below the range of human hearing (less than 20 Hz).

Insulators − materials that are poor conductors of heat or electricity (e.g., wood or glass); materials with air pockets slow down the movement of heat because the air molecules are far apart.

Intensity − a measure of the energy carried by a wave.

Interference − the redistribution of energy due to the superposition of waves with a phase difference from coherent sources, resulting in alternate light and dark bands.

Intermolecular forces − interaction between molecules.

Internal energy – the sum of the kinetic energy and potential energy of the molecules of an object.

Inverse proportion – the relationship in which the value of one variable increases while the value of a second variable decreases at the same rate (in the same ratio).

Ion exchange – a method of removing hardness from water, and it replaces the positive ions that cause the hardness with H^+ ions.

Ion – a charged atom or group of atoms, e.g. Na+.

Ionic bond – a force of attraction between oppositely charged ions in a compound, resulting from a transfer of electrons.

Ionization – a process of forming ions from molecules.

Ionized – an atom or a particle with a net charge because it has gained or lost electrons.

Isobaric process – pressure remains constant.

Isochoric process – volume remains constant.

Isostasy – a balance or equilibrium between adjacent blocks of Earth's crust.

Isothermal process – in which temperature remains constant.

Isotope – atoms of the same element with the same atomic number (i.e., number of protons) but with a different mass number (i.e., number of neutrons).

J

Joule (J) – the unit used to measure work and energy; can also measure heat; $1\ J = 1N{\cdot}m$.

Joule's Law of Heating – states that the heat produced when current (I) flows through a resistor (R) for a given time (t) is given by $Q = I^2Rt$.

K

Kelvin scale of temperature (K) – the lower fixed point is taken as 273.15 K (0 °C), and the steam-point (the upper fixed point) is taken as 373.15 K (100 °C); the interval between these two points is divided into 100 equal parts; each division is equal to 1 K.

Kelvin's statement of Second Law of Thermodynamics – it is impossible that, at the end of a cycle of changes, heat has been extracted from a reservoir, and an equal amount of work has been produced without producing some other effect.

Kepler's Laws of Planetary Motion – the three laws describing the motion of the planets.

Kepler's First Law – in planetary motion, each planet moves in an elliptical orbit, with the Sun located at one focus.

Kepler's Second Law – a radius vector between the Sun and a planet moves over equal areas of the ellipse during equal time intervals.

Kepler's Third Law – the square of the period of an orbit is directly proportional to the cube of the radius of the major axis of the orbit.

Kilocalorie (Kcal) – the amount of energy required to raise the temperature of 1 kg of water by 1 °C; 1 Kcal = 1,000 calories.

Kilogram – the fundamental unit of mass in the metric system of measurement.

Kinetic energy (KE) – possessed by a body due to its motion; $KE = \frac{1}{2}mv^2$, where m is mass and v is velocity.

L

Laser – a device that produces a coherent stream of light through stimulated emission of radiation.

Latent heat – energy released or absorbed by a body during a constant-temperature phase change.

Latent heat of vaporization – the heat absorbed when one gram of a substance changes from the liquid phase to the gaseous phase; also, the heat released when one gram of gas changes from the gaseous phase to the liquid phase.

Latent heat of fusion – the quantity of heat required to convert one unit mass of a substance from a solid state to a liquid state at its melting point without a change in its temperature; the SI unit is $J\ kg^{-1}$.

Latent heat of sublimation – the quantity of heat required to convert one unit of mass of a substance from a solid state to a gaseous state without a change in its temperature.

Law of Conservation of Energy – states that energy can neither be created nor destroyed but can be transformed.

Law of Conservation of Mass – mass (including single atoms) can neither be created nor destroyed in a chemical reaction.

Law of Conservation of Matter – matter can neither be created nor destroyed in a chemical reaction.

Law of Conservation of Momentum – the total momentum of a group of interacting objects remains constant in the absence of external forces.

Law of the lever – when a lever is balanced, the sum of the clockwise moments equals the sum of the anti-clockwise moments.

Lenz's Law – the induced current always flows in such a direction that it opposes the cause producing it.

Lever – a rigid body, which is free to turn about a fixed point called the fulcrum.

Light – a form of energy.

Light-year – the distance that light travels in a vacuum in one year (365.25 days); approximately 9.46×10^{15} m.

Line spectrum – an emission (of light, sound, or other radiation) spectrum consisting of separate isolated lines (discrete frequencies or energies); can be used to identify the elements in a matter of unknown composition.

Lines of force – lines drawn to make an electric field strength map, with each line originating on a positive charge and ending on a negative charge; each line represents a path on which a charge would experience a constant force; having the lines closer indicates a more energetic electric field.

Liquids – a phase of matter composed of molecules that have interactions stronger than those found in gas but not strong enough to keep the molecules near the equilibrium positions of a solid, resulting in the characteristic definite volume but the indefinite shape of a liquid.

Liter – a metric system unit of volume; usually used for liquids.

Longitudinal strain – the ratio of change in the length of a body to its initial length.

Longitudinal waves – the particles of the medium oscillate along the direction of propagation of a wave (e.g., sound waves).

Loudness – a subjective interpretation of a sound that is related to the energy of the vibrating source, related to the condition of the transmitting medium and the distance involved.

Lubricant – a substance capable of reducing friction (i.e., force that opposes the direction of motion).

Luminosity – the total amount of energy radiated into space each second from the surface of a star.

Luminous – objects that produce visible light (e.g., the Sun, stars, light bulbs, burning materials).

Lunar eclipse – when the Earth passes between the sun and the moon.

Lyman series – a group of lines in the ultraviolet region in the spectrum of hydrogen.

M

Magnetic domain – tiny physical regions in permanent magnets, approximately 0.01 to 1 mm, have magnetically aligned atoms, giving the domain an overall polarity.

Magnetic field – the region around a magnet where other magnetic objects experience its magnetic force; a model used to describe how magnetic forces on moving charges act at a distance.

Magnetic poles – the ends, or sides, of a magnet about which the force of magnetic attraction seems to be concentrated.

Magnetic quantum number – from the quantum mechanics model of the atom, one of four descriptions of the energy state of an electron wave; describes the energy of an electron orbital as the orbital is oriented in space by an external magnetic field, a kind of energy sub-sublevel.

Magnetic reversal – the changing of polarity of the Earth's magnetic field as the north magnetic pole and the south magnetic pole exchange positions.

Magnetic wave – the spread of magnetization from a small portion of a substance from an abrupt change in the magnetic field.

Magnification – the ratio of the size of the image to the size of the object.

Magnitude – the size of a measurement of a vector; scalar quantities that consist of a number and unit only.

Malleable – can be hammered into sheets (e.g., metals).

Malus Law – the intensity of the light transmitted from the analyzer varies directly as the square of the cosine of the angle between the plane of transmission of the analyzer and the polarizer.

Maser − microwave amplification by stimulated emission of radiation.

Mass (m) − the quantity of matter in a body; the SI unit is the kg; remains the same everywhere; a measure of inertia, which means resistance to a change of motion.

Mass defect − the difference between the sum of the masses of the individual nucleons of a nucleus and mass of nucleus.

Mass number − the sum of the number of protons and neutrons in a nucleus; used to identify isotopes (e.g., Uranium-238).

Matter − anything that occupies space and has mass.

Mean life − the average time during which a system (e.g., atom, nucleus) exists in a specified form.

Mechanical energy − the sum of the potential energy (PE) and the kinetic energy (KE) of a body; energy associated with the position of a body.

Mechanical waves − require a material medium for propagation (e.g., sound waves and water waves); also *elastic waves*.

Megahertz (MHz) − unit of frequency; equal to 106 Hertz.

Melting – the changing of a solid to a liquid state.

Melting point − the temperature at which a phase change of solid to liquid takes place.

Metal − matter having the physical properties of conductivity, malleability, ductility, and luster.

Meter − the fundamental metric unit of length.

MeV − a unit of energy; equal to 1.6×10^{-13} joules.

Millibar − a measure of atmospheric pressure equivalent to 1,000 dynes per cm^2.

Miscible fluids − fluids that can mix in any proportion.

Mixture − matter made of unlike parts with variable composition and separated into their parts by physical means.

Model − a mental or physical representation of something that cannot be observed directly; used as an aid to understanding.

Modulus of elasticity − the ratio of stress to the strain produced in a body.

Modulus of rigidity − the ratio of tangential stress to the shear strain produced in a body.

Mole − the amount of a substance that contains Avogadro's number of atoms, ions, molecules, or any other chemical unit; 6.02×10^{23} atoms, ions, or other chemical units.

Molecule – two or more atoms chemically combined.

Moment − a measure of the turning effect of a force. Moment of a force = force × perpendicular distance from the fulcrum.

Momentum − a measure of the quantity of motion; the product of the mass and the velocity of a body; SI units are kg·m /s.

Monochromatic light − consisting of a single wavelength.

N

Natural frequency – the frequency of oscillation of an elastic object in the absence of external forces; depends on the size, composition, and shape of the object.

Negative electric charge – one of two types of electric charge; repels other negative charges and attracts positive charges.

Negative ion – atom or particle that has a surplus or imbalance of electrons and a negative charge.

Net force – the resulting force after vector forces are summed; if a net force is zero, the vector forces have canceled, and there is no unbalanced force.

Neutralization – the reaction between an acid and a base to give salt and water.

Newton (N) – a unit of force defined as $kg \cdot m/s^2$; 1 Newton is needed to accelerate a 1 kg mass by 1 m/s^2.

Newton's First Law of Motion – a body continues in a state of rest or uniform motion in a straight line unless an external (unbalanced) force acts upon it.

Newton's Law of Gravitation – the gravitational force of attraction acting between two particles is directly proportional to the product of their masses and inversely proportional to the square of the distance between them; the force of attraction acts along the line joining the two particles; real bodies having spherical symmetry act as point masses with their mass assumed to be concentrated at their center of mass.

Newton's Second Law of Motion – the rate of change of momentum is equal to the force applied; the force acting on a body is directly proportional to the product of its mass and acceleration produced by force in the body.

Newton's Third Law of Motion – for every action, there is an equal and opposite reaction; the action and the reaction act on two different bodies simultaneously.

Noise – sounds made up of groups of waves of random frequency and intensity.

Non-uniform acceleration – when the velocity of a body increases by unequal amounts in equal intervals of time.

Non-uniform speed – when a body travels unequal distances in equal intervals of time.

Non-uniform velocity – when a body covers unequal distances in equal intervals of time in a direction, or when it covers equal distances in equal intervals but changes its direction.

Normal (N) – a line perpendicular to the surface of a boundary.

Nuclear energy – the form of energy from reactions involving the nucleus.

Nuclear fission – the splitting of a heavy nucleus into more stable, lighter nuclei with an accompanying release of energy.

Nuclear force – one of four fundamental forces; a strong force of attraction that operates over short distances between subatomic particles; overcomes the electric repulsion of protons in a nucleus and binds the nucleus.

Nuclear fusion – a nuclear reaction of low mass nuclei fusing to form a more stable and more massive nucleus with an accompanying release of energy.

Nuclear reactor – a steel vessel in which a controlled chain reaction of fissionable materials releases energy.

Nucleons – a collective name for protons and neutrons in the nucleus of an atom.

Nucleus – the central, positively charged, dense portion of an atom; contains protons and neutrons.

O

Octet rule – during bonding, atoms tend to reach an electron arrangement with eight electrons in the outermost shell.

Ohm − unit of resistance; 1 ohm = 1volt/ampere.

Ohm's Law – the current flowing through a conductor is directly proportional to the potential difference across the ends of the conductor. At a constant temperature, the voltage across a conductor is proportional to the current flowing through it. Voltage = current × resistance (V = IR).

Open system − a system across whose boundaries matter and energy can pass.

Optical fiber − a long, thin thread of fused silica; used to transmit light; based on total internal reflection.

Orbital − the region of space around the nucleus of an atom where an electron is likely to be found.

Origin − the point on a graph where the x and the y variables have a value of zero at the same time.

Oscillatory motion − the to and fro motion (periodic) of a body about its mean position; also, *vibratory motion*.

Oxidation – the addition of oxygen or the losing of electrons.

P

Pascal − a unit of pressure equal to the pressure resulting from a force of 1 N acting uniformly over an area of 1 m^2.

Pascal's Law − states that the pressure exerted on a liquid is transmitted equally in all directions.

Paschen series − a group of lines in the infrared region in the spectrum of hydrogen.

Pauli exclusion principle − no two electrons in an atom can have the same four quantum numbers; a maximum of two electrons can occupy a given orbital.

Peltier effect − the evolution or absorption of heat at the junction of two dissimilar metals carrying current.

Period (of a wave) − the time for a wave to travel through a distance equal to its wavelength; denoted by T; period of a wave = 1/frequency of the wave.

Period (of an oscillation) − the time to complete one oscillation; does not depend upon the mass of the bob and amplitude of oscillation; directly proportional to the square root of the length and inversely proportional to the square root of the acceleration due to gravity.

Periodic wave − a wave in which the particles of the medium oscillate continuously about their mean positions regularly at fixed intervals of time.

Periodic motion − a motion that repeats at regular time intervals.

Permeability − the ability to transmit fluids through openings, tiny passageways, or gaps.

pH scale – a scale from 0 to 14. If the pH of a solution is 7 it is neutral; if the pH of a solution is less than 7 it is acidic; if the pH of a solution is greater than 7 it is basic.

Permanent hardness – hardness in water that cannot be removed by boiling. It is caused by calcium sulfate.

Phase – when particles in a wave are in the same state of vibration (i.e., in the same position and the direction of motion).

Phase change – the action of a substance changing from one state of matter to another; always absorbs or releases internal potential energy that is not associated with a temperature change.

Photons – quanta of energy in the light wave; the particle associated with light.

Photoelectric effect – the emission of electrons in some materials when the light of a suitable frequency falls on them.

Physical change – a change of the state of a substance but not in the identity of the substance.

Pitch (sound) – depends on the frequency of the wave.

Planck's constant – proportionality constant in the ratio of the energy of vibrating molecules to their frequency of vibration; a value of 6.63×10^{-34} J·s.

Plasma – a phase of matter; a hot highly ionized gas consisting of electrons and atoms that have been stripped of their electrons because of high kinetic energies.

Plasticity – the property of a solid whereby it undergoes a permanent change in shape or size when subjected to a stress.

Plastic strain – an adjustment to stress in which materials become molded or bent out of shape under stress and do not return to their original shape after the stress is released.

Polarized light – light whose constituent transverse waves are vibrating in the same plane.

Polaroid – a film that transmits only polarized light.

Polaroid or polarizer – a device that produces polarized light.

Positive electric charge – one of the two types of electric charge; repels positive and attracts negative charges.

Positive ion – atom or particle with a net positive charge due to an electron or electrons being torn away.

Positron – an elementary particle having the same mass as an electron but an equal and positive charge.

Potential difference (or *voltage*) – the force, which moves the electrons around the circuit. Unit is Volt (V).

Potential energy (PE) – possessed by a body by its position or configuration; see the *Gravitational potential energy* and *Elastic potential energy*.

Power – scalar quantity for the rate of doing work; the SI unit is Watt; 1 W = 1 J/s. The rate at which energy is converted from one form to another. Unit is Watts (W). Power = voltage × current (P = VI).

Pressure – a measure of force per unit area (e.g., kilograms per square meter (kg/m^2)). Unit is Pascal (Pa).

Primary coil – part of a transformer; a coil of wire connected to a source of alternating current.

Primary colors – three colors (red, yellow, and blue) combined in various proportions to produce any other color. When red, green, and blue are combined, it results in white. For example, red + green + blue = white.

Principal quantum number – from the quantum mechanics model of the atom, one of four descriptions of the energy state of an electron wave; describes the main energy level of an electron regarding its most probable distance from the nucleus.

Principle of calorimetry – states that if two bodies of different temperature are in thermal contact, and no heat is allowed to go out or enter the system; heat lost by the body with higher temperature is equal to the heat gained by the body of lower temperature (i.e., the heat lost = the heat gained).

Products – chemicals produced in a chemical reaction.

Progressive wave – a wave that transfers energy from one part of a medium to another.

Projectile – an object thrown into space horizontally or at an acute angle and under the action of gravity; the path followed by a projectile is its trajectory; the horizontal distance traveled by a projectile is its range; the time is taken from the moment it is thrown until the moment it hits the ground is its time of flight.

Proof – a measure of ethanol concentration of an alcoholic beverage; double the concentration by volume (e.g., 50% by volume is 100 proof).

Properties – qualities or attributes that, taken together, are usually unique to an object (e.g., color, texture, size).

Proportionality constant – a value applied to a proportionality statement that transforms the statement into an equation.

Pulse – a wave of short duration confined to a small portion of the medium at any given time; also a *wave pulse*.

Q

Quanta – fixed amounts; usually referring to fixed amounts of energy absorbed or emitted by matter.

Quantum limit – the shortest wavelength; present in a continuous x-ray spectrum.

Quantum mechanics – model of the atom based on the wave nature of subatomic particles and the mechanics of electron waves; also *wave mechanics*.

Quantum numbers – numbers that describe the energy states of an electron; in the Bohr model of the atom, the orbit quantum numbers could be any whole number (e.g., 1, 2, 3, etc.); in the quantum mechanics model of the atom, four quantum numbers are used to describe the energy state of an electron wave (n, m, l, and s).

Quark – one of the hypothetical fundamental particles; has a charge with magnitudes of one-third or two-thirds of the charge on an electron.

R

Rad – a measure of radiation received by a material (radiation-absorbed dose).

Radiant energy – the form of energy that can travel through space (e.g., visible light and other parts of the electromagnetic spectrum).

Radiation – the emission and propagation of waves transmitting energy through space or some medium. Heat transfer through invisible rays, which travel outwards from the hot object without a medium.

Radioactive decay – the natural, spontaneous disintegration or decomposition of a nucleus.

Radioactive decay constant – a specific constant for a isotope that is the ratio of the rate of nuclear disintegration per unit of time to the total number of radioactive nuclei.

Radioactive decay series – series of decay reactions that begins with one radioactive nucleus that decays to a second nucleus that decays to a third nucleus and so on, until a stable nucleus is reached.

Radioactive Decay Law – the rate of disintegration of a radioactive substance is directly proportional to the number of undecayed nuclei.

Radioactivity – spontaneous emission of particles or energy from an atomic nucleus as it disintegrates.

Rarefaction – a part of a longitudinal wave where the density of the particles of the medium is less than the typical density.

Real image – an image generated by a lens or mirror that can be projected onto a screen.

Reactants – chemicals that react together in a chemical reaction.

Rectifier – converts alternating current to direct current.

Rectilinear motion – the motion of a body in a straight line.

Reduction – the removal of oxygen or the gaining of electrons.

Reflected ray – a line representing the direction of motion of light reflected from a boundary.

Reflection – the bouncing back of light from a surface.

Refraction – the bending of a light wave, a sound wave, or another wave from its straight-line path as it travels from one medium to another.

Refractive index – the ratio of the speed of light in a vacuum to that in the medium.

Relative density – (i.e., *specific gravity*) is the ratio of the density (mass of a unit volume) of a substance to the density of given reference material. *Specific gravity* usually means relative density concerning water. The term *relative density* is more common in modern scientific usage.

Relative humidity – the percentage of the amount of water vapor present in a specific volume of the air to the amount of water vapor needed to saturate it.

Resistance (R) – the opposition of a conductor to current (i.e., the flow of charge). A good conductor has a low resistance, and a bad conductor has a high resistance.

Resolving power – the ability of an optical instrument to produce separable images of different points of an object.

Resonance – when the frequency of an external force matches the natural frequency of the body.

Restoring force – the force which tends to bring an oscillating body back to its mean position whenever it is displaced from the mean position.

Resultant force – a single force, which acts on a body to produce the same effect on it as done by other forces collectively; see *balanced forces*.

Reverberation – apparent increase in the volume of sound caused by reflections from the boundary surfaces, usually arriving within 0.1 seconds after the original sound.

Rigid body – an idealized extended body whose size and shape are fixed and unaltered when forces are applied.

S

Salt – when a metal replaces the hydrogen of an acid.

Saturated air – air in which an equilibrium exists between evaporation and condensation; the relative humidity is 100 percent.

Saturated solution – the apparent limit to dissolving a given solid in a specified amount of water at a given temperature; a state of equilibrium exists between dissolving solute and solute coming out of solution.

Scalar quantity – a physical quantity described entirely by its magnitude.

Scientific law – a relationship between quantities; usually described by an equation in the physical sciences; describes a broader range of phenomena and is more important than a scientific principle.

Scientific principle – a relationship between quantities within a specific range of observations and behavior.

Second – the standard unit of time in the metric and English systems of measurement.

Second Law of Motion – the acceleration of an object is directly proportional to the net force acting on that object and inversely proportional to the mass of the object.

Secondary coil – part of a transformer; a coil of wire in which the voltage of the original alternating current in the primary coil can be stepped up or down by electromagnetic induction.

Secondary colors – formed when two primary colors (i.e., red, green, blue) are mixed. The three secondary colors are yellow, magenta, and cyan. For example, red + green = yellow; red + blue = magenta; and blue + green = cyan.

Second's pendulum – a simple pendulum whose period on the surface of the Earth is 2 seconds.

Semiconductors – elements whose electrical conductivity is intermediate between that of a conductor and an insulator.

Shear strain – the ratio of the relative displacements of one plane to its distance from the fixed plane.

Shear stress – the restoring force developed per unit area when deforming force acts tangentially to the surface of a body, producing a change in the shape of the body without any volume change.

Siemens – the derived SI unit of electrical conductance; equal to the conductance of an element with a resistance of 1 ohm; also written as ohm^{-1}.

Simple harmonic motion – the vibratory motion occurs when the restoring force is proportional to the displacement from the mean position and is directed opposite to the displacement.

Simple pendulum – a heavy point mass (a small metallic ball) suspended by a light inextensible string from frictionless rigid support; a simple machine based on the effect of gravity.

Snell's Law – states that the ratio of *sin* i to *sin* r is a constant and is equal to the refractive index of the second medium concerning the first.

Solar eclipse – happens when the moon passes between the sun and the Earth.

Solenoid – a cylindrical coil of wire that becomes electromagnetic when current passes through it.

Solids – a phase of matter with molecules that remain close to fixed equilibrium positions due to strong interactions between the molecules, resulting in the characteristic definite shape and definite volume of a solid.

Solution – a mixture of a solute (usually a solid) and a solvent (usually a liquid).

Sonic boom – sound waves that pile up into a shock wave when a source is traveling at or faster than the speed of sound.

Sound – a form of energy.

Specific gravity – see *relative density*.

Specific heat – the amount of heat energy required to increase the temperature of 1 g of a substance by 1 °C; each substance has its specific heat value.

Speed – a scalar quantity for the distance traveled by a body per unit of time; if a body covers the distance in time, its speed is given by distance/time; SI units are m/s.

Spin quantum number – from the quantum mechanics model of the atom, one of four descriptions of the energy state of an electron wave; describes the spin orientation of an electron relative to an external magnetic field.

Stable equilibrium – a body is in stable equilibrium if, when slightly moved, its center of gravity rises.

Standing waves – the condition where two waves of equal frequency traveling in opposite directions meet and form stationary regions of maximum displacement due to constructive interference and stationary regions of zero displacement due to destructive interference.

State of motion – when a body changes its position concerning a fixed point in its surroundings; the states of rest and motion are relative to the frame of reference.

State of rest – when a body does not change its position concerning a fixed point in its surrounding; the states of rest and motion are relative to the frame of reference.

Steam-point – the temperature of steam over pure boiling water under 1 atm pressure; taken as the upper fixed point (100 °C or 212 °F) for temperature scales.

Stefan-Boltzmann Law – the amount of energy radiated per second per unit area of a perfectly black body is directly proportional to the fourth power of the absolute temperature of the surface of the body.

Sublimation – the changing of a solid directly to a gas. (Iodine is an example of a substance that sublimes).

Superconductors – some materials in which, under certain conditions, the electrical resistance approaches zero.

Super-cooled – water in the liquid phase when the temperature is below the freezing point.

Supersaturated – containing more than the average saturation amount of a solute at a given temperature.

Surface tension – the property of a liquid due to which its surface behaves like a stretched membrane.

Suspension – a mixture of a liquid and a finely divided insoluble solid.

T

Temperature – a measure of the hotness or coldness of a body; according to the molecular model, measures the average kinetic energy of the molecules; heat flows from a body at a higher temperature to a body at a lower temperature.

Temporary hardness – hardness in water that can be removed by boiling. It is caused by calcium hydrogen carbonate.

Tensional stress − the opposite of compressional stress; when one part of a plate moves away from another part that does not move.

Tesla (T) − SI unit of magnetic flux density; the magnetic flux density of a magnetic flux of 1 Wb through an area of 1 m^2.

Thermal capacity − the quantity of heat required to raise the temperature of the body by one degree (1 K or 1 °C).

Thermal equilibrium − when two bodies in contact are at the same temperature, and there is no heat flow between them; also, the average temperature of the bodies in thermal equilibrium.

Thermal expansion − the increase in the size of an object when heated.

Thermometer − a device used for the measurement of temperature; the mercury thermometer is commonly used.

Third Law of Motion − when two objects interact, the force exerted on one object is equal in size and opposite in direction to the force exerted on the other object; forces always occur in matched pairs that are equal and opposite.

Titration – the process of adding one solution from a burette to a measured amount of another solution to find out exactly how much of each is required to react.

Total internal reflection − a condition where all light is reflected from a boundary between materials; occurs when light travels from a denser to a rarer medium, and the angle of incidence is greater than the critical angle.

Transformation of energy − converting one form of energy into another (e.g., when a body falls, its potential energy is converted to kinetic energy).

Transverse wave − a wave in which the particles of the medium oscillate in a direction perpendicular to the direction of propagation of the wave (e.g., water waves, light waves, radio waves).

Trough − the point of maximum negative displacement on a transverse wave.

U

Ultrasonic − sound waves too high in frequency (above 20,000 Hz) to be heard by the human ear.

Unbalanced forces − when some forces act on a body and the resultant force is not zero.

Uniform acceleration − when the velocity of a body increases by equal amounts in equal intervals of time.

Uniform circular motion − the motion of an object in a circular path with uniform speed; accelerated motion.

Uniform speed − when a body travels equal distances in equal intervals of time.

Uniform velocity − when a body travels along a straight line in a direction with equal distance in equal time intervals.

Universal Law of Gravitation − every object is attracted to every other object with force directly proportional to the product of their masses and inversely proportional to the square of the distance between the centers of the two masses.

Unpolarized light − light consisting of transverse waves vibrating in all possible random directions.

Unstable equilibrium – a body is in unstable equilibrium if, when slightly moved, its center of gravity falls.

V

Van der Waals force – general term for weak attractive intermolecular forces.

Valency – the number of electrons an atom wants to gain, lose, or share to have a full outer shell.

Vapor – the gaseous state of a substance that is generally in a liquid state.

Vector quantity – a quantity that needs magnitude and direction to describe it.

Velocity (v) – distance traveled by a body in a direction per unit time; the displacement of the body per unit time; a vector quantity; the SI units are m/s.

Vibration – a back and forth motion that repeats itself.

Virtual image – an image formed when the reflected or refracted light rays appear to meet; this image cannot be projected on a screen.

Volt (V) – a unit of potential difference equivalent to joules/coulomb.

Voltage drop – the difference in electric potential across a resistor or other part of a circuit that consumes power.

Volume – the amount of space an object occupies.

W

Watt (W) – SI unit for power; equivalent to joule/s.

Wave – a disturbance or oscillation that moves through a medium.

Wavelength (λ) – the distance between the two nearest points on a wave in the same phase; the distance between two adjacent crests or two adjacent troughs.

Wave (mechanical) – a periodic disturbance produced in a material medium due to the vibratory motion of the particles of the medium.

Wave mechanics – alternate name for quantum mechanics derived from the wavelike properties of subatomic particles.

Wave motion – the movement of a disturbance from one part of a medium to another involving the transfer of energy but not the transfer of matter.

Wave period – the time required for two successive crests (or successive regions) of the wave to pass a given point.

Wave velocity – the distance traveled by a wave in one second; depends on the medium through which it passes.

Weight – the force with which a body is attracted towards the center of the Earth; the SI unit is N; the gravitational units are kg·wt and g·wt; the weight of a body is given by mg. Weight = mass × acceleration due to gravity.

Weightlessness – the state when the apparent weight of a body becomes zero; objects while falling freely under the action of gravity are seemingly weightless.

Wien's Displacement Law – states that for a black body, the product of the wavelength corresponding to its maximum radiance and its absolute temperature is constant.

Work − work is done when a force acting on a body displaces it; work = force × displacement (W = Fd) in the direction of the force; work is a scalar quantity; the SI unit is Joule.

Y

Young's modulus of elasticity − the ratio of normal stress to the longitudinal strain produced in a body.

Z

Zeeman effect − the splitting of the spectral lines in a spectrum when the source is exposed to a magnetic field.

Zeroth Law of Thermodynamics – states that if body A is in thermal equilibrium with body B, and B is also in thermal equilibrium with C, then A is necessarily in thermal equilibrium with C.

Customer Satisfaction Guarantee

Your feedback is important because we strive to provide the highest quality prep materials. Email us comments or suggestions.

info@sterling–prep.com

We reply to emails – check your spam folder

Highest quality guarantee

Be the first to report a content error for a $10 reward
or a grammatical mistake to receive a $5 reward.

AP Physics 1 Review provides a comprehensive review of topics tested on the AP Physics 1 exam. The content covers foundational principles and concepts necessary to answer exam questions.

This review book will increase your score.

Visit our Amazon store

AP Chemistry, Biology and Physics online practice tests

Our advanced online testing platform allows you to take AP practice questions on your computer to generate a Diagnostic Report for each test.

By using our online AP tests and Diagnostic Reports, you will:

Assess your knowledge of subjects and topics to identify your areas of strength and weakness

Learn important scientific topics and concepts for comprehensive test preparation

Improve your test-taking skills

To access these and other AP questions online
at a special pricing for book owners, visit:
http://ap.sterling-prep.com/bookowner.htm

AP prep books by Sterling Test Prep

AP Biology Practice Questions	AP Psychology
AP Biology Review	AP U.S. History
AP Physics 1 Practice Questions	AP World History
AP Physics 1 Review	AP European History
AP Physics 2 Practice Questions	AP U.S. Government and Politics
AP Physics 2 Review	AP Comparative Government and Politics
AP Environmental Science	AP Human Geography

Visit our Amazon store

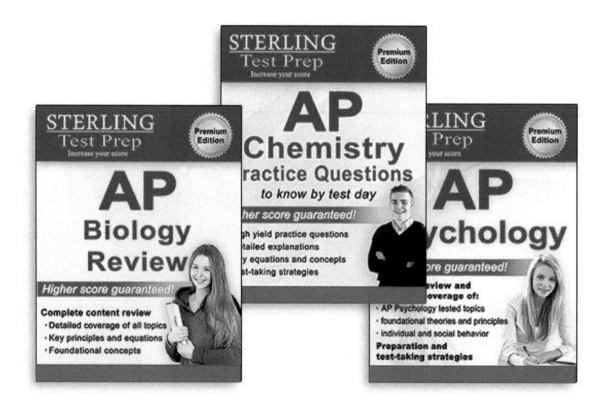

College Level Examination Program (CLEP)

Biology Review

Biology Practice Questions

Chemistry Review

Chemistry Practice Questions

Introductory Business Law Review

College Algebra Practice Questions

College Mathematics Practice Questions

History of the United States I Review

History of the United States II Review

Western Civilization I Review

Western Civilization II Review

Social Sciences and History Review

American Government Review

Introductory Psychology Review

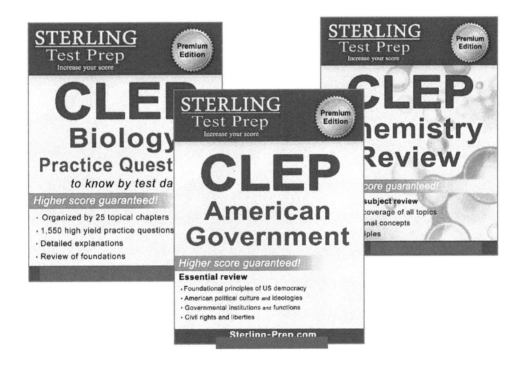

Visit our Amazon store